HUMAN RIGHTS
AND
NARRATED LIVES

HUMAN RIGHTS AND NARRATED LIVES: THE ETHICS OF RECOGNITION

Kay Schaffer
Sidonie Smith

© HUMAN RIGHTS AND NARRATED LIVES

First published 2004 by
PALGRAVE MACMILLAN™
175 Fifth Avenue, New York, N.Y. 10010 and
Houndmills, Basingstoke, Hampshire, England RG21 6XS
Companies and representatives throughout the world

PALGRAVE MACMILLAN is the global academic imprint of the Palgrave Macmillan division of St. Martin's Press, LLC and of Palgrave Macmillan Ltd. Macmillan® is a registered trademark in the United States, United Kingdom and other countries. Palgrave is a registered trademark in the European Union and other countries.

ISBN 1–4039–6494–7
ISBN 1–4039–6495–5

Library of Congress Cataloging-in-Publication Data
Schaffer, Kay, 1945–
    Human rights and narrated lives : the ethics of recognition / Kay Schaffer, Sidonie Smith.
        p. cm.
    Includes bibliographical references and index.
    ISBN 1–4039–6494–7 (hardcover)
    ISBN 1–4039–6495–5 (paperback)
    1. Human rights. 2. Personal narratives. I. Smith, Sidonie. II. Title.

JC571.S354 2004
323—dc22   2003067786

A catalogue record for this book is available from the British Library.

Design by Newgen Imaging Systems (P) Ltd., Chennai, India.

First edition: August 2004
10 9 8 7 6 5 4 3 2 1

Printed in the United States of America.

Transferred to digital printing in 2006.

*To activists and witnesses involved in
human rights struggles around the world*

CONTENTS

ACKNOWLEDGMENTS

The idea for an extended study of the uses of personal narratives in campaigns for human rights arose during the first meeting of the International Auto/Biography Association in Beijing in June 1999. "All I have is my story" became a phrase challenging us to consider peoples' rights to their own stories. With that nub of an idea we applied to the Rockefeller Center program in Bellagio, Italy, for a joint fellowship that would enable us to begin our collaborative mapping of the relationship between storytelling and human rights as they intersect across the domains of law and literature. The month at Villa Serbolini not only delighted our senses, it also enabled us to do preliminary reading and thinking about the history and philosophical foundations of the human rights regime and its many critiques. Most particularly, we thank José Antonio Aguilar Rivera, fellow Serbolini confrérè and Mexican political scientist, for his generous reading of our first attempt at presenting this background. José complicated our arguments and returned us to the drawing board to reconsider how we wanted to situate our larger argument about life writing in the field of human rights.

Fortunately, we have been able to work side-by-side frequently over the last four years. Our debts of gratitude for making these meetings possible go to the Humanities Research Centre (HRC) at the Australian National University (ANU) in Canberra and to the School of Humanities at Curtin University of Technology in Perth. In Spring 2003, the HRC at the ANU sponsored a year-long project on "The Humanities, Culture, and Human Rights." For six uninterrupted weeks we were able to pursue our project and to engage in dialogues with colleagues whose interests we shared, among them Norbert Finch, John Docker, and Margaret Jolly. Carolyn Turner, deputy director of the HRC, welcomed and supported us in our fellowship. To the Feministas, a collaborative of feminist historians at the ANU, which includes Georgiana Clauson, Ann Curthoys, Desley Deacon, Rosanne Kennedy, Jill Matthews, and Ann McGrath, we owe a special debt for their rigorous critique of an early version of the introduction.

Their challenge to us, as we sat before them soaked from the late afternoon rains of mid-February Canberra, forced us to hone our larger argument, refine our methodology, and begin the book from another angle. We also thank Susan Andrews for talking through with us the place of Holocaust studies in the contemporary study of trauma.

From Canberra we moved to Curtin University in Western Australia, where Sidonie held the Hadyn Williams Fellowship in the School of Humanities and Kay joined her as a visiting scholar in the humanities. At Curtin, we owe our thanks to Barbara Milech who organized our visits under the auspices of the Human Rights and Globalization Project and hosted us with unfailing generosity and graciousness. We thank Brian Dibble for lending us his parking space and office, Dean of Humanities Tom Stannage for hosting our residency, and colleagues Krishna Sen and Jon Stratton for their conversation and suggestions.

A number of colleagues offered invaluable advice and support. We extend our deep appreciation to Dorothy Driver and Joan Wardrop for their insights on the context of South African human rights campaigns; Dorothy Driver, Rosanne Kennedy, and Gillian Whitlock for their critiques of the chapter on Indigenous narratives in Australia; Nicolas Jose, Wei Jingsheng, and Xianlin Song for their contributions to the chapter on narratives in post-Tiananmen China; and to Xianlin for providing the Chinese characters therein. Joan Wardrop brought us books from the stores of South Africa and Dorothy Driver generously lent us her library of materials on the Truth and Reconciliation Commission. Conversations with Anthony Langlois at Flinders University extended our thinking on contemporary legal theory and challenges to the human rights regime. With his usual responsiveness, Mark Selden read and commented on an earlier version of our introduction. If prizes were awarded for getting books to print, the Australian honor would undoubtedly go to Gail Carnes, who naïvely offered to read through the final draft and make suggestions for clarity, without imagining the austere days and sleepless nights that lay ahead as deadlines loomed.

We owe debts to our universities as well. The University of Michigan provided funds for travel and research assistance through the Martha Guernsey Colby Collegiate Professorship. The Global Ethnic Literatures Seminar, sponsored by the Comparative Literature Program directed by Tobin Siebers, offered release time from teaching and a semester-long occasion to gather with faculty and graduate students across the humanities engaged in work on new global formations at the intersection of politics and cultural production. In Australia, the University of Adelaide provided several one-year grants; and the Australian Research Council provided a three-year Discovery Grant to assist the project. Margaret Hosking at the Barr Smith Library at the University of Adelaide was unfailing in her assistance in ordering books and searching for research materials.

We thank hosts and audiences at the University of Michigan, the University of Pittsburgh, the University of Adelaide, the University of Western Australia, Murdoch University, Latrobe University, Deakin University, the University of Sydney, the Chinese University of Hong Kong, the second International Auto/Biography Association Conference in Melbourne, the Association for the Study of Australian Literature Conference in Brisbane, and the American Studies Conference at the University of Mainz for their invitations to present papers and their enthusiastic and incisive questions and comments. And we thank the anonymous readers of the manuscript for St. Martin's/Palgrave who supported this project at the same time that they urged further refinement of its arguments.

Our research assistants have been the mainstay of the project at all stages. They have prepared background material and kept track of the bibliography, growing at an exponential rate. Sidonie thanks Cary Burtt, Emily Crandall, Emily Lutenski, and Tomomi Yamaguchi. To Emily Crandall and Emily Lutenski we owe an especial debt for their meticulous preparation of the final manuscript. Kay is deeply grateful to her research assistants, each of whom enthusiastically offered specialist expertise at various phases of the research—Simone Bignall, Jennifer Jones, Kelly Layton, and Natasha Vorassi; her perspicacious research associate, Emily Potter; her editorial assistants, Shannon Dowling and Pam Papadelos; and Mary Lou Burger and Juliet Fuller, whose dedication to a friend/mother in need exceeded the obligations of friendship and family. Kay is also indebted to her postgraduate student, Sonja Kurtzer, and the Honours students in the Centre for Aboriginal Studies at Curtin University of Technology for sharing their stories about the forced removal of children from their families and the ongoing legacy of Stolen Generation experiences on their lives.

We are indebted to our editor Farideh Koohi-Kamali for her immediate and enthusiastic support, and to Melissa Nosal and Theresa Lee for their patience in moving us through the production process. For permission to reprint excerpts from "Land of the Free?: Circulating Human Rights and Narrated Lives in the United States" in chapters 1, 3, 6, and 7, we thank the editors of *Comparative*

American Studies 1.3 (2003), and the editors of *biography*, 27.1 (2004) for permission to reprint a version of chapter 1, "Conjunctions: Life Narratives in the Field of Human Rights." Passages in chapter 4 appeared in "Legitimating the Personal Voice: Shame and the Stolen Generation Testimony in Australia," in *Resistance and Reconciliation: Writing in the Commonwealth*, edited by Bruce Bennett, Susan Cowan, Jacqueline Lo, Satendra Nandan, and Jennifer Webb (Canberra: ASAL [Association for the Study of Australian Literature] and UNSW-ADFA, 2003), 47–63; "The Stolen Generation and Public Responsibility," in *Antipodes: A North American Journal of Australian Literary Studies*, 16.2 (June 2002), 5–10; "Manne's Generation: White Nation Responses to the Stolen Generation Report," in *Australian Humanities Review* (July–September 2001) at www.lib.latrobe.edu.au/AHR; "Cultural Studies at the Millennium: Tributes, Themes, Directions," in *Continuum: Journal of Media and Cultural Studies* 14.3 (November 2002), 265–75; and *"Rabbit-Proof Fence*, Relational Ecologies, and the Commodification of Indigenous Experience," in *Australian Humanities Review*, 31.2 (April 2004) (with Emily Potter). Portions of chapter 7 originally appeared in "Transforming Trauma: Post-Tiananmen Narratives and the Chinese Intellectual Diaspora" in *The Regenerative Spirit*, Volume 1, *Polarities of Home and Away*, edited by Nena Bierbaum, Sid Harrix, and Sue Hosking (Adelaide: Lythrum Press, 2003), 245–65.

Our partners, Robert and Greg, have remained committed to our work even as we have left them behind to meet together for extended periods long distances from home. Their energetic arguments with us have reminded us to sharpen our questions and deepen our thinking.

INTRODUCTION

The post–Cold War decade of the 1990s has been labeled the decade of human rights, the decade in which, Michael Ignatieff claims, "human rights has become the dominant moral vocabulary in foreign affairs" (2002, A29).[1] Not incidentally, it has also been described as the decade of life narratives, what commentators refer to as the time of memoir. Many of these life narratives tell of human rights violations. Victims of abuse around the world have testified to their experience in an outpouring of oral and written narratives. These stories demand that readers attend to histories, lives, and experiences often vastly different from their own. As people meet together and tell stories, or read stories across cultures, they begin to voice, recognize, and bear witness to a diversity of values, experiences, and ways of imagining a just social world and of responding to injustice, inequality, and human suffering. Indeed, over the last twenty years, life narratives have become one of the most potent vehicles for advancing human rights claims.

In Argentina, the mothers of the Disappeared take their bodies and their stories to the Plaza de Mayo and thereby make public the continuing silence of the State about the fate of daughters and sons. Stolen Generation narratives in Australia collectively reframe "well-intentioned" policies of assimilation as forms of cultural genocide. Testimonies and published life narratives by women in East and Southeast Asia, forced into sexual slavery by the Japanese Imperial Army during World War II, expose the institutionalized rape culture of forced prostitution during wartime as a violation of women's human rights. Narratives of political dissidents, like the letters from prison by China's champion of democracy Wei Jingsheng, often banned in their country of origin, find publishers elsewhere in nations receptive to their politics and only too ready to invoke the story told in order to exert pressure on non-compliant nations to address, justify, and modify their human rights record. Life narratives of displacement and cultural marginalization, such as those written by ethnic Turks in Germany, bring stories of second-class citizenship to the bar of public opinion around the world. Coming-out stories, such as Charlene Smith's narrative of rape and of her subsequent struggle to join other women to protest the inadequacy of HIV-AIDS counseling and treatment in South Africa, have focused national and international attention on the silenced stories of sexual assault and the scourge of AIDS in Africa. In the United States, Europe, and elsewhere, coming-out stories have played a critical role in the campaign to achieve human rights legislation for lesbians and gay men. Narratives of disability direct attention to the failure of advanced democracies to address the particular needs of the disabled as denials of basic human rights. The accumulation of these narratives from diverse cultural locations, often written by people with limited political purchase in a national arena, often competing and conflictual in their appeals, accumulate nonetheless into a chorus of voices demanding response and responsible action.

These two contemporary phenomena—human rights as the privileged mode of addressing human suffering and the rise in popularity of published life narratives—have commonly been understood to exist within the separate domains of politics and literature, respectively. *Human Rights and Narrated Lives*, in concert with more recent interdisciplinary studies, understands "the political" as inclusive of moral, aesthetic, and ethical aspects of culture. It treats life narratives and human rights campaigns as multidimensional domains that merge and intersect at critical points, unfolding within and enfolding one another in an ethical relationship that is simultaneously productive of claims for social justice and problematic for the furtherance of this goal.

The Universal Declaration of Human Rights (UDHR), adopted in 1948, and all subsequent Conventions and Covenants, have signaled to the imagined international community as a whole, to the nation-states within that imagined community, and to individuals and communities within those nation-states, a collective moral commitment to just societies in which all people live lives characterized by dignity, equality, bodily inviolability, and freedom.[2] These instruments of the United Nations position the victims of rights violations as potential legal claimants in the international arena. They provide platforms and mechanisms for redress for those whose rights to life, liberty, and security have been denied: whether by slavery, torture, rape and other forms of physical abuse, genocide, terrorism, racial and gender discrimination, ethnic cleansing, arbitrary detention, or denial of cultural integrity. Human rights platforms and mechanisms make possible a legitimating process of telling and listening that demands accountability on the part of states and international organizations.

The UDHR recognizes the "rights of individuals...to challenge unjust state law or oppressive customary practice" (Ignatieff 2001b, 5). Individuals initiate this process in a number of ways—by telling their stories to human rights advocates working for NGOs, by testifying before national inquiries and official or quasi-official tribunals, and by presenting their stories to the court of world opinion. Significantly, human rights discourses, norms, and instruments depend upon the international commitment to narratability, a commitment to provide, according to Joseph Slaughter, "a public, international space that empowers all human beings to speak" (415). That is, for rights discourse to become activated victims need to come forward and testify to their experience. Their testimony brings into play, implicitly or explicitly, a rights claim. The teller bears witness to his or her own experience through acts of remembering elicited by rights activists and coded to rights instruments.

These acts of remembering test the values that nations profess to live by against the actual experiences and perceptions of the storyteller as witness. They issue an ethical call to listeners both within and beyond national borders to recognize the disjunction between the values espoused by the community and the actual practices that occur. They issue a call within and beyond UN protocols and mechanisms for institutions, communities, and individuals to respond to the story; to recognize the humanity of the teller and the justice of the claim; to take responsibility for that recognition; and to find means of redress. In the specific locales of rights violations and in the larger court of public opinion, life narrative becomes essential to affect recourse, mobilize action, forge communities of interest, and enable social change.

Rights workers and rights campaigns make use of life narratives as they bring forward claims of human rights abuses. Stories provide necessary evidence and information about violations. They put a human face to suffering. They command international attention, spurring the interest of NGOs and the media, building awareness of events at home and in other parts of the world. As individual stories accumulate, the collective story gains cultural salience and resonance, sparking further interest in life narratives. Activist organizations enlist stories as a form of moral suasion to reach potential advocates and volunteers, to raise money to underwrite campaigns, and to persuade governments to honor their commitments to the UDHR, other UN covenants, and, in some cases, their own national policies. NGOs and quasi-judicial government forums provide legitimating platforms for stories to be heard, sometimes resulting in official inquiries and, in rare cases, official apology, reparations, and the recasting of official and textbook narratives. Stories unsettle private beliefs and public discourses about the national past, generating public debate, sympathy, and outrage. In response, publishers seek out narratives for mass distribution. Public displays and events, occurring in national, and international venues—the AIDS quilts, the Sea of Hands displays in Australia, the Madres de the Plaza de Mayo in Argentina, the caravan of Aung San Suu Kyi in Myanmar—make rights activism visible to increasing numbers of people, generating broader awareness of human rights movements.

Storytelling in action accumulates political import. In local contexts, life storytelling constitutes a social action on the part of individuals or communities, resonating through multiple cultural contexts, including the moral, aesthetic, political, and legal (Wilson 1999, 7). As stories circulate beyond local contexts through extended national and transnational communication flows, they enable claimants to "speak truth to power," to invoke Michel Foucault. The stories they tell can intervene in the public sphere, contesting social norms, exposing the fictions of official history, and prompting resistance beyond the provenance of the story within and beyond the borders of the nation—in relation to the communities affected as well as the institutions and discourses of history, religion, ethics, aesthetics, politics, and the law. Such disruptions of storytelling unfold through "piecemeal aggregation, rupture and upheaval and continue to be transformed by social action" (Wilson 1999, 7).

Stories enlisted within and attached to a human rights framework are particular kinds of stories—strong, emotive stories often chronicling degradation, brutalization, exploitation, and physical violence; stories that testify to the denial of subjectivity and loss of group identities. Sometimes these stories are told in the immediacy of catastrophic conflict, sometimes only years or decades after the recollected event. Some stories, formerly locked in silence, open wounds and re-trigger traumatic feelings once they are told. Some stories, recounted in the face of oppression and repression, of shame and denial, reinvest the past with a new intensity, often with pathos, as they test normative conceptions of social reality. All stories invite an ethical response from listeners and readers. All have strong affective dimensions for both the tellers and their audiences, affects that can be channeled in negative and positive ways, through personal, political, legal, and aesthetic circuits that assist, but can also impede, the advance of human rights. Whether or not storytelling in the field of human rights results in the extension of human justice, dignity, and freedom depends on the willingness of those addressed to hear the stories and to take responsibility for the recognition of others and their claims. In the transits of this multi-vectored space there are many flows, but also many detours, undercurrents, dams, and blockages.

DEFINING CONJUNCTIONS

Human Rights and Narrated Lives traces the transformations of stories in the field of human rights as they connect with human rights platforms, discourses, and campaigns. These transformations occur within the contexts of story production, circulation, and reception. The study also attends to the efficacies of storytelling for tellers and their audiences, specifically the affective, emotional, and cognitive dimensions that activate or fail to activate ethical imperatives in the social field where literature enfolds into politics.

By *production* we signal the conditions enabling and constraining the telling of stories. Distinctions between immediate contexts of telling and subsequent contexts of reception become important to processes of production. In certain instances stories are told in person before a hearing, commission, or tribunal, in the context of a direct and political relationship between telling and listening. In other instances, stories are reproduced in media broadcasts and state-sponsored publications, or published as life narratives using modes of production that expand the imaginative possibilities of dialogic exchange between narrators and more distanced readers. All stories emerge in the midst of complex and uneven relationships of power, prompting certain questions about production: Who tells the stories and who doesn't? To whom are they told and under what circumstances? Why, when, how, and where do narratives become intelligible as stories of human rights? What historical, cultural, and institutional conditions affect the shapes stories take? What are the personal, social, political, and ethical effects of stories and their venues of production for both tellers and listeners?

By *circulation* we signal the conditions enabling and constraining the movement of stories across time and location—that is, their reproduction in dispersed sites and their silencing in others. Stories originate in local contexts already transected by global concerns and forces. They enter and travel through global circuits of exchange that affect the import of the stories: through official UN mechanisms for recognition and redress; through national inquiries and international tribunals; through talk shows, news broadcasts, the web, rights brochures, and the like; through publication channels dependent on the popularity of narratives of victimization; through personal appearances in activist- or state-organized venues; and through other people's stories. Issues of circulation raise another set of questions: How do diverse and dispersed circuits affect the ways in which stories are framed, presented, and reinterpreted, often for successive generations or scattered communities of affiliation? How do modes of circulation impact upon the expectations of the teller, the structure of the story, and the mode of address to different kinds of audience? How are stories taken up in legal/political as opposed to literary/aesthetic domains? How do stories in circulation invite conflicting responses— among them empathetic identification, political advocacy, apathy, and backlash, some of which exceed, some of which frustrate the desires of tellers for recognition and redress?

By *reception* we signal the conditions enabling and constraining the ways in which stories are received and interpreted by multiple audiences in their immediate contexts of production as well as those distant from the originating event. Storytellers take risks. They hope for an audience willing to acknowledge the truthfulness of the story and to accept an ethical responsibility to both story and teller. There is always the possibility, however, that their stories will not find audiences willing to listen or that audiences will ignore or interpret their stories unsympathetically. Questions arise: In what venues— transnational, national, local, personal—do stories find audiences? What historical and cultural landscapes of collective memory do stories enter and unsettle? What are the terms of judgment directed to the stories in different forums of interpretation? How are stories enlisted in other peoples' causes? How do contexts of reception direct and contain the ethical call of stories and their appeals for redress?

Affective dimensions always attend the telling and reception of stories. Stories may generate strong sensations, feelings, and embodied responses for tellers and their audiences, at times of first and subsequent witnessing. As a sensation, capacity, or force felt in the body, affect lends intensity and amplification to responses, suffusing the conditions of reception. Cultures contain reservoirs of affect, residues of the unspoken, what Brian Masumi describes as "a state of suspense, potentially of disruption" (1996, 220). Sensations, such as embodied pain, shame, distress, anguish, humiliation, anger, rage, fear, and terror, can promote healing and solidarity among disaffected groups and provide avenues for empathy across circuits of difference. They can activate interest, excitement, vicarious enjoyment, shock, distress, and shame. They can also produce pleasure out of another's pain, turn subjects of story into spectacle, reduce difference to sameness, and induce exhaustion. While affect offers a potential for change, for becoming, it is impossible to predict how sensations will be channeled into knowledge or practice. What affects do stories that trouble knowledge of the past activate in audiences, as individuals and collectivities? Given the charged context of acts of remembering for tellers, what affects are reactivated in the diverse sites of storytelling?

Guided by these questions about the production, circulation, reception, and affective dimensions of storytelling, *Human Rights and Narrated Lives* explores how narratives that bear witness to suffering and impact differently upon dominant and marginalized, subaltern and outgroup communities, emerge in local settings that are inflected by and inflect the global; how in these settings rights discourse enables and constrains individual and collective subjects of narration; how the generic shapes that stories take are contingent upon the specific cultural, historical, and political contexts in which they arise; how acts of narration affect survivors, their communities, and dispersed audiences; how they raise questions about the status of evidence, the historical past, and narrative truth; how the affective force of stories impacts upon political, legal, cultural, and aesthetic vectors of experience, knowledge, and action; how life narratives are transformed as they become attached to a range of different desires, politics, and interpretations in arenas far from their immediate locus of meaning; and how and under what conditions their calls for recognition, response, and redress are mediated by the formal and informal structures of governments, politics, and culture.

We are using the term "life narrative" in its broadest sense, as an umbrella term that encompasses the extensive array and diverse modes of personal storytelling that takes experiential history as its starting point. These modes can range from oral or written testimony that bears witness to human rights abuse; to published narratives that unfold as retrospective, ethnography, confession, memoir, *testimonio*, letters, journals, recorded oral history; to autobiographical and semi-autobiographical fiction that adheres to some invocation of historical events or persons. Modes of address in personal storytelling vary depending on whether the contexts of telling are juridical, political, communal, social, imaginative, or some overlapping combination. Since personal storytelling involves acts of remembering, of making meaning out of the past, its "truth" cannot be read as solely or simply factual. There are different registers of truth beyond the factual: psychological, experiential, historical, cultural, communal, and potentially transformative. The present of personal narrating becomes a fulcrum, that point where the pressure of memories of a traumatic past and the hopes for an enabling future are held in balance. As balancing acts, directed back to a past that must be shared and toward a future that must be built collectively, acts of personal narrating can become projects of community building, organizational tools, and calls to action.

By the phrase "the field of human rights" we signal formal networks and informal meshworks of intersecting domains through which life narratives are enjoined to human rights activism. Networks refer to independent, organized, hierarchical, and geographically dispersed organizations and institutions that investigate, promote, monitor, and adjudicate rights claims. The United Nations and its regional commissions constitute one formal network; NGOs, such as Amnesty International and Human Rights Watch and affiliated websites, another. The term "meshworks," coined by Wendy Harcourt of the Society for International Development, signals self-organized, fluid, and ever-mobile cyberworlds and spontaneous actions that grow in unplanned or unexpected directions around human rights activism (Harcourt n.p.). Webs of alliances within and among various groups resisting oppression—women, racial and ethnic minorities, First Nation peoples, environmental and other groups—constitute these meshworks of the human rights regime—the dense flows of connections among groups and peoples working on behalf of human rights that transcend national, ethnic, racial, class, gender, and other social boundaries. Networks and meshworks intersect and interpenetrate in ways both mutually supportive and unpredictably contentious and adversarial.

Human rights activism unfolds in the networks and meshworks linking the United Nations, nation-states, and NGOs, and scattered venues or sites of action. The United Nations continually exerts a persuasive power to mobilize action by member states and extend understanding of human rights principles and modes of redress. Some nations, attentive to their international obligations and eager to appear progressive in the eyes of the world, establish national bodies to assess, monitor, and implement human rights principles. Some nations in the midst of political transformation—such as South Africa, East Timor, and Bosnia—enlist storytelling in processes of transformative justice. Others, such as China, espouse rights primarily in order to protect themselves against international pressures and to provide a forum for projecting their own version of human rights internationally. Others insist that the issues are purely domestic and reject international pressures *tout court*. Others, autocratic Asian nations and fundamentalist Islamic nations, contest Western-based principles and propose alternative schema of rights. NGOs, with their in-between status as neither sanctioned nor official, shuttle between local sites of abuse and international sites of redress, monitoring human rights progress, and bringing ongoing violations to international attention. Internet communication, public events, and their scatter effects disseminate awareness of human rights through everyday interactions and targeted events, such as anti-globalization interventions in World Trade Organization meeting sites.

In and between the intersections of local, national, and transnational interests, a multitude of consensual and conflictual forces—material, legal, historical, affective, personal, and intersubjective—blend, clash, veer off, dissipate, and transform in ways that test human rights ideals and complicate local campaigns. There are the material practices of human rights: the campaign strategies, the daily coalition-building, the media of global circulation, especially the Internet and network conglomerates; the legal principles and contestations that spur negotiations around rights and the geopolitical environments in which rights-talk and activism takes place; the architectures of memory structured by spatialities (the there of the event, the here of the telling, listening, and the space in-between) and temporalities (the then, the now, the not yet), which imbue acts of remembrance with cultural and historical significance; the affective environments of cultural memory, particularly those deriving from the Holocaust and its residue of remembering which precede and impinge on traumatic storytelling and its reception; the subject positions available for narrators to occupy in telling stories and the narrative forms accessible by them; and the embodiments of physical and emotional pain that victims experience and to which they testify.

All of this we take to constitute the contested and mediated field of human rights.

CASE STUDIES

We have chosen five sites that enable us to consider the conflicted and indeterminate ways in which storytelling connects to human rights campaigns that have been and are taking place around the globe: apartheid and post-apartheid South Africa before, during, and subsequent to the Truth and Reconciliation Commission hearings; Australia and the National Inquiry into the Forced Separation of Indigenous Children from their Families; East and Southeast Asia and the belated narratives of World War II sex prisoners; the United States and prison rights narratives; and China in the wake of the Tiananmen Square massacre. All of these are sites where human rights abuses have gained international recognition and tested the efficacy of human rights platforms in action.

Three of our case studies look to locations—South Africa, Australia, and East and Southeast Asia—where rights violations and campaigns have been widely publicized. In South Africa, the Truth and Reconciliation Commission (TRC) process captured worldwide attention as it marked the transition from and apartheid system that had denied freedoms to the majority black population and thus rendered South Africa a pariah state in the eyes of the world. The Commission promised a new era of racial reconciliation and nation building in South African history. The Human Rights and Equal Opportunity Commission (HREOC) Inquiry in Australia, prompted by the UN Decade of Indigenous Peoples, came in the wake of South Africa's TRC hearings. Although not as broadly reported around the world, the inquiry galvanized political controversy and upset narratives of nation within Australia and became linked to similar Indigenous campaigns in other postcolonial, white settler nations. It gathered further attention through the global media when Australia hosted the Sydney 2000 Olympic Games. The case of former sex prisoners (often referred to as "comfort women"), gained international attention when linked to transnational feminist agendas associated with the International Decade of Women and events leading up to and surrounding the fiftieth anniversary of the end of the War in Europe and the Pacific. In all three cases, local initiatives combined with international attention and the moral suasion of the United Nations brought about national inquiries or, in the latter case, a transnational citizens' tribunal that provided a legitimating forum for recognition and calls for redress.

The inclusion of prison narratives in the United States and post-Tiananmen Square narratives in and outside China might seem unusual choices. These latter chapters stand in contrast to the other three. Although the United States purports to be a defender of human rights on the international stage, it rarely looks within at sites of widespread violations. The areas of incarceration rates and prisoner rights, while taken up by AI and HRW, do not gather public attention and spark moral outrage that human rights claims provoke in other global locations. In part, this is because of the complicated issue of the incarcerated subject as a subject of human rights within the United States. It is more difficult for prisoners to garner sympathy as victims of the justice and penal systems because they are perceived to be guilty and thus outside the domain of human rights. But it is also due to America's privileged status as superpower and arbiter within the human rights regime. While United States officials have been slow to recognize the human rights of prisoners at home, it protests often about the treatment of dissidents and political prisoners in "enemy" or "pariah" states, as has occurred relative to China, Burma, the former Soviet Union, and apartheid South Africa.

The Tiananmen Square massacre in 1989 turned world attention to China as one of the world's major violators of human rights.[3] Within China, the government censored stories about the event. Because of its authoritarian regime, calls for redress for violations of human rights and dignity have had no purchase in a national arena. Nonetheless, Tiananmen discourse continues to circulate within China through underground channels, forcing the government to maintain vigilance around the Square, particularly on the June 4 anniversaries. Accounts of the Tiananmen massacre, however, have begun to be told by members of the Chinese diaspora to audiences outside China. In addition, new stories are emerging within and beyond China's borders that channel and transform trauma into new desires and imperatives. While framed outside a human rights language, they assert new rights and freedoms for Chinese citizens at home and in dialogue with dispersed, diasporic communities.

Exploration of these five sites enables us to attend to the specific aspects of human rights campaigns and engage with the contradictions and conundrums that attend the production, circulation, and reception of personal stories in the field of human rights. Each has its own defining problematic. In South Africa storytelling within the context of the Truth and Reconciliation process was yoked to nation building, including the imagining of new South African citizen-subjects. After the TRC, citizens of post-apartheid South Africa faced new imperatives that challenged the unity-building frameworks promoted by the Commission and its Report and set new counter-narratives into circulation. In Australia, Indigenous storytelling challenged British common law, setting in motion contested claims for Indigenous rights and racial reconciliation that were forestalled rather than advanced with the publication of the Inquiry's Report and its framing of child removal as a form of cultural genocide. In the case of former sex prisoners, the end of the Cold War opened new discursive opportunities for remembering and understanding World War II differently; but it was only when transnational activism around the trafficking of women and military prostitution forced a recognition of women's rights as human rights that the stories could enter an international arena of human rights adjudication. In the United States, inmates and their advocates have found it difficult to position the incarcerated as claimants to human rights, given that inmates have been denied state-guaranteed constitutional rights and are positioned beyond the boundaries of the citizen-subject. Their status as convicted and incarcerated tests the limits of entitlement and the representation of "victim." It also confounds the ethical call for empathetic identification with prisoners abused within the system. And in China, the government has sought to substitute Western-based human rights discourses with ones that challenge those of the United States, transnational NGOs, and Chinese dissidents. In this context, alternative modes of storytelling disperse traumatic memories and attach citizen desires, to China's rush to modernization, yoking them to global markets and global youth cultures.

The intersections of storytelling and rights claims develop differently at each site. Each site has its specific local dimensions, mobilized through particular global transits. Each unfolds through unpredictable developments and outcomes involving overlapping and contradictory networks and meshworks of advocacy. Taken together, the cases we have chosen allow us to peruse First and Third World concerns; consider national, postcolonial, and transnational histories and frameworks; engage with Western and Asian values debates across democratic and authoritarian contexts; address trauma and the different paths to healing; and flag some of the many challenges to the human rights regime in the aftermath of the attack on the World Trade Center and the U.S.-led war on terror.

As these five case studies demonstrate, in the midst of the networks and meshworks of the regime of human rights, personal storytelling continues to command attention, however unpredictable or inadequate, and to call on people around the world to listen and to act. *Human Rights and Narrated Lives* is our attempt to listen, to follow the strands of personal storytelling, and to respond through an ethics of recognition.

CHAPTER 1

CONJUNCTIONS: LIFE
NARRATIVES IN THE FIELD OF
HUMAN RIGHTS

The last decades of the twentieth century witnessed the unprecedented rise in genres of life writing, narratives published primarily in the West[1] but circulated widely around the globe. This "memoir boom" has certainly occurred in English-speaking countries, from Australia to Jamaica, from England to South Africa, and in European countries, especially France and Germany.[2] However, there has been a relative boom in personal narratives coming from elsewhere in the world as well. In many global locations, in post-Maoist China and Latin America, in North Africa and the Philippines, in Northern and Eastern Europe, life narratives have been told, transcribed, published, and translated, gaining both local and international audiences.

This rise in the popularity of published life narratives has taken place in the midst of global transformations, both cataclysmic and gradual, that have occurred in the decades since the end of World War II: a succession of wars of prolonged and short duration; repeated instances of mass genocide in Cambodia, Rwanda, Bosnia, and elsewhere; violent and nonviolent decolonization movements in South America, Asia, and Africa; the intensification and dissipation of the Cold War in Europe; mass migrations of peoples; the acceleration of change and fragmentation of contemporary life. These geopolitical and temporal transformations form not so much a backdrop, but rather a fractured web of intersecting geographic, historical, and cultural contingencies out of which personal narratives have emerged and within which they are produced, received, and circulated. These global transformations have spurred developments in the field of human rights as well, developments that demand, for their recognition in the international community, multiple forms of remembrance of and witnessing to abuse. To situate the contemporary interest in life narratives in the field of human rights it is necessary to recall briefly the origins of the UDHR in the contentious and passionate debates of the mid-twentieth century.

At the end of World War II, the incontrovertible evidence of the violence unleashed in the Japanese and German war efforts and of Nazi mass killings created an international climate of moral indignation. As this moral indignation attached itself to the modernist values and principles of the victors, the international community renewed its commitment to a "United Nations" of peoples dedicated to the pursuit of peace and the protection of human rights. In relatively swift succession came the signing of the Charter of the United Nations in 1945; the Nuremberg and Tokyo war crimes trials in 1945–46 and 1946–48 respectively; and the adoption by the United Nations of the UDHR in 1948. The Nuremberg trials in particular issued a call to the world community to remember crimes against humanity. As an expression of ideals, the UDHR became the point of origin binding an international community together in service to a more just future.

Debates about, refinements of, and votes on the UDHR and its accompanying Covenants, one on Civil and Political Rights (ICCPR) and a second on Economic, Social and Cultural Rights (ICESCR), took place in the two decades following 1948 amidst movements of decolonization and Cold War anatagonisms. Whether violent or relatively peaceful, movements of national liberation from colonial rule, founded on the right to the self-determination of peoples laid out in the ICCPR, involved complex negotiations—by states, communities, and individuals—of the psychological, political, economic, and cultural legacies of a colonial past that had to be remembered, made, and remade for the sake of national futures. For its part, the Cold War effectively remapped the globe through spheres of influence that displaced earlier spheres of colonialism. Cold War politics also sparked contentious debates within the United Nations about the nature of rights, particularly the relative priority of "negative" rights that protect individuals from the state and "positive" rights that pertain to aspirational goals and an enabling standard of living that might extend human dignity and freedom for everyone.

In the aftermath of decolonization movements and Cold War *realpolitik*, over sixty human rights treaties, declarations, and Conventions have come into effect to address specific rights. For the last fifty years, differences in philosophical perspectives related to negative, positive, and group rights, as well as disagreements about appropriate interventions and modes of redress have been rehearsed in local, national, and international venues. Campaigns have ensued. Conventions and Declarations have taken shape after heated negotiations. The reach of rights discourse has extended beyond the institutional settings of the United Nations and the official bodies of nation-states responding to rights initiatives to formal NGO networks and informal meshworks of advocacy—the dense and nonhierarchical flows of connections among groups and peoples working on behalf of human rights that transcend national boundaries. Within these global information flows, the very meaning of a human right, and the foundational assumptions supporting it, have been challenged, critiqued, and redefined. At the heart of these debates, voices of dissent have prompted ongoing critiques of human rights discourse, frameworks, and mechanisms for implementation.

RIGHTS AND STORIES

By the last decades of the century, the modernist language of rights had become a *lingua franca* for extending—sometimes explicitly, sometimes implicitly—the reach of human rights norms, not everywhere, but across an increasingly broad swath of the globe. Post–World War II struggles for national self-determination and equality for women, indigenous peoples, and minorities within nation-states led to the rise of local and transnational political movements and affiliations—movements for black and Chicano civil rights, women's rights, gay rights, workers rights, refugee rights, disability rights, and indigenous rights among them—all of which have created new contexts and motivations for pursuing personal protections under international law. In each instance, personal storytelling motivated the rights movement. These collective movements have gained momentum and clarified agendas for action through attachment to the goals of the UDHR and attendant discourses, events, and mechanisms. The collective movements have also argued for new claims, pressing for reinterpretations of rights frameworks, and lobbying for

Covenants and Declarations that expand the kinds of rights that require recognition and protection.

In the 1960s, group action and advocacy led to the adoption of the Convention on the Elimination of All Forms of Racial Discrimination (1969). In the 1980s, women's and feminist activism led to the adoption of the Convention on the Elimination of All Forms of Discrimination against Women (1981). In the 1990s, trade union and indigenous advocacy led to the adoption of the International Labor Organization Convention 169 on Indigenous and Tribal Peoples (1991) and the Draft Declaration on the Rights of Indigenous People (1993). Together, these latter two instruments, if and where ratified, can significantly alter the parameters of rights discourse in that they acknowledge and support group rather than individual rights, encompassing the aspirations of indigenous and minority peoples for self-determination and their claims to culture, language, religion, and land rights, sometimes in opposition to states' claims of sovereignty. In the early 1990s, rights activists lobbied for the Convention on the Rights of the Child. In this evolving culture of rights, personal witnessing plays a central role in the formulation of new rights protections, as people come forward to tell their stories in the contexts of tribunals and national inquiries. In its role as an advocate for peaceful forms of civic engagement within nations and across nations, the United Nations itself has generated audiences for local stories muted within the dominant cultures of member states through its "decade" strategy, that is, through the targeting of a particular group and the concentration of attention on its issues for a decade, as in the International Decade of Women and the International Decade of Indigenous Peoples.

Local movements that "go national" or "international" often generate climates that enable the reception and recognition of new stories, attaining what Gillian Whitlock refers to as a "discursive threshold" (2000, 144). Emergent in communities of identification marginalized within the nation, such movements embolden individual members to understand personal experience as a ground of action and social change. Collective movements seed local acts of remembering "otherwise," offering members new or newly valued subject positions from which to speak and to address members of their own community in acts of solidarity. They also offer members of the dominant community occasions for witnessing to human rights abuse, acknowledging and affirming the rights of others. Through acts of remembering, individuals and communities narrate alternative or counter-histories coming from the margins, voiced by other kinds of subjects—the tortured, the displaced and overlooked, the silenced and unacknowledged—among them. These counter-histories emerge in part out of the formerly untold tales of those who have not benefited from the wealth, health, and future delivered to many others by the capital and technologies of modernity and postmodernity. Individuals and groups may also engage in narrative acts of critical self-locating through which they assert their cultural difference and right to self-determination, or they may imagine leaving the past behind for a new social order or a newly empowered collective subjectivity. Members of collective movements deploy personal narrating to witness many forms of trauma—sexual violence and abuse, economic and political degradation, racism, terrorism, and forms of genocide. Their stories enable new forms of subjectivity and radically altered futures.

In nations where freedom to speak publicly is circumscribed, for instance, in authoritarian, fundamentalist, and, for some groups, in democratic states, victims may be unable or unwilling to speak publicly. Professional rights advocates may seek out stories of abuse from victims, speak on their behalf, and frame their stories within the field of human rights. Often these stories must be solicited and circulated anonymously by NGOs. This has often been the case in relation to Islamic women telling stories of sexual, domestic, religious, and cultural inequality and oppression. In such contexts, activist framing may enfold the narrative within the individualist, humanist, and secular frameworks of Western rights, overwriting the customs and beliefs of the victims. And yet, local campaigns, particularly those that involve stories of violence against women, are often most successful when harnessed to an international rights movement. In these instances, transits between the local and global and within pockets of modernity involve complex negotiations of traditional and modernist discourses and practices.[3] In other instances, stories may be framed within traditional, communal, religious, or philosophic frameworks different from, but arguably consonant with, modernist aspirations for human dignity and social justice.

Since the late 1980s, wide-scale transformations—geographic, economic, political, cultural, and psychic—have also impelled people to tell their stories. These include the opening of the Berlin Wall, the collapse of the Soviet Union into ethnic states pursuing agendas of ethnic nationalism, the end of the policy of apartheid in South Africa, the global movements of indigenous peoples to reclaim lands and have their cultures acknowledged, the changing demography of the new Europe through immigration, the rise (and collapse) of Asian economies and the expansion of the Asian diaspora, the refugee crises around the globe, and before and after September 11, 2001, the rise of international religious fundamentalisms. Unprecedented global unrest has called forth and called for repeated acts of remembering, through which people reclaim identities at home, in transit, and in new communities and nations.

The violence unleashed by resurgent ethnic nationalisms at the end of the Cold War has multiplied the number of people displaced into refugee camps, and dispersed into welcoming and not-so-welcoming nations. The proliferation and increasing reach of ethnic diasporas through mass migrations has brought about displacements of peoples, values, and identifications, often motivating the reconstitution of communities of tradition in exile. Ongoing processes of decolonization have led people released from their colonized status to struggle with the communal and psychic legacies of colonization. In white settler nations, indigenous struggles to survive state-sponsored acts of oppression compel acts of witnessing to a past erased in official histories of the nation. Within different democratic nation-states, the rise of the politics of multiculturalism and diaspora and calls for recognition of the claims of indigenous groups have challenged conventional understandings of the relationship of ethnicity and indigeneity to citizenship. As a result, new or newly identified citizen-subjects reimagine the grounds of their communal identities, test the individualist ethos of the UDHR, and contest master narratives of national belonging and identity.

Forces of turmoil, often violent, move individuals, communities, ideas, cultural forms, and economic wealth around the globe in ways that unsettle old identities and understandings of the past, and presage the imagining of possible futures. Such dislocations of identity unsettle psychically experienced understandings of time (the before, the now, the possible future), space (the old place, the new place), subjectivity (the me I used to be and the me I am becoming), and community (the ones to which I used to belong and the ones of which I am now a member). The scrambling of zones of time, space, subjectivity, and community engenders new patterns of remembering and new modes of response on the part of individuals, communities, and nations. The condensations and expansion of temporal and spatial dimensions of past and present set in motion rememberings of old selves and imaginings of new selves, rememberings of old belongings and allegiances and new ones in the diasporic spaces of dispersed, postmodern communities and nations (Baucom 160–2). While some people may be reluctant narrators, preferring to forget or forestall the pain of unrest, dislocation, and exile, others may be energized to tell their stories in order to work through the political and social, psychic and embodied residues of trauma and loss. Furthermore, displaced, migrant, and diasporic people arrive at destinations where different discursive fields and different histories of activism offer new terms and storytelling modes (sometimes foreign, sometimes familiar; sometimes shunned, sometimes embraced) through which they might remember, interpret, understand, reconstruct, and comes to terms with a complex past.

In the midst of dislocations and relocations, personal and collective storytelling can become one way in which people claim new identities and assert their participation in the public sphere. It can also become a way of maintaining communal identification in the face of loss and cultural degradation. Or it can be enlisted in witnessing to the failures of democratic nations to realize and live up to their democratic principle of inclusive citizenship, making visible rents in the social fabric that undermine unified narratives of national belonging. In all cases, storytelling functions as a crucial element in establishing new identities of longing (directed toward the past) and belonging (directed toward the future).

THE LITERATURE OF TRAUMA AND THE HOLOCAUST

Stories emerging from collective rights movements and the cataclysmic geopolitical displacements of the last two decades have become identified with a larger body of literature concerning trauma and traumatic remembering. The cultural focus on "trauma" in the last decades of the twentieth century, arising out of feminism, psychoanalysis, and ethnic identity studies, motivated life writing that mapped and mined the disruptive effects of significant events in the past. Circulating within professional, academic, and popular perceptions of and discourses about trauma in the West, this literature has become a prominent genre of personal narrating. Journalistic reports, popular magazine articles, academic studies, feminist activisms around sexual abuse, and medical diagnoses of Post Traumatic Stress Syndrome (officially accepted in 1980) as a condition suffered by victims of the war in Vietnam; all have contributed to the public awareness in popular and academic domains of multiple forms of trauma and traumatic remembering.

In English-speaking and European cultures, the experience of trauma has been understood predominantly through psychoanalytic frameworks of interiority that describe trauma as self-altering and self-shattering, and acts of traumatic remembering as fitful, incomplete, and belated, caught in a "dialectic between dissociation and compulsory repetition" (Ball 2). The literature of trauma at once compels and sustains the contemporary practice of trauma therapy specific to the West. Once this psychoanalytic understanding of trauma and the healing process it underwrites becomes enlisted in human rights frameworks for telling and listening to stories, the psychoanalytic model spreads through global circuits into dispersed local sites, providing a framework for narrations of suffering. In this way, narratives produced in dispersed global locations are drawn into the field of trauma and reinterpreted as part of the contemporary literature about trauma.

Exemplary of the literature of traumatic remembering in the West have been Holocaust stories and all that has come to signify "the Holocaust" as the emblematic limit case of human rights abuse in the twentieth century. In the last two decades of the past century, an imperative for Holocaust survivors to work through the trauma of the past took on particular urgency with the passing of the last generations of survivors. Popular and scholarly audiences throughout the United States, Europe, Australia, and other Western nations have reacted profoundly to the resultant outpouring of Holocaust stories as they confront the challenge of the ethical in the face of radical suffering. So important and influential have Holocaust stories become, that this signal event has become a template for all forms of traumatic telling, response, and responsibility within the contemporary field of human rights.

It is instructive to review the history through which the Holocaust and Holocaust stories came to be exemplary of the literature of trauma, linking that history back to the Nuremberg Trials at the end of World War II. The Nuremberg Trials, so much a part of the environment of outrage out of which the regime of human rights had its inception, may have called Nazi leadership to account, but they did not focus on the systematic, mass killing of Jews and others labeled "undesirable" by the Nazi regime as a crime against humanity. The event that would later be labeled "the Holocaust," and become paradigmatic in defining the limits of unimaginable and unspeakable trauma in the latter part of the twentieth century in the West, had not yet reached a discursive threshold of intelligibility. That would take another thirty years.[4]

The first turning point came in 1961 when the Eichmann Trial in Israel televised to the world the testimony of survivors of the Nazi Judeocide, testimony that was accepted as evidentiary and took on juridical authority. While the Eichmann Trial brought the horrors of the Nazi genocide to an international audience, it did not, however, provide a unifying discursive framework for understanding the nature of the event as Holocaust, as an unprecedented traumatic world event exceeding the understanding of Jewish history as a succession of pogroms (Arendt 35). Israeli success in the 1967 Six Day War marked another turning point, affecting as it did the re-masculinization of the Israeli nation. It also promoted transnational identification and affiliation between an Israeli and an American Jewry (Breines 72). The emergence of an Israeli state with a history of victory, coupled with "the revival of the public culture of countries humiliated by occupation and collaboration" (Winter 55) provided an environment in which stories of the traumatic past could be told and heard.

By 1978, the word "Holocaust" came to signal not only an event within Jewish history but also a unique and unprecedented "world" experience. Personal memories of the Nazi genocide became part of a public discourse beyond the personal, resonating within world cultural memory. This transformation was aided by the proliferation of published life narratives, films, and the immensely popular television miniseries, *Holocaust*, broadcast in the United States and subsequently in Europe (Breines 72). Over the next decade, at academic conferences and in university courses, scholars and students debated the ethics, politics, and aesthetics of Holocaust representation with reference to the growing body of Holocaust narratives. Exploring the status of witness "truth" and "genocide," this work seeded the emergence of the field of Holocaust Studies. "It is only when the Judeocide becomes discursively constructed as the Holocaust, and as traumatic," notes Jon Stratton, "that there is a public space in which the traumas of Holocaust survivors make sense, not just as individual trauma, but as experiences within a greater, cultural trauma" (6). In the context of the culture of trauma, the Holocaust story became commodified and reified as the premier instance of traumatic remembering.

By the final decades of the twentieth century, as scenes of personal witness gave way to processes of historical recovery (Wajnryb 2), Holocaust remembrance took many forms. The first and second generations of children of Holocaust survivors enacted what Marianne

Hirsch describes as "postmemory," "a powerful form of memory" attached not to the event but to images, stories, and transgenerational hauntings "mediated not through recollection but through projection, investment and creation" (9). In painting, websites, videos, and personal narratives, these children gave meaning and structure to an event that had occurred outside their lifetimes but nonetheless persisted through received memories and the residues of personal and cultural affect.[5] Artists and activists, dedicated to building and maintaining an archive of testimony, produced documentary and feature films and assembled exhibitions, oral histories, and video archives at various places—in Israel, the United States, Australia, the United Kingdom, the Netherlands, and elsewhere.[6] Communities built and sponsored memorials and museums housing collections of photographs and witness testimony.[7] All of this occurred in an era when anti-Semitism and Holocaust denial were on the rise (Winter 55).

The literature of trauma in the West, exemplified by Holocaust narratives, has become the dominant paradigm for understanding the processes of victimization, remembering, witnessing, and recovery. And pychoanalysis has provided the explanatory framework through which the survivor's embodiment of traumatic memory, explorations of the traumatic past, and mourning and "working through" of trauma's radical disruption in the present has been understood.[8] Responses to these stories focus on ethical processes of responsibility and psychoanalytic understandings of the processes of healing, both personal and cultural. Because of the paradigmatic status of Holocaust stories and their interpretation as limit cases of trauma, the production, circulation, and reception of these stories have shaped modes of response to other events, histories, and contexts of suffering.

Recently, however, the universal applicability of a psychoanalytic model, with its emphasis on the closed interiority of trauma, has been contested as inadequate to address the diverse experiential histories, languages of suffering, structures of feeling, and storytelling modes evidenced in diverse cultural traditions around the world (see Bennett and Kennedy). Critics argue that the psychoanalytic model privileges stories suffused with traumatic remembering and suffering, and silences other kinds of stories that may not unfold through the Western trope of trauma (see Ball; Berlant; and Boler). They argue that it universalizes diverse and multiple structures of feelings, eliding gender, racial, and ethnic differences. It renders individual suffering and psychic interiority the ground of trauma, making it difficult to register the cultural transmission of stories and their imbrication in institutional and political structures and practices. Furthermore, the psychoanalytic model of trauma cannot adequately address the genealogies and architectures of cultural memory, such as those characterizing the evolution of "the Holocaust" as it has come to be represented not only as story, but as preeminent event, emblem, haunting, history, and transcendent myth on a world stage.

Though foundational to Holocaust studies, for millions of people elsewhere in the world this model for addressing trauma and processes of healing limits understanding of the many ways in which people respond to and deal with a past of suffering. Many cultures have adopted other ways of understanding and figuring cataclysmic events, including genocide. For example, in indigenous struggles in South America liberationist theology provides a model for resistance within the struggle and recovery in its aftermath. In some East-Asian countries, shamanic inscription and Daoist modes of spirit possession become experiential models and embodied forms of dealing with a traumatic past. In some Islamic fundamentalist contexts, Jihad becomes a form of recovery from the past of degradation. In the immediate face of radical suffering and distress, telling and healing can take more pragmatic forms, even in Western settings (see Rall n.p.).

STORIES AND MARKETS

These historical contingencies help us to understand larger global contexts for the production of narratives of displacement, suffering, and trauma, some but not all of which arise out of or are enlisted in human rights activism. In order to more fully comprehend the force of storytelling in the late twentieth century, we need also to consider the economic and cultural forces imbricated in the local and global transits of circulation and reception of life narratives.

Life narratives have become salable properties in today's markets. They gain their audiences through the global forces of commodification that convert narratives into the property of publishing and media houses (Baxi 40–1). Publishing houses in turn convert stories of suffering and survival into commodified experiences for general audiences with diverse desires and also for an increasing number of niche audiences interested in particular kinds of suffering. The expanding market for life stories coincides with the increasing education, disposable income, and leisure time of the post–World War II generations in Western democratic nations and pockets of modernities elsewhere around the globe. Postwar educational initiatives and modernization campaigns provided greater access to higher education, resulting in a broader-based reading public and wider markets for stories.

Different communities around the globe, however, have differential levels of affluence, education, leisure, and access to media and print technologies. In relationship to print technologies, Philip G. Altbach notes that developing countries, which may have a public eager for stories from home and elsewhere, often have a poorly developed publishing industry (2). In such locations, a paucity of publishing venues seriously affects the ability to "communicat[e] a culture" at the local and national levels, and within a global marketplace of commodities and ideas (3). The same point could be made about the access of people in developing countries to nascent local and national media outlets in the face of the globalizing force of Western syndicated and corporate media transmission. At this historical moment, telling life stories in print or through the media by and large depends upon a Western-based publishing industry, media, and readership. This dependence affects the kinds of stories published and circulated, the forms those stories take, and the appeals they make to audiences. That is, stories coming from local sites around the world or from sites of exile, as they are taken up within Western-dominated global information flows, may lose their local specificity and resonance in translation. What is lost and gained in the local to global transits affects patterns of recognition and redress in diverse and often unpredictable ways.

The "triumph" of global capitalism and the dominance of the West, particularly the United States, have meant that the culture of the individual, the belief in the individual's uniqueness and unique story, and his or her individual rights, has gained an international currency as it has been exported to ever-expanding areas of the globe. Interlocking media venues, serving the interests of global capital, keep personal stories in various kinds of circulation. Talk shows feed audience desires to hear other people's stories. Publishers seek out and put in print the personal narratives of celebrities of all kinds, actors, politicians, sports figures, and the little people whose small stories are made newsworthy for a brief moment due to a traumatic or freakish event (Massumi 1993, 3–4). Television producers turn out video biographies, called biopics, to feed to the history channels or the channels and programs aimed at engaging the emotional sympathies of women. Olympics coverage, broadcast around the world every two years, features mini-biographies of star athletes, stories that enhance viewer investment in the games, stimulating identification with personal struggles to overcome adversity. The desire for personal stories, often telling of individualist triumph over adversity, of the "little person" achieving fame, of people struggling to survive illness, catastrophe, or violence, seems insatiable in the West and is expanding with the reach of global media. Publishers and media conglomerates recognize that stories of suffering and survival sell to readers. The marketing of these life stories takes place in different cultures—of fear, suspicion, trauma, recognition, and advocacy. If the post–World War II era began with new hopes for a transcendent future and faith in democratic governments, the century ended with a sense of nostalgia, melancholy, and cynicism in the midst of communities fractured and unsettled. Cataclysmic shifts in power relations and the movements of populations abroad and within a nation have bred a culture of fear, borne of insecurities. Local identity movements within Western democratic states (gay, feminist, and indigenous rights, to name a few) also foster insecurities, raising fears in others by challenging beliefs, relationships, and seemingly stable identities and by demanding recognition of different experiences and pasts.

Markets feed these insecurities and provide commodified stories through which readers can reinvent imagined securities. Some readers may respond to insecurities by enacting empathetic identification that recuperates stories of radical differences into their more familiar frameworks of meaning. Such acts of consumption of other peoples' lives enable some to dispel the fear of otherness by containing it. This type of recuperation occurred when Western feminist readers of Iman's *I Am Iman* sensationalized African and Islamic women's lives and translated their empathetic identification with Iman into a, Western-inflected campaign against the practice of clitoridectomy. In this case, empathetic identification became a means to the reader's own self-affirmation as an empowered agent, here an agent of social change and humanitarian betterment.

Some readers may respond to the insecurities of fragmenting national environments by recuperating stories of difference in ways that reconfirm national myths and heroic fictions, as occurs when immigrant stories such as Frank McCourt's *Angela's Ashes* and *'Tis* or indigenous stories such as Sally Morgan's *My Place* are read as assimilation success stories. In the midst of insecurities, some readers seek out stories as a means to displace their fears and supplement the sense of their own modernist anxieties through the vicarious consumption of other people's lives. Or they may seek in those lives opportunities for trying on different, more exotic, exhilarating, romantic, or outlaw identities. This kind of reading occurred when readers adopted characters from Armistead Maupin's *Tales of the City* as if they were fragments of their own imagined lives.

Life narratives may also provide ways for readers to imagine the security of a common past or common future in the midst of the fragmentation and unnerving pace of change of the present. If, as Jay Winter suggests, memory is "a metaphor for a broader movement of uncertainty about how to frame the past" (65), then narratives of personal remembering become sites for knowing the past differently in the present. Winter describes the capacious absorption of stories of suffering in the United States as the compulsion to recover the past, particularly for privileged, wealthy, educated urban elites. For Andreas Huyssen, the commodification of storytelling is one way for the culture to forestall postmodern fragmentation and the uncertainty of contemporary life by anchoring belief on some imagined foundation around which people can keep at bay the impending forces of chaos. This openness to remembering the past through the consumption of stories of trauma and suffering reverberates with a desire of readers to believe in the promissory note of modernism within the postmodern condition. Andreas Huyssen calls this preoccupation with memory a "new imaginary of temporality" (2003, 16) in which Western audiences feed their need to believe in the achievable goals of justice and freedom, to keep faith in narratives of progress, and to believe in the efficacy of collective action against the overwhelming forces of fragmentation.

For other readers, sensationalized stories of suffering feed the darker passions of what Kirby Farrell labels the posttraumatic "wound" cultures of postmodernity. Farrell describes posttraumatic culture as a culture desensitized to suffering, "a world in which power and authority seem staggeringly out of balance, in which personal responsibility and helplessness seem crushing, and in which cultural meanings no longer seem to transcend death" (Farrell 7). In a posttraumatic environment, some readers seek out spectacles of suffering and trauma to fuel sado-masochistic fantasies and voyeuristic pleasures. Identifying with perpetrators rather than victims, they may turn to another person's potential violence to both experience and exorcize their own "posttraumatic demons" (Farrell 7). Others may turn to narratives of suffering and trauma to feed their needs to "feel" something, anything, any sensation, to experience some concatenation of affects and pleasures. This "recourse to traumatic narratives," argues Ball, "paradoxically serves simultaneously to defer, to organize, and to reproduce the low-grade angst" (19).

Despite the vagaries of the cultures of trauma and posttrauma, the insatiable reach of capital, the commodification of narratives of suffering, and the standardizing forces of globalization, a counter desire for local knowledge arises as local communities struggle to distance their stories from a "panoptic mastering viewpoint" (Clarke 242; Baucom 161).[9] In local sites of struggle, a culture of disbelief and cynicism about "official" or normative narratives of history, identity, and nation motivates people to narrate as well as read stories that contradict, complicate, and undermine the grand modernist narratives of nation, progress, and enlightenment. These stories of cultural difference proliferate as voices of dissidence claim the legitimacy of their local experiential histories. These are the stories that are told by people who have been displaced into new communities and nations, or who have been previously subjugated within their respective nations, who have broken silence to tell the stories of racism, discrimination, degradation, but also of survival, resilience, and transformation. For readers who identify with collective movements, whether they are active participants or not, narratives coming out of a shared experience offer new avenues for activism and self-understanding, new models of remembering. Such narratives can enable access to and potential recognition of the incommensurable differences between the teller's experience and that of the reader, making possible circuits of connection across differences, and circuits of difference across connection. Although always compromised, stories offer readers new ways of gaining knowledge about peoples around the globe, calling into existence new cultural forms, new modes of circulation, and new forms of civic engagement.

In the midst of the transits that take stories of local struggle to readerships around the world, NGOs and activists enlist stories from victims as a way of alerting a broader public to situations of human rights violations. They also solicit and package stories to attract readerships. The kinds of stories they choose—sensationalized, sentimentalized, charged with affect—target privileged readers in anticipation that they will identify with, contribute to, and become advocates for the cause. The frames they impose on stories are designed to capture the interest, empathy, and political responsiveness of readers elsewhere, in ways they have learned will "sell" to publishers and audiences. NGOs harness their rights agendas to the market and its processes of commodification. And yet, the processes of commodification are never fully complete, nor are the efficacies of stories in action entirely predictable. Given their imbrication in the flows of global capital and the commodification of suffering, stories are received and interpreted in unpredictable ways by the audiences whose attention they seek and garner.

PUBLISHED LIFE NARRATIVES AND
HUMAN RIGHTS CAMPAIGNS

Published life narratives have contributed directly and indirectly to campaigns for human rights. Although this chapter addresses the conjunction of narrated lives and human rights discourses and activism in the last twenty years, this linkage between stories and actions extends back to the earliest discussions of an international rights movement. As David Rieff notes, it was a memoir that spurred the adoption of the Geneva Convention of 1864. In *A Memoir of Solferino* (1859), Swiss humanitarian Henri Dunant witnessed the carnage of the decisive battle of the Franco-Austrian war. The memoir provided an affective springboard for subsequent debates about just and unjust wars, leading to the founding of the International Committee of the Red Cross and the adoption of the Geneva Convention.[10] Rieff goes so far as to suggest that "the conference at Geneva succeeded in translating the reaction to the book into a body of law" (68–9).

In the last decades of the twentieth century countless numbers of published narratives have fueled and been fueled by campaigns for human rights. Told from diverse locations by diverse people, many of whom have been previously silenced, they offer hybrid modes of telling stories, and hybrid modes of mediating political, ethical, and aesthetic imperatives. Latin American *testimonio*, the recorded and transcribed testimony of indigenous and/or poor peoples, bears witness to collective struggles against massive state violence and oppression. Postcolonial *bildungsroman*, the story of education into and for national citizenship, explores the possibilities for and constraints limiting the decolonization of subjectivity in postcolonial worlds. Survivor narratives tell stories of abuse through which narrators turn themselves from victims to survivors through acts of speaking out that shift attention to systemic causes of violation. Prison narratives of political dissidents, like the letters from prison by China's champion of democracy Wei Jingsheng, while often banned in their country of origin, find publishers elsewhere, and thereby exert continued international pressure on noncompliant nations to address, justify, and modify their human rights record.

Sometimes narratives published previous to the public recognition of a specific rights campaign are recirculated and resituated within the context of that campaign, as has been the case with Sally Morgan's *My Place*. Published in the year of Australia's bicentenary of white settlement/invasion, Morgan's hybrid narrative reconstructs her coming to consciousness as an Indigenous Australian and incorporates the oral histories of her mother, grandmother, and uncle. Initially received as an individual journey in search of a lost identity, *My Place* was reinterpreted as a "Stolen Generation" narrative about lost childhoods after the publication of the *Bringing Them Home* report issued by the National Inquiry into the Forced Separation of Indigenous Children from their Families (Wilson 1997). In such cases, a narrative's popularity, built up through years of new editions, provides a threshold that seeds different perceptions of the narrative by succeeding generations.

Sometimes published narratives serve as lightening rods in rights campaigns. Take, for example, the case of Rigoberta Menchú's powerful *testimonio, I, Rigoberta Menchú: An Indian Woman in Guatemala*, published originally in Spanish in 1983 and issued in English in 1984, Menchú's book found a responsive audience, particularly in the United States. "This is my testimony," she begins: "My experience is the reality of a whole people" (1). Menchú's *testimonio* chronicled the means through which the ruling elites and the military sustained their power and maintained their control over the Quiché Indian population through physical violence, economic dependency, and cultural denigration. It chronicled as well the passionate commitment of the indigenous community to withstand degradation and forge a politics and an activism of resistance. Throughout her testimony, Menchú provided graphic details of her own personal and familial tragedy at the hands of a repressive army that tortured her mother to death, murdered her father, and burned her brother alive. Menchú's narrative and her extensive activism directed world attention to the plight of the Quiché Indians in Guatemala, contributing to the efforts of indigenous Guatemalans, united in local guerilla resistance movements, to bring an end to state-sponsored massacres and an increased respect for Mayan culture.

Through her narrated life, Menchú told the story of her people, performatively enacting the culturally specific mode of collective testimony that exposed the oppressive conditions within Guatemala and secured her authority to speak as a representative of her people elsewhere. The attention generated by the *testimonio* produced an aura-effect around Menchú herself, elevating and legitimating the Quiché woman as an international authority on the struggles of indigenous peoples. In 1992 Menchú was awarded the Nobel Peace Prize, international acknowledgment that brought increased sympathy for her cause and increased interest in her narrative. She was subsequently appointed Goodwill Ambassador for the UN-sponsored International Year (and now decade) of Indigenous Peoples, becoming a spokesperson for indigenous communities around the world that are engaged in local campaigns and are claiming rights to self-determination and cultural integrity.

Taken up in the United States as testimony to human rights abuse and promulgated largely through the advocacy of the urban left, Menchú's narrative became a symbol of the revolutionary spirit and struggle of a people. It also entered mainstream academe when selected as a core text in the undergraduate curriculum at Stanford University and when placed on the reading lists of courses in literary and cultural studies, Spanish languages and literature, and anthropology at many other colleges and universities. These modes of circulation and reception in the United States reified the narrative as an exemplary *testimonio*. When taken up in university classrooms and scholarly journals, the text became a locus of postcolonial critique in the United States. It spurred debates among Latin Americanists, postcolonial critics, anthropologists, and women's studies and cultural studies scholars about the nature of the postcolonial condition, the evidentiary status of *testimonio*, and the intersections among cultural formations, reading publics, and politics. The combination of popular and scholarly attention turned close attention back on the narrative itself.

In the late 1990s, *I, Rigoberta Menchú* provoked a scandal in academic and activist circles in the United States with the publication of David Stoll's analysis, *Rigoberta Menchú and the Story of All Poor Guatemalans*. Stoll, an American anthropologist, challenged the text's status as *testimonio*. While sympathetic to the Quiché cause espoused by Menchú, he charged Menchú with fabricating details of her own history, of the violent oppression of her family, of the deaths of family members, and of the extent of her leadership role in the resistance.[11] His critique fueled yet another set of contestations. Amongst other issues, commentators questioned the nature of the collaborative relationship between Menchú and Elisabeth Burgos-Debray, the anthropologist/collaborator who is sometimes listed as the "author" of the text. Debray's role as interlocutor and editor of the text called into question the "authenticity" of Menchú's narrative as witness documentary. Readers, critics, and activists took sides. Menchú's cause was joined. In fiercely contested debates, advocates and detractors invoked Menchú's narrative in newspaper columns, academic journals articles, and conference sessions in the United States where they took up issues having to do with personal and collective forms of remembering, narrative authenticity, and juridical versus nonjuridical understandings of truth telling.

The circulation and reception of Menchú's narrative demonstrates the contested and unpredictable impact such stories can have. In some contexts, as Bain Attwood and Fiona Macgowan suggest, published stories can become a form of cultural and political capital for oppositional groups (xi), and the knowledge they represent can generate proprietary claims within communities that distinguish insiders from outsiders. In others, readers and audiences can impose competing demands and tools of interpretation through what Leigh Gilmore terms "extrajudicial 'trials'" or "forums of judgment" that provoke engagements around the evidentiary status of narrative meanings. Through these contradictory channels of circulation and reception a "levering forward of ethics, truth telling, and scandal" unfolds, setting in motion many potential outcomes (Gilmore 2002, 695–6).

The history of reception of *I, Rigoberta Menchú* suggests that those who publish their stories of oppression, abuse, trauma, degradation, and loss can neither know nor control how that story will be received and interpreted. A story can generate recognition, empathy, critical awareness, advocacy, and activism elsewhere that helps to empower people struggling locally to extend their campaigns for human rights. The same story can become a commodity, and the teller a celebrity on a world stage as the narrative is dispersed through book clubs, radio and television interviews, and talk shows, classrooms, and living rooms, picked up by independent documentary filmmakers and distributed internationally. The same story can become a "scandal" overseas that produces resistance within and beyond the boundaries of the nation as it generates, as did *I, Rigoberta Menchú*, controversy that turns international attention to claims and counterclaims having to do with juridical veracity.

Through the rise in publication of "minority" life stories, the literature of trauma, and hybrid forms of life writing, storytelling has become a potent and yet highly problematic form of cultural production, critical to the international order of human rights and movements on behalf of social change. Personal narratives in all their generic variety and locational specificity reveal the effects of the traumatic past (Kennedy 1997, 236)—whether the past be one of radical dislocation, terrorism, physical torture, profound loss, forced assimilation, discrimination, oppression, or sexual abuse. The very aesthetics of form, the very forms of narrative address to the reader, enable victims to speak truth to power. As meta-sites for social critique, published narratives sometimes unsettle received conceptions of personal and national identity, sometimes dismantle the foundational fictions through which nations and imagined communities construct and reconstruct their histories, sometimes promote new platforms for and forms of political action, and sometimes produce a backlash of actions that forestall recognition and redress. In local communities and through global flows, stories sometimes enable the reconstitution of lost subjectivities, call forth new narratives of affiliation and belonging, and open up new international debates on the practical means through which to achieve justice with respect for the historical, national, religious and philosophic traditions both consonant with and different from those foundational to the UDHR.

At other times, however, their efficacy remains severely limited. The personal voice, as it is picked up, edited, translated, published, and disseminated by dispersed media, institutions, and advocacy groups around the world becomes at once reified as the authentic voice of suffering and depersonalized through various forms of recontextualization. The narrative reaches broader audiences beyond the local community, but those audiences subject the narrative to different and unpredictable readings, put the narrative to different and unpredictable uses. At any historical moment, only certain stories are tellable and intelligible to a broader audience.

OTHER SITES OF NARRATION

Published life narratives, although widely circulated and influential, are only one site of personal storytelling in the field of human rights. Storytelling in the context of human rights takes place in diverse venues and occurs for a variety of intentions. Sometimes it occurs in the field where abuses are ongoing or in commission hearings or national inquiries. In these instances the taking of testimony is purposeful and directed at a particular goal or specific aspect of a human rights campaign. Sometimes the narrating is embedded in UN-sponsored documents and NGO handbooks and Internet sites or framed by the UN-sponsored aims and objectives of national forums and reports. At others, it is gathered into anthologies of testimony assembled by activists, academics, and publishers. Sometimes stories are produced by local campaigners and circulated through dispersed media. At other times the aims and objectives of personal storytelling are more diffuse, as in the many scattered sites of rights activism and in mediascapes (Appadurai 328 ff.) where reporting on rights and rights advocacy is advanced. Some sites are organized and supported by human rights institutions. Some operate underground in opposition to state laws, constantly subjected to surveillance, censorship, and possible prosecution. Other venues of public culture, sporting events or rock concerts for example, may seem entirely unrelated to human rights activism but can suddenly be mobilized to call attention to rights violations.

In chapter two, we investigate features of storytelling in seven sites of human rights activism additional to the domain of published life narratives.

Chapter 2

The Venues of Storytelling

In chapter one we surveyed some of the historical and sociocultural formations affecting the rise in publication of life narratives in the last several decades. We were particularly interested in the motivations prompting stories of displacement and exile and stories of mass genocide and traumatic loss for which the Holocaust has served as a paradigmatic event. We briefly canvassed some of the factors contributing to a broad readership for personal narratives, among them the rise of global capital and the cultures of fear and suspicion. Since our project is about storytelling in the larger field of human rights, we rehearsed some of the ways in which local and global transits of storytelling interpenetrate and are enfolded within the evolving human rights regime, as exemplified by the controversies surrounding *I, Rigoberta Menchú*. Turning from the domain of published life narratives, we now consider in more detail seven additional sites: fact-finding in the field; handbooks and websites; nationally based human rights commissions; human rights commission reports; collections of testimonies; stories in the media; and other scattered venues through which narratives circulate.

Fact-Finding in the Field

On the ground, incidences and circumstances of human rights violations require documentation before UN-sponsored investigations and processes of redress can be initiated. UN rapporteurs and working groups, representatives of NGOs and other advocacy groups, and claimants themselves gather information on location in order to accumulate credible and reliable data about violations and to build a case that can be presented to an official body established to study, recognize, and perhaps adjudicate rights violations. Often coming together across national boundaries, groups of activists form alliances to publicize issues and to seek redress for rights violations. As a case accumulates—through attention, testimony, documentation, fact-based argument, moral suasion—its human rights dimensions sharpen into a campaign that becomes international in scope.

Information gathering takes many forms. Fact-finders seek information in and through heterogeneous sources, among them legislation, court opinions, ordinances, regulations, newspapers articles, government reports, photographs, documentary evidence, and reports by local NGOs. They gather evidence from personal testimony found in letters, affidavits, depositions, video footage, and interviews. Lawyers observe trials and interview witnesses (Ravindran et al. 12–20). This process of fact-finding and documentation is followed by the preparation of documentary statements, sometimes in the form of a letter of concern to be directed toward authorities within a country, sometimes in the form of a major report to be published and circulated in national and international arenas.

For advocates, the goal of fact-finding is to provide credible and reliable data about rights abuses, since, in a juridical frame, there can be no case without evidence and that evidence must stand up to cross-examination. Mindful of the demands of the adjudicating frameworks in which testimony is presented and received, activists must approach testimony through the methods of positivistic social science research, applying principles of rationality and tests of truthfulness and authentication and seeking corroborative evidence that protects against the unreliability of individual memory. Further, they must conform the case to defined violations deriving from the UDHR or UN conventions ratified by the nation in which the violations took place or to which the perpetrators belonged.

Charged with the responsibility for interviewing claimants, rights advocates in the field assume the status of "professionals," coming from elsewhere. Implicitly, this positioning makes professional activists the objective arbiters of a rights claim and the claimant a victim and object of fact-finding.[1] As "judges of narrative" in the juridical sense, advocates are enjoined to determine the truth-value of the testimony they collect, evidentiary testimony they cannot assume to be true.[2] In most cases, therefore, a witness's story has to be corroborated through the testimony of others, family members and strangers among them. In the case of torture victims, doctors may be called in to make determinative judgments based on their reading of embodied behavior and the sources of body trauma. In this way, the mute evidence of the body serves as corroboration for the truth-status of the narrative.

Personal testimony, understood and judged unproblematically as evidentiary, turns the speaker into a victim and molds his or her story into a case history, a piece of positivist evidence, with attendant gains and losses. The primary gain comes with the legitimating of individual loss and suffering and the embedding of the individual story in a larger story of human rights violations for the purposes of building a case and motivating action. The constraining aspects of the practices of fact-finding are several. The need to build a credible case renders the individual story less important than the accumulation of many stories of violation, told in a certain way, and told again and again. The high level of concern about the reliability and credibility of "oral information" in fact-finding and documentation means that the affects attached to recollections of pain and suffering become particularly suspect, and are treated as potentially subversive to the project at hand (Thoolen and Verstappen 19). The pressure to conform the "messiness" of personal testimony to the protocols for codification of a human rights abuse, to contain it within a standardized, often chronological, format that more easily addresses the series of questions the inquiry has established as critical to the goal of documenting a particular human rights issue, subsumes local knowledge and conceptual frameworks for understanding different cultural experiences and traditions to the national and international frameworks of human rights law. Finally, the reduction of testimony, of remembered experience, to evidence, judged either as purely factual or mendacious, obscures the ways in which narratives of suffering offer bits of evidence that cannot easily be reduced to evidence (Hesford and Kozol 5).

HANDBOOKS AND WEBSITES

Handbooks, published documents, and (more recently) websites offer other sites for personal narrating in the context of human rights struggles. Documents and websites have multiple uses and appeals. Some handbooks incorporate the voices of witnesses, victims, and survivors to frame and offer vivid reporting on specific human rights violations. The 1991 *Amnesty International Handbook*, for instance, incorporates first-person testimony in the introductions to chapters on specific domains of rights abuses. Here the introduction of the personal voice functions in ways distinct from the uses of personal narrative in the context of documentation. Directed to people who might be persuaded to work on behalf of human rights campaigns, the *Amnesty International Handbook* utilizes personal testimony in order to engage potential human rights advocates. In particular, it serves as a means to recruit and train possible AI members, sponsors, and activists, encouraging them to "be part of the action."

Websites now enable globally based advocates around the world to attract local rights activists and victims of human rights violations and give them a voice. One such website, *Witness* (www.witness.org), pioneered innovative strategies for strengthening advocacy through the use of digital technologies. Established by an unusual blend of celebrity, professional, and commercial interests, bringing together British musician and activist Peter Gabriel, the United Nations Lawyers Committee for Human Rights, and the Reebok Human Rights Foundation, the site offers training in collecting testimony in local communities, documentary-making for an international audience, and video streaming for grassroots advocacy. It also advises visitors on how to use the site for public service announcements and how to prepare formal testimony for use at an international tribunal.

With a variety of low-tech (text-based) to high-tech (video streaming) interactions, *Witness* offers maximum flexibility for people in less developed and/or remote rural areas to gather evidence and tell their stories. The organization loans camcorders to groups otherwise without access to digital technologies and offers on-site, on location, and hands-on virtual training for activists and victims of human rights violations.[3] At the receiving end, high-capability on-line viewers gain immediate access to mini-documentaries made by locally based advocates from around the world. In 2002 the website featured seventeen short video documentaries, among them stories of refugees in Senegal, massacres in Sierra Leone, genocide in Rwanda, and the international trafficking of girls and women. Professionally edited and introduced by celebrity supporters like Susan Sarandon, Tim Robbins, Lou Reed, and Laurie Anderson, the mini-documentaries allow viewers to engage with the issues, access additional information, and take action through petitions and protests directed at those in authority via Internet links.

When testimony circulates through human rights handbooks and websites to transnational audiences, it helps build coalitions and extend spheres of suasion. For website users, stories make an affective appeal, often through the inclusion of provocative and personalizing visual images. They arouse compassion for victims of rights violations. Told through AI or Western venues, they also enhance the credibility and reputations of such organizations as central, and successful, champions of human rights. These latter effects matter in the recruitment of volunteers. In the context of human rights handbooks and websites, then, personal narratives personalize statistics, motivate grassroots activity, compel readers and potential volunteers to action, and raise money through humanitarian appeals.

Website initiatives like *Witness* are not without detractors. Some critics contend that the new relation between aesthetics, commerce, and politics puts a "humane" corporate face on human rights issues that contradicts the resistant identities of human rights victims. Others argue that human rights websites like *Witness* provide access for some but not all victims, setting up competition between claimants and producing a polarization of "infocrats" and "cyber paupers" (Havemann 2000, 25). Paul Havemann further cautions that the infotainment format of websites can turn the ground of suffering into web-surfer spectacle. Most importantly, uneven access to technology enables the consolidation of global hierarchies of power based not only on gender, ethnicity, class, and region but also increasingly on differential access to technology, particularly between North and South America, and between Europe, Asia, and Africa (2000, 25). Nonetheless, new media technologies extend the scope for the production of testimony, sustaining new social movements and styles of political activism. They engage victims on the local level in ways that help to destabilize state power and build transformative transnational alliances, albeit in uneven, contingent, and unpredictable ways.

HUMAN RIGHTS COMMISSIONS AND TRIBUNALS

Multiple platforms of human rights activism also provide opportunities for victims of rights abuses to testify before nationally based human rights commissions, UN-based tribunals and rapporteurs, and activist-sponsored tribunals and hearings. Pressure from the international community or from shifts in political power inside a nation can prompt governments and statutory bodies in reluctant nations to establish formal commissions of inquiry. The most prominent of these forums involve truth commissions, like those conducted in the 1990s in a number of Latin American countries; truth and reconciliation commissions, like those held in postcolonial nations like South Africa,

Canada, and Australia; and international World Court Tribunals conducted at The Hague, like those investigating the genocidal wars in Rwanda, Uganda, and Bosnia. Often these inquiries are established only after years of pressure from defendant or victim groups within the nation. Often they delve into areas of human rights abuse buried in the nation's history and memory.

Once commissions, tribunals, or hearings are called, public discourse begins to "catalyze" private discourse, "send[ing] out the message," suggests Peter Novick, that " 'This is something you should be talking about' " (107). Such forums allow previously silenced voices to be heard in new legitimating contexts. Yet, when witnesses give themselves over to UN and NGO protocols and processes, they give their stories over to institutional shaping. As a result, a great deal can be lost to them.

In becoming the legal subjects of human rights within a national inquiry, witnesses participate in and thus reinforce the legal structures of the nation, paradoxically effecting an exclusion of recognition of their different laws, customs, and protocols that operate in their distinct and separate cultures. For example, in cases of First Nation peoples, spiritual affiliations with land, relations within family and kinship networks, and guardianship over secret and sacred knowledge built up through oral traditions, sacred rituals, and spiritual practices, all ontologically foundational to speakers, cannot be accommodated by human rights protocols. To tell a story consonant with group traditions requires a different voice, the "we" of a group narrative; a different structure that might seem fragmented and discontinuous; a different logic of connection to place, not time; and a different speaking position in which agency and self-conscious reflection is subsumed by a collective "we" (Attwood and Macgowan xiv). These group imperatives can be overwritten when personal stories are transformed into testimony in preparation for an official inquiry. Further, tribunals and commissions exercise a "will to know" about the buried past. They operate on the assumption that people, when given the occasion, will and should want to tell their stories. This presumption occludes the cultural rights of potential witnesses who may need to protect themselves, their community, their history, and their secret knowledges by remaining silent (see Povinelli 2000).

Entering the arena of an official inquiry or tribunal, witnesses and their advocates are also constrained by legal norms of argument. When Japanese Americans sought reparative justice through the U.S. Congress for their internment during World War II, they sought to argue their case *as a group* on the grounds of systemic and structural ethnic discrimination. At the Tribunal, lawyers for the claimants tried to introduce social and systemic arguments concerning long-term discrimination of one group (the Japanese American plaintiffs who had been interned during the War) by another group (the American government). Tribunal officials excluded these arguments, however; and plaintiff lawyers had to present their plaintiffs in purely legal terms as individuals seeking individual damages. In this process, individual plaintiffs could not tell stories of differential war experiences, or claim differential reparations. Paradoxically, then, those individuals making claims before the Tribunal had to present themselves at once as individuals and as "representatives" of the group, and mount a case that effaced the differential experiences of individuals within the group. In other words, only certain kinds of stories of injustice could be told and legitimated within the Tribunal's terms of reference. On the one hand, Japanese Americans won their case and gained reparations because, as Eric Yamamoto contends, they were able to frame their case tightly within the American law/Enlightenment paradigm of individual rights (493, 498). On the other hand, rather than challenging universal principles that exclude differences, these processes strengthened the political integrity and efficacy of a system of law that the claims themselves contested.

In the context of tribunals and truth and reconciliation commissions not all stories can be told. For example, Hilary Charlesworth and Christine Chinkin, addressing specifically gendered violations, contend that international human rights law "has retained the deeper, gendered, public/private distinction" that obscures and overlooks women's experiences of rights violations because human rights law has understood "women's lives" as "generally conducted within the sphere deemed outside the scope of international law, indeed also often outside the ambit of 'private' (national) law" (69). Thus, until the emergence of international outrage at the systematic rape of women during the Bosnian war as a form of ethnic cleansing, women's stories of sexual violation have been particularly vulnerable to exclusion. Islamic women living in fundamentalist nations also suffer disadvantage in relation to bringing charges of sexual violence to public account, having little recourse to the religious Shari'a courts and being under obligation to protect the honor of their fathers and brothers. Moreover, any testimony they might give jeopardizes their position of respect and belonging within their community. Although rape and other forms of violence against women have been recognized as war crimes since the Versailles Treaty of 1919, prosecutions have been rare (Brown and Grenfell 348). In the aftermath of the

Bosnian war, several international UN-sponsored forums, including the Vienna World Conference on Human Rights (1993) and the Fourth International Conference on Women held in Beijing (1995), passed resolutions that focused world attention on rape as a war crime and a fundamental violation of women's human rights. More recently, gender-based persecution and rape have been classified as crimes against humanity in the Rome Statute of the International Criminal Court (1998). The international conferences facilitated the gathering of testimony of former World War II sex prisoners, presented at the Japanese War Crimes Tribunal hearings, and of Bosnian victims, whose documentaries were prepared for presentation at the International Criminal Tribunal for the former Yugoslavia (ICTY) at The Hague. In the latter case, former military officers received jail sentences, albeit minimal, for participation in the systematic rape of women. Still, as the South African TRC demonstrates, where few raped or sexually abused women testified on their own behalf, whether because their violations were deemed to fall outside the political mandate of the commission or for fear of shaming or reprisal, patriarchal relations on a local level and legal definitions of gender-based abuse as "domestic" or "private" continue to constrain women to positions of silence.

At their best, hearings and tribunals become sites where some aspects of national histories of progress and modernity are countered, contested, and contradicted by stories presenting a counter-history of conquest, dispossession, oppression, and discrimination on the one hand, and (always limited) forms of resistance and self-determination on the other. Truth and reconciliation commissions and rights tribunals also offer opportunities, both individual and collective, to heal the lingering wounds of injustice and to project a new future of reconciliation, and sometimes reparations. Commissions rarely, however, lead to a national will to make more than symbolic gestures toward apology and limited material reparation. And their terms of reference and protocols for presentation reproduce exclusionary norms that perpetuate the silencing of many stories of difference.

HUMAN RIGHTS COMMISSION REPORTS

Oral testimony, heard, broadcast, and recorded at commissions and hearings, creates an ever-broader public attentive to human rights violations and the narratives of inquiry witnesses. Individual stories, presented at tribunals, are subsequently reported in newspapers and on radio and television. They are mounted on websites, circulating nationally but also more broadly through international networks and meshworks of advocacy. The testimonies of Indigenous witnesses to the HREOC inquiry in Australia were put on the Aboriginal and Torres Strait Islanders Commission (ATSIC) website; the testimonies of witnesses to the TRC in South Africa were mounted on the African National Congress (ANC) website. Archived on human rights advocacy websites, commission hearings can be accessed by interested parties for future reference.

Inquiries also produce and circulate, in hard copy and digital formats, official reports that document the findings of human rights claims. The HREOC and TRC reports in Australia and South Africa, for instance, were widely distributed free-of-charge to Indigenous and black communities in their respective countries. The publication of an official report (on-line or in print) ensures that stories remain in circulation, providing a counter-history to national narratives that elide histories of violence, exploitation, and degradation of some of the nation's subjects; and projecting new cultural and national alignments of belonging, ownership, and custodianship consonant with the restorative aims of the commissions.

Official reports document the legacy of the past for readers in the present. Sometimes, as in the case of the truth commissions in South America, where intentions are retributive, commission reports contain little testimony from victims. In an attempt to restore social and political stability to the nation, the reports sanitize the abuses of the past and issue summative accounts of punishments to perpetrators of past violations. When the intent of a commission is restorative, as in the case of the TRC in South Africa, and of the Canadian, New Zealand, and Australian inquiries into indigenous rights, commission reports can include testimony to provide a ground for active processes of reconciliation in the future. Commissioners direct their findings to a national audience, often with an intention of healing and reconciliation. In such cases, the final reporting can legitimate the testimonies of the victims, turning witnesses into survivors of abuse. Affirmation of the testimony allows those who testified to take up agentic social positions in the present even as they bear witness to their objectification in the past, although it can also, at least partially, instate their identity status as victims.

Even so, official reports strategically deploy personal testimony to achieve political ends. The translocation of personal narration from live testimony to published report repositions the narrating voice, making it part of the larger narrative of nation. Moreover, reports frame personal testimony in specific ways as they address national or transnational audiences. Victim testimony is often thematized in different sections of a report, or juxtaposed against perpetrator testimony, or segmented to document specific human rights violations. Thus the voice, structure, style, intentions, and ownership of an individual story can be appropriated to and subordinated by the larger intentions of the reporting commission. Testimonies can be reduced to forensic evidence, denuded of emotion, and removed from the individual lives and experiences of suffering and trauma. They can be excerpted and joined to other excerpts to produce corroborative evidence through de-individualized repetition. They can be placed within ethical and moral frameworks in order to solicit empathy and understanding. Such framing can enhance awareness of human rights abuse for previously unknowing readers, but it can also induce a sense of shame on behalf of the nation for both witnesses and audiences whose shadowed and hidden pasts are exposed and opened to scrutiny.

The legitimation of stories through human rights reports builds solidarity within disaffected groups and generates a new awareness of the crimes embedded within the nation's past that can lead to significant social change. But the circulation of stories in reports can also be contentious and fraught with uncertainty. If victims experience trauma at the time of retelling their stories, often after years of protective shielding and the active forgetting by the nation, they may suffer re-traumatization and continued wounding once their testimony becomes public. Once in the public domain and secured within the pages of a human rights commission report, their stories can be subjected to further scrutiny and response, including acceptance and recognition but also challenge, rebuttal, scorn, and denial. Victim healing may require apology, responsibility, recognition, and reparations; but the government may or may not respond to commission recommendations. National political leaders and resistant national governments, desirous of protecting themselves from the implications of a UN-sponsored human rights inquiry, may reject the report's findings, challenge the authenticity of the speakers, question their motives or those of the presiding commissioners, and subject the testimony to legalistic tests of credibility. Further, the moral and ethical imperatives of restorative justice, like those of the South African TRC, may set up expectations of social transformation and hopes for the future that prove impossible to meet. Or, as in the case of Canada, commission reports and their recommendations can result in redistribution of land and recognition of indigenous self-determination for some but not all victims of a colonial history of dispossession. Or, as in the case of Australia, they can prompt contentious national debates, denials of redress, and forums of blame and suspicion. Finally, the conflicts and contestations that attend the publication and circulation of personal stories within local communities and the nation can intensify the pain suffered by victims and their communities.

COLLECTIONS OF TESTIMONIES

Another way in which personal narratives circulate in the context of struggles for human rights is through published collections of testimony. Such anthologies gain their ethical force by gathering multiple narratives of shared victimization into one volume whose purpose is to challenge and rewrite history, call the reader to recognition, and spur action. Such anthologies are almost always, though not invariably, introduced and edited by advocates or activists who provide scholarly commentary on the contexts that gave rise to the testimony and propose interpretative human rights frameworks through which to read and make sense of the stories.

The collective presentation of multiple stories of loss and suffering enforces the horror and impact of the wrongs of the past, but it has other effects as well. The purposeful repetition of stories often produces what might be called an "ur" narrative of victimization. A common story emerges out of the accumulation of voices telling stories that conform to a similar structure, thematically organized to invoke similar histories of abuse, violence, or degradation, and utilizing similar modes of address that make an emotive appeal. These edited versions "fix" the life and identity of the tellers in their victimhood, often locking the survivors' stories and lives to the past. Such collections solicit empathetic identification between the tellers and their audiences and encourage cognitive awareness of discriminatory practices, both of which serve to enliven the scholar/activist/editor's mandate for human rights activism.

Inger Agger's *The Blue Room: Trauma and Testimony among Refugee Women: A Psychosocial Exploration* (1994) offers an example of the way in which activist/scholars organize testimony according to their disciplinary jurisdiction. A Danish psychologist who has worked extensively with victims of trauma, Agger structures her psychosocial exploration of trauma around the notion of the ritual space of rooms. The "blue room" of her title refers to both the blue-walled room in her apartment where the interviews were conducted, and the ritual, metaphorical space of psychological healing. Composed of chapters with titles such as "The Daughter's Room," "The Father's Room," the structure of the book builds a "house" of remembering, the remembering necessary for her subjects to "work through" the trauma in psychoanalytic terms, to make themselves whole after the survival of trauma. Agger focuses each chapter on a first-person account of sexual abuse, torture, imprisonment, or other violations of human rights, giving first place in her project to the particular voices of women from Latin America and the Middle East living as refugees in Denmark. While giving priority to the voices of victims, the psychologist nonetheless situates those voices and stories within a therapeutic model of recovery, thus imposing a Western-based paradigm on structures of feeling and languages of suffering.

In Australia after publication of the HREOC's *Bringing Them Home* report, readers across the country sought out more stories from survivors of what had been a hidden national history of child separation. Within six months of the release of *Bringing Them Home*, Carmel Bird edited the collection *The Stolen Children: Their Stories*, an anthology containing stories and excerpts from seventeen witnesses to the Inquiry, gathered with their cooperation and collaboration. (Bird collaborated with witnesses and negotiated royalties for those whose stories were included.) In addition to the stories, *The Stolen Children* anthology includes responses and reactions to the report from thirteen leading political figures, historians, philosophers, and community leaders, lending different perspectives to the import of the Indigenous victim stories. The excerpts from anonymous witnesses, from "Paul," "Karen," "William," and others, tell of traumatic dislocations of culture and identity, stories that delimit an entire life to the experience of separation that stands in for and provides an explanatory framework for the complexities of the larger lives and experiences of the tellers. Attesting to the impact the Inquiry made on the general public, the anthology helped to inform the larger non-Indigenous population within Australia of the paralyzing effects of separation on Indigenous communities. Yet, it also had the effect of reducing informants to victims of separation, infantilized as figures of lost childhood. *The Stolen Children*'s emotive form of address, making an empathetic appeal to the non-Indigenous reader to identify with the victims of forced childhood separation, as would a bereaved mother, provokes an imagined parental sympathy in the reader (Whitlock 2001, 203ff.). In terms of human rights discourse, Bird's anthology asks the reader to understand governmental policies of child separation as "nothing but a policy of systematic genocide" (Bird 1998, 1), a claim also made in the HREOC Report that prompted widespread shock among Australian readers, initially garnering sympathetic support but subsequently prompting resistance and backlash.

As these examples suggest, anthologies of personal narratives, organized around targeted human rights abuses or targeted issues in survival, personalize stories of rights violations and make them available to a wider audience. Although they provide evidence of a range of experiences that particularize the effects of rights violations and government policies and practices on individual lives, they also, however, format the different stories in standardized structures and thematics of presentation. Juxtaposing multiple narratives, they cast a patina of anonymity (even if names are included) and uniformity upon the witnesses. Framed by scholar/activists, they impose frameworks from the cultural location of the editor onto narratives coming from distinctively different cultural locales. And, while they encourage empathetic identification, that identification comes at the potential cost of reducing differences to sameness.

STORIES AND THE MEDIA

Even before people had access to the Internet they were utilizing media technologies to tell their local stories, spurring activism and intervention. For example, in China during the hunger strikes on Tiananmen Square, students maintained contact with supporters in Hong Kong via fax machines. The Hong Kong contact proved vital to support for ongoing protests both inside and outside mainland China.[4] In South Africa, one of the most successful independent media projects was the establishment of independent community radio networks in the townships prior to the release of Nelson Mandela.[5] Through these underground networks local communities could track anti-apartheid activism across South Africa and elude the reach of state-sponsored censorship. In South Africa, China, and elsewhere, underground newspapers have been a major source of opposition to government oppression throughout the last fifty years of the rights regime.

If the pace of human rights awareness and activism dramatically quickened in the 1990s, this is undoubtedly due to the influence of the Internet, which extended the reach of independent media across the globe. In 1994, the indigenous Mexican groups known as the Zapatistas were the first to utilize the Internet to publicize their campaign for indigenous rights in Chiapas. Referring to the importance of a global media, Subcommandante Marcos, the movement's leading spokesperson, declared: "We did not go to war on January 1 to kill or have them kill us. We went to make ourselves heard" (quoted in Knudson 508). The Zapatistas, whose claims for land went virtually unheard for five centuries, achieved a victory in this instance. Blending local voices, utilizing the vernacular, and linking indigenous stories to the Internet, the Zapatistas tackled the consequences of modernization for people's survival through postmodern technological strategies, initiating a new kind of politics that trespassed the borders of the nation-state.[6] Telling their stories to the world through the capacities of the Internet, local *Mestizo* and indigenous communities in Mexico were brought in touch with one another. Their voices, heard outside the State, brought the plight of ten million indigenous people living in abject conditions to international attention, opening up new public spaces for indigenous peoples, and fundamentally transforming rights discourse and politics along the way. Since that time, indigenous peoples in other locations have adopted similar strategies, utilizing international communication technologies to "build sites of counter-hegemonic power which give unprecedented exposure to their politics of naming and shaming to reclaim their traditions and lands through the assertion of rights" (Havemann 2000, 21). In this local campaign, the voices of activism carried across virtual communities of affiliation to national and transnational settings.

Countless other sites continue to bring the voices of human rights victims to an ever-increasing community of international listeners. Those like www.universalrights.net, created to promote the fiftieth anniversary of the signing of the UDHR, feature people telling their stories. Stories about democracy and freedom, equality and justice, peace and well-being. Stories from indigenous people, women, and children. Stories from victims of poverty, torture, environmental catastrophe. Stories about successful human rights campaigns and human rights heroes like Martin Luther King, Jr, Rigoberta Menchú, Nelson Mandela, Patrick Dodson, and Aung San Suu Kyi. Visitors to this site are invited to tell their own stories about victims and heroes, and are instructed about how to report human right violations, get involved in campaigns, and find links to other sites. Websites like *Witness*, mentioned previously in the context of producing narrative accounts to promote advocacy, enable local groups that have no access to the national domain to tell their stories and document their experiences with the use of a camcorder.[7] In the words of one recent storyteller, "this camera means that someone in this world cares about us, about our struggle, seeing this camera here today means that we are not alone" (Datu Makapukauw, qtd. on *Witness* website newsletter, Fall 2000–September 2001).

State-based media may also bring about change beneficial to rights victims from within the nation. Although rights advocates have been reluctant to acknowledge the efficacy of government web-based initiatives (often the only ones available in authoritarian states like China), the extension of e-government and e-commerce sites has the capacity to foster social change even in more or less authoritarian regimes. In other words, it is not only cyber-dissidents whose net-based initiatives pressure regimes for change. An increasing number of states, from Singapore to Vietnam, from China to Egypt, have launched sophisticated "e-government" initiatives that effectively increase people's access to information about social services, link state bureaucracies with even the most remote citizens, and offer the potential for political liberalization and an increase in "government transparency" and "accountability" (Kalathil 4 of 6). The downside to these initiatives, in terms of political efficacy, is that they also enable governments to increase levels of surveillance, censorship, and propaganda.

Internet media, then, are not without their limitations. Not everyone can gain access to Internet technologies, as the case in Myanmar vividly illustrates. There, according to Shanthi Kalathil, "a 1996 decree makes possession of even an unregistered telephone (much less a computer) illegal and punishable by imprisonment" (Kalathil 3 of 6). Even with access, the distinctive and incommensurable aspects of culture for which campaigns seek recognition can be diluted, possibly even effaced. In the transnational flows of rights activism, the distinctive nature of the local may be too fully absorbed by the global. Web-based activism connects rights campaigns to the market forces of global capital, facilitating the commodification of stories and media, sometimes in an uneasy collusion.

SCATTERED VENUES

Finally, the regime of human rights unfolds in scattered venues and scattered media. People tell their stories in films and documentaries, in museum displays, on television and radio talk shows, at union meetings and political rallies, at rock concerts, at book fairs, literary festivals, and speaking tours, in alternative newspapers, on T-shirts, lapels, and bumper stickers. Alongside official human rights apparatuses, and operating simultaneously with them, these scattered events make visible various dimensions of human rights campaigns in local contexts. These eruptions of human rights claims in venues distant from official networks of advocacy foster meshworks of awareness and lift claims to new levels of national and international visibility.

Cultural institutions have also become locations of political activism on behalf of rights violations and injustices. Theater companies stage

performances that disseminate information and catalyze moral indignation about particular situations, as did Tony Kushner's *Angels in
America* in the United States and Jane Harrison's *Stolen* in Australia.
Museums promote mutual recognition of diverse social and cultural
groups through new approaches to public space and public display.
Presenting a polyphony of divergent voices rather than univocal interpretations of the nation's cultural history, they disrupt dominant structures of power. Museums can also become venues for exhibitions and
installations about human rights violations by artists and photojour-
nalists, such as the Australian artist/activist George Gittoes, the
American videographer Carol Jacobsen, and the Japanese artist Taeko
Tomiyama. Alternative video and photographic exhibits document the
lives of people living in circumstances in which violations of human
rights occur on a daily basis, as did the exhibits about life in El
Salvador and Palestine mounted by the photojournalist Larry Towell
and life in the "killing fields" mounted by Cambodian photojournalist
Dith Pran.

Public displays outside institutional contexts become spontaneous
and popular sites for recognizing, remembering, and mourning victims and survivors of human rights abuses. The multiple appearances
of AIDS quilts around the globe in the 1990s, for instance, called
attention to the AIDS pandemic as a human rights concern. As the
size of the quilt grew, and as it was replicated in many nations, so did
the extent of the population aware of the devastations of a disease that
had been stigmatized and of people marginalized and abandoned.
After the *Bringing Them Home* report was published in Australia,
hundreds of thousands of citizens signed Sorry Books as a gesture of
sympathy and personal apology. Sea of Hands, a ground display of
multicolored plastic hand shapes that appeared first as a part of the
1997 Reconciliation Week activities, alerted the nation and the world
not only to indigenous human rights claims but also to their widespread support throughout the nation. Currently, over 250,000 people have registered their commitment to and support of native title
claims for Indigenous Australians through the Sea of Hands.

Even more dispersed in their effects are the signs individuals wear
as they go about their everyday lives. Through tee-shirts, ribbons,
arm bands, tattoos, decals, bumper stickers, and the like, people
announce their identification with particular persons—Mumia Abu-
Jamal, or Nelson Mandela, or the Mothers of the Disappeared—or
with particular causes and campaigns—various indigenous, anti-war,
or "solidarity" movements. In 1998, a group of Italian observers surprised locals when they traveled to Chiapas, Mexico, to protest

against human rights violations. Wearing T-shirts that read "*Todos somos Indios del mundo*" ("We are all Indians of the World"), they expressed solidarity with the indigenous Chiapas Indians in their battle with the Mexican government (Jornada.unam website). Here people's bodies display their identification with other persons and causes, often remote from their own local and national contexts, effectively serving as a kind of body billboard to call attention to and support other people's stories.

Spontaneous and unexpected events become especially important when circumstances on the ground may not yet be framed or recognized as legitimate in human rights terms, or when issues have not achieved international recognition as human rights violations, or when member states refuse to acknowledge violations on a local level. Because they take place in the realm of popular culture and affect people's everyday life experiences, these events and actions can draw attention to the specific situations and create a larger audience knowledgeable about and invested in human rights issues. As a result, issues become attached to human rights discourse, an attachment that creates an atmosphere of instability out of which new initiatives for social change can form.

Scattered sites move human rights claims into an international sociality of language, commitment, and action for justice. But, as with all the sites we have surveyed, the scattered sites of storytelling and rights activism have a qualified efficacy. Channeled through the interests of global capital, some sites augment the coffers of advertisers; some make witnesses into spectacles of suffering; some address their audiences through emotive confrontation, setting in motion affective appeals that have a "feel good" effect for their far-flung advocates, but may not further recognition, ethical judgment, or redress.

CONCLUSION

All sites surveyed above signify far more than their geographical or institutional locations. As affective sites, they disperse embodied forces of intensity into political, legal, aesthetic, ethical, and moral discourses and actions. As ideological sites, they test the notion of the universal, generating multiple contestations and contradictions. As dialogical sites, they join tellers and listeners/readers in communicative exchanges about the meaning of rights. As cultural sites, they unsettle familiar knowledge frameworks by introducing different interpretations across the boundaries of cultural difference. As nodal sites, they engage local and global transits, opening new possibilities for becoming. Taken together, fact-finding in the field, handbooks and websites, commission hearings and reports, published narratives and anthologies of witness testimony, stories in the media, and scattered events offer multiple and proliferating occasions, forms, and usages for storytelling in the field of human rights.

The production, circulation, and reception of stories within any particular campaign unfold unevenly across these sites. Some forms are more prominent in specific campaigns than others. Some produce rights claims that contradict claims from other sites. Some enable new stories to be told by people previously silenced in public forums. Some organize and some disrupt terms on which rights can be taken up. Some forestall and some advance human freedoms. Some intend to make objective, juridical claims on specific listeners, while others evoke emotive responses that prompt popular awareness and activism. Each site, with its own mix of formal, contextual, social, historical, and cultural particularities, contributes to an international human rights agenda, in ways that contest, constrain, and advance the principles embodied in the UDHR.

With these multiple circuits of activism and advocacy in mind, we turn now to South Africa, the first of our five case studies.

CHAPTER 3

TRUTH, RECONCILIATION,
AND THE TRAUMATIC PAST OF
SOUTH AFRICA

*It is our contemporary history—which began in 1960 when the
Sharpeville disaster took place and ended with the wonderful inau-
guration of Nelson Mandela (1994) as the first democratically-
elected President of the Republic of South Africa—it is this history
with which we have to come to terms. We could not pretend it did
not happen. Everyone agrees that South Africans must deal with
that history and its legacy. It is how we do this that is in question.*

—*Desmond Tutu*, opening the South African Truth and
Reconciliation Commission Hearings

*In 1994, South Africa finally threw off apartheid and elected
Nelson Mandela in its first democratic elections. But the human
rights abuses, and the contempt for the humanity of others that gave
birth to apartheid has not left us.*

—*Charlene Smith*, Proud of Me

On February 11, 1990, tens of thousands of jubilant well-wishers
lined the streets and squares of Cape Town. On that momentous day,
the seventy-one-year-old Nelson Mandela left Victor Verster Prison,
Paarl, after spending over twenty-seven years in prison there and on
Robben Island. Mandela remembers the scene as "a happy, if slightly

disorienting, chaos" (1994, 553). The huge crowds waited for hours for a first sight of their hero, frequently erupting with the shouts "Viva! Viva! Viva Nelson Mandela!" (DeVeaux 49). Finally, near dusk, Mandela appeared before a rally on Cape Town's Grand Parade. His raised fist brought a roar from the crowds that swelled above the ululations of the women and thunderous sounds of feet pounding the *toyi toyi* on the pavement as supporters sang and danced to celebrate the return of Mandela, Prince of the Madiba clan.

Mandela's release (and the release of other prisoners, as well as the un-banning of anti-apartheid organizations) signaled a new departure for South Africa. Although it would be four years before the country held its first democratic elections, the long walk to freedom for the majority black population had just about reached its destination. But even on this day, as the crowds waited for Mandela to arrive, arm in arm with his wife Winnie, visible signs of the fear that bound black lives for 300 years—most particularly during the fifty years of apartheid rule—were evident. Helicopters buzzed overhead as police reinforcements lined the streets. With patience strained to breaking point, segments of the crowd became disruptive. When a minor scuffle broke out police released their dogs and fired rubber bullets and tear gas into the crowd.

This was not the only sign of discontent to trouble the euphoria of the day.[1] Some ANC supporters feared, at that time and later, that Mandela was out of touch with the grassroots political activities that had brought the country to this point—campaigns by the trade unions, women's groups, and the Youth League. Some feared that, in his negotiations with government officials, already begun in the years prior to his release, he would be too conciliatory (Gibson 2001, 81). Others distrusted Mandela's moves toward rival groups, especially the conservative Inkatha Freedom Party under the direction of Chief Buthelezi.[2] In addition, many in the crowd, active in the anti-apartheid people's movement and the multiracial umbrella group Mass Democratic Movement (MDM),[3] had concerns about the authoritarian strands of the ANC. The question remained: Would the ANC be able to bring about unity and heal the ideological rifts across and within the racial divides of those blacks and whites who opposed apartheid? (Saul 1990, 69; Ross 2003, 70.)

Some members within the ANC worried about the continued importance of a "leader" figure, and particularly a male leader, especially given the important leadership role that Albertina Sisulu had played in the MDM in South Africa during the previous six year struggle to end apartheid.[4] Some worried that, in the wake of the collapse of the Soviet Union and socialist states in Eastern Europe, the radical politics of worker and social movements would be sidelined or that the ANC would "co-opt" people power to silence opposition, disenfranchising the workers whose actions had made this day possible (Gibson 68, 70, 75). Anti-apartheid activists questioned whether bourgeois democracy was the best they could anticipate and whether the creation of new political elites would lead to cronyism and corruption. Clearly, as John Saul cautioned, it was not yet time to pop the champagne corks (63).

While they experienced jubilation and a sense of relief for Mandela on a personal level, many people also felt apprehensive about where the struggle would now go. The ANC, operating a government in exile from 1983, was rife with internal tensions between factions: the former long-term prisoners; the exiles who had been living abroad and could now return; those who had been labeled dissident within the ANC; those who were not exiles living abroad but guerillas fighting in Southern Africa; and those who had survived in South Africa and there planned the guerrilla warfare tactics that rendered the country ungovernable under the National Party's apartheid regime. Although the National Party had unbanned anti-apartheid organizations, released political prisoners, and embarked on a platform of reform leading to a new constitution and democratic elections, it still had to negotiate with its supporters as it responded to the demands of the popular movement. "Struggles within struggles" still remained to be fought and won within the country (Gibson 2001, 72).

During the next four years, the violence in South Africa worsened. In 1990 alone, 1,500 people were killed. The police arrested ANC and Communist Party leaders and fomented violence between Inkatha and the ANC (Mandela 1994, 574–8). Strikes, demonstrations, and boycotts culminated in a national strike on June 16, 1992, the sixteenth anniversary of the Soweto children's revolt of 1976, a movement that had brought the horrors of South Africa's apartheid government to the eyes of the world. Amidst the violence, the strikes, and the sabotage, negotiations for new government elections, a new Bill of Rights, and a new constitution came to a standstill. Two significant events threatened the negotiations: a massacre at the Joe Slovo squatter camp at Boipatong in June, 1992, and the assassination of a revered leader of the Communist Party, Chris Hani, on April 10, 1993. Paradoxically, the sense of shock and the realization of how close civil war was in the days and nights after Hani's killing helped push the negotiators toward setting a date for the election. That "dark night" (Mandela 1993, 601) of Hani's death, Mandela delivered one of the most moving and politically significant speeches he had ever made.

But on that day in 1990, the man, the myth, and the walk to freedom came together in a moment of hope and promise for a new future. If anyone could unite the country, it was Mandela. His release was hailed as a victory, not only for the country, but also for the world. In human rights terms, Mandela embodied the hopes of an international community of anti-apartheid activists inside and without South Africa who had campaigned for nearly thirty years for his release and for an end to the heinous regime.

In 1993, Mandela shared the Nobel Peace prize with National Party President F.W. de Klerk. Months later, on another great day, April 27, 1994, the first free democratic elections took place. That event, too, would overwhelm South Africans, bonding masses of them in a spirit of common humanity. Snaking through the streets in voting lines with day-long waits, businessmen and nurses, church women and politicians, white and black women who shared the mothering of children, night watchmen and students, university-educated and illiterate voters, all stood together "on new ground," the ground of equality (Gordimer 2003, 468–9). The project of national reconciliation had begun.

APARTHEID AND CENSORSHIP

In his autobiography *The Long Walk to Freedom*, Mandela writes, "the violence and bombings ceased, and it was as though we were a nation reborn" (611). In his election address he made reference to the immortal "Free at Last" speech of Martin Luther King and preached a message of love and forgiveness: "This is a time to heal the old wounds and build a new South Africa" (612). Many wondered if those old wounds could ever be healed. With the opening of the TRC in 1995, one of the most courageous attempts at reconciliation through truth telling that had yet been attempted, the process of healing would begin. The "leaking tap" (Krog 311) of witnesses to the violence of South Africa's apartheid past would turn into a flood of remembering as personal narrative yoked itself forever to the reconciliatory processes of nation building within the regime of human rights.

It had not always been thus. Up until the release of Mandela there was no discourse on human rights that extended to blacks within the country, no history of published or public storytelling in a human rights context, and no public record of the violations of the majority black population's human rights.[5] In response to criticism by the United Nations, the National Party had argued that its "homelands" policy accorded with the purposes and founding principles of the United Nations and with certain principles relating to the self-determination of peoples enshrined in the second generation of human rights principles and covenants (Manzo 101). Homelands policy segregated citizens in racial and ethnic categories, in effect banishing black South Africans to (bogus) independent homelands and dependent Bantusan areas. Although the National Party denied blacks citizenship and many basic human rights protections, it argued cynically that segregation protected the distinct cultures of South Africa, and it used second-generation social and cultural rights discourse to its advantage while censoring discussion of first-generation political and civil rights.

The independent Union of South Africa, established in 1911 at the end of the South African War (sometimes referred to as the Anglo-Boer War), had guaranteed civil and political rights to whites-only through a constitution that codified white supremacy (Manzo 136). Under the National Party regime that came to power in 1948, the State introduced a number of laws to reinforce the segregation of the races, acts clearly in breach of UDHR principles. It extended the "Pass laws"[6] that regulated the movement of blacks in all parts of the country, provoking mass protests and anti-pass campaigns throughout the decade of the 1950s, culminating in the Sharpeville Massacre of 1960 and the withdrawal of South Africa from the Commonwealth (Posel 1991, 237). The 1949 Prohibition of Mixed Marriages Act and the 1950 Immorality Amendment Act prohibited interracial marriages, as well as all forms of sexual contact across color lines. The Group Areas Act of 1950 made possible the mass relocation of any population, including whites, that inhabited areas designated for other race groups. It had the effect of reserving more than 80 percent of the country for whites (who made up about 14 percent of the population of some 42 million people). It also led to the destruction of integrated communities and the impoverishment of the black and coloured populations.[7] The Bantusan system designated separate "nations" or homelands for blacks according to complex ethnolinguistic criteria. Through the Bantusan system, black South Africans were accorded some compensatory tribal rights that effectively kept them divided from one another and intent on differences rather than solidarity. The Separate Amenities Act of 1953 specified that all public amenities and facilities (parks, libraries, zoos, beaches, sports grounds, and so on) would be for the exclusive use of specified racial groups. And the 1950 Suppression of Communism Act allowed for the suppression of all forms of dissent by any means.

The Bantu Education Act in 1953 further disempowered black South Africans by replacing mission schooling, which ensured literacy for those blacks prepared to convert to Christianity and fostered an educated elite, with a system of inferior education, destined to prepare the majority of blacks for labor and service jobs.[8] Coupled with the Bantusan system, strict state-enforced censorship laws functioned to contain knowledge production and dissemination. Censorship was an integral part of the apartheid regime, a way for the State, its leaders, and its bureaucrats to control the information that became "public," a way to render invisible critiques of the regime, to render invisible to history the discontent and resistance of the black majority population and the extent of state-sponsored violence required to "secure" the apartheid system. These measures secured white privilege and supremacy—through separation, surveillance, censorship, and Bantu education.

THE UNDERWORLD OF APARTHEID AND THE CIRCULATION OF NARRATIVE

The election of the National Party in 1948 marked the beginnings of a legally enforced system of apartheid. Before it took hold, Alan Paton's international bestseller *Cry, the Beloved Country*, published by Charles Scribner and Jonathan Cape in 1948, issued an early alert to the world about the conditions of South African racial oppression. Published to universal acclaim in England and the United States, the book was taken up by the Book-of-the-Month Club, widely distributed throughout the English-speaking world, and added to the reading lists for junior high school English classes during the 1950s and 1960s. Paton's narrative of the experience of black Africans in a racist society resonated with those abroad as a text that exposed the palpable realities of white racism and black struggle for dignity and citizenship rights.

In the ensuing decades, the international transmission of news reports on violence—stories of the Soweto Uprising of 1976 and the ensuing student protests, the Black Consciousness Movement, and the murder of its leader, Steve Biko—kept in circulation knowledge of the conditions of life for South Africa's black population, intensifying pressure on various international players to take action. So too, personal narratives, smuggled out of the country or written in exile, kept knowledge about State violations of human rights in circulation, supplementing and adding personal immediacy to news reports. Resistance leaders, white radicals, and survivors in exile wrote personal narratives that were published in Europe and the United States. Prison narratives chronicled the apartheid regime's assault on political activists. Journalist and historian Ruth First's[9] *117 Days* (1965), for instance, told not only of her time in prison but also of her long years as an anti-apartheid campaigner and ANC activist. It became prescribed reading for London schoolchildren in the 1970s (Daymond et al. 36).[10]

Along with published narratives, plays and performance poetry that dramatized the conditions of life under apartheid also found receptive audiences within and beyond South Africa. In the 1960s and 1970s, dramatist Athol Fugard, working with black performers John Kani and Winston Ntshona, among others, developed collaborative modes of creating (and portable modes of staging) productions that played in township halls, university campuses, and other underground locales in attempts to elude the ubiquitous censors. Fugard, Kani, and Ntshona toured cities in Angola, Zambia, and Tanzania where ANC guerrillas maintained a party in exile. Fugard's *The Island, Boesman and Lena, My Children! My Africa,* and *Sizwe Bansi is Dead* toured Europe, the United States, and Australasia, unleashing a revolutionary theater movement that turned drama into a tool of empowerment.

With the rise of the Black Consciousness Movement in the 1980s, more black and coloured writers produced narratives that aided the Struggle (Coullie 42). Coloured author Dan Mattera in *Memory is the Weapon* (1987) and black trade unionist Emma Mashinini in *Strikes Have Followed Me All My Life* (1989) addressed specific international readerships of trade unionists and socialists, building coalitions and enlisting broader support for sanctions. These autobiographical narratives were acts of witnessing to degradation and to acts of survival and resistance.

Autobiographical narratives and Fugard's touring plays offered glimpses to the wider world of the "realities" of life lived in the midst of apartheid, of the social and psychic cost of living under surveillance, of blacks and coloureds living as outsiders in a white South Africa. In other words, they attached flesh and blood reality to the facts and statistics reported in the news by overseas journalists.[11] Potent sites for challenges to the legitimacy of the South African government and its vast legal and extra-legal machinery of enforcement, they motivated member nations of the international community to take steps, such as boycotts and divestment campaigns, that would begin to put increasing pressure on the South African government to end apartheid.[12]

Inside South Africa, many forms of orature, including protest poetry, township riddling sessions, impromptu travelers' songs of Lesotho migrant workers, and migrant women's music, carried on a politics of resistance by transforming the traditions of oral literature (Hofmeyr 89, Coplan xiv).[13] Funerals of slain South Africans provided other contexts for public performances that subverted state censorship. In the townships and homelands Xhosa women's storytelling, long the provenance of men, played a crucial role in subverting state mechanisms of authority.[14] Through these oral traditions, circulating within black cultures, the tellers maintained some degree of cultural agency. But beyond these local forms, black voices of resistance addressed themselves to an audience of anti-apartheid exiles, strangers outside South Africa, and a public requiring education about the system of apartheid and its violations of human rights.

In exile, the ANC set up Radio Freedom, beaming news and propaganda into the Republic from station facilities across Southern Africa. It established a Fighting Fund and sent activists, choirs, writers, and actors abroad to raise money. The tours promoted other sources of support and advocacy campaigns—from the United Nations Human Relations Commission, the Soviet Union, India, Oxfam, and the World Council of Churches. Around the world, NGOs, trade unions, women's groups, churches, governments, corporations, sporting organizations, and cultural workers joined the cause of anti-apartheid struggle, seeding pressure for official sanctions; trade and economic boycotts; campus divestment campaigns directed at corporations doing business in South Africa; sports, music, and cultural boycotts; and corporate decisions to move operations out of South Africa. Rock stars held benefit concerts. American actors, like the cast of the popular and progressive television show *Cagney and Lacey*, voted to donate their South African royalties to the cause of black liberation. In the late 1980s the ANC collected significant funding from the West and China, Third World countries, and a multitude of private institutions, enabling a formidable underground movement in South Africa to build a foundation for public confidence (Davis 1987, 75).

FRAMING NARRATED LIVES IN COUNTRY AND IN EXILE

Diverse forms of witnessing to life in this apartheid State recorded, spurred, and sustained the Struggle inside South Africa and informed and motivated activism internationally. But the politics of framing and the location of critical reception invariably influenced how particular life narratives would be received by reading audiences. The histories of critical reception for two such narrated lives, Elsa Joubert's semi-fictionalized biography, *The Long Journey of Poppie Nongena* (1978) and Mark Mathabane's *Kaffir Boy* (1986), attest to this complex politics of recognition in the context of apartheid.

The Long Journey of Poppie Nongena, as told to and edited by Elsa Joubert, was originally published in Afrikaans in 1978, and subsequently translated into English (by Joubert) in 1980. Poppie (not her real name) had arrived at Joubert's doorstep in Cape Town in the midst of the Soweto uprisings of 1976, that "year of fire" after black schoolchildren organized mass demonstrations in opposition to the introduction of a mandatory Afrikaans language instruction in schools. Arriving in Cape Town in a destitute and outlawed state, Poppie told her incredible story to her Afrikaner writer-employer who in turn produced the life narrative for publication. Thus, *Poppie* was a project born out of the Soweto uprising, that violent moment of black resistance to apartheid law and to the imposition of an inferior Bantu education system.

Although the actual voice of the anonymous black woman would be muted in Joubert's biography, the highly political text could be read as the ur-story of black African women under apartheid. It tells of an impoverished black woman, a figure largely absent from published South African history and culture, and her collective identity within several black communities. It tells of her experience of child labor; multiple family displacements; a reluctant marriage in which she loses her identity and civic status; banishment to her (largely absent) husband's Bantusan; domestic violence; alcoholism; unemployment; restrictions under the pass laws; life as an outlaw lived in illegal squatter communities; police raids; murders; horizontal violence involving both whites and blacks, including frequent neck-lacing;[15] evictions; forced removals; surveillance and indignities at the hands of the police; and frequent acts of resistance.

State censors never banned the book, even though Poppie's narrative told of the everyday realities of the pass laws, for instance, and of forced removals and police surveillance. Indeed, the book proved to be immensely popular in South Africa as well as overseas. It was serialized in South African newspapers and women's magazines. It won three literary awards. Its reception prompted over one hundred reviews, countless articles, letters to the editor, and reports. And it was translated into English, French, Spanish, and German. Curiously, Anne McClintock observes that most black leaders and critics applauded the text while, for the most part, the white Left ignored it (299–302). Many white reviewers raved about the book (Driver, 2004). Others, McClintock notes, called the book "scandalous" for its violation of racial, class, gender, and aesthetic boundaries, and its challenge to white certainties (300).

Poppie's power to gain a wide readership and move readers to identify with this black woman captures the paradoxes of literary production in an apartheid state. On the one hand, the collaborative dynamic of the production of the text accords with the structures of black–white relationships promoted through apartheid laws and policies as does the reception of the book on the part of some readers as a family saga, a framing that would allow some reviewers and readers to evade the ethical call of "Poppie's" narrative voice of resistance (see McClintock 304). On the other hand, Joubert, who claimed copyright for the text, also negotiated the distribution of royalties with "Poppie" prior to publication.[16] *Poppie*'s broad readership also suggests how difficult it is to predict the kinds of reception a narrative will receive from diversely located audiences within and beyond the oppressive system of its construction. From one point of view *Poppie* can be read as an account of a Xhosa woman's struggle, a political struggle not unlike that of millions of other black women living in apartheid South Africa. From another point of view, the narrative, as framed by Joubert, can be read as a "universal" story of human tragedy and individualist struggle and survival. In the latter case, a reader might foreground the narrative of individualist struggle and survival and resist, actively or unconsciously, the political impact of a narrative about struggles in Soweto.[17]

The diverse and mixed readings of the text point to the complex social positionings and alliances, structures of affinity and division, cross-cultural crossings and intersections between dominant and "outgroups" across multiple forms of community and diverse cultures of oppression and resistance. No ultimate "reading" can ever be possible. A text like Poppie might better be understood as a "singular event," to invoke Félix Guattari's concept,[18] that sets off multiple responses with unpredictable outcomes. Subaltern stories, even when told "anonymously" through collaboration with white writers, build solidarity for their own groups and make possible new awareness, understanding, repositionings, and collectivities for those in positions of difference from the storytellers.

The story of Mathabane's *Kaffir Boy* reveals the ways in which stories of apartheid suffering became commodified as they circulated outside South Africa. As one of the broadly circulated autobiographical narratives written by a black South African and published in England and the United States in a decade marked by increasing international opposition to the apartheid regime, *Kaffir Boy* generated considerable interest in the United States. Mathabane had been fortunate to escape apartheid when in 1978, at the age of eighteen, he won a tennis scholarship to a small college in the United States. His narrative told the story of a young South African boy's struggle to survive everyday violence and gain an enabling education despite the Bantu education program through which the South African apartheid government reproduced subordination and limited aspiration among its subject population. Its visibility and popularity in the United States stands in stark contrast to its status in South Africa. The autobiography, ironically, is little known and has never been reprinted by a South African press.

Overseas, however, particularly in the United States, the narrative gained widespread attention. After the publication of *Kaffir Boy* and its sequel, *Kaffir Boy in America* (1989), Mathabane attracted broad media attention, none perhaps surpassing the impact of his appearance on *The Oprah Winfrey Show*. Winfrey's overt sympathy, as an African American, toward Mathabane, and her advocacy of his anti-apartheid story and politics, prompted the widespread identification with his coming-of-age story and anti-apartheid politics, particularly among, although by no means limited to, African Americans. His appearance and Winfrey's promotional support for his book generated increased popular knowledge about the apartheid regime and the struggles of the ANC in the United States. It also increased profits from book sales, profits used to establish scholarship programs and to seed international anti-apartheid activism.

Mathabane's appearance on *Oprah* initiated a five-year national "interest" in the Mathabane family in South Africa, the family's battles against the National Party regime, and the political transformations taking place inside the country. Mathabane made several appearances on the *Oprah* show that intermittently reactivated audience interest in his family's fortunes in the manner of a mini-soap opera. Winfrey eventually offered to provide a scholarship and a new start in the United States for his sister Miriam, still embattled in the upheavals that marked the demise of National Party's hold on South Africa. After Nelson Mandela assumed the South African presidency in 1994, Miriam finally made the trip to the United States, appeared on *Oprah*, and took up the proffered scholarship. With her brother Mark, she published her own narrative in 2000, *Miriam's Song*. Miriam's exodus from oppression and the bestowal of the scholarship fed directly into the American myths of progress according to which education provides the means for the committed individual to overcome class, ethnic, gendered, and racial oppressions.

The manner of his debut on the U.S. stage via the talk show circuit raises important issues about the media of awareness and political advocacy in human rights struggles. As is the nature of the medium, the talk show format directs audience responses affectively toward an empathetic identification with an individual success story of resistance and survival. This emotional appeal reduces the complexities of apartheid politics in South Africa to a personal story of one man or woman's opposition to the State, aimed at garnering the sympathetic attachment of the audience. Yet, it can also promote awareness and activism if viewers channel their affective responses into critical self-awareness of the politics of racism, poverty, class divisions, and oppressions both at home and abroad. In relation to the Mathabane family story, coming from South Africa but delivered to television viewers in the United States, such attention to South African apartheid muted awareness and concerns for injustice at home, transferring the outrage and activism on behalf of human rights to an "elsewhere" halfway around the globe.

As the discussions of the Joubert and Mathabane narratives demonstrate, different dynamics attended the production, reception, and circulation of life stories under apartheid. The politics of reading and response is never clear-cut, nor can audience interests and interpretative frameworks be predicted in advance. Sometimes and in some situations the life story can lead audiences to greater awareness, identification, recognition, advocacy, and activism on behalf of the human rights of victims. Sometimes stories told by activists are collapsed into the politics of the struggle. At other times the political efficacy of the narrative can be diverted into generative moral, aesthetic, historical, or legal assessments. If told at home, in the case of *Poppie* through Afrikaner agency, a story can be hailed as "universal" in a way that provokes limited forms of empathetic response. If told overseas and situated within the popular media like that of *The Oprah Winfrey Show*, it can be commodified to enlist the "do-gooder" sympathies of a wide audience, ennoble Western myths of exceptional individualism, and deflect national attention away from human rights issues in the readers' neighborhoods. Despite a myriad of disparate responses by different reading publics both in South Africa and beyond its borders, the cumulative effect of stories told, particularly through the decade of the 1980s, gave worldwide witness to the struggle against apartheid and the South African regime of gross human rights violations.

COMMISSIONING OF TRUTH

With the passing of the apartheid era new forums for storytelling emerged. In 1995 the new Parliament passed the Promotion of National Unity and Reconciliation Act, mandating the establishment of a Truth and Reconciliation Commission (TRC) that would engage in an extensive project of individual and collective remembering. Charged with bringing to the public "as complete a picture as possible of the nature, causes and extent of gross violations of human rights" committed from March 1, 1960 to December 5, 1993, the Commission sought to "restor[e] the human and civil dignity of such victims by granting them an opportunity to relate their own accounts of the violations of which they are the victims" (TRC 1:140). Seeking national consensus about the new terms of identification in South Africa—across racial and ethnic divides, across the divide of contested history—the TRC sought to confront South Africa's violent, rights-violating past, what Anthony Holiday describes as "its protracted birth pangs during the apartheid era" (46), and to mark, according to Dorothy Driver, "the birth of a new South African consciousness" (2001, n.p.).

Given its mandate to promote "national unity and reconciliation in a spirit of understanding which transcends the conflicts and divisions of the past" (Promotion of National Unity and Reconciliation Act of 1995), the Commission inaugurated an ambitious and idealistic theater of personal storytelling, modeling for the world what Michael Ignatieff describes as the "essential problem" of "balanc[ing] peace and justice, forgetting and forgiving, healing and punishment, truth and reconciliation" (2001a, 15). Through the establishment of the TRC, South African leaders acknowledged and exercised the commitment to narratability acknowledged in the signing of the UDHR in 1948 (Slaughter 415). Going beyond the mandates of truth commissions elsewhere, the Act "explicitly recognized the healing potential of telling stories" (TRC 1:112) and the importance of oral storytelling traditions to the transmission of culture. In effect, a massive project of storytelling became the foundational event symbolizing the transition from apartheid to the post-apartheid State.

Commissioning the truth in service to nation building has become an integral part of the international regime of human rights. In the last thirty years there have been numerous truth commissions in action around the world.[19] Such commissions promote the idea that governments, to be legitimated in the eyes of the people, have an obligation to search for the "truth" of the past in order to "provide a fair record of a country's history and its government's much disputed acts" (Hayner 607). More precisely, commissions help build a broader consensus about what version of the past will be credited, for, it is not that the truths of the past of massive violations of human rights are not known to people and thus in need of discovering or uncovering; it is, rather, that certain people have not had access to a national forum in which their experiences and their truths of the past can be acknowledged and credited. In the context of truth commissions, the commitment to narratability—to witness and confession—contributes to the mandated retelling of the nation's past, to establish an archive, open the country to new narratives of identity, and legitimate the authority of the "new" State for all its citizens.

Several defining features distinguished the TRC from earlier truth commissions. Most notably, the South African TRC sought truth telling in pursuit of restorative, not retributive, justice. In a move motivated by the goal of reconciliation, the TRC defined four different notions of truth: "factual or forensic truth, personal or narrative truth, social or 'dialogue' truth and healing and restorative truth" (TRC 1:110). Factual or forensic truth provides corroborative evidence for establishing the "what" of what happened in the past, a truth necessarily privileged for the purposes of determining reparations for victims and amnesty for perpetrators. Personal or narrative truth comes from witnessing to the subjective experience of suffering and victimization, a truth based on people's "perceptions, stories, myths and memories" (TRC 1:112) and necessary to the reconstitution of their subjectivities. The constitutive process of fitting together an understanding of, or knowledge about, the context of everyday life under apartheid produces social or "dialogue" truth, a new foundation for national unity. Healing and restorative truth emerges out of the production of a collective, consensual narrative of nation through which the new South Africa can remember its past and find its future, a narrative of nation that listens for the voices of the formerly voiceless and disenfranchised.

Second, the TRC included an amnesty provision through which perpetrators of human rights violation could be granted amnesty provided they gave a "full confession" regarding their participation in the violent events of the past, as long as those deeds were deemed to be political acts and not acts of personal violence. Third, it set up a process of one-to-one direct witnessing between victims and perpetrators, many of whom faced each other in the hearingroom. And fourth, the process was organized, presented, and represented as a public event, dependent on public participation and broad media coverage. The South African Truth Commission was the first such commission to open its hearings to the public, although only about 10 percent of the over 21,000 victim testimonies were aired in public hearings (Posel 1991, 3). Segments from the hearings were broadcast live on national and local radio stations, televised through nightly headline stories, and reported widely around the world.

The charismatic figures of Nelson Mandela, the first democratically-elected president of South Africa, and Archbishop Desmond Tutu, the chief commissioner of the TRC, added not only stature but public faith and confidence in the Commission's work of nation building. The two visionary figures coupled the Christian message of forgiveness and reconciliation with the African concept of *ubuntu*. "Ubuntu," comments Driver,

> is the Xhosa and Zulu term for a concept that entered South African English literary and political discourse during the Black Consciousness era of the 1970s and 1980s, although its genealogy is considerably older. Associated with African humanism and African socialism, ubuntu ... serves to oppose European greed, selfishness and the dehumanizing treatment of black South Africans, and to delineate a psychological dynamic in which each individual—whatever their class status—is accorded equivalent dignity and personhood. (2001, n.p.)

Thus, the South African version of commissioning the truth in service to nation building and human rights enfolds the principles of Enlightenment individualism and African *ubuntu*, fusing local traditions within global politics, tradition within modernity. African principles are in this way articulated (albeit imperfectly) with Western conceptions of law. In the realm of ethics, the traditional African principle of *ubuntu* is articulated with the Judeo-Christian principles of forgiveness and redemption.

THE NATIONAL INSTITUTION OF STORYTELLING

For the victims, the TRC, its philosophy and its process, promised restoration of their human and civil dignity through organized storytelling (TRC 1:57). Through its ritualized scene of witnessing, victims could bring their personal stories of suffering and pain to a public realm, transforming private stories into public myth (Bozzoli 185–6). They could confront perpetrators, demand justice, and claim the right to compensation. Participation in the process could bring public apology, recognition, and vindication, as well as the possibility of compensation. In return, witnesses were asked to forgive and forget. For the perpetrators, the Commission offered the possibility of amnesty and legal protection from further civil action, as long as they offered a full and open disclosure of crimes, including full details of accomplices. In return, they risked the indignity of public exposure. For the nation as a whole, the TRC activated a fuller archive about the past and utilized reconstructed memories to reframe a story of nationhood. The TRC also demanded that the nation face hard moral questions about its past and about the terms of its future.

The TRC process structured an ethics of recognition for victims, perpetrators, and the nation as a whole; but the process brought its own constraints, with potentially negative effects on witnesses to suffering and loss. According to its terms of reference, the TRC limited the scope of its activities, placing certain stories inside and some outside its scope. The Commission was charged with gathering "truth" about particular kinds of gross violations of human rights specifically to do with the "public, political and bodily nature of human rights" (Van Schalkwyk 185). As a result, attention was directed to killings and murders, abductions and disappearances, and incidents of torture and physical maiming. Vigorous critique of these terms of reference came from women's advocates who argued early in the process that the focus on abuses of bodily integrity rights limited the purview of the Commission in ways that erased women's experience of apartheid from consideration and thus limited the history collectively reconstructed through the processes of the TRC.

Women's advocates argued that men and women experienced the everyday violence of apartheid and the environment of resistance differently.[20] Consequently, the individualist model of human rights discourse and protocols obscured the ways in which women shouldered the burdens of racist oppression visited not just on individuals but on entire communities (Van Schalkwyk 185). Annalet Van Schalkwyk, among others, argues that this failure to account for the gendered effects of the apartheid regime meant that women were largely precluded from becoming "victims" of human rights violations (185), though they could give witness to the violations of the rights of their loved ones.

The Commission took steps to address the critiques of women's advocates, holding special women's hearings in Durban, Johannesburg, and Cape Town. In these spaces women were encouraged to come forward with stories of their own victimization, particularly in relation to their experiences of rape and sexual abuse. Some women did come forward; but others did not, in part due to the shame of public exposure. "In many cases, too," suggests Driver, "assault would seem difficult to define, to separate out from occasions of coercion and the terrible negotiations of power open to women with nothing but sex to exchange" (2001, n.p.). In the end, the TRC organized its project in ways that narrowed its conceptualization of women's rights as human rights and thus limited its projection of gender equality, guaranteed in the Constitution, as a critical feature of the new nation. As one of the commissioners noted, "we only began to scratch the surface of the horror" (Joyce Seroke, qtd. in Driver 2001, n.p.).

For some witnesses, testimony before the TRC had salutary effects; but for others, the act of personal storytelling exacerbated rather than assuaged their experience of traumatic suffering and loss. Telling reopened wounds and triggered further suffering, intensified in instances when perpetrators did not respond with recognition or contrition or even acknowledgment. The TRC could not demand contrition on the part of perpetrators, who were required to tell a certain kind of story to earn amnesty but could not be required to exude a particular affect.[21] Victims, on the other hand, were asked implicitly and explicitly to adopt particular affects. "Virtues of forgiveness and reconciliation were so loudly and roundly applauded," notes Richard Wilson, "that emotions of revenge, hatred and bitterness were rendered unacceptable, an ugly intrusion on a peaceful, healing process" (1999, 17). In its quest for reconciliation, the TRC demanded that witnesses cede their right to seek redress through the courts and then enjoined acts of forgiveness and censored affects such as anger and rage, thereby suppressing certain affective dimensions of storytelling unleashed through the process of witnessing.[22]

Nor could the TRC control the reception of victim stories as they circulated through the media. Although victims gained some forms of limited agency over their lives and their stories as a result of testifying before the Commission and having their stories validated, they lost control of their stories as they circulated beyond the immediate context of telling. Many experienced dismay at becoming a model for "the compelling drama of exposé, confession, and, at times, repentance in a 'mediasized' arena" (Posel and Simpson 7). When republicized in the media or in other people's writing, witness stories became commodified trauma narratives enlisting audience sympathies in ways that were not always conducive to the victims' processes of healing.

As for the TRC's role in nation building, the results of the TRC process were mixed. For some, but not all participants, the victim hearings enacted the democratization of the former apartheid State in the language of universal human rights. As a result, the hearings validated their lives and legitimated them as new subjects of history assuming a role in constructing the larger narrative of nation. Their witnessing also contributed to the reimagining of a nonracialized South Africa and nonracialized South African citizen-subject. But witnessing also positioned those who testified as victims, eliding their agency and resistance during the struggle and homogenizing differences—between women and men, old and young, black and white (Ross 2003a, 5, 128).

The TRC reified the identities of victim and perpetrator, and set them in opposition to one another. Deborah Posel and Graeme Simpson (citing the work of Philip Bonner and Noor Nieftagodien) argue that this binary leaves no place "to explore the moral ambiguities born of a politics of complicity or collaboration under apartheid; nor to explore the complexities of social causation where individuals are caught up in structural processes that both motivate and constrain their actions, in ways that may not be intelligible to the actors themselves" (10). Further, the narrative collectively produced through victim witnessing and perpetrator confession represents "a revised official history as one of a shared, non-ethnically marked nation" (10). Such a narrative occludes tensions and antagonisms within different groups and obscures the different motivations for victims and perpetrators to testify at the hearings.

Finally, for the nation, the rhetoric of the TRC promoted the legitimation of a new political order, enabling South Africa to claim full membership in the community of nations. The South African version of commissioning the truth modeled a new ethics of advocacy for the rest of the world, an ethics melding the literal and symbolic meaning of human rights principles with the traditional African principle of *ubuntu*. It signaled the enfolding of indigenous and Western traditions as integral to post-apartheid relations. As a number of commentators suggest, however, this utopian desire for a unifying and healing discourse could only ever be fraught with contradiction, given the different imperatives of African customary traditions and Western law, the different usages of testimony, the deep historical divisions of the past, and the gaps and fissures of memory (Attwell and Harlow, Ross 2003b, Sanders 2000, Driver 2001). Despite its valiant attempts at reconciliation, in the end the TRC could not manage all the uncertainties that lay ahead in the journey toward social, economic, and political reconstruction.

NARRATED LIVES AND NATION BUILDING

During the course of its tenure, the TRC held eighty hearings across South Africa, took testimony from over 21,000 witnesses, identified

46,696 gross violations of human rights suffered by 28,700 victims. Nightly television broadcasts and documentaries of the hearings took this testimony into the homes of all South Africans. The broadcasts brought home to viewers, who believed they had an understanding of the realities of apartheid, more than the common knowledge they assumed. According to Gunther Pakendorf, the testimonies invoked "heterogeneous memories of the gruesome details, the extent of operations, the breathtaking depravity and cold cynicism of those involved, the heart-wrenching heroism of most victims, the intensity and unrelenting nature of it all" (n.p.). Pakendorf goes on to suggest that, in making visible the realities of apartheid, the TRC hearings made it imperative for people privileged by the apartheid system to confront the common knowledge of racism that they had refused to admit to themselves, "the daily humiliation people of color had to endure as second and third class citizens in the land of their birth, the denial of their human dignity" (n.p.). The broadcasts challenged viewers to accept complicity for their role in the appropriation of land and dispossession of peoples, to admit the everyday banality of racial oppression that their lives had supported and benefited from, to become witnesses to the victims' stories, and to respond ethically to the TRC's aims of healing and reconciliation. These demands elicited powerful and contradictory passions and prompted complex, deeply felt, and ambiguous responses.

In 1998 the Commission issued a 2,500-page, five-volume report that was broadly available in print, on CD, and over the Internet.[23] The TRC Report, as distinct from the broadcasts, frames the history of the past, providing an "official" version of events, apportioning blame, weighing evidence, and presenting testimony for compensation and amnesty. It renders findings on the majority of those cases and names 400 perpetrators. Wilson suggests that in the public theatricalization of victim testimony, the commissioners individually and collectively did the cultural work of ethical recognition, responding to witnessing by embedding individual stories in the larger narrative of the nation. In the published Report, commissioners framed the narratives by situating them within the context of historical events and practices of resistance; "teleologizing" death as self-sacrifice for a new future; grafting individual testimony onto the larger "allegory of liberation"; and encouraging acts of forgiveness (1999, 15–16). Through its power to frame personal testimony and to make decisions about whose testimony to include in its final Report, the TRC enacted a closure of sorts on the hearings and attempted to constitute new South African identities for people whose individual stories became part of the new story of a nation, liberated from its pariah past. The Commission hearings and the final Report, taken together, however, would have different efficacies for the different groups of people involved—victims, perpetrators, newly-constituted South African citizen-subjects, white and black, young and old, the wealthy and the impoverished, and the nation as a whole.

For the victims, the TRC's praxis of recognizing personal truth as one of the truths sought by the Commission inaugurated a partial healing process. The extensive media reporting of the hearings to the larger public issued a general ethical call to the community to respond, to acknowledge the dignity and humanity of the other, and to struggle toward redress. The public staging of testimony required of perpetrators a confession to past crimes and a tacit acknowledgment of the power of the new State (Wilson 1999, 12). But not all told the truth, or the whole truth. And as many victims complained, perpetrators often confessed and appealed for forgiveness not to the victims they had harmed but to the commissioners who were empowered to grant them amnesty. The published Report of the Commission produced a patchwork allegory of liberation, but not all South Africans were prepared to accept the rhetoric of forgiveness nor prepared to heed the call of reconciliation. The Commission's attempt to produce a unifying national narrative of reconciliation muted these contradictions and, for many victims, opened new wounds.

Critics of the Commission process claimed that powerful political parties and individuals could and did short-circuit the work of the Commission. Government officials could vet testimony; they could refuse to appear before the TRC to request amnesty; perpetrators could seek injunctions in the courts to forestall testimony before the TRC. Critics claimed that few whites came forward with testimony, and few came to listen to the hearings. Women remarked that men did not attend sessions in which they gave testimony. And, as Goldblatt and Meintjes, Driver, and Ross document, many women came forward only to tell of the victimization and suffering of their sons, husbands, and brothers. Their own suffering, including rape by police and anti-apartheid activists and sexual servitude in ANC military camps, remained unwitnessed. Disenfranchised youth complained that the TRC did not speak for them. Their concerns were sidelined, their voices not attended to, their lives marginalized. Determined to maintain their radical resistance, they recoiled from the framing of testimony through the rhetoric of Christian suffering and redemption. Many of the victims who gave testimony before the Reparations Committee, telling of the loss of financial support due to the death of fathers, husbands, and sons, felt deprived of just compensation when they received the paltry sum of about ZAR 20,000 (USD 2,500). Some white South Africans might have been shamed into recognition of the personal and social costs of the apartheid system for those whose rights were violated. Others were turned off by the "leaking tap" of victim testimony, denying the violations of the past, refusing the politics of guilt, recoiling from responsibility in willful acts of forgetting. During the hearings they tuned out and turned off. There were also widespread concerns about the lamentably slow pace of the reparation hearings and the inadequacy of reparations that were issued.

Although it provided a healing catharsis for many victims who testified, releasing them from the burden of the silenced past, and radically altered public consciousness, the TRC has been judged as a partial success, as only the beginning of an indeterminate future. It offered a new narrative of nation building, but it also opened up fissures within the "rainbow" nation and inaugurated a healing process that would be impossible to adequately fulfill (Posel and Simpson 10–12). The recent history of post-apartheid South Africa has borne out the limited possibilities of the dream imagined in the initial excitement about South Africa's commissioning of truth.

IN THE WAKE OF THE TRC: SOUTH AFRICA'S POST-APARTHEID NARRATIVES

In the aftermath of the TRC hearings, the stories of victims and perpetrators have been incorporated in a variety of vehicles, subsumed into different political and aesthetic agendas, framed amidst a variety of affective appeals. Shortly after the conclusion of the TRC hearings, Antjie Krog, an Afrikaner poet and journalist who had covered the hearings for the South African Broadcasting Company, published her account of the Commission, *Country of My Skull*. In a retrospective assessment she comments, "The last victim hearings finished five months ago, and the focus has been lost. No more the voices, like a leaking tap in the back of your mind, to remind you what this Commission is all about" (311). In the post-TRC era, life narrating continues to be enlisted, explicitly or implicitly, in the project of nation building. Though the tap of narrative turned off with the conclusion of the hearings, the voices of witness have continued to circulate within and beyond South Africa.[24] "What seems to have happened," suggests the writer and social critic Njabulo Ndebele, "is that the passage of time which brought forth our freedom has given legitimacy and authority to previously silenced voices. It has lifted the veil of secrecy and state-induced blindness. Where the State sought to hide what it did, it compelled those who were able to see what was happening not to admit the testimony of their own eyes. In this connection, the stories of the TRC represent a ritualistic lifting of the veil and the validation of what was actually seen" (19). These two perceptions—Krog's nearly numbing and guilt-suffused Afrikaner reactions to the disclosures of South Africa's repressed and repressive history and Ndebele's expression of new potentials opened up by the "lifting of the veil of secrecy and state-induced blindness"—expose fragments of the conflicted responses through which South Africans negotiate paths into an indeterminate future.

In post-apartheid South Africa numerous forms of life writing have emerged that contribute to the ambiguities of transition. Some narratives seek new forms of national unity as they variously address the difficult and contentious task of confronting the apartheid past; enlarge debates about shame, guilt, denial, forgetting, and responsibility; provide healing narratives of heroic resistance and ethical responsibility; and assume a role in the project of reconciliation and nation building. Others refuse this imperative, instead challenging unified or reconcilable perspectives, positions, and identities in recognition of heterogeneous histories and subjectivities. These latter writings exceed the borders of both nation and identity; allow experimentation with new narrative forms in imaginative and playful ways not possible in the morally exigent climate of the past; refuse the authority of voice; destabilize the language of nation building; and open up spaces for contradiction and incommensurability. Post-TRC narratives advance the extension of human rights and freedoms within South Africa. While some remain committed to the universal humanism of the foundational principles of the United Nations and attempt to establish them as normalizing within the social fabric, others reach beyond these presumptions and bear witness to the fractures, ambiguities, and dissonant voices that speak from below.

Nation Building

Since the close of the TRC and the publication of the Report, a number of memoirs have appeared, authored either by previously exiled activists, many of whom returned with the release of Nelson Mandela and the first democratic elections, or by those who were participants in the TRC process, either as commissioners or witnesses. These texts attempt to recover the suppressed history of the apartheid regime and to respond from new positions of critical awareness and ethical responsibility. Autobiographies by key black activists include Nelson Mandela's (ghost-written) *The Long Walk To Freedom* (1994) and Desmond Tutu's *No Future Without Forgiveness* (1999), two persuasive texts addressed to diverse readerships that testify to the full humanity and subjectivity of black Africans and open paths to reconciliation through forgiveness. These personal narratives, written by South Africa's elder black statesmen and heroes, provide a narrative context for the enactment of the work of reconciliation. They also supply heroic stories of celebrated figures to model for the nation an ethics of transcendence of apartheid, of heroic resistance, and of reconciliation.

Other memoirs attempt to rewrite the nation's history from the "other" side. These include Mamphela Ramphele's *A Life* (1995), an autobiographical narrative that details Ramphele's involvement with the black consciousness movement and its leader Steve Biko through the 1970s;[25] James Gregory's *Goodbye Bafana* (1995), a narrative of tribute to Mandela written by his jailer at Robben Island; and Joe Slovo's *Slovo: The Unfinished Biography* (1995), a posthumously published narrative by the former chairman of the South African Communist Party and reputed genius behind the ANC. Slovo's daughter Gillian has also written *Every Secret Thing: My Family, My Country* (1997), a narrative that attempts to come to terms with the lives of her father, Joe, and her mother, Ruth First, the radical journalist, historian, and ANC activist assassinated in a car bomb explosion in Mozambique in 1982. Collectively, these narratives fill gaps in the historical record of anti-apartheid struggle, contributing to an expanded archive upon which South Africa will construct its revisionist history.

Architects and politicians of the apartheid regime have also published narratives, not all of them accommodating to the changes that swept through the nation. The revelatory memoir of Eugene de Kock, *Long Night's Damage* (1998), riveted readers with its exposé of secret government deals with rival groups and involvement, as a former commander of Vlakplaas, a farm that became notorious as the base of a police death squad that operated with impunity during apartheid, in the torture, murder, sabotage, fraud, and theft that marked the corrupt dealings of the National Party. Recounted in neutral tones uninflected by expressions of personal accountability, his chilling narrative reveals, in Hannah Arendt's terms, the banality of evil. More than this, as Michiel Heyns notes, it underscores the pointlessness of confession if it comes without recognition or remorse.

F.W. de Klerk also published a politically motivated and barely apologetic defense of the apartheid regime in *The Last Trek: A New Beginning* (1998). These narratives mark the writers' "liberation from the bonds of the past" and their entrance into the new South Africa. Often confessing to ignorance, innocence, political naiveté, or good intentionality, they signal a break that distances them from early, and, in post-apartheid terms, unacceptable versions of themselves without taking on responsibility for those harmed by apartheid policies.

Other writers, like Jo-Anne Richards in *The Innocence of Roast Chicken* (1996), Damon Galgut in *The Beautiful Screaming of Pigs* (1998), and Mark Behr in *The Smell of Apples* (1995) trace fictionalized journeys of conversion from childhood innocence to adult awareness of white privilege and its costs. Behr's text, in particular, gained notoriety when, shortly after its publication, the author, a radical white student at Stellenbosch University, confessed that he had been a police informant. Through this confession, which evoked a range of responses from anger and dismay (from former friends) to praise (from more distanced readers), the former informant framed himself as a victim-hero of a post-apartheid South Africa. Through this and similar confessional narratives, Sarah Nuttall and Carli Coetzee suggest, "good" white South Africans gain entitlement "to membership of the new nation by means of [...] confession and a performance of a purge" (3). Part confessional, part apology, and part defense, these fictionalized memoirs by people associated with the apartheid regime give rise to the depth of anger, fear, prejudice, and disavowal that continues to forestall a politics of reconciliation.[26]

Other white South Africans, notably those who participated in some way in the TRC hearings, have published narratives of their journeys of self-transformation. Krog in *Country of My Skull* (1998) and Wendy Orr in *From Biko to Basson* (2000) attempt to reconcile European and African heritages by reflecting on their post-apartheid identities. Orr, a commissioner of the TRC and a member of the Reparations Committee, pens a memoir in which she enjoins the reader to her "human rights wake-up call" (15). That call came for Orr in 1985 when, as a district medical officer in Port Elizabeth, she attended to a torture victim held in jail, and subsequently filed a case in the Supreme Court in opposition to the practices she witnessed in prison. "Overnight," she writes, "I became worldwide headline news; a hero and a traitor; an object of praise and one of vilification; a recipient of bouquets and death threats... My human rights wake-up call had forced me into activism and, try as I might, it would be difficult to turn away from this path" (15). Thus Orr frames her narrative in terms of her "conversion" to the cause of human rights and uses this opportunity to justify her role in the national institution of witnessing. Throughout, Orr allows the voices of witness to speak, reproducing long sections of testimony, calling on readers to attend to the stories and recognize the suffering of apartheid's victims. Although occasionally referring to the emotional cost of her involvement, for the most part Orr positions herself as a nonpolitical participant in a way that renders her role as commentator on the inside story of the TRC, as neutral, not invested, and therefore, perhaps, "more objective." Addressing her narrative primarily to white South Africans, she asks that they witness the testimony she presents as a touchstone in the national movement toward reconciliation.

Krog's *Country of my Skull* also performs a politics of reconciliation. From her insider's perspective as a journalist (and poet) who worked for the ANC before covering the TRC for the South African Broadcasting Company, Krog presents a commanding narrative that combines the genres of reportage, memoir, and meta-fiction. As reportage, *Country of my Skull* records the details of the TRC hearings, often reproducing the testimony of victims and perpetrators as well as the tenor of the testimony and its reception; it also records the everyday labors of reporting on the content and the drama of the TRC hearings. As memoir, *Country of my Skull* becomes an occasion for Krog to reflect on her Afrikaner heritage and her previously unacknowledged complicity with apartheid policies as well as the complexities of reconciliation. Remarking on this aspect of the narrative, Michiel Heyns argues that, for Krog, the narrative's construction was "a personal rite of passage from the relatively secure world of the liberal Afrikaner to a frightening sense of complicity with the perpetrators and the horrors recounted at the hearings" (44).

Country of my Skull also engages readers in a meta-narrative on the importance of testimony, the meaning of truth, and the modes of communicative exchange among the victim, the victim's story, the absent perpetrator, and the listener as witness. Like Elaine Scarry, and Shoshana Felman and Dori Laub, Krog attests that testimony depends on the address to the other. If the Commission served as proxy perpetrator for victims during the hearings, standing in for the South African nation in order to set right the misuse of power in the past, Krog positions herself in the text as a proxy for listeners to whom "truth" is addressed (Sanders 2000, 29–31). Furthermore, as the hearings progressed, Krog and other journalists experienced themselves pulled into a vortex of psychological instability. In this, her personal trauma parallels the trauma that the hearings induced, not only for victims, but also for the nation as a whole. The author's recognition of a profound responsibility to witnesses and her own testimonial agency engages the reader in what Mark Sanders, citing Jacques Derrida and Anne Dufourmantelle, describes as a "drama of hospitality," "an enactment of hospitality between strangers, towards those who have been strangers in their own country and strangers to each other" (2000, 31).[27]

Some critical responses to Krog's narrative, however, expose the profound complexities of witnessing to another's suffering through an ethics of recognition. A number of witnesses, finding themselves represented on the pages of Krog's narrative, responded with surprise and anger. Some recoiled from her profiling of their pain; others failed to recognize themselves through the perceptions of the writer; still others resented what seemed to them as an appropriation of their pain to her project of reconciliation (see Ross 2003b, Bennett, Sanders 2000, and Libin). Commenting on the circulation of his testimony through the media as well as Krog's text, ex-ANC combatant Yazir Henri notes that "the disembodiment of my testimony has made the struggle to reclaim my voice, memory, and agency, harder. The dispossession of my voice, through a continuous recycling of my, by now, unmoored testimony, was compounded by the superimposition of other voices and narratives onto my own" (qtd. in Grunebaum and Henri 111). This is not to say that Krog acted irresponsibly in incorporating witness testimony into her text; it is to suggest that the incorporation of testimony, however well-intentioned and sensitively framed, changes the contexts of telling and the affective dynamics across the victim-perpetrator-beneficiary circuit of exchange (Ross 2003b, 148). This dissociation and relocation can become especially fraught when the testimony of witnesses such as Henri is transformed "into a figure, an emblem around which white guilt and affective transformation is elaborated" (Bennett 183). Henri's response cuts directly to the difficulties inherent in an ethics of recognition. Using the voices from the hearings to explore her own complicity with apartheid and responsibility for the pain and suffering of others, Krog produces an emotionally charged and passionately felt ethics of recognition, while at the same time muting the profound alterity and incommensurable difference of the other. In his highly critical reading of the Krog narrative, Mark Libin goes so far as to suggest that Krog "foregrounds her emotional response ... her guilt and sorrow, as well as self-loathing ... [in a way that] ultimately overflows, engulfs and finally overwhelms the testimony of witnesses she endeavors to record" (123).

In the final pages of *Country of My Skull*, Krog reflects upon the impact of the TRC on her own life and that of her country, committing herself and her text to the ongoing project of nation building and reconciliation. She writes that despite

> its mistakes, its arrogance, its racism, its sanctimony, its incompetence, the lying, the failure to get an interim reparation policy off the ground after two years, the showing off—with all this—it has been so brave, so naively brave, in the winds of deceit, rancor, and hate. Against a flood crushing with the weight of a brutalizing past onto new usurping politics, the commission has kept alive the idea of a common humanity. Painstakingly it has chiseled away beyond racism, and made a space for all of our voices. For all its failures, it carries a flame of hope that makes me proud to be from here, of here. (364)

Despite the cautionary concerns expressed by witnesses and critics, Krog's deeply moving text, of all the narratives intent on nation building in the post-apartheid era, comes closest to taking up the call issued by Archbishop Tutu when he opened the hearings.

Krog's *Country of My Skull* is perhaps the post-TRC narrative most familiar to overseas readers. Shortly after publication, it became a bestseller in South Africa, was republished in Italy, the United States, and the United Kingdom, and attained an almost legendary status. Krog herself has made many overseas trips since its publication where she has given international lectures and multiple interviews to the media, produced prize-winning videos that have screened in film festivals and aired on independent television around the world, and opened up the difficult and contentious debates about guilt, shame, denial, forgetting, and reconciliation in South Africa.

Dissemi-nations

Not all South Africans responded to the TRC and its commitment to a human rights discourse in search of reconciliation and unifying nation building. The editors of a special issue of *Modern Fiction Studies* (*MFS*) in 2000 identify a number of contrapuntal impulses evident in the new writing as post-TRC authors attempt to articulate the "experimental, ethical, and political ambiguities of transition... and the role of culture—or representation—in limiting or enabling new forms of understanding" (Attwell and Harlow 3). A number of recent texts explore new directions into the future, refusing the positionalities inherent in South African identity politics. For some, there can be no unity, no rainbow nation, no reconciliation, given the 300 years of white rule and the rifts in the social fabric. Part of this pattern of alternative response has to do with the discontent expressed by radical youth and women who felt betrayed or disgusted by the post-apartheid politics of conciliation that continued to protect white and male privilege. Part has to do with a more postmodern impulse toward recognition of the ghosts and remnants of the nation's past that haunt the present, and the dissidence, ambiguity, and multiplicities of identities that will not cohere, but nonetheless make possible a new politics of becoming.

A recent example of life writing projects that destabilize hierarchies of power and blur boundaries of identity and nation is the collection of personal stories, *Finding Mr. Madini* (1999). *Finding Mr. Madini* arose out of a collaborative storytelling workshop for homeless youth that utilizes the power of literacy to empower writers beyond a politics of racial reconciliation. Jonathan Morgan, a white psychiatrist visiting Johannesburg to conduct research for a proposed novel in which a homeless youth figured, facilitated a series of writing workshops for homeless youth. While he assembled the collection of personal narratives, he speaks neither for nor on behalf of the writers in the text. The stories he encouraged and the stories writers shared contribute not to building a nation, but to tentatively exploring points of contact, conflict, affiliation, and diversion for blacks living in South Africa but exploring identities that refuse confinement within the borders of nationhood. The storytellers live in South Africa, but they have come from many countries on the continent, seeking survival on the fringes of a more economically advanced country. The narratives contest one another, reveling in a contradictory assemblage. Morgan himself assumes no more expertise than any other writer in the group. There is no named author or editor of this text; rather he is ascribed the function of "director" with The Great South African Spider Writers, in the authorial attribution of the book.[28]

The success of *Finding Mr. Madini* enabled the establishment of many writing cells throughout the country, utilizing the techniques of narrative therapy. Collectively known as the Arc-Hive initiative, this narrative therapy movement prompts "a new wave of 'truth' and reconciliation" (Morgan et al. 281), forcing the healing power of storytelling into different and decentralized directions. With its mission to "circulate stories of protest, survival, and triumph, and to bring together a web of members for the purposes of consultation, information, and support" (281), the Arc-Hive initiative has gained the support of a wide range of governmental, professional, and charitable organizations. As "the first official African Story-Telling, Capturing and Lending Body" (281), Arc-Hive conducts workshops, and collects and publishes stories that circulate through the body politic of South Africa, expanding the reach of storytelling amongst the homeless and enfolding stories into one another and the contours of the nation.

Other writers have begun to exploit the ambivalences resulting from South Africa's new historical and political imperatives through imaginative fictions that explore writing as a space of possibility. These new narratives, argues Driver, imbue characters with a consciousness of the ironies of their contradictory positions. Zoë Wicomb, for example, adopts a feminist stance, informed by black consciousness, but strategically deconstructs race and gender categories in ways that destabilize identity and "open up new spaces for subjectivity" (Driver 1996a, 49). In her semi-autobiographical short story collection *You Can't Get Lost in Cape Town*, published before the end of apartheid in 1987, she had already begun to undermine a white order without positing a new, black monolithic authority in its place (Driver 1996a 50). Her more recent *David's Story* (2000), set in 1991 following the release of Nelson Mandela, deals with post-apartheid issues. It allows ancestral histories, colonial and apartheid regimes, and the muted voices of the dispossessed to commingle in a historical novel that refuses history. It is a novel about South African identity, fractured by myth, memory, and desire; a telling that links oral traditions and African orature to English and Dutch records and interpretations; a narrative that allows the gaps and silences enfolded within to yawn open, exposing the white masks of politics, religion, and history. "David" is the ostensible narrator, but "Dulcie," the voice of alterity linked to the land and metaphors of ongoing connection, haunts and dissembles David's story. "The importance of Wicomb's transformations—of stereotypes and subjectivities," writes Driver, "cannot be overemphasized [...] It is a writing, let's say, fully worthy of the history of black women's resistance to racist and capitalist exploitation and suppression, and of the ongoing battle to bring gender into current political negotiations" (Driver 1996a, 52).

Wicomb's might be seen as the most radical exploration of possible post-apartheid subjectivities, but her work exists in relation to other texts, other stories, that would have been impossible to tell given the censorship regime of the old South Africa. New fictionalized, semi-autobiographical narratives by feminist and gay writers, in particular, challenge the sexual repressions of the past. Marita van der Vyver's *Entertaining Angels* (1994) utilizes fantasy techniques and fairy tales to explore new realms of female sensuality and subjectivity.

It opens up imaginative spaces to explore issues of gender and sexuality previously forbidden from public discourse. K. Sello Duiker's *The Quiet Violence of Dreams* (2001) offers readers a shocking and violent account of the shattered life of an urban black youth who turns to an underworld of drugs, sex, corruption, and prostitution. Writers such as Duiker have become an integral part of South Africa's "remaking and reimagining of itself," testing the country's new discourse on human rights that decriminalized homosexuality and troubling its construction of a new history of the apartheid past.

The narratives of nation building contribute to a unifying project in a number of ways: by eliciting inclusive narratives by exiled ANC leaders; by offering former National Party leaders and sympathizers ways to carve a niche in the new post-apartheid State; and by enabling beneficiaries of the apartheid regime to signal their movement away from the past and commitment to reconciliation. The narratives of dissemi-nation explore diffuse subjectivities and subject positions within the new South Africa. In both modes of life writing, the voices of witness, the scenes of testimony, the incommensurate stories told, and the promises and failures of the national institution of storytelling instated by the TRC return to register the multiple dispersals of memory, affect, and identity and to provide new points of departure.

CONCLUSION: NEW STORIES, NEW HUMAN RIGHTS CAMPAIGNS

The TRC and its promoters imagined a revolutionary human rights project that would deliver a new truth about the apartheid past, heal individuals and the community, produce the conditions for a new post-apartheid subjectivity, and set the course for the yet-to-come founded centrally on the protection of universal human rights for all people in the rainbow nation. It did not wholly succeed. In many ways, however, the TRC achieved a great deal more than anyone had the right to expect, given South Africa's violent history. The national investment in the institution of storytelling did help the nation avoid the bloody confrontation of a civil war. It offered the promise of a way forward through the collective remembering of the national past. But its achievements as a vehicle for the international regime of human rights have to be weighed along with the continuing legacies of the apartheid regime.

Change has come at an exasperatingly slow pace for South Africa's non-white majority that still suffers from limited educational opportunities, poor health and housing, unacceptable levels of unemployment, especially for black youth, and the worsening crisis of HIV/AIDS. In fact, material conditions in the sprawling townships have worsened, as women and children utilized their freedom of movement to migrate from homeland environments to the cities where they joined their husbands, living with them in overcrowded conditions. In the Guguletu township of Cape Town, for example, male migrant-worker barracks that had previously housed three men per room, with inadequate cooking, plumbing, and sanitation facilities, now have upward of twenty people occupying the same space, the same small bedroom designed for three occupants. The children of these workers, many of whom had been involved in the radical politics of change, find themselves without access to education, training, or employment, even though they live only ten kilometers from the center of Cape Town. Wives have been left to cope with unhealthy and dehumanizing conditions, as relatives and older family members join them, constructing makeshift tin shelters for access to a communal water tap or toilet. The project of land redistribution has yet to proceed with any significant change in the material conditions of the majority of black South Africans.

Now, more than a decade after Mandela's release, the country turns its attention to other campaigns for human rights targeted at government corruption, soaring crime rates, violence and sexual assault, and the HIV/AIDs pandemic leaving in its wake hundreds of thousands of homeless orphans. Performance artist and rights activist Pieter-Dirk Uys remarks that statistics can be numbing in a country where 40 percent of the workforce, 60 percent of the Army, and 30 percent of the teenagers are said to be HIV-positive; where researchers estimate that some one million rapes occur each year (some of which are perpetrated repeatedly on the same victim); and where predictions are that within five years there will be over three million infant orphans. And so life writing continues to be enlisted in the call for new kinds of rights for South Africans, rights to medical technologies, medicines, adequate health care, and freedom from sexual violence among them.

After the long decades of state-based censorship, the TRC placed human rights at the center of political and cultural life. As an institution the TRC modeled new modes for collectively rewriting history, gathering into its national narrative same stories formerly unacknowledged, and yet eliding other, dissident stories. The TRC attempted to mediate contesting narratives through a language of reconciliation; and yet set in motion generated heterogeneous dialogues whose aftereffects have yet to play themselves out. In the wake of the TRC, many writers and critics have returned to narrative to reflect on the transition, some like Nelson Mandela and Desmond Tutu writing themselves into the narrative of nation as elder statesmen for the new South Africa, others like Antje Krog taking personal responsibility for healing and reconciliation, still others utilizing the contested terrain of post-apartheid culture to explore the contradictions, contestations, fractures, and discontinuities that were present on the days of Mandela's release and made manifest during the hearings of the TRC.

CHAPTER 4

INDIGENOUS HUMAN RIGHTS IN AUSTRALIA: WHO SPEAKS FOR THE STOLEN GENERATIONS?

It is my belief that when the Aboriginal and Torres Strait Islander story of Australia is heard and understood then there will be a true reconciliation. The abstract language of human rights and justice will settle down on the realities of the lives and aspirations of individual men, women and children who wish simply to have their humanity respected and their distinctive identity recognised.

—*Michael Dodson*, Social Justice Commission:
First Report 1993

I believe Australia is still illegally occupied. . . . This is my land and . . . we are in the 208th year of occupation and we have never been given any justice or any rights.

—*Murrandoo Yanner*, Carpentaria Land Council
activist (1996), Sydney Morning Herald

On January 26, 1988, the Australian government staged a grand Bicentennial celebration to mark two hundred years of continuous European settlement. On that day, two separate but interconnected events drew the nation's attention to the disparities between the lives of Indigenous and non-Indigenous Australians and their very different investments in the nation's history. While (mainly white) officials and crowds gathered at Sydney Cove to watch a reenactment of Captain Arthur Phillip's arrival and landing of the First Fleet, delivering officers, soldiers, and convicts to the shores of Botany Bay to establish a penal colony in Britain's far-flung outpost of Empire in 1788, Indigenous Australians and their supporters began a march through the streets of Sydney to protest against what for them was Invasion Day.

The protest had been planned. In the lead-up to the Bicentennial, Aboriginal activists had issued an invitation for others to join what they termed a "party" to "support the Aboriginal struggle for peace, justice and freedom" (*Sun* 315). No one, however, could have predicted what occurred, nor contain the event as it happened, nor represent it in any coherent way. The size of the crowd, the carnival atmosphere on the streets, the spontaneous mini-happenings that erupted within and between groups assembled, and the outpouring of mixed emotions that the "party" generated for spectators and participants alike—all were among the unexpected and unpredictable elements of the nation's counter-celebration. This counter-remembrance of settlement-as-invasion contested what other Australians celebrated in their patriotic tribute to the unified fictions that sustained their belonging as citizens of Australia.

There were two separate events on Australia/Invasion Day, 1988: the formal, orderly, structured, and commemorative official celebration of Australia as a white settler nation and the informal, unscripted, and disruptive protest of an alter-nation. One event enacted an often-told story about the origins of Australia—that is, what was already known and visible to history and codified in politics and law. The other dislodged the certainties that sustained the national narrative. It exposed fissures—previously invisible, hidden, or denied—in the discursive contours of nation. The highly visible, visual, and spirited counter-celebration displaced the official story of white settlement, raised significant human rights issues, and opened multiple possibilities for the future.

The clash of cultures was built on a number of fictions: the fiction that the first British flag planted by Captain James Cook—who was greeted as he disembarked from the ship Endeavour by the Gadigal tribe of the Eora people—was sufficient to establish British sovereignty over the land; or the fiction of the continent as *terra nullius*, empty, unoccupied, and open to European possession, without negotiation or compensation to its indigenous occupants. These fictions have constituted the nation of Australia as a legal and political entity. They have become doctrine, largely unquestioned, by the dominant public. And they have also underwritten the dispossession of Aboriginal and Torres Strait Islander peoples of their land, and also of their cultures, laws, and languages, effectively depriving them of their own sovereignty and self-determination on a continent they have inhabited throughout millennia.[1]

In Sydney, the parade of some 20,000 Indigenous marchers and their supporters took off from Redfern and snaked its way among cheering crowds to Hyde Park. Led by Galarrwuy Yunupingu, Chairman of the Northern Land Council, elders from remote Arnhem Land began a traditional dance. At the same time, a radical, urban-based student contingent made their way to Mrs. Macquarie's Chair, a prominent vantage point on Sydney Harbour first favored by the wife of Lachlin Macquarie, an early governor of New South Wales. Narrowly avoiding potentially violent stand-offs with the police, protesters hastily erected a tent embassy, hoisted the Aboriginal flag, and greeted the re-enacted First Fleet with catcalls of "murdering dogs" and "convict scum" (Attwood and Markus caption for illus. 34 and 35). With attendance estimated at 100,000, it was, Yunupingu recalled, "the biggest crowd ever seen to mourn the injustice of the past" (*ibid.*).

Yunupingu told the throng of supporters, "For us, this [landing of the First Fleet] was an act of war that led to genocide." Aboriginal rights activists argued that the doctrine of *terra nullius* had been counterfeit from the start in that it contravened the instructions of the British Admiralty to Captain Cook to "take possession *with the consent of the Natives* [emphasis added]."[2] Protestors displayed on their bodies visible signs of their increasing frustrations with the government. Dressed in black clothing, layered with tee-shirts sporting defiant slogans, and wearing flag-motif headbands designed in the Aboriginal colors of red, yellow, and black, they waved Aboriginal flags, greeted each other with Black Power salutes, and marched behind banners that proclaimed "White Australia has a Black History." The exuberant demonstration announced to the wider public: We are here; we have survived; we did not consent. Picked up in sound bites and broadcast with stunning visuals across the country by a greedy media more intent on sensationalism than substance, the march unsettled received narratives of nation.

The Bicentennial counter-celebration represented an unprecedented form of Indigenous intervention into the formation and perpetuation of national identity and marked a clear departure from the confining politics of accommodation that had largely silenced the demands of Australia's first peoples. It contrasted sharply with earlier commemorative events, such as the sesquicentennary celebrations of 1938 and those surrounding the Royal Visit of Queen Elizabeth in 1954, at which Indigenous people were forced to serve as props in First Fleet reenactments or exotic entertainment for visiting dignitaries.[3] Although emanations of the nation's counter-memories to settlement, circling below the surface of appearances, had arisen in many smaller moments of protest in the past, what emerged during the alter-native celebration of survival channeled those counter-memories into new, and sometimes incommensurable, imperatives that continue to motivate Indigenous rights activism today.

NATIONAL AWARENESS

Prior to the Bicentennial, few Australians knew of the history of Indigenous dispossession. People identifying as Aboriginal and Torres Strait Islander constitute only two percent of the present population of some twenty million people. They live in widely disparate communities, both geographically and culturally. Some Aboriginal people, residing in remote areas of Central and Northern Australia on lands ceded to their control and management through Native Title Acts in the 1970s (some with acknowledgement of their continuous occupation on traditional land, others granted after a series of government-controlled dislocations), survive with many of their cultural traditions intact. Others live in debased conditions, their lands encroached upon by pastoralists and the mining and forestry industries, their voices and concerns seldom heard or acknowledged in national forums until recently. Although intersecting and interrelated through language, custom, and skin groupings, these disparate groups constitute separate cultures and have different affiliations to land. The Torres Strait Islander population of Australia stands at about 28,000, 80 percent of whom live outside of the Torres Strait (APG 1992a, 323). Even the descendants of those dispossessed of lands and subjected to Australia's nineteenth- and twentieth-century policies and practices of segregation and assimilation—who now live modern lives in urban centers—had been largely invisible to the wider public. Their history had not been taught in schools. Their claims to land rights had been largely ignored. Indigenous groups had little knowledge of each other's stories. Children of mixed descent, raised on government reserves and Church missions and "brought up white" in an assimilationist era, were denied access to their cultural knowledge and traditional heritage. Whether residing on traditional lands or missions, raised and surviving in remote or urban areas, a majority of Aboriginal and Torres Strait Islanders live their adult lives in Third World conditions in one of the First World's most affluent nations. They suffer from poor health and housing standards; high rates of infant mortality; low life expectancy; poor education; unemployment and poverty; high rates of incarceration and deaths in custody; intolerably high youth suicide rates, especially for males; and high levels of stress that lead to unacceptable levels of community violence, rape and domestic abuse, family disintegration, alcoholism, and drug addiction.

Difficult though it has been to call the nation's attention to Indigenous human rights issues, the Bicentennial offered a threshold, in terms both of registering rights violations and offering a platform for storytelling. There were, however, omens that portended problems for the future, stemming not only from a lack of knowledge about Indigenous lives but also from an apparent unwillingness to listen. From the 1920s, Indigenous activists, faced with governmental indifference, had mounted numerous local campaigns and had been involved in community, national, and international networks of advocacy, including, after 1950, human rights organizations and UN-sponsored conferences and forums. Since 1982 they had actively participated in the UN Working Group on Indigenous Peoples, drawing upon their knowledge of UN conventions and covenants to support grassroots activism.

One highly visible campaign that had gained momentum during the 1980s concerned the inordinate number of Aboriginal deaths in custody. The government's 'blind eye' to the problem had led Aboriginal leaders to send two representatives to Geneva in 1987 to address the Working Group on the Rights of Indigenous Peoples and seek UN support (*Age* 317–18). Bicentennial enthusiasts may have chosen to ignore the issue, but they could not have been unaware of it. Indeed, on January 29, 1988, the day after the Bicentennial commemorations, an inquiry was scheduled to open in Adelaide to investigate circumstances surrounding a 19-year-old Aboriginal youth found dead in his cell. Justice Michael Kirby, speaking to the alternation assembled at the Bicentennial, acknowledged the inquiry and the ongoing deaths in custody campaigns, while also lamenting that, by 1988, the white Australian public had become "bored with the subject of Aboriginal justice" (APG 1992b, 325).

ROYAL COMMISSION TO INVESTIGATE
ABORIGINAL DEATHS IN CUSTODY

It had only been months before, in late in 1987, that the Hawke Labor government announced a Royal Commission to investigate Aboriginal Deaths in Custody (RCADIC). For decades, Aboriginal leaders had expressed outrage concerning the high number of black youth held in prisons. Aboriginal rage came to a head in 1983 after 16-year-old John Pat was kicked to death by five off-duty police officers in Roebourne, Western Australia, and three officers were acquitted at trial in 1982. Forming a Committee to Defend Black Rights, activists demanded action. The committee organized an effective media campaign that included speaking tours for the families of those who had died in custody, thus enlisting storytelling as a compelling tool of resistance against governmental indifference (Mickler 174). Shock headlines appeared regularly in the press detailing conditions of incarceration, intra-racial victimization, and an inordinately high number of deaths in custody as a result of suicide in suspicious circumstances. According to Paul Wilson "the proximity of the bicentenary celebrations in 1988, and the prospect of Aboriginal protest, 'embarassed' the Hawke [Labor] Government into holding the inquiry." He continues, "The Australian Government was all the more sensitive to international scrutiny because it had been vocal about the mistreatment of black South Africans..." (Harris 210). In this instance local activists, deploying the techniques of embarrassment and moral suasion, successfully utilized storytelling, conjoined with the international auspices of the United Nations, to counteract their inability to effectively influence a national political agenda.

The Royal Commission noted that although Aborigines comprise approximately 2 percent of the population, they represent 24 percent of the prison population, are significantly younger, have significantly higher rates of re-incarceration, and are three times more likely to receive custodial sentences than their non-Aboriginal counterparts (Harding, Broadhurst, Ferrante et al. 79–103).[4] The terms of reference for the Commission involved not only investigating the circumstances surrounding the deaths, but also studying the legacies of colonialism inherent in Australia's social, cultural, and legal policies and practices of discrimination. To investigate the problem, the Commission solicited testimony from representative Aboriginal groups and family members of the victims as well as government departments, the police, and state legislatures. The Commission collected over 100,000 pages of transcripts, individually investigated every death in custody, prepared detailed reports concerning the death of each victim, and commissioned twenty-one research papers. The final, 5,039-page, eleven-volume report not only disclosed extensive racialized abuse within the justice system, it also addressed the "underlying issues of...historical and political dispossession of the Aboriginal people and their subsequent impoverishment and disenfranchisement...as precursors to the high contact between police and Aboriginal people" (Harding, Broadhurst, Ferrante et al. 118 f.f.). Foremost among its 339 far-reaching recommendations was a sweeping call for measures to aid the self-determination of Aboriginal people and an education campaign to alert the larger public to the "deliberate and systematic disempowerment of Aboriginal people starting with dispossession from their land and proceeding to almost every aspect of their life" (Johnson 1991, 8). Lowitja (then Lois) O'Donoghue, serving as Chair of the Aboriginal and Torres Strait Islander Commission, called the Report the "most important social document for Aboriginal people in [the twentieth] century" (qtd. in Harris 212).

The RCADIC Inquiry was unprecedented and unparalleled, "the most comprehensive social inquiry into a population ever carried out in Australia," according to Steve Mickler (173). Yet while it sought Aboriginal testimony and acknowledged Aboriginal authority, the Inquiry also limited and contained Aboriginal involvement. Only one of the commissioners was Aboriginal; an overwhelming proportion of the dry, legalistic document cited official, non-Indigenous sources; and many Aborigines who could have testified declined to do so because of their distrust of the police and the legal system and their cynicism concerning the ability of the government to effect change (Harris 201). The Report framed the limited amount of witness testimony it contained within the Commission's terms of reference, often describing victims in derogatory fashion and presenting men of stature within the Aboriginal community through racist and patronizing police stereotypes of the shiftless, lazy, vagrant, or drunken Aborigine (204). In the end, although the Report amounted to what Mickler calls "a $30 million dollar act of state confession" (186), it found insufficient evidence to convict any prison official of wrongdoing. When released, it garnered little interest in the larger non-Indigenous community; and the government failed to act on a majority of the recommendations.[5]

The Report framed its arguments and findings in ways that conformed to normative racial categories of deviance that would have long-term consequences. It constructed "Aboriginality" with reference to a legal system in which young offenders were seen to be victims of a criminal justice system, thus marking Aborigines off from mainstream Australian society and framing Aboriginal life in terms of criminality and victimization. Although the Report itself constitutes a significant milestone, the failure of States to act, the continued rise of Indigenous incarceration, and ongoing instances of death in custody showed that, despite the compassion and anger elicited by the storytelling tours and graphic testimony from police and members of victims' families, the Commission's findings failed to compel the nation to responsive action or to deliver needed change. And through the refusal of states to take up the recommendations, the Royal Commission served to further alienate Aboriginal groups and sowed seeds of further distrust (Harris 1996). Despite the urgency of the issues, it remains difficult to gain a national audience and move potential advocates to action when the victim of rights violations has been detained in custody, especially if that victim is black.

INDIGENOUS STORYTELLING

The Bicentennial year provided Australians with multiple opportunities to consider the disparities between living white and living black. With an awareness of storytelling as a critical tool for building knowledge and connection, mainstream presses published two important Indigenous life narratives supported and subsidized by the Bicentennial Committee. Although not the first published narratives, they were the first to be actively celebrated, heavily marketed, and critically promoted. Sally Morgan's *My Place* (1987) and Ruby Langford's (now Ruby Langford Ginibi') *Don't Take Your Love to Town* (1988) presented two very different stories that shocked and surprised their (mainly white) readers who had little knowledge of Aboriginal life and experience. These texts raised issues that have since emerged as matters of urgent concern on Australia's human rights agenda. *My Place* told of forced child removal, Indigenous loss of identity and culture, government control of (limited) educational and employment opportunities, and of the struggles of family elders who grew up to work as a stockman for slave wages or as a domestic servant who suffered physical, sexual, and psychological abuse from white bosses. *Don't Take Your Love to Town* detailed a resourceful single mother's unceasing struggle against poverty and prejudice, frequent family dislocations, a series of devastating relationships with alcoholic partners, and the police harassment and imprisonment of two of her sons, one of whom tragically died in custody during the time of writing. Of the two, *My Place* was embraced by the larger, white Australian public. *Don't Take Your Love to Town* found less favor.

A comparison of the reception of these landmark texts and the shifts in their reception over time reveals the unstable political and aesthetic, moral and ethical terrains that influenced critical reception and the willingness of non-Indigenous readers to engage with the stories. *Don't Take Your Love to Town* appeared during the Deaths in Custody hearings. It spoke directly to issues of national concern. Some advocates promoted it, but without drawing specific attention to its politics. In an early review in *The Australian*, the national newspaper, Billy Marshall-Stoneking commented: "If you pick up this book, you pick up a life. . . . The life Langford has lived in Australia is as close to the eyes and ears as print on the page makes it." He introduces the narrative as "the ultimate battler's tale."[6] Yet *Don't Take Your Love to Town*, even when marketed within a dominant white myth of nation, failed to find a major audience. Although it has become a best-seller over time, and is taught regularly in universities and secondary schools, this hard-hitting, politically-informed story of Aboriginal survival in inner city and fringe environments struck most readers and critics in 1988 as too political, too strong, too distasteful, and too unsettling. Despite, or perhaps because of, the RCADIC hearings, most non-Indigenous readers were unwilling or unable to confront the gritty realism of the text, the streetwise tactics of survival it presents as the narrator struggles against the indifference or hostility of white bureaucrats, the social factors that lead to the incarceration and death of Aboriginal youth, and the everyday effects of prejudice and racism on Aboriginal lives.

Ginibi's searing accounts of her sons David's and Noddy's drift to crime and altercations with the police parallel elements of Colin Johnson's *Wild Cat Falling* (1965), the first autobiographical novel depicting Aboriginal life published by a major press.[7] Johnson's novel dealt with the brutality of institutionalized violence encountered by a nameless protagonist in orphanages, prison, and urban Sydney—a kind of deprived, extreme urban existence. Indigenous speakers testified to similar experiences in Kevin Gilbert's anthology *Living Black: Blacks Talk to Kevin Gilbert* (1977). Youth violence, incarceration, and confrontation with police were depicted in the contemporaneous short stories of Archie Weller in his collection *Going Home: Stories* (1986) and formed part of the abject fringe-dweller existence detailed in Robert Bropho's *Fringedweller* (1980). In the Bicentennial year, Jack Davis published his biting anthology *John Pat and Other Poems*, dedicated to the memory of the murdered youth. These narratives from "the other side" exposed the failure of assimilation and the cruelty and indifference of white bureaucrats and citizens. At the time of publication, they fostered an awareness of Aboriginal experience through storytelling, but they failed to garner widespread sympathy for or advocacy on behalf of Aboriginal rights. With virtually no dialogue on a national level between Indigenous authors and white audiences, with no informed understanding of the links between "well-intentioned" policies of assimilation and the degraded conditions of Indigenous lives, the readerships for such personal narratives were poorly equipped to respond to these stories on any level, let alone to register them as stories of human rights violations. Readers had neither the informed knowledge about the past nor the moral, ethical, political, and aesthetic wherewithal to enable alternative readings.

My Place, however, was hailed as a Bicentennial event: widely read, warmly embraced, heavily promoted and marketed in Australia and overseas. This story, chronicling the self-education of a fair-skinned Aboriginal child who grew up believing herself to be "Indian" in a household of members attempting to "pass," was received as a coming-of-age narrative. Sally, the protagonist, reflects upon her childhood, questions her reluctant elders about certain family "secrets," and traces the gradual discovery of her Aboriginal heritage. After presenting her own story, Morgan includes three oral testimonies transcribed verbatim from her mother, grandmother, and great-uncle in the last third of this intergenerational text. This testimony, regarded when published as a curious addendum by white readers, highlights the consequences for several generations of Aboriginal people of the government's policy regarding the forcible removal of Indigenous children from their families and their placement in institutional care. It documents government surveillance over family members' lives; restrictions on behavior, movement, living arrangements, choice of marriage partners and employment; lost wages; and the legacy of shame and despondency. Early readers of *My Place* approached the narrative as a coming-of-age story rather than a narrative of rights violations. Only when another decade passed and the Human Rights and Equal Opportunity Commission's (HREOC's) Inquiry into the Forced Separation of Indigenous Children from Their Families concluded with a devastating report, *Bringing Them Home*, in 1997, did other readings become possible. At the same time, the public acclaim and critical attention that *My Place* has received over time has had the unfortunate effect of eclipsing other histories and experiences of assimilation and child removal (van Toorn 1999; Hosking). Nonetheless, having sold in excess of 500,000 copies worldwide, the book has alerted an international audience to critical aspects of Indigenous life in Australia.

The HREOC's *Bringing Them Home* report contains an overwhelming accumulation of testimony from victims of forced assimilation, thereafter referred to as the "Stolen Generation/s." Issued at a time when people around the world were especially attentive to social justice and reconciliation, the Report shocked the nation into understanding that massive human rights violations had occurred, that they had resulted from government policies and programs, and that those (failed) policies were continuing to have devastating effects. The testimony presented in the report documented the history and consequences of the forcible removal of Indigenous children from their families between 1910 and 1970. During that time it is estimated that up to 100,000 children, a majority of them female, were removed from their communities and placed in orphanages, mission schools, and foster care (Manne 2001). *Bringing Them Home* linked the survivors' testimony to UN conventions to which Australia is a signatory nation, and served as the basis for charges against the Australian government for gross human rights violations.

Prior to the release of *Bringing Them Home* in 1997, most Australians were largely ignorant of the experience of Indigenous Australians living under forced assimilation. A decade earlier, readers had embraced Morgan's *My Place* not in politicized terms but in individualist, liberal humanist terms, placing it alongside other "battler" narratives that told the stories of "typical" Australians struggling for recognition. After the inquiry, however, Morgan's family history took on new salience as a text that documented a separate and distinct Indigenous cultural reality.[8] It became intelligible in revised terms of cultural memory as a human rights story.

As in the case of the Royal Commission's Deaths in Custody Report, *Bringing Them Home* relies heavily on life narratives, the former framed within legalistic rhetoric directed to the judicial system, the latter framed in human rights terms addressed to the general public. *Bringing Them Home*'s narratives also recall written stories dating back to the 1970s, authored in the main by women who themselves had been stolen as children, including Margaret Tucker's *If Everyone Cared* (1977), Monica Clare's *Karobran* (1978), Ella Simon's *Through My Eyes* (1978), Shirley Smith's *Mum Shirl: An Autobiography* (1981), Elsie Roughsey's *An Aboriginal Mother Tells of the Old and New* (1984), and Ida West's *Pride Against Prejudice*

(1984). These stories told by Aboriginal elders and activists who had been or became engaged in civil rights campaigns from the 1950s to the 1970s fighting for prison reform, housing, health, employment, and education initiatives[9] foreshadowed and were preparatory to what Ruby Langford Ginibi has called a "revolution" of Aboriginal writing that was triggered by the subsequent publication of *My Place* and *Bringing Them Home*. The foundational narratives and the resurgence of stories published after the Bicentennial had an important influence on Indigenous communities in Australia. According to Ginibi, "Their stories, our stories that we write, they are our histories. They are our reclaiming of territory and culture and identity" (Honeysett 9).

The influence of Indigenous narratives on non-Indigenous readers, however, had less of an impact on a national politics of recognition. The foundational narratives of the 1970s, published largely with the support of political, union, women's, or church advocacy groups, were made accessible to a white audience through the processes of collaboration that brought Indigenous storytellers together with white editors and publishers in the production of the narratives. Couched in assimilationist ideologies, Christian optimism, or neo-Marxist critique; utilizing polite forms of audience address; mediated through the work of publishing professionals; and framed in designated categories of fiction or autobiography, the early narratives compromised Indigenous knowledge and experience, made few political demands on their readers, and received little publicity.[10] Yet, in the light of stories contained in *Bringing Them Home*, these foundational texts fostered an environment that enabled Indigenous authors to share their experiences, build solidarity within their intersecting communities of affiliation, and heighten general awareness of the Indigenous experience in Australia, thus providing a context for the reception of *Bringing Them Home*. They preceded and also made possible shifts in power relations. Their efficacy is discernible in the mediated processes of production and reception they elicited; in the microclimates of change, however random or contingent, they stimulated; and in their opening up of a space for dialogue between peoples previously separated by the politics of segregation and assimilation (See van Toorn 1999, 255).

Since the publication of *Bringing Them Home*, hundreds of Indigenous life narratives have been published. In the 1990s, international attention to racial reconciliation and the links between the experiences of Stolen Children in Australia, victims of apartheid in South Africa, Maori disputations over treaty rights in New Zealand, and the Indian removals in Canada produced different political climates for these stories and more knowing, diversified reading audiences.[11] Tales like those depicted in Philip Noyce award-winning film, *Rabbit-Proof Fence*, based on the auto/biographical narrative of Doris Pilkington Garimara, now gain widespread sympathy and empathetic identification.[12] This evocative and moving film enacts the endurance of three separated children as they trek a 1,600-kilometer journey in which two return to their community rather than endure the hardships and indignities they confronted at the Moore River Mission in Western Australia. Critically acclaimed for its power to move audiences and educate them about the experience of forced removal, it has been widely adapted as a teaching tool, although its appeal to the emotions and potential to universalize and commodify Stolen Generation experiences triggers suspicion and invites debate about the politics of reception (Birch 2002; Hughes-D'Aeth 2001; Potter and Schaffer 2004).

HIDDEN HISTORIES OF RESISTANCE

Since the first decade of the arrival of the British, Aborigines resisted the incursion onto their lands. As Penny van Toorn notes, far from being silenced, Aboriginal people not only told their stories but also "recount[ed] small segments of their lives, in piecemeal, fragmentary, written forms in hundreds of handwritten letters, petitions, and submissions to official inquiries and court testimonies" from as far back as 1796 (2001, 1–2). Despite considerable constraints, there have been many instances of tactical intervention "within a cultural, political and moral order established by a foreign power" (20)—in attempted gestures of reciprocity and supplication, in local news chronicles, and through evidential testimony in pursuit of recognition and redress before numerous official inquiries into what would now be recognized as human rights abuses.

In the past, a range of factors mitigated the scope and effectiveness of Indigenous protest, including the distance of many groups from metropolitan centers, their distinct and different cultures, their oral traditions, and the fact that English was for many a second language. What they began to share, however, was a common history of dispossession under the practices and policies of colonial oppression that encroached upon their lives and made them increasingly vulnerable to cultural, environmental, and political upheavals. Over the course of the nineteenth century, with the incursions of exploration, the pastoral industry, forestry, mining, and rural and urban settlement, Indigenous communities suffered the loss of land and sustenance, as well as injury and death from frontier violence, massacres, poisoning, the importation of European diseases, sexual exploitation, and abuse. Although contemporary historical research indicates that Indigenous protests were frequent, spirited, and vigorous, the geographic, linguistic, and cultural differences among Indigenous communities and their limited access to Western legal systems of justice have severely limited, without ever fully containing, their powers of protest.

One issue for contemporary critics is the relative absence of reliable evidence to support instances of injustice and Indigenous resistance in the past. There were many settlers who expressed outrage or acknowledged what Henry Reynolds calls "the whispering in their hearts" (1998)—a gnawing moral ambivalence about the effects of white settlement on the Aboriginal population and their own implied or explicit complicity in it. But the expanding population largely turned a blind eye to the cruelties of "frontier justice" and the consequent decline of Aboriginal cultures, suppressing knowledge, awareness, and recognition.

Until the late 1960s little historical research had been conducted to build an awareness of the impact of colonialism on Indigenous populations or to document the nascent political campaigns and organizations formed from the 1920s and 1930s to support Aboriginal activism. Until the 1970s, with the exception of *Wild Cat Falling*, there were no published life narratives or a supportive publishing industry to enable the transmission of stories. Until the 1990s there were no critical texts by Indigenous theorists and activists or anthologies that articulated Indigenous cultural and political perspectives.[13] Public knowledge of the devastating treatment of Australia's indigenous peoples and awareness of their stories as civil or human rights issues are recent phenomena. It was not until the RCADIC (1987–89) and HREOC (1996–97) inquiries that Indigenous life experience was seen as integral to the politics of human rights. Only in the last ten years have more complex and nuanced sets of narratives, knowledges, and critical perspectives been available to provide evidence and commentary about the complex, multi-layered, intersecting, and divergent paths that led from invasion to the present.

THE DIFFERENTIAL IMPACT OF INVASION

When the First Fleet arrived, the vast continent of Australia was occupied by approximately 500,000 Indigenous people represented by more than five hundred clan groups, two hundred and fifty languages, and distinctly different cultures. Over time, Indigenous communities experienced the incursion of an unceasing succession of white explorers, settlers, pastoralists, timber workers, gold prospectors, mining companies, tourists, and other demanding newcomers. Those like the Eora who met the First Fleet at Botany Bay (and many other groups in southeastern Australia) suffered rapid dispossession of lands and decimation of people and cultures as a result of early white settlement. Some groups, like the Meriam people of Mer Island in the Torres Strait, continuously occupied their traditional lands, eventually securing Native Title rights in the landmark Mabo High Court decision of 1992. Others, like the Anangu, the Pitjantjatjara, and other semi-nomadic groups in Central Australia were moved from their traditional desert lands to reserves as recently as the late 1960s, after the British conducted, without sufficient warning, a series of aboveground atomic tests at Maralinga and Emu Flats that exposed adjacent and downwind populations to radioactive fallout dubbed "The Black Mist." The health consequences were devastating, and included death, radiation-related illnesses, stillbirths, and genetic birth defects, and environmental impacts that rendered the land unsafe for inhabitation. In the 1970s, state governments resettled affected communities onto tracts of land, vested in Land Trusts, "for the benefit of Aboriginals entitled by Aboriginal tradition to the use and occupation of the land concerned..." (Reconcililation and Social Justice Library, 74). After a 1984 Royal Commission into the nuclear testing program and protracted negotiations over responsibility and reparations, the Australian and British governments finally accepted financial liability for the health and environmental consequences of the testing and negotiated measures of compensation and redress for affected communities, as well as responsibility for remediation of the land. Nonetheless, the devastation was immense and could never be fully compensated.

Others groups, like the Thirroul living in the Lake Tyers Gippsland region of Southeastern Victoria, the Mapoon mission communities on the Cape York peninsula, and the Yolngu at Yirrkala in the far North, were forced from large areas of reserved lands in the 1960s to make way for mining and forestry operations. In the 1960s, in the more populous southeast region of the country, Welfare Boards in Victoria and New South Wales decided to close down the few reserves that remained in the states to make way for housing that was culturally insensitive to the needs of the people, inadequate in scope, and slow in coming. These mid-century displacements prompted widespread rage that evoked civil and human rights campaigns and fuelled a contemporary land rights movement.

Whenever protests have occurred, from colonial times to the present, they have taken place at the intersections between local and global transits of authority, power, advocacy, and resistance. For semi-traditional communities, English was a second language, although some members quickly learned to interact with the invaders in pidjin or Creole. But when negotiating issues of concern across cultures, Indigenous protocols required, out of respect for traditional authority, that only the elders could speak, although the elders did not always have the English language skills necessary to communicate effectively with white officials. From the 1830s, humanitarian, Christian, and anti-slavery organizations in Britain, soliciting support from the Home Office to assert the rights of Aborigines as British subjects, mounted intermittent campaigns around the abusive treatment of "the natives" and the adverse effects of colonial expansion on Indigenous lives. Often campaigns ensued in response to rumors of frontier violence, poisoning, exploitation, and massacre. When local alarm failed to be heeded by local authorities, others, such as missionaries, welfare officers, and concerned politicians, officially petitioned humanitarian organizations and the Home Office in Britain. The Home Office commissioned inquiries, but even when inquiries substantiated claims and colonial or state governors supported measures of redress, little changed to alter attitudes, behaviors, and practices within the shifting and contested conflict zones on the frontier between settlers and the first inhabitants. In a late nineteenth-century response, and as a way of protecting a "dying race," state governments introduced paternalistic forms of protection that attempted to segregate Aborigines from settlers. These policies resulted in a further loss of Indigenous human rights, including limitations to freedom of movement, rights to land, and custody of children (See Attwood and Markus 1999; Goodall 1996; and Reynolds 1987, 1992, 1998).

One of the main differences between Australia and other white settler nations, such as Canada and New Zealand, is that the British government signed no foundational treaties with Indigenous Australians and the nation established no Bill of Rights. Protections, rights, and remedies, therefore, were limited. When recognized at all, Aborigines were incorporated into legal and political frameworks as objects to be controlled and manipulated by the states in which they lived. It was not until the Constitutional Referendum of 1967, overwhelmingly approved by Australian voters, that Indigenous people were counted in the census and brought under the conjoint jurisdiction of the States and the Commonwealth government.[14]

STORYTELLING AND RIGHTS

For a highly oral culture, storytelling has been the primary mode of passing knowledge, maintaining community, resisting government control, and sharing the burden of hardship. Without a political base or a national forum of their own, Aborigines shared stories among themselves, gradually relating them to advocacy groups. The effectiveness of storytelling as a form of communal solidarity should not be underestimated. As Richard Delgado remarks, stories shared in community, although largely invisible to the larger public, "create their own bonds, represent cohesion, shared understandings, and meanings. The cohesiveness that stories bring is part of the strength of the outgroup." He continues, "[s]tories, parables, chronicles, and narratives are powerful means for destroying mindset—the bundle of presumptions, received wisdoms, and shared understandings against a backdrop of which legal and political discourse takes place" (Delgado 1989, 2412, 2413).

During the 1930s and after the Second World War, with the signing of the UDHR, Aborigines conjoined their stories to ILO and UN civil, worker, and human rights platforms, often with the collaboration of white supporters. Sometimes, as in the case of the Yolngu bark painting petition, Indigenous communities utilized traditional forms of communication to bring their demands to the public. In 1963, Yirrkala members of the Yolngu people from Arnhem Land presented a bark petition to Parliament as a formal protest against mining company and government incursions onto their ancestral lands. Written in traditional language, framed with carved designs that were owned by the two petitioning clans, and signed by the elders representing them, this bark painting utilized Indigenous protocols, including a storytelling mode of presentation and traditional art practices, to assert sovereign rights to land. This form of protest, in dialogic relation across separate and distinct cultures, was unprecedented and caused a sensation in the press. The *Melbourne Age* reported it under the headline "House Hears Plea in a Strange Tongue" (Attwood 2003, 228–30). The bark petition marked the beginning of direct negotiations for land rights, attempted in specifically Indigenous terms.

For the most part, through the 1950s and 1960s political campaigns took root locally and in consort with non-Indigenous advocacy groups. Many groups advocated racial segregation for remote Aborigines, deeming it as necessary to their survival, without recognizing Indigenous claims to sovereignty through prior ownership (Reynolds 1996; Watson 2002). The groups' supporting campaigns, many of which were aligned to the Communist Party, left-wing labor unions, activist church organizations, women's, peace, and Moral Re-armament groups, subscribed to different political philosophies, policies, and practices. Although membership included Aboriginal people, and some offered full-membership and leadership positions exclusively to Aborigines, in many instances the leadership was dominated by whites and activated by white conceptions of Aboriginal "betterment."

Although advocacy campaigns for racial equality were radically in advance of what the nation was willing to accept, their civil rights emphasis actually accorded with the government's policies of assimilation. Resting on principles of equal rights that denied the existence of racial and cultural differences, campaigns had no platform on land rights, nor did they recognize the rights of minority peoples. That would come later, prompted by pressure on the United Nations from indigenous groups around the world to protect minority cultures under the jurisdiction of sovereign states. Although when threatened, remote, semi-traditional communities fought fiercely for control over their own lands, many church-raised, urban-based Aboriginal leaders accepted civil or equal rights platforms and the premises of assimilation. For example, the Federal Council for Aboriginal Advancement (FCAA), the most radical political organization to voice Aboriginal perspectives, adopted the first article of the UDHR as its slogan in 1958: "All human beings are born free and equal in dignity and rights...and should act towards one another in the spirit of brotherhood" (cited in Attwood 2003, 153). They engaged in campaigns in favor of anti-discrimination, social and political equality, voting rights, welfare entitlements, health and housing opportunities, and wage equity.

Advocacy groups understood "Aboriginality" variously. White members believed that by "breeding out the race" assimilation would bring about equality over time. Aboriginal leaders began to object, arguing that assimilation amounted to a patronizing and demeaning form of "white racism." Increasingly, they spoke in pursuit of integration "as a separate people" and demanded a national representative platform to hear and adjudicate their claims (Attwood and Markus 19–20). What emerged were two distinct, conflicting, but overlapping sets of claims: one in pursuit of human rights protections and freedoms within international guidelines established through the ILO, the UDHR, and related UN conventions; the other arguing for self-determination, land rights, sovereignty, and a recognition of customary law, in advance of international principles and platforms to protect the minority rights of distinct cultural groups within sovereign nation-states. The first, with the will of government, could be addressed by equal rights and anti-discrimination legislation passed in the 1970s to overcome discriminatory practices in health, housing, employment, education, social welfare, and prison reform. The second required that the government recognize the much more contentious call for minority rights of a culturally distinct people residing within a sovereign nation. Though necessary to the activist agenda of ensuring Indigenous human rights, neither would proceed without protracted political campaigns and interventions with reference to local and national politics and the acceptance of responsibilities under international human rights covenants.

The 1970s were a transformative decade for Indigenous rights. Advocates compared the situation of Indigenous Australians with native peoples in other countries, adopting their slogans and tactics— from the swell of support to end South African apartheid to the civil rights and Black Power movement in the United States. In 1972 defiant Aboriginal leaders set up an Aboriginal Tent Embassy on the lawns of Parliament House. Stan Grant remembers it as "an ingenious masterstroke that would graphically highlight the Aboriginal struggle and catapult black issues onto the front pages of the country's newspapers and onto television screens in every home in the nation" (Grant 190). He recalls, "the Tent Embassy hosted visits from the international media, Soviet diplomats, Canadian Indians, Native Americans and members of the Irish Republican Army" (192). Utilizing the headline-grabbing tactics of radical struggles elsewhere, and extending the reach of a radical politics of Black Power, indigenous activists took their demands to the streets.

These demands met with mixed responses within Aboriginal communities and from successive Labor and Liberal governments. Under the Whitlam, Hawke and Keating Labor governments (1972–96) Australia strove to recognize its obligations to Indigenous people under international law. The government set up a National Aboriginal Consultative Committee (NACC) (1973) to initiate dialogue on rights claims; passed the Aboriginal Land Rights (Northern Territory) Act (1976) that allowed Aborigines living on traditional lands in the Northern Territory to claim limited rights to reserves on Crown land on the basis of their ongoing occupation; passed the Racial Discrimination Act (1975) which implemented Australia's signing of the UN Covenant for the Elimination of all Forms of Racial Discrimination (CERD); and established the Aboriginal and Torres Straight Islander Commission (ATSIC) in 1990, the first representative national forum and elected decision-making body for Indigenous people (which was abolished by the Howard Liberal government in 2004). In anticipation of the UN International Year of Indigenous Peoples (1994), the Keating Labor government established the Human Rights and Equal Opportunity Commission (HREOC), which appointed Mick Dodson its first Indigenous Social Justice

Commissioner in 1993. In June of 1992, the High Court of Australia delivered the important Mabo land rights decision, allowing land rights for Aborigines living on Crown lands if they could prove continuous occupation. The High Court decision overturned the nation's doctrine of *terra nullius*.[15] Labor Prime Minister Paul Keating committed his government to a program of redress in his famous Redfern Speech delivered in December 1992 on International Human Rights Day. The speech electrified the nation, as the prime minister, for the first time, accepted responsibility for past discriminatory policies towards Indigenous peoples. He told the crowd:

> We took the traditional lands and smashed the traditional way of life. We brought the diseases. The Alcohol. We committed the murders. We took the children from their mothers. We practiced discrimination and exclusion. It was our ignorance and prejudice. And our failure to imagine those things being done to us. (qtd. in Aboriginal and Torres Strait Islander Commission Report 1993)

Although drawing on an assimilationist rhetoric that homogenized the "we" of the nation, the speech established a new agenda of national responsibility.

BRINGING THEM HOME

In 1995, the Human Rights and Equal Opportunity Commission, with the support of the Keating Labor government, established the Inquiry into the Forced Separation of Indigenous Children from their Families. It enabled Indigenous speakers who testified to their past experiences to be heard and acknowledged. Prompted by the UN Decade of Indigenous Peoples, it came in the wake of South Africa's Truth and Reconciliation hearings and mirrored similar Inquiries in Canada and New Zealand. Although not broadly reported around the world, the inquiry galvanized political controversy within Australia and linked Australia's history more broadly with the oppressive practices of white settler colonialism.

The Commission met over a period of eighteen months, collecting testimony from 585 witnesses in every state of Australia, including the Northern Territory. The witnesses (whose anonymity was protected in the Report) told how children who had been removed typically lost their language, cultural knowledge, and connection to family and cultural heritage. They were lied to and denied knowledge about their families. They suffered long term mental, physical, emotional, social, and economic consequences as a result of their separation, including a loss of empowerment and responsibility for their own affairs, and geographic disruptions that would prevent them from being able to take up native title right claims. Victims' stories of separation and abuse shocked readers, but the telling provided a legitimating context that recognized the irreparable harm caused by government-sanctioned policies and practices that were only glimpsed in earlier Indigenous life narratives.

The first-person testimony of multiple voices, legitimated through the Report and interleaved with the narrative contexts provided by HREOC, opened up new discursive spaces for witnesses to articulate the pain and trauma of the past. Through giving testimony, Indigenous victims gained a new form of (mediated) direct address to a "white" audience. Their experiences were no longer cloaked in Communist, Christian, or Moral Re-armament optimism, but rather evidence of massive human rights abuse. The commission also enabled new understandings of the import of past government policies on Aboriginal lives. Commenting on the import of the testimony and drawing on Articles 1, 2, 3, 7, 10, 12, and 26 of the UDHR and the Genocide Convention of 1948, Sir Ronald Wilson, Chair of the Inquiry, argued that "the policy of forcible removal of children from Indigenous Australians to other groups for the purpose of raising them separately from and ignorant of their culture and people could properly be labeled 'genocidal' in breach of binding international law from at least 11 December 1946," and, preceding this date, was contrary to acceptable legal principles under British common law (275).

The inquiry validated Indigenous claims and recognized their legitimacy through the HREOC, a statutory body with a quasi-judicial status. It acknowledged the denial of selfhood suffered by so many children who had neither family, nor community, nor institutional caregivers to sustain them. It told of the continuing consequences of separation, including rape and sexual abuse, loss of contact with parents, and lies by authorities regarding their removal. The long-term effects of separation, not only from family but from heritage and cultural identity, have produced numerous social and psychological consequences—drug and alcohol abuse, youth suicide, domestic violence, and lives too often marked by despondency and despair. In all, the Report made fifty-four recommendations "directed to healing and reconciliation for the benefit of all Australians" (Wilson 1997, 4). First and foremost, it called for the acknowledgment of the truth of the testimony and the delivery of a national apology as a way of admitting responsibility, in line with the principles and guidelines formulated by UN Special Rapporteur Theo van Boven (1993). Other recommendations included the pursuit of measures to restore separated victims access to land, language, and culture and to ensure self-determination and non-discrimination in line with international standards; monetary compensation according to international "heads of damage" claims; the provision of counseling services; the extension of Link Up services to enable reunions between the children and their families; and the facilitation of family history projects. The Report also called for measures to educate the Australian public about past policies so that such policies would never be repeated. It called for a number of reparations, including financial compensation; and it proposed an annual Sorry Day to commemorate the history of forced separations.

Bringing Them Home bestowed legitimacy and official recognition to the stories of dispossession, loss of family, kinship ties, language, and country—and the consequences of that loss. The sheer accumulation of so many stories, told through first-person narratives and grouped thematically through the Report, framed within the public discourse of the Inquiry, enabled Indigenous speakers a place and a space within a national culture they had not been able to occupy before. It offered not one story but a multitude of stories; not an individualized, polished text but an official, public government document punctuated with first person accounts of trauma. Not a private narrative but one sanctioned by the authority of the commission itself. Not one disseminated through publisher catalogues and bookshop posters but through national and international news networks. When it was published, demand far exceeded supply. Over twelve thousand copies sold within months of publication, prompting the publication of the popular anthology edited by Carmel Bird, *The Stolen Children—Their Stories* (1998), and re-publication of Peter Read's earlier neglected history on "The Stolen Generation" (1988, 1998).

Beyond the borders of Australia, Stolen Generation stories circulated in a number of global arenas. Overseas commentators prepared documentaries on Australia's shameful past and its growing reputation for human rights violations.[16] Broadcasters of the Sydney 2000 Olympic Games prepared profiles on Indigenous athletes and mini-documentaries on the Stolen Generation/s to coincide with Cathy Freeman's anticipated gold medal victory in the 400-meter run. Indigenous groups used the Games as leverage, threatening a boycott and massive public protests. Nelson Mandela toured Australia, intensifying media interest in Indigenous politics to maintain pressure on the government. In March 2000, the UN delivered a negative report card to Australia. Of particular alarm were the rise in deaths in custody, the mandatory sentencing of youths, widespread racial discrimination, and lack of consultation with Indigenous groups. As news of the report circulated around the world, Australia's human rights violations came under the international spotlight.[17]

APOLOGY AND BACKLASH

In its address to readers *Bringing Them Home* did more than expose the abuses of the past. It asked that "the whole community listens [*sic*] with an open heart and mind to the stories of what has happened in the past and, having listened and understood, commit itself to reconciliation" (Wilson 1997, 9). In this way, HREOC not only presented the testimony of witnesses within a human rights framework, it also called for an active ethical engagement on the part of its readers. The broader public was asked to become involved in a process that might bring about justice by acknowledging the loss and harm that had been done to Indigenous witnesses and their families.[18] The Inquiry modeled itself on the South African TRC in its attention to restorative justice and its call for national healing based on ethical responsiveness. Unlike the TRC, the Inquiry collected confidential testimony in private. It did not stage confrontations between victims and perpetrators. Its activities were not reported in the daily news. Nonetheless, when the written report appeared, it opened a dialogue between people previously separated by a racial divide and initiated a process of healing for the nation and for the survivors and their communities.

The Report seeded a range of political and cultural activities. Many Australian citizens engaged in local processes of healing and reconciliation. State Parliaments and church groups issued apologies. Sorry Day commemorations and Bridge Walks in every major city attracted hundreds of thousands of Australians intent on actively participating in gestures toward healing. Indigenous communities advanced action on many of the recommendations of the *Bringing Them Home* Report, developing social and political networks, tracing their family connections, telling stories in community-based reconciliation forums, and activating a range of public initiatives—in education, health, archaeology, history, human rights, the law, land rights, community development, and Indigenous media. But the Liberal government under the leadership of Prime Minister John Howard, not having commissioned the Inquiry, queried its conclusions, especially those that related to charges of genocide. This finding caused massive public outrage, denial by the government, and rebuttal by some historians, spurring ongoing debate (see Windshuttle; and Manne 2003).

The newly-elected Liberal government initiated a few small gestures toward reconciliation in the form of funding for counseling services, Link Up, and the founding of a National Oral History Project through the National Library, which enabled hundreds of stories to be recorded, hundreds of lives acknowledged.[19] It refused, however, to admit to the finding of genocide, issue an official apology, or open up the possibility of financial compensation as reparation, arguing that the present generation of Australians is not responsible for the policies of the past, and that those policies, however devastating, arose out of good intentions. In what Eric Yamamoto calls the "reconciliation decade" (1997) of the 1990s, national leaders in South Africa, the United States, Canada, England, France, Germany, and elsewhere apologized for policies and practices of racial oppression. But not Prime Minister Howard. In Australia neither apology nor reparations of any significance have been offered.[20]

Backlash and denial, spurred by the claims of genocide and the government's refusal to apologize or offer compensation to Stolen Generation victims, stalled national reconciliation as the country shut down its remembering processes. During the election campaign of 2001 a people's poll showed concern for indigenous issues among only 14 percent of the population. In the seven years since the Report was released, sympathy for Indigenous claims has waned. The human rights discourse, with its emphasis on social justice and welfare practices has been replaced by a rhetoric of accountability and personal responsibility, sometimes labeled by its supporters as "practical reconciliation." Nonetheless, *Bringing Them Home* profoundly unsettled the nation, channeling affect into multiple forms of micropolitical engagement. It seeded thousands of local initiatives towards racial reconciliation and Indigenous autonomy, including dinners and memorials, storytelling workshops and healing houses, educational awareness and stolen wages campaigns, land rights and environmental initiatives, mediation workshops, national arts and culture festivals, international exchanges for Indigenous writers, artists, dancers, and musicians. Such sites of rights activism, largely initiated and directed by Indigenous communities, continue to contribute to a micro politics that feeds into national and global realignments of power.[21]

THE HEALING PROCESS: TELLING AND LISTENING

The Indigenous life narratives that preceded the Inquiry and the testimonies taken before it expose the internalized oppression suffered by Indigenous people. Narrators witnessed to their own shaming and abjection within white culture; they told of lives compromised by a lack of recognition and validation. As Kelly Oliver comments, such forms of systemic racial violence deny the subjectivity of the victim as self-constituting. They render the teller an "other," a subject without subjectivity (Oliver 2001, 17).[22] The inquiry validated the subjectivity of those who testified. Wilson noted, "the Commission became convinced that the process of storytelling was itself the beginning of a healing process" (Bird 1998, xiv).

Psychoanalyst and Holocaust survivor Dori Laub writes, in a language commonly invoked by Indigenous speakers and their supporters in the wake of the Report, that the process of telling and listening is an essential first step toward healing. He maintains that the giving of testimony is a two-fold process: the telling itself, which breaks previous frameworks of knowing and what goes on beyond the words. This second process, beyond the words, allows emotional healing, the key to a rediscovery of a lost identity (Laub 63). In *Testimony: Crises of Witnessing in Literature, Psychoanalysis, and History*, Dori Laub and Shoshana Felman examine the fundamental role of literature in the process of healing. The reader as witness "in the second person" becomes "at the same time a witness to the trauma and a witness to himself [*sic*]" (58). That is, the reader acknowledges his or her role in identifying with the victim of trauma and taking responsibility for recognizing the victim's trauma. Shocked Australians engaged in this role after the release of *Bringing Them Home*, taking up the position of witness and experiencing a sense of dis-ease, shame, and responsibility. Writer, biographer, and critic Drusilla Modjeska expressed such sentiments shortly after the Report's release. She commented, "I am sure I am not the only one to have had the sensation of waking up to find myself in an Australia I barely recognise. Or, rather, more to the point, in an Australia I would rather not recognise" (158).

The Inquiry set up expectations within the community that the government would accept responsibility on behalf of the nation, apologize for its role in perpetrating human rights abuses, and initiate material changes necessary for reconciliation. Indigenous people expected it. When the prime minister refused to apologize at a national reconciliation conference, the assembled audience registered its contempt by standing and turning its collective back. His refusal exacerbated their individual and collective pain. Indigenous activists stressed the importance of apology for their communities, for whom the pain and trauma of recounting memories of experiences in the past had redoubled, opening new wounds.

In the words of Katrina Power, delivered in a speech to a national conference, "If we are given an opportunity to forgive, we are given the opportunity to heal." This dynamic of healing continues to be affirmed. For example, in their introduction to *Many Voices*, an oral history project conducted by the National Library of Australia, Doreen Mellor and Anna Haebich write:

> most of us...would wish to find a way to heal the sadness, abuse and deprivation that children undoubtedly suffered as a result of the policies that led to their separation, and have subsequently led to generations of grief, hurt and bewilderment. The [oral history] project has been established with the intention of making it possible for people to listen with an open mind to the complex array of experiences that make up this history, and in doing so, to participate in a restorative process for our whole community. (14)

The Oral History project, Link Up services, and related narrative therapy projects all contribute to the work of healing and to building an archive of stories, thus filling a gap in cultural memory, particularly for Indigenous communities.

While the telling and listening process may be restorative in the immediate environment and positive context of witnessing, some critics, including Indigenous and non-Indigenous researchers working together in dialogue, like Jan Tikka Wilson and Rosanne Kennedy, suggest that the healing process outlined by trauma theorists like Felman and Laub may be too confining a paradigm, particularly for previously colonized people in colonizer nations, when stories circulate in public domains beyond the immediate contexts of telling. The psychoanalytic model requires an empathetic relationship that pre-supposes that the listener will vicariously identify with the teller. If victims fail to receive affirmation through the telling of their stories, they remain entrapped within the trauma. Even if readers empatheti-cally identify with the tellers, tellers can receive affirmation only as the "other." In addition, listeners experience a variety of reactions to shock and shame, and their responses are intensified by affect. Affect, as Silvan Tomkins' studies have shown, can be channeled in a range of negative or positive ways. Shock and shame can lead to an ethics of recognition and gestures of reconciliation. They can also provoke feelings of guilt and denial. Drusilla Modjeska identified with the tes-timony and expressed responsibility in a positive channeling of affect, as did thousands of like-minded Australians who became involved in Sorry Day ceremonies, Reconciliation Bridge Walks, Sea of Hands installations, and other communal activities. Other listeners, however, identified not with the victims but with the officials and institutions coming under scrutiny. They affirmed, with the prime minister, that assimilationist policies were well intentioned and, at any rate, present-day Australians were not responsible for the abuse that occurred in the past. Their responses, triggered by the negative affect of shaming, prompted emotional outrage, cognitive rebuttal, and willful forgetting/denial. Yet, as Anne Brewster notes in reflecting on the backlash, forgetting is a supplement to memory; not an end of the story but part of the processes of ongoing interaction (Brewster n.p.).

Even when the process does succeed, it has different dynamics for Indigenous and non-Indigenous listeners. When non-Indigenous listeners or readers accept an ethical responsibility to acknowledge the story and the veracity of the tellers, narratives of shaming place tellers in the position of victim, with listeners as advocates and agents, thus reinforcing pre-existing power relations. Validation of the teller's story can lead to new forms of subjectivity, beyond victimhood; but, in the context of a human rights regime, it also requires the teller to take up a particular performative stance—as the subject of human rights whose testimony is given and received in the pursuit of social justice, with enabling and constraining effects.

Gillian Whitlock notes that the emotive force of *Bringing Them Home* testimony engaged readers in a particular way, one that was "generated by the figure of the child as victim, most specifically through the tropes of the stolen child, and the rhetoric of 'coming home'" (Whitlock 2001, 203). Carmel Bird's anthology, *The Stolen Children: Their Stories*, extends the trope, as does Philip Noyce's internationally-acclaimed film *Rabbit-Proof Fence*. These responses rebound on those who testify. It locks them into a child-centered identity, thus collapsing a full life history into a singular event. Further, if their stories are not validated, as has been the case of many in Australia, tellers can be called upon to reiterate and justify their testimony, thus becoming trapped within the painful and limiting confines of victimhood. If adult survivors contest the label "stolen," as did Lowitja O'Donoghue in an interview in which she related that she was not "stolen" but "removed" since her mother agreed to her separation, believing it to be in the best interests of the child, the media can exploit the remarks, casting doubt on the whole phenomenon (Bolt 2001a,b). If Stolen Generation survivors want to tell a different story, as did Nancy Barnes in *Munyi's Daughter*, a story that highlights the narrator's triumph over adversity and traces her successful journey into relationships and employment, they find no ready audience, even in their own communities (Hosking). In addition, the production, circulation, and interpretation of stories as trauma tales rely heavily on a psychoanalytic model in which gaps in memory, effaced by trauma, are recovered and subjectivity is restored in the interaction between teller and listener in a therapeutic context. Such a model leaves little room for the expression of a critical consciousness on the part of tellers of their knowledge of the politics of oppression.

The HREOC Inquiry initiated a process of healing with the aim of national reconciliation between Indigenous and non-Indigenous Australians. But there have been other imperatives for Stolen Generation survivors, their families, and community. Their pain required, and they engaged in, different processes of personal and communal healing, beyond the psychoanalytic model.[23] Link Up engaged Stolen Generation survivors in narrative therapy sessions that allowed for more diffuse, agentic and cognitive forms of storytelling. Kennedy and Wilson analyzed those interviews (now housed at the National Library) noting that they deploy a different mode of address than those taken in the HREOC context. Narrative therapy encourages tellers to consciously reflect on the political dimensions of their experiential history. Interviewees reveal a critical consciousness of the role of the nation "in the practices of denial, including the denial of Aboriginal history and Aboriginal dispossession" (128–29), and a political awareness of unequal power relations, and the consequences for themselves of internalized racism (131).

As Aboriginal consultant Jaqui Katona had noted at the "soul-searching" Going Home conference held in Darwin in 1994 (before the Inquiry) official witnessing would have the potential to generate a greater awareness for dispossessed urban Aborigines of the loss of their connections to land. But it also had the potential to position witnesses as "a separate class of Australian citizen, confined to live in towns without culturally appropriate administrative measures to deal with their needs." They would have neither the birthright required to lodge native title claims nor the genealogies and family histories needed to reconnect easily with their ancestral cultures (*Australian* 341). These potential consequences of the telling, listening, and healing processes complicate understandings of the dynamics of the healing process.

NEW NARRATIVES AND THE HEALING PROCESS

Our growing awareness of the limitations of the psychoanalytic model led us to seek out Indigenous narratives published in the wake of the HREOC Inquiry, to look to life narratives for other signs of healing.

We noted several distinctive characteristics that appear to be new to the writing. Rather than tentatively explore the scars and wounds of the past in search of understanding, as many pre-Inquiry narratives had done, these confident narrators reveal astute political awareness, utilizing a language of human rights when exploring the meanings of their past experience. In adopting this narrative stance, they move from objective to subjective positions under the law, from being victims to agents; from expressing passivity and suffering to exercising critical awareness; from feeling shame to expressing anger, pride, and collective healing; from recounting their individual experiences to understanding themselves as collective subjects, connected not only to other Indigenous communities in Australia, but also to victims of human rights abuse around the world. This sense of communal identification signals an important shift in narrative voice that reflects new arenas of political activism and communal forms of healing in the absence of government initiatives.

The narratives attest to many, varied subject positions for Indigenous narrators. They tell of different kinds of separation. Some recount growing up in government dormitories or reserves like Ruth Hegarty's *Is That You, Ruthie?* (1999), Veronica Brodie's *My Side of the Bridge* (2002), and Albert Holt's *Forcibly Removed* (2001). Others tell of Christian Mission experiences, like Ambrose Mungala Chalarimeri's *The Man From the Sunrise Side* (2001), Edie Wright's *Full Circle: From Mission to Community—A Family Story* (2001), and Iris Burgoyne's *The Mirning: We are the Whales* (2000). An increasing number are cultural maintenance narratives, told by the old people in remote semi-traditional communities, for whom English is their second language. They address their stories to family and community, as does Jessie Lennon in *I'm the One That Know This Country!: the Story of Jessie Lennon and Coober Pedy* (2000), and Tex and Nelly Camfoo in *Love Against the Law: The Autobiographies of Tex and Nelly Camfoo* (2000). And some narratives, written by third-generaton, urban-based, and Western-educated authors, like Stephen Kinnane's *Shadow Lines* (2003), Fabienne Bayet-Charlton's *Finding Ullagundahi Island* (2002), and Stan Grant's *The Tears of Strangers* (2003), investigate the transsections of two separate but interrelated cultures—one lived in cities as beneficiaries of assimilationist "betterment," the other lost but now retraced, through historical, familial, and imaginative reclamations, to ancestrally-linked Indigenous pasts.

These recent Indigenous life narratives differ significantly from those published prior to the HREOC Inquiry. Notable elements of difference include: a concern with the politics of collaboration; narrative authority and ownership of knowledge; a critical awareness of heritage and modes through which it was threatened; and interpretative frameworks that locate the speakers as subjects of human rights.[24] The authors confidently link agentic and communal subjectivities to other histories of oppression around the world. The difference in tenor, tone, and tactics of transmission signals validation of Stolen Generation testimonies, the political framing of those testimonies in terms of human rights violations, and the ethics of recognition called into play by the Report, coupled with an expanding knowledge-base, derived from historical, genealogical, and oral history projects.

Politics of Collaboration

In many stories, Indigenous elders relate the government/dormitory and religious mission narratives. In contrast to life stories that emerged earlier, these texts overtly attend to the politics of collaboration. The Wright, Chalarimeri, Burgoyne, and Brodie stories all consist of oral narratives that have been transcribed from tapes in an overt process of negotiated collaboration with editors. Edie Wright's intergenerational text was written by a granddaughter and based on tape-recorded and transcribed narratives of her mother and grandfather. Ambrose Chalarimeri's story was taped and transcribed by his partner Traudl Tan. Iris Burgoyne and Veronica Brodie worked with non-Indigenous collaborators whose roles they delineate in the preface and the acknowledgments. All comment overtly on the different cultural legacies and negotiations of differential power relations involved in the processes of production that were largely absent in previously published collaborative texts.

The Lennon and Camfoo texts are cultural maintenance narratives told by traditional elders to anthropologists. Their primary address is to family. Not being members of the Stolen Generations, these storytellers detail other consequences of the Aboriginal Protection Acts on their lives. Both texts were transcribed from oral narratives that utilize Indigenous storytelling techniques, blending traditional and pidgin languages and cadences. For example, in Jessie Lennon's narrative, *I'm the One That Know This Country!*, compiled by Michele Madigan, the first words of the text that appear on the title page are in Anangu language and are addressed to the Indigenous reader. Madigan provides a counter-text to Jessie Lennon's narrative through the extensive use of annotated photographs and maps that visually narrate for non-Indigenous readers the traditional elements in Jessie's transcribed stories. She also includes prefatory notes on language,

a pronunciation guide, a glossary of abbreviations, a contextual introduction, an Aboriginal timeline and a list of references that facilitate
the use of the text in secondary schools. In *Love Against the Law*,
recorded and edited by Gillian Cowlishaw, the anthropologist relates
the different processes of transmission that occurred between herself
and Nelly as opposed to herself and Tex, and the difficulty in eliciting
and recording Tex's biography because of her ambiguous ascribed
kinship relationship to him. She negotiates the distance between
Indigenous storytellers and non-Indigenous readers by presenting a
polyvocal text. This approach enables the Indigenous storytellers to
communicate directly and in familiar modes of address to family and
community, and to render their stories as closely as possible to oral
discourse. It also means that stories are accompanied by the sometimes-
intrusive appearance of bracketed translations of language and the use
of textboxes and other aids that visually interrupt the flow of story in
order to make the text accessible to non-Indigenous and Indigenous
readers from other geographic and language areas. Through hybrid
forms and methods of presentation, these texts become valued
resources to the local community and prized by families while also
engaging in a dialogic exchange across cultures. These cultural maintenance narratives preserve Indigenous stories while at the same time
offering accessibility to non-Indigenous readers.

Narrative Authority

All of the stories adopt narrative modes of address made possible by
knowledge obtained from government records, new revisionist histories, and the human rights framing of the *Bringing Them Home* testimonies, as well as the legitimacy given to Aboriginal witnessing by the
HREOC Inquiry. These are storytellers with agency, attesting to traditional and adapted knowledge, customs, and practices that speak to
power from the other side. They tell of recorded and unrecorded
massacres and murders and encounters with characters from white
history. Lennon testifies to displacements of her people through
processes of colonization and the destruction of lives caused by the
British nuclear tests at Maralinga, connecting historical evidence and
data recovered from government reviews in the 1980s and 90s to her
own knowledge of miscarriages and cancer that resulted for many
members of the Anangu community. From the assertive title of the
book to the final words of the author "I'm the one who know every-
way. *Ngura nyangatja nyayuku*—This is my home!"(147), Lennon
retains control over her story.

Tex and Nelly Camfoo reside in traditional country in Arnhem Land. Their story attests to ongoing cultural traditions and black-fella ways against the incursions of white Australian politics and politicians. "I didn't get my culture from Mr Keating," says Nelly (107). "Aboriginal law is still here," states Tex (102). *My Side of the Bridge* provides Veronica Brodie with an opportunity to express the "heart-wrenching and heartbreaking" trauma her people endured as a result of Hindmarsh Island Bridge Royal Commission (1995). The Commission inquiry denied Njarrindjeri women's claims to secret, traditional knowledge, accepting only the "facts" discernable through written records. The decision against the women's claims not only deeply offended the so-called dissident women, but also opened painful rifts between factions in her already divided community.[25] Iris Burgoyne's stories in *The Mirning* recollect a past suffused with episodes of sexual abuse, poisoning, and other racist practices that only recently have been exposed by contemporary historians. She responds, however, not with shame and guilt but with anger, accusing the missions of multiple human rights violations. A comment made at the end of her narrative underscores her agentic position. She writes in hope that her reminiscences "may have provided some insight into the spiritual and cultural wealth of a nation that has endured hardship and injustice with stoicism and good humour" (136). The nation here is not the white settler nation, but the nation constituted in, by, and through Indigenous histories and their ongoing traditions. In this instance, Burgoyne confronts white Australian readers, asking them not to fit Indigenous stories into white accounts of nationhood but, rather, to alter their frame of reference and confront their own roles in Indigenous histories of separation.

Language of Human Rights

One of the most striking features of this collection of texts is the deployment of the language of human rights. The texts include chapter titles made familiar by *Bringing Them Home*, like "Removal," "Stolen Generation," and "Reconciliation." They include words and phrases that resonate with the language of the HREOC Inquiry and its terms of reference—separation, institutionalization, destruction of culture and heritage, the loss of language, limited educational opportunities, restrictions on freedom, segregation, physical and sexual abuse, mental and physical cruelty, unjust detention, coercive practices, and the intergenerational effects of separation on families and communities. The narrators understand their treatment in terms of a violation of human rights: "Our people knew they were deprived of basic human rights" (Burgoyne 56); "We had no rights!" (Brodie 61). Through reference to past histories of suffering around the world, enjoined to the moral weight of the UHDR, narrators connect their experiences to a world memory of human rights violations.

At the same time, many narratives assert the rights of their communities as a separate and distinct people, with ongoing languages, laws, traditions, and ways of life. Lennon and Burgoyne "know" their country, maintain cultural traditions, and attest to their survival as a distinct people. Tex and Nelly Camfoo, growing up across two cultures, two laws, reveal the ambiguities of their culturally divided lives. These narratives attribute retrospective awareness and agency to those being dispossessed: "My grandfather knew he was entitled to something" (Burgoyne 28). "The Mirning in general were very shy or 'shame.' We didn't argue with Europeans and just accepted the situation" (56). Prior to *Bringing Them Home*, Indigenous life stories had told of victimization and subordination in which tellers were shamed into positions of "little nobodies" (Nannup 47), denied subjectivity within the dominant culture. In these recent narratives the tellers establish themselves as knowing subjects of history and of human rights violations. Some, however, exceed these parameters to acknowledge entitlements to land, law, culture and language as a culturally distinct people.

Indigenous narrators also align their stories with the suffering and abuse of minority peoples in other parts of the world. Many compare their experiences to the Jews in Nazi Germany, the Blacks in Apartheid South Africa, the Catholics in Northern Ireland, West Bank Palestinians, the slave and black militants in U.S. civil rights history, and the victims of the Khmer Rouge in Cambodia. Brodie, breaking her indirect mode of authorial address in a way that implicates the reader and the nation in relation in the process of tattooing full-blood Aborigines proposed by the Northern Territory authorities, asks, "Do you realise that Hitler's system of tattooing Jews comes from what they wanted to set up in the NT?" (Brodie 102). She uses the simile "like a concentration camp" (72) to describe the look of an Aboriginal woman's home in South Australia. Brodie, Burgoyne, and Holt all describe their separation and mission experiences through similes from the Holocaust: "the mission felt like a concentration camp" (Burgoyne 41). A number of narrators compare their experiences and express a solidarity with victims elsewhere: "they said black Americans were treated badly, but the Aboriginal people were equally oppressed" (Burgoyne 129); "toilets were sign-posted 'not for the convenience of natives'" (Holt 16); "we were like placid zombies because we were under absolute control" (Holt 71). About the Worrabindia Mission, Holt comments dryly, "it had nothing to recommend it....[T]hird world conditions prevailed" (83). Authors imbricate their stories with the cultural memory of oppression from elsewhere, enabling new scripts of identity, affiliation, solidarity, and belonging.

Transected Lives

The publication of *Bringing Them Home*, the collection and housing of oral histories, extension of Link Up services, and opening of archival government and Mission records to descendents of separated families made possible many projects of recovery and reclamation. A new generation of young writers, like Stephen Kinnane and Fabienne Bayet-Charlton, whose grandmothers and great-grandmothers were removed from country, now track the invisible traces of their transected lives and tell stories that model new paths to the future.

Shadow Lines, writes Kinnane, are "wide lines of negotiation that we all use to make sense of our differences and interconnections" (379). His lines lead back to his great-grandmother's Miriwoong country in the remote Eastern Kimberley region of Northwest Australia, from which she was removed at the age of five and sent to the Moore River Mission in 1906. Bayet-Charlton's journey returns her to the mud flats of the Northern Rivers area of New South Wales where her Bundjalung great-grandmother was born in 1903, and from which ancestors were removed, then displaced to the dry, dusty desert region of Coober Pedy. Utilizing submerged and invisible stories, following "knowledge" through totem dreaming and scraps of memory passed down by family, augmented by sometimes unreliable or insufficient records, their memoirs trace two lines of connection, not easily separated or demarcated, in pursuit of a reclaimed heritage, and place of belonging.

"Cuts leave scars. Scars leave tracks. Tracks can be followed," writes Kinnane (12). Reconnection to country entails pain, surprise, shock, and serendipitous discovery for both writers. Kinnane and Bayet-Charlton find "mountains of misrepresentation"[26] in records over which their ancestors had no control. Kinnane traces his London-born grandfather's nine-year battle with the Aborigines Department to obtain permission from the Protector to marry his Aboriginal grandmother. Bayet-Charlton battles the Institute of Aboriginal and

Islander Studies in Canberra that denies her access to records leading back to her great-grandfather's country and later family mission experience. *Finding Ullagundahi Island*, the title of the book and her grandmother's ancestral home, becomes a project induced by melancholy and nostalgia, dreamings and desires, intuitions and fortuitous luck. Travelling by car, she finds two countries in a single landscape, "divided neither by borders nor language, distance nor time" (186). Both authors follow invisible tracks that reconnect them to country, following countless dislocations experienced by their families, eventually leading to reunions and reconnection with surviving relatives. "Memories," writes Bayet-Charlton, "are old but alive like pain, like blood. It never stops flowing... Rivers and dust flow in our blood." (240). Their journeys reinvest hopes and dreams and connections from the past into the present where, layered and intermingled with urban lives and experiences, the two cultures, two worlds, two lines of connection intersect.

Of all the third generation narratives to appear that recover a lost history and reclaim the past, Stan Grant's *The Tears of Strangers* (2002) has the potential to receive the widest international attention. Published and promoted by Harper Collins, an international press, and written by a respected and controversial media personality, it presents a complex, critically-informed account of Grant's family history in which he validates the "dark history" of separation that affected his family, friends, and other community members. Throughout, he refers to official documents, histories, government records, and scholarly accounts understood through contemporary critical theories of identity construction. A third-generation, urban-based, tertiary-educated descendent of an Aboriginal great-grandmother and an Irish convict great-grandfather, Grant melds family and community genealogies with historical and anthropological perspectives on black struggle and survival. Raised in a black world of death, danger, and violence, with an alcoholic father who "beat him with all the fury only a black man could muster, hitting someone he imagines to be white" (14), he harbors no sympathy for urban Indigenous nostalgia for a lost Aboriginal culture. Nor does he support a divisive radical politics of confrontation. All positions, in fact, come under scrutiny for their failure to deal with a messy and constantly shifting ground.

An internationally successful journalist and news reporter living in Hong Kong,[27] Grant declares, "I am a white success.... [I]n my whiteness, I've gained the world but I've lost something of myself. I can't pretend to be a black success. There's really no such thing" (155).

This comment contrasts sharply with the approaches to transected lives taken by Kinnane and Bayet-Charlton, both of whom find openings to the future through connection to ancestral identity, place, and belonging. The narrative trajectory of *The Tears of Strangers* moves outward from personal reconciliation with Grant's family history as an Indigenous Australian to a future in a global arena, marked but not determined, by his indigeneity. The narratives by Kinnane and Bayet-Charlton imagine futures through a reinvestment of hopes, dreams, and belongings in the present to ancestors living and long dead. They are acts of connection. Although written with an attachment a to personal and communal loss, *The Tears of Strangers* imagines a future untethered from the pull of connection to the past.

At the end of the book, Grant cites three important turning points of Aborigines in contemporary national life: Paul Keating's Redfern speech, that defining moment of a new nation that "turn[ed] pain into hope" (234); the 1992 Mabo decision and the minority judgments of the High Court Justices Deane and Gaudron that "separate[d] mere law from the higher ideal of justice" (236); and Cathy Freeman's gold medal win at the 2000 Sydney Olympics. For Grant, these turning points effected a "spiritual revival, one which rendered denominations obsolete, that dispensed with dogma" (233). All powerfully affective, these events signaled an ethics of recognition. Missing from this list is the Stolen Generation Report. Indeed, Grant eschews the title "Stolen Generation": "A life can't be reduced to a catchy slogan," he cautions (145). He views the "history wars" and debates about guilt, shame, blame, and responsibility as whitefella business.[28] *The Tears of Strangers* imagines a future for Australia beyond racial divisions in which the black and white heritages of second- and third-generation descendants of stolen children might be more closely intertwined. It presents a perspective from one connected to but moving beyond the national imperatives of reconciliation.

CONCLUSION

This brief summary of some recent Indigenous life narratives leads us to offer several concluding observations. First, contemporary Indigenous narratives, however conflictual in juxtaposition, engage in dialogue on equal terms with non-Indigenous readers. Second, narrators pursue many separate and distinct paths to identity. For some, living semi-traditional lives on native title lands, cultural traditions and affiliations remain strong and viable. For others, the fight for recognition of native title claims, sovereignty, and self-determination through dialogue, debate, and an activist politics of resistance remain fundamental. Other third-generation survivors of stolen children track life-lines back through creative journeys of memory and desire that follow the traces of a silenced past. Still others explore new openings forged from the in-between spaces of transected lives, hybridized cultures, and indeterminate futures. Third, there are many paths to healing. A national apology has not been forthcoming, but neither have Indigenous people remained trapped in an impasse.

These texts mark a departure from the past, from mainly white-controlled monologues to mutually-constituted dialogues between differently-positioned Indigenous and non-Indigenous participants in the production, reception, and circulation of stories. They enable new conversations in productive textual spaces of reconciliation otherwise occluded by the national politics of denial. Engaging readers and writers alike in an ethics of intersubjective exchange and critical responsiveness, they create ethico-political and aesthetic terrains that challenge Eurocentric, secular humanist polarities that attend the politics of sameness and difference.

CHAPTER 5

BELATED NARRATING:
"GRANDMOTHERS" TELLING STORIES
OF FORCED SEXUAL SLAVERY
DURING WORLD WAR II

Our policy should henceforth be to draw the sponge across the crimes and horrors of the past—hard as that may be—and look, for the sake of all our salvation, toward the future.

—*Winston Churchill*, as quoted in George Hicks

The authority for this tribunal comes not from a state or intergovernmental organization but from the peoples of the Asia-Pacific Region and, indeed, the peoples of the world to whom Japan owes a duty under international law to render account.

—Summary Judgment of the Women's International War Crimes Tribunal 2000 for the Trial of Japanese Military Sexual Slavery

On March 11, 2001 Korean "grandmother" Kap Soon-Choi walked onto the stage of a lecture hall at the University of Michigan in the United States and sat down between two younger women, one her interlocutor, the other her translator. After leaning toward her interlocutor for the first question, she began her testimony, translated into English as "We were so very poor." For over an hour Kap Soon-Choi told her harrowing tale of abduction and forced sexual slavery in a Japanese military "comfort station" to a hall full of hushed college students. She told her story; she wept; she resumed. After her formal testimony, Kap Soon-Choi responded to audience questions for another hour. Throughout the two hours of testimony to her radical degradation, the *Michigan Daily* photographer shot photos for the next day's paper.

In the last decade, some fifty years since the end of World War II, former "comfort women"[1] such as Kap Soon-Choi have circled the globe bringing their histories of sexual slavery to ever-broadening audiences of activists, jurists, government officials, and college students. They have addressed UN commissions, national tribunals, and Japanese courts. Survivors and activists have lobbied in national capitals such as Tokyo, Seoul, and Washington, D.C. Anthologies of testimonies, websites, and documentary films produced by scholar/activists and NGOs have brought their stories and their faces to global audiences. Contemporary artists, such as Tomiyama Taeko in Japan and Yong Soon Min in the United States, have incorporated histories of the World War II sex prisoners in their installations and paintings.

For fifty years after the end of the Pacific War, a virtual silence reigned regarding the Japanese Imperial Army's institutionalization of forced sexual slavery. Immediately after the war, documents related to "comfort stations" were destroyed or packed away in forgotten archives—both in Japan and in the United States. Prosecutors at the Tokyo War Tribunal (1946–48), officially known as the International Military Tribunal for the Far East, did not raise the issue of enforced military prostitution, despite the fact that investigators had gathered information about the "comfort stations" and the systematic rape of women by the Japanese military in occupied territories (see Dolgopol 130–6).[2] In the tribunals, the Allies focused on crimes against peace rather than crimes against humanity, crimes that would occupy the Nuremberg Trials (Rumiko 214–5). The Dutch did hold war crimes trials in Batavia (now Jakarta), Indonesia, in 1948, during which they prosecuted Japanese military officers for complicity in forcing Dutch women into military brothels, but the names of victims and accused were sealed in archives that will not be made available to the public until 2025. In 1965, the Japanese–South Korean Basic Treaty established terms for compensating Korea for unpaid labor and damages to the country and its people. In return for restitution and reparation payments, the Korean government absolved Japan of its debt (Hicks 131).[3] At no time during treaty negotiations did the issue of former Korean sex prisoners arise as a case of forced labor.

And yet, Ueno Chizuko insists, "the existence of the comfort women was common knowledge even in Korea" (136). As early as 1965, the Modern History Research Society of Japan issued *Memoirs of a Korean Comfort Woman* by the pseudonymous Kim Chun Ja (Barkan 52). Then, in the early 1970s, the Japanese journalist Kako Senda published *Jugun Ianfu* (1973), an account of the extensive comfort station system based on analysis of memoirs and testimonies of Japanese soldiers. Kako's book, which sold half a million copies and was translated into Korean, was followed by Kim Il Myon's 1980 book *The Emperor's Forces and Korean Comfort Women*. Kim's book provided detailed information that would later become vital for activists (Barkan 52); but, as did the others mentioned, it presented the women "as victims of Japanese colonial and military aggression, with little attention paid to the specifically sexual exploitation they suffered" (Mackie 42). Sekiguchi Norika's 1989 documentary film, *Senso Daughters*, told of the comfort stations and of the sex prisoners but did not include any first-person testimony. To that date, no former sex prisoners living in the lands of former Japanese colonization and occupation had come forward of their own initiative to make their stories public (Freiberg 234). Common knowledge had yet to be translated into a public discourse fueled by witness testimony.

All that changed in August of 1991 when Kim Hak Sun testified publicly to her experiences as a sex prisoner during the Pacific War. Four months later, a small group of Korean women, among them three former sex prisoners, brought a class-action suit against the Japanese government. In their suit, the women sought apology, reparation, prosecution of perpetrators, and a commitment to educate successive generations about these crimes against humanity. The next year the history of World War II "comfort women" hit the international news when representatives of two NGOs, the International Education Development Group of East Asia and the Korean Council for the Women Drafted for Military Sexual Slavery by Japan,[4] brought the issue to the UN Commission on Human Rights Subcommission Working Group on Contemporary Forms of Slavery (Soh 2001, 69).

Through a confluence of forces at the intersections of geopolitics, transnational feminist activism, and the memorial politics surrounding the fiftieth anniversary of the end of World War II, the stories of former sex prisoners entered into the field of human rights. The belated "coming-out" stories (Barkan 53) of a relatively modest number of "grandmothers," as they are often called, all of them in their seventies and eighties, most of them living lives of poverty, many of them living alone and without family, had finally become "internationally newsworthy" (Hein 1998, 109). In what follows, we trace the history of this belated narrating, a history that begins in shame and moves to ur-story. We also explore the contradictory effects of this arena of personal storytelling, as stories move from local communities to transnational venues of witnessing.

HISTORICAL CONTEXTS

Jugun ianfu ("military comfort women") is the euphemistic term for women forced into sexual slavery in military brothels by the Japanese Imperial Army from 1931 to the end of World War II.[5] In the early years of World War II Japanese women, many sold into prostitution, accompanied troops into occupied territories.[6] When the spread of venereal disease threatened military preparedness, however, sex brokers turned to the recruitment of native girls and women throughout Japan's extensive lands of occupation where a licensed system of prostitution had already been instituted. According to Gay J. McDougall, Special Rapporteur of the United Nations Commission on Human Rights (UNCHR), official documents reveal that the Japanese Imperial Army established brothels in occupied areas to maintain military morale; to contain the effects of sexually transmitted disease and keep the army fit; to curb uncontrolled sexual violence directed against occupied communities that tarnished the image of the Imperial Army at home and abroad, as had occurred with "the rape of Nanking"; and to limit espionage (McDougall; Soh 2002).

The exact numbers of sex prisoners are hard to establish, primarily because of difficulties in documentation. Various estimates put the figure anywhere between 80,000 and 200,000 women, and some suggest numbers in excess of 200,000. Most of the women (some 80 percent) came from Korea, but others came from the Philippines, Dutch colonial Indonesia, Taiwan, the Pacific Islands, Malaysia, Burma, and northeast China (Soh 2002). (Recent research suggests that the number of Chinese women coerced into sexual slavery may be far higher than previously believed.) Some of the women were as young as eleven and most were in their late teens and early twenties. Most came from poor families. However they got to the military brothels, by deceptive recruitment or abduction, once there the girls were systematically raped, forced to service from thirty to seventy soldiers a day, violently attacked and abused, and rarely allowed to leave. In addition, a racial/class hierarchy determined the availability status of the girls. Japanese women and, in colonial Indonesia, Dutch women were reserved for officers. Enlisted soldiers visited brothels where impoverished Korean women, or impoverished women from other occupied areas, were held prisoner.

Some estimates suggest that only a quarter to a third of the women forced into sexual slavery survived. Many of the girls disappeared, assumed by others to have been killed. At the end of the war, some were systematically executed and some were forced to commit suicide with the Japanese retreat. Others may have committed suicide when they returned home. Evidence suggests that many of those who survived did not return home due to shame and the expectation of rejection by families (Ueno 131). Wherever they settled, the former sex prisoners suffered from mental and physical disabilities, including the effects of venereal disease, sterility, asthma, insomnia, and nervous breakdowns (Watanabe 5). Survivors lived lives of poverty, disability, and isolation, their painful past "sedimented in the body" as material memory (Lee 1999, 93).[7]

The Legacy of Shame and Silence

Gendered shame, in this case women's internalization of the judgments of others, has much to do with the long silence about this physically and psychically horrific past. During their months or years as sex prisoners, the girls and women forced into organized prostitution had been stripped of their names and assigned Japanese names. They had often been forbidden to communicate with other women in the brothels. They had lived under the constant threat of violence, disappearance, and death. If they became pregnant, they had been forced to undergo abortions. They had been subjected to the unrelenting, dehumanizing, and shaming gaze of commandants, doctors, officers, and rank soldiers. In effect, they had been made into the living dead, subjects without social value. Hwang Kumju (sometimes Hwang Keum-ju), whose narrative is excerpted in three anthologies of testimonies of survivors, witnesses to the social death imposed upon and internalized by the young girls and women in the stations. "We were told to behave as if we didn't see anything or hear anything," she recalls. "So we walked about with our hands covering our eyes. If we tried to take a walk outside the barracks we were kicked back inside. So we had no opportunity to look around at where we were" (Howard 76).

Returning to "normal" life at the end of the war, survivors lived with the legacies of routine fear, physical abuse, psychic numbing, and social "disgrace." The effects of sexual slavery—the infertility, the damaged sexual organs—meant that many of the women would no longer be able to claim the social identities available to young girls and women as wives and mothers. Hyunah Yang suggests that most survivors lived out a form of " 'voluntary' resignation from the normal woman's life"; and that such resignation involved "a self-shaming mechanism" that made victims "apologize" for themselves (66). In effect, many survivors "died" to everyday life. The families and communities to whom survivors returned enforced their shame and self-contempt by refusing to acknowledge this past, obscuring it in secrecy, and rejecting or abandoning them.

Within this shadow of gendered shame, there could be no anguish and suffering to narrate that would be credited in the public sphere. There could be no community of identity for collective acts of remembering. There could be no story for the women to narrate without its recuperation into the culturally powerful "prostitution script," the degraded version of the cultural script of woman's embodied passivity and availability to serve the needs of men. Assigning survivors the social identity of "prostitute" rather than innocent victim, the script limited the cultural "forms of representation" (Van Alphen 26) available to them for understanding the life lived during their horrific months and years of sexual slavery and social death, and their years of survival in old or new homes. Finally, there could be no recovery without the possibility of social exchange, the route out of shame. The past of suffering would go un-narrated for these women, most of whom had little access to or impact on the terms of public discourse because of their impoverished backgrounds. "The comfort women system," writes Ueno, "succeeded in keeping the women who had been made comfort women silent" (131).

Nor were there receptive audiences within the nations involved willing to accept ethical responsibility for recognition of their suffering. The persistence of privatized shame, therefore, cannot fully explain the long silence about the wartime fate of the women. The silence has to be understood in part as an effect of broader cultural and political forces, particularly the gendered dynamics of war and other catastrophic events (Lentin 97; Brunet and Rousseau 36). To the degree that "women are seen as the tropes of the collectivity's honour or shame," observes Ronit Lentin, "their narratives are all too often officially, or unofficially, silenced" (100), particularly if they are narratives of sexual violation.

Nationalist leaders, rebuilding the nation out of the ruins of war, would find the gains of revealing the atrocities of the Japanese military less compelling than the gains of refiguring a virile modern nation coming out of the nightmare of "symbolic emasculation" attending occupation and colonization (Chungmoo Choi 398; Hyun Sook Kim 100–1). Narratives of heroic resistance of the nation's men would, and did, become more desirable stories of wartime than those of enforced degradation of the nation's women and girl-children (Chungmoo Choi 398). In the ensuing decades, a past of national shame needed to be repudiated in service to a desired future of full membership in the big league of Pacific Rim nations and emulation of the "big boys" in Tokyo (Freiberg 233). Despite their radically divergent trajectories of modernization, South Korea and Indonesia, the Philippines and China, all shared the desire to claim and demonstrate a virile national identity through flexing economic and/or military muscle. Thus, there was reluctance to press the Japanese government to acknowledge this massive violation of human dignity, to apologize for the system, or to make restitution to the victims. The fact that the majority of the girls and women coerced into organized prostitution for the Japanese military came from impoverished backgrounds and had little access to political influence, and that they remained silenced by shame, meant that there was little political capital to be gained in pursuing information about, advocating on behalf of, and resolving the national "problem" of survivors of forced prostitution.

Nor did the victors of World War II go looking for their testimony. As the injunction of Winston Churchill suggests, the global order of the Cold War rendered certain kinds of rights violations visible from the point of view of the West and other violations invisible. In the face of the alliance between the Soviet Union and Communist China, a generation of Cold Warriors rebuilt and rehabilitated Japan as a democratic bastion in the threatened Pacific Rim region. Years of war crimes trials would only extend the longevity of wartime stereotypes. Later, in the 1960s, the goal of the West was to promote Japan as its chief ally and buffer to the Soviet sphere in East Asia. The Cold War promoted selective amnesia, particularly with regard to "crimes against humanity" in the Pacific War. Neither the victors nor the Cold Warriors went looking for stories of massive violations of human rights.

Within Japan another logic rendered the history of forced prostitution un-memorable. As elsewhere around the world, wartime exploitation of women's bodies through licensed brothels could be normalized as "prostitution," an ordinary commercial aspect of warfare, rather than criminalized as systematic rape (Stetz 91–2). With sexual slavery so easily framed within the circuits of a commercial wartime economy, the Japanese nation could deflect charges of war crimes and project responsibility back onto the women themselves.[8] Moreover, the ease with which women with sexual experience outside marriage could be labeled unchaste and contaminated within male-dominated cultures meant that women who spoke publicly of sexual slavery became the ones put "on trial." Survivors could be, often were, and continue to be positioned as "prostitutes" who chose their fate rather than innocents who were forced to their fate. Additionally, in the post–Hiroshima era, the Japanese represented themselves as victims of the Pacific War to themselves and to the world—as victims of the Japanese military regime and of the atomic bomb (Chin 233; Field 17–22). In this context of remembrance of radical suffering, the nationalist figure of Japanese victim occludes that of the culpable Japanese perpetrator of war crimes against girls and women.

"Both the rulers and the ruled," notes Hyun Sook Kim, "are guilty of a masculinized nationalism that has selectively absented and marginalized the memories of comfort women" (101). The intersection of the privatized shame of social death experienced by the former sex prisoners and the specter of the public shame of the nation-states directly involved ensured that for almost fifty years the women did not tell their stories publicly and that national leaders did not go looking for their stories. After World War II there would be no receptive public for the narratives of former sex prisoners, no cultural intelligibility to their stories, no urgency attached to their particular acts of remembrance and recovery, no juridical or public recognition of their claims, no identity as victim of a rights violation. "Without recognition," comment Ariane Brunet and Stephanie Rousseau, "there can be no punishment, reparation nor rehabilitation. Worse still, there are neither victims nor aggressors" (38).

SILENCE BROKEN

After 1989, the Cold War imaginary no longer organized the retrospective understanding of World War II. International attention turned to human rights as the successor global project, spurring a number of campaigns designed to archive oral testimonies of survivors of the Nazi Holocaust and to recover the "forgotten" war crimes of the Pacific War, especially as the fiftieth anniversary of World War II began to generate commemoration activities. Increasing numbers of people began to imagine and position themselves as victims of human rights violations in the past (Park 123). In the case of the former sex prisoners, however, human rights had to be linked to women's rights through transnational feminist activism.

By the early 1990s what Vera Mackie describes as "discursive social change" had taken place whereby "the range of possible statements about militarism, sexuality and violence" expanded, enabling "the framing of new political campaigns on gender, sexuality and human rights" (40).[9] In Japan in the 1970s and 1980s feminist activists (in the Asian Women's Association and Women Questioning the Present) laid the groundwork for subsequent feminist analysis of military prostitution as a systematic part of Japanese imperial aggression (Mackie 44–5). But the impetus for organizing World War II victims of that aggression came from Korea. By the late 1980s, two developments in Korea prepared the way for a shift in the interpretation of the national past, and thus a shift in explanatory paradigm from "war situation" to "crimes against humanity": democratization and women's activism (Ueno).[10] As Korea adjusted to the transition from military dictatorship to democracy in the mid-1980s, women came forward to speak publicly about the use of rape as a form of torture during the military dictatorship. Their public testimony forced the issue of sexual violence against women into national consciousness in such a way that the moral and legal indictment of the perpetrator overrode the culture of shame silencing victims. The second development involved the emergence of an organized women's movement in Korea with transnational links to women's movements across Pacific Rim countries and to women's activism elsewhere around the globe.[11] Several groups, most prominently the South Korean Church Women's Alliance and the Korean Council, began to focus national attention on Japanese sex tourism and the sex trade attached to military bases in Korea as forms of neo-imperial and state-sponsored exploitation of Korean women. That military personnel still used the term *wianbu*—in Japanese *ianfu* and in English "comfort women"—to refer to women in the sex trade pointedly reinforced the continuing relationship of earlier and contemporary forms of sexual oppression (Mackie 46).

Activists needed testimonial evidence to make the legal case for apology and reparations for survivors of forced prostitution during World War II. Around 1990, activists in Korea issued a call for former sex prisoners to come forward with their stories, and a Korean Council Victim's Hotline opened in 1991.[12] Following that call, women activists elsewhere in the Pacific region put out calls for testimony. The call came across the radio in the Philippines in 1992. As survivors came forward, women's NGOs gathered and documented what by then had become human rights violations.

They called for hearings. They filed lawsuits. They organized international tribunals.

Pressured by the Korean Council and international media coverage, the Japanese government issued official reports in 1992 and 1993.[13] The 1992 Report acknowledged the existence of the comfort station system and the Japanese military's complicity in the system but failed to concede that women were forced into service in the stations. With this refusal, the Report effectively denied the legitimacy and authority of the testimony presented by survivors. After Dutch, Korean, Chinese, and Filipina survivors testified *en masse* at the International Public Hearing Concerning the Post War Compensation of Japan in Tokyo in late 1992, Japan issued a second report in 1993 acknowledging the "possibility of 'forcefulness'" in the system but attributing such practices to civilians rather than the military (Hyunah 54; Chin 242). In response to continued challenges by the North and South Korean governments and the Korean Council, the Japanese government conceded that women and girls were coerced into sexual slavery and that the Japanese military was officially involved in recruitment efforts (Soh 2001). But the Japanese government issued no apology or reparation plan.[14]

The public demands made by former sex prisoners for recognition, apology, and reparation gained increasing international attention after 1992 as activists around the world organized transnationally to reframe women's rights as human rights, particularly in the domain of violence against women. While member states ratified the UDHR in 1948, another thirty-one years passed before the UN adopted the Convention on the Elimination of All Forms of Discrimination Against Women (CEDAW) in 1979. Even then, CEDAW did not list freedom from violence against the self as an inalienable, universal right. Two things needed to happen: Violence against women had to be labeled a violation of women's human rights, and rape had to be reaffirmed as a war crime. The World War I War Crimes Commission of 1919 had listed rape and forced prostitution among thirty-two violations of the laws of war, but the Allies failed to prosecute these offenses after the two world wars. Moreover, international law and human rights instruments related to women and gender have until recently rendered systematic rape and military prostitution invisible aspects of war and its remembrance (Askin 42–5). As Brunet and Rousseau note, "rape and other gender-specific violations have never been, and still are not recognized in humanitarian law as crimes of violence committed against women *by reason of their gender*" (44, emphasis ours).[15]

In 1992 CEDAW finally included gender violence as one form of discrimination, "placing it," according to Sally Engle Merry, "squarely within the rubric of human rights and fundamental freedoms and making clear that states are obliged to eliminate violence perpetrated by public authorities and by private persons" (87). In 1993 the Global Campaign for Women's Human Rights, participating in the World Conference on Human Rights held in Vienna, televised tribunal hearings on the systematic rape of Bosnian women as a form of ethnic cleansing. The Vienna Conference marked a turning point for activists on behalf of women's rights when conferees acknowledged that "the human rights of women and of the girl-child are an inalienable, integral and indivisible part of universal human rights." They also acknowledged that the formal platforms, mechanisms, and bodies of the rights regime had to be reconstituted to ensure that "the equal status of women and the human rights of women" could be pursued through "the mainstream of United Nations system-wide activity" (*Vienna Declaration* para. 18, 37).[16] After the Vienna Conference, activists and scholars from around the world lobbied for the incorporation of gender perspectives within the theoretical, structural, and organizational dimensions of the human rights project (Gallagher 283–8).

By the time of the UN-sponsored Fourth World Conference on Women in Beijing in 1995, violence against women was at the center of conference attention, Declaration discourse, and activist mobilization. Survivors of forced prostitution attended the Beijing conference, witnessing to their experiences of sexual slavery, and feminist and NGO activists presented workshops on military prostitution. "That reconceptualisation of rape as a violation of fundamental human rights and as something that should be judged by a single global standard," Laura Hein claims, "was a crucial step in shifting popular opinion in Japan and elsewhere toward sympathy for the former comfort women" (1999, 347).

It is important to note, however, that stories of sexual violence told by European and Australian women paved the way for the broader internationalization of the stories of former sex prisoners from Southeast Asia. In the early 1990s, widely disseminated media stories exposed the systematic rape of Bosnian women as part of a plan of ethnic genocide. Then in 1994 Australian Jan Ruff-O'Herne published *50 Years of Silence*, the first extended life narrative written by a former sex prisoner in English. Ruff-O'Herne had testified at the Tokyo tribunal in 1992; but, as she explicitly makes clear in her narrative, she came to recognize that the international community, particularly Western nations, would take more notice of the campaign on behalf of the former sex prisoners if the cause became identified not only with impoverished Korean, Chinese, Taiwanese, Malaysian, and Filipina women in Southeast Asia and with ethnic Koreans in Japan, but also with a Dutch-born, Indonesian-raised middle-class woman. Due to her privileged status as Western and white, her narrative could not so easily be dismissed as the retrospective fabrication of a former prostitute. Moreover, the Dutch had held war crimes trials in 1948 for which they had assembled a record of verification, even if that record would not be made available until 2025. The publication of *50 Years* in 1994, and the production of the video based on the narrative by Ruff-O'Herne's daughter Carol that same year, thus brought the story of sexual slavery during the Pacific War to the attention of a broader public in Australia and other Western countries. Undoubtedly, Ruff-O'Herne's narrative has been critical to gaining recognition of claims for apology and reparation in the West. Undoubtedly, its embeddedness in the geopolitics of recognition raises fundamental questions about whose stories count as credible, and about whose voice of suffering carries more political weight in the global marketplace of competing victimages.

Rights Discourse and the Past

The discourses through which events that happen to people become "experience," and are thereby given individual and social meaning, cannot be understood as "a static, timeless phenomenon" but need to be understood as "changeable and transformable" (Van Alphen 26). If before the 1980s, as Ueno claims, "no one, not even the participants themselves, understood what had happened as a 'crime'" (136), by the 1990s national and international climates had dramatically altered, making possible new representational frames through which the survivors could tell their belated stories of suffering and begin to regain social dignity. When they finally came forward to tell their stories in acts of coming-out, they entered a public sphere in which the international discourse of women's rights as human rights could be mobilized to put the past in a new framework.

Human rights discourse offered women isolated in dispersed local communities across many nations a communal identity, that of "former comfort woman" (Howard 114). This communal identity is not founded on ethnicity or race, or on national affiliation or geographical proximity. It is founded on the generational and gendered identity the women share with one another across national boundaries. In their personal narratives, they characterize their connection with one another as a founding condition of their public testimony. Again and again they testify to the embodied connection they feel to one another, a connection that carries the ethical force of collective witness. As ethical subjects of rights, the women speak to, with, and on behalf of other former sex prisoners (the ones who survived and the ones who disappeared and died).

Rights discourse gave survivors not only a new identity, but also a new discursive framework through which to reconstitute past experiences. In the act of narration, the former sex prisoners claim a legal subjectivity acknowledged in the international public sphere and thereby claim the right to have their suffering recognized as organized and systematic rape rather than voluntary prostitution. Going public, they refuse the prostitution script and the internalized shame that secures the script precisely because there is another script through which to understand their radical dehumanization. Moreover, rights discourse gave these women a language for naming the perpetrator of violence. Claiming a legal identity as a subject of rights violations, survivors have been able to shift the scene of recognition and apology from the self-directed charges of the socially dead self to the international platforms of the contemporary global order through which perpetrators are addressed and called to account.

The collected testimonies of survivors reveal the ways in which rights discourse motivates the emplotment of their reconstructed histories. Survivors begin by situating their past selves in their places of origin and family circumstances. They then tell of the deception whereby they were forced into the comfort station, the journey to the brothel, the first rape. They detail the abjection of life in the station, including emotional and physical violence and tell of the deaths and disappearance of other women and girls. They describe the end of the war, the arduous return home, and the difficulties of survival, the physical disabilities, the isolation, the loneliness. In the course of the ten years that survivors have been telling their stories to activists and to officials in tribunals and hearings, this has become the ur-story of forced prostitution and social death. This is the narrative that Kap Soon-Choi told in her appearance on the campus of the University of Michigan.

Paradoxically, the women position themselves in the remembered past as victims of human rights violations, a subject position claimed in the present. The voice of the subject of human rights can be heard in phrases and terms that encode contemporary understandings of human rights. In the repeated deployment of the term "rape" for naming what has been experienced in the past, we hear the voice of the subject of human rights framing the past through new discourses of rights and their denial. Thus, while the story survivors tell of their younger selves is the story of social death, their acts of telling situate them as performative subjects of narration testifying in the present. As subjects of universal human rights, the women become subjects with subjectivity (see Oliver).

As they rewrote the past away from the prostitution script, the survivors of sexual slavery engaged in a new kind of remembering with consequences rather than "memory without consequences" (Young 82). Claiming this legal subject position, survivors were empowered to address governmental and nongovernmental instrumentalities—activists, rights organizations, UN rapporteurs, lawyers, courts, and so on. Subjects of rights, survivors achieved the public status to challenge their own governments and the government of a nation-state not their own, effectively situating themselves as world-citizens in an international civic sphere. Agents in an international debate about the narratives through which the Pacific War would be remembered in the future, they connected with allies in their struggle for recognition, apology, and reparation, from women's activists in Manila and Seoul to college students on campuses in the United States, Canada, and Australia. As Hyun Sook Kim remarks: "By telling their stories of forced recruitment, hunger, confinement, torture, beatings, disease, rape, death, and humiliation, the women reconstitute both private and public memories of the past" (96). They also speak counter-truth to official histories of the Pacific War (see Howard 103).

In their public witnessing within the human rights regime, survivors were awakened from the social death of the unshared past. A new social subject came into being whose memories were "sharable" (Van Alphen 37) with a community of women with similar silenced pasts and with the younger generations they hoped to educate about the truth of the Pacific War. Being a subject of universal human rights, former sex prisoners remembered and imagined themselves outside the gendered identities reproduced through local and national gender relations, outside the self-negating horizon of privatized shame. Thus global flows in the international civic sphere have made this new identity a new lived experience with a new relationship to the past, present, and future.

FRAMING CONSTRAINTS

The call for testimony in the early 1990s offered the former sex prisoners a discourse through which to understand their past anew and an occasion through which to enact the agency of storytelling with consequences. Participation in the scattered venues and officially sponsored activities of the United Nations and its rights apparatuses, however, meant that the stories they told came to be framed by the imperatives of specific contexts of telling and resolicited and reframed by activists working on their behalf. UN-sponsored rapporteur reports are a case in point. The narrative testimony of the former sex prisoners provided the evidentiary basis for rights abuses cataloged by such rapporteurs for the UNCHR McDougall, but official reports needed to present cumulative evidence and carefully argued conclusions and recommendations rather than personally-inflected stories. The authority of the report, its official status as a truth-telling document, depended at once on witness accounts that told the same story and on the suppression of individual differences. Thus the witnessing of survivors cannot be disentangled from the agendas of activists working in various rights organizations and the organizations through which their narratives have circulated.

In some ways, for instance, the women have been held hostage to the ur-narrative of crimes against humanity. Rights activists require for their activism and expect from their informants a particular story of victimization: the ur-story of childhood poverty, abduction, forced sexual slavery, and lonely survival. Changing the story, going beyond the expected narrative, can be seen as a deviation from the work of collective remembering that must be done. Moreover, the narrator is expected to position herself as "victim" of the Japanese military aggression and thus as a victim of the "past" rather than an active agent in the present. Paradoxically, the agency promised through rights discourse requires the ceding of agency regarding the kind of story that can be told.

The repetition of the ur-story can be seen in such anthologies as *Comfort Women Speak*, with its common format of multiple (in this case, nineteen) abbreviated testimonies. The force of the volume, its affective appeal to a global audience, comes from the constraint of the narrative template, the common plotting, the common self-characterization as innocent victim, and the repetition of the ur-story. But in the very serializing of versions of the ur-story, the agency of individual women fades, and the differences in their experiential histories become blurred.

Survivors have also been asked by activists to tell their story of abject victimization repeatedly. They have been enlisted in global tours. Asked to rehearse their stories of suffering and degradation one more time for one more audience, the survivors can be put on "display" as victims, made into a spectacle of "the oppressed" and "the abject." In the name of bringing the silenced story of sexual slavery to the civic sphere, these women might be seen to be victimized once again. Describing her many visits with former sex prisoners, the activist-scholar Dai Sil Kim-Gibson cautions: "If indeed the old women had disclosed material beyond '*that* period,' it rarely made its way into the stories. It was as if their existence was justified by the horrendous years they suffered; nothing before or after *that* seemed to matter. Saddest of all, the grandmas themselves were convinced of that. They have become issues, numbers, and objects of studies, not full-blooded human beings" (1997, 259).

A second constraint at the site of story production has to do with the issue of stories told and untold. LaShawn Jefferson of the Women's Rights Division of HRW cautions that focus on violence against women, in this case systematic rape in wartime, occludes larger issues of systematic discrimination against women. Kap Soon-Choi alludes to such larger societal issues in her opening testimony: "We were so very poor." The occasion for her testimony, however, does not direct attention to the intersection of gender and poverty and to the gendered structures of Korean society within the context of Japanese colonialism. The force of the narrative is directed to the Japanese government in the form of demand for reparation rather than being directed to the reform of the local society in terms of gender inequalities. In anthologies, too, the story of colonial domination and sexual exploitation occludes the story of gender inequalities and class oppression in the homeland. In some narratives, however, the women allude to these stories. "Let me finally say something I consider to be important," insists Yi Young-Sook: "The Japanese were bad. But the Koreans were just as bad because they put their own women through such terrible ordeals for personal profit" (Howard 56).

The former sex prisoners are held hostage to rights discourse in another way. Both the women who testify and the activists working on their behalf have invoked the discourse of shame and honor to frame the call for official apology and reparation from the Japanese government. Yet the meta-narrative of lost-and-found honor encodes and thus reproduces traditional values in which women's honor is understood as sexually based and constitutive of patriarchal authority. Womens rights, as Brunet and Rousseau argue, must be "recognized as such; that is, as forms of violence that deprive them of their fundamental rights, not as attacks on their honour and reputation" (49). Further, the call for official apology and reparation for this violation of honor places "the key" to restoration "in the hands of the Japanese government." "Under the circumstances," argues Chungmoo Choi, "the victims continue to be kept in the position of passive recipients of honor" (404). Since the Japanese government is itself a gendered institution, the ceding of the power to restore honor to the State maintains the gendered construction of rights that marginalizes women and their interests. The women speak themselves as subjects of human rights, claiming legal subjectivity; but the site, occasion, and normative form of testimony can contribute to their continued capture within the circuit of demand and apology/reparation (see Chungmoo Choi) and within the call for recognition that puts the agent of recognition outside the self. As Norma Field cautions, "The longer the Japanese government refuses to substantiate its acknowledgment of this truth, the longer these women will be compelled to, in effect, commodify their bodies and their stories—until the public loses interest" (26–7). Testimony in and of itself may not affect a subjective solution to the sufferings of the past.

In the contexts of rights activism dispersed across heterogeneous sites of reception, the prostitution script persists as an explanatory paradigm for dismissing the legitimacy of survivor claims and stories. Often the women insist on the ways in which they attempted to resist being raped, by hiding, by showering the soldiers with insults, or by jumping out of windows. By presenting themselves in the past as agents of resistance, however unsuccessful, the women claim some site of human dignity in the time of social death. They also reveal their recognition of the force of the prostitution script readily available to their audience. Given the suspicion of female sexuality outside of marriage, a suspicion persisting across fifty years of silence, and the cultural valuation of female chastity, they recognize how convenient and comfortable it is for others to mediate the horror of the suffering and the implications of the demand for apology by assigning survivors the identity of "prostitute," especially if they came from impoverished backgrounds. Because the prostitution script pervades contemporary symbolics of gender across diverse cultures, and because it is inextricable from the symbolics of class and ethnicity, it cannot be kept outside these narratives of sexual slavery and social death.

Yet another constraint on these scenes of witness involves the ways in which the framing of the narratives of former sex prisoners within the contexts of human rights law, discourse, mechanisms, and activism occludes different cultural traditions of telling stories and producing social meaning. Whatever alternative storytelling traditions might be available to the women, who come from at least nine different countries and even more local communities, those alternatives are in little evidence in the carefully scripted testimony gathered for tribunals, and in the edited collections of testimony published in different languages and translated primarily into English for circulation to global audiences. Perhaps this is why several survivors turned to the visual arts to explore the past and its structures of feeling. Other imaginative realms may offer more freedom to tap into, adapt, and mine their history through aesthetic forms attached to their own cultural traditions, traditions incompatible with the forms of telling necessary to the human rights regime and activist agendas.

Finally, continued requests for repetition of the ur-narrative of sexual slavery can become part of the lingering structures of feeling attached to the earlier social death. Certainly, some women testify to the healing power of witnessing, as Mun P'ilgi does when she concludes her testimony: "To release my pent-up resentment, I reported to the [Korean] Council in June 1992. I hesitated a lot, but I feel so relieved to pour out the things that have been piled up in my heart for so many years" (Howard 87). But there are others who testify to the debilitating aspects of witnessing. As Jadranka Cigelj admits in the film *Calling the Ghosts* (about the systematic rape of Bosnian women during the war in the former Yugoslavia): "Without the live witness, one can only speculate about the crime. The crime has not been filmed with a camera! It is only recorded in the memory of the witness." Then she continues: "In order to expose the crime, you violate the witness" (qtd. in Hesford, 214). To be asked to make visible the shame of the past is to be put in the position of being shamed once again. Such acts of remembering attach the survivor once again to the degradation of social death. "Nowadays, people often come here to interview me about my life as a 'comfort woman.' I cannot see them as often as I used to. My nightmares become worse after remembering the past at these interviews," says Kim Soon-duk (Schellstede 40). In such a comment, Kim Soon-duk implicates activists working for justice in the ethical violence of extracting one more version of the story of social death. "Occasionally people come to hear my story of a former 'comfort woman,'" explains Yi Yŏngsuk, and then she continues: "I am reluctant to talk about it because it is my shameful, terrible past. Recollecting such a past is so emotionally draining" (Schellstede 101).

ALTERNATIVE FRAMES

The power of the ur-story and its repetition to frame, constrain, exploit, and commodify the anguished suffering of former sex prisoners is partially mediated when activists approach their oral history projects with critical awareness of the politics of collaborative life narrating and when survivors themselves write and publish their own extended narratives. Unlike the editors of *True Stories* and *Comfort Women Speak*, for instance, Dai Sil Kim-Gibson in *Silence Broken: Korean Comfort Women* (1999) puts herself in the text, presenting historical background and analysis in dialogue with the testimony and the voices of survivors.[17] In her refusal to erase her presence and her role as interlocutor, she insists on the intersubjective context of collaborative storytelling as ethical imperative. This insistence can be seen in her presentation of the testimony of Hwang Keum-ju (whose story is also included in *True Stories* and *Comfort Women Speak*). Rehearsing the history of their relationship, Kim-Gibson describes the context of her interview with Hwang and Hwang's response to her request for her story:

> *"But you have already heard my story twice. What would you like me to tell you?" "Anything that comes to your mind. Don't worry about repeating yourself. In fact, I wouldn't mind hearing the same story again. I doubt, though, that it would be the same." "What do you mean? Facts are facts." "Oh, I know, but this time I am sitting in your apartment, eating your Kimchi and listening to your story alone." "That is true." There was no need for me to explain what I meant. Her story began. (14)*

In this brief exchange, Hwang signals the codification of her story—"you have already heard my story twice"; she reveals her tacit understanding that the ur-story has become obligatory. In return, Kim-Gibson signals to Hwang that stories, apparently repetitious, change in the moment and site of narration and through the intersubjective relationship of teller and listener. "That is true," Hwang concludes, engaging her interlocutor in an ethics of storytelling.

The version of Hwang's story contained in *Silence Broken* stands in stark contrast to the flattened version of Hwang's story in *Comfort Women Speak*. In a more intimate setting, Hwang seems less pressured to tell the formulaic story. She expands on the circumstances of her childhood, explaining that her father's illness, which eventually led to the impoverishment of the family, was a venereal disease picked up while he was studying in Japan. She narrates her family's willingness to give her as a concubine to a much older man in order to get money to pay for her father's medicine. In the flattened version, Hwang says only: "When I was 11 years old, I had to leave home because my family was very poor" (3). In the expanded version she comments on the traditional sacrifice of young girls to the needs of the patriarch of the family; to female complicity in patriarchal social relations; to the sexual illness her father introduces into his family; to the suicide of her grandmother, devastated by her granddaughter's self-sacrifice; and to her own desire to "ma[k]e something of myself" (16). In effect, Hwang tells the story of the oppression of the girl-child in the patriarchal Korean family as well as the story of Japanese exploitation of impoverished Koreans.

As telling as her expansion on the circumstances of her childhood and detailed description of life in the station, however, are the disruptions of the narrative that announce Hwang's powerful presence as an agent of narration. She includes an angry speech she made in Japan challenging new regulations for fingerprinting Koreans living in Japan. She criticizes other survivors who express love for some Japanese, calling them "those mother fucking bitches" (22). She critiques movies she has seen about the former sex prisoners, concluding that there's "no way any movie can depict our past" (22). She expresses the desire for some recognition from people in the United States for her strength of character in enduring hardships, asking for an "honorary doctorate in hardships" (23). She states, "so many Japanese are afraid of me; they are afraid to talk to me...At the sight of them, curses run out of my mouth like a river" (24). Hwang's direct discourse as the subject of narration accumulates to project her in the present moment as wise, angry, combative, irreverent, ironic, and proud of her power to unsettle people. Through the rhetorical moves and affective valences of her narrative, the narrator explodes the hold of the ur-narrative and its figuration of the former sex prisoner as passive victim and silent sufferer.

The two individually authored narratives written by survivors, Ruff-O'Herne's *50 Years of Silence* and Maria Rosa Henson's *Comfort Woman* (1999), also offer opportunities to write beyond the ur-story and thus resist being fixed by rights discourse. In *Comfort Woman* Henson does tell the ur-story of childhood poverty in the Philippines, abduction in adolescence, sexual bondage, survival, shame, and silence (in the middle three chapters). She reimagines the experience of social death through animal metaphors: "When the soldiers raped me," she writes, "I felt like a pig. Sometimes they tied up my right leg with a waist band or belt and hung it on a nail on the wall as they violated me" (40). In her chapter on "recovery," Henson carries forward the description of herself in the past as an animal, crawling on four legs, virtually mute. She figures herself as the unhuman, cowering in corners away from the light, drooling uncontrollably from her mouth, her body bearing and baring the somatic marks of remembering. With the expansive possibilities of an extended personal narrative, however, Henson does not situate herself only as a victim of the Japanese military system of organized rape, nor does she constitute the meaning of her life solely in terms of the identity of "former comfort woman."

"My story begins in the barrio of Pampang" (1), announces Henson, insisting from the first words of her personal narrative on the salience of place—the geographical place of her birth, the social place of class in Filipino society, the sociocultural place of poverty in the narrative of rape, the cultural place of collective origins in personal storytelling. Henson's originary story is itself a story of rape, but not the story of her rape. Rather it is the story of the rape of her mother at age fifteen by the landlord and patriarch for whom her mother worked (Henson's beloved father). Through the framing of sexual violation that rights discourse provides, the older narrator can present the mother's rape as a narrative of forced prostitution, sexual violence rooted in class hierarchy and oppression;[18] she can link the scene of domestic violence to the wartime violence of the Japanese, both instances of patriarchally organized violation.

In her extended life narrative, Henson incorporates a biographical narrative of her mother, telling of the multigenerational fate of daughters in impoverished families. "This story comes from my mother's own lips," she writes: "She told me all that happened to her before I was born. She told me not only once but many times. That is why this is written in the diary of my mind" (6). Thus, the daughter situates her narrative in the larger story of class exploitation and resistance, thereby locating her sexual slavery as an effect of colonial and class oppression rather than in the story of woman's fallen nature. Moreover, in the narrator's commentary on the source of her story of origins in the mother's oral testimony, Henson links her published narrative to the oral traditions of her illiterate and economically impoverished community.

Entwined in the story of sexual victimization and social death, Henson weaves the story of resistance and heroic agency. Describing herself as a young girl, unacknowledged but financially supported by her father, she remembers a younger self dedicated to hard work and educational achievement, avenues through which to escape the social death of illegitimacy and poverty. "My dream was to redeem [my mother's] sad life, " (13) she recalls. She narrates how, after Japanese occupation shattered that dream, she enlisted with the resistance fighters of the Huk, carrying messages and medical supplies for the movement. In the story she tells of her marriage after the War to a resistance fighter named Doming, she emphasizes the continuing resistance of the impoverished and exploited workers to the capitalist class and the political system supporting it. Throughout her narrative, she refuses to represent the members of her community as passive victims of the Japanese occupation and capitalist oppression.

The venue of extended life narrative provides the opportunity for Henson to write beyond the script of "comfort woman." Having been released from the shame of the past through the act of testifying before activists and commissioners, having joined with other survivors of sexual slavery during the Pacific War to produce a collective narrative of sexual oppression, Henson can reclaim her past as one that holds the memory of sexual degradation but does not hold itself constrained by that time. Life begins before her abduction and continues after her survival of the horrors of the War. Moreover, Henson reclaims her identity as a woman of integrity by reconstructing her past as one in which she identifies herself as daughter to a devoted mother; as quietly devoted wife; as mother to two daughters and a son—imagines herself, that is, in traditionally feminine roles of daughter, wife, and mother encoded within the discourses of Catholic Christianity. If *Comfort Woman* is haunted by the nostalgia the older narrator feels for the younger self of promise lost in the wake of sexual degradation, it is released from the past as well by the embrace of the ethical subject who redeems that earlier self-esteem, redeems her mother's life, and redeems the lives of the women with whom she shares this past of degradation. This is the subject looking toward the future: "I realized I had a responsibility to come out with my story" (86).

Like Henson, Ruff-O'Herne opens her narrative by positioning herself as a grandmother whose grandchildren ask for her stories of childhood and representing her life narrative as an act of generosity and love carried from one generation to the next. As is the case with Henson, Ruff-O'Herne presents a narrative of childhood and early adolescence, a time before the forced prostitution of the comfort station. The first half of *50 Years* narrates the story of an idyllic childhood as the daughter of Dutch colonists in Indonesia and her adolescent immersion in the rituals of colonial femininity (the first ball, first ready-made dress, first infatuation). "They were happy days," she recalls, "without a care in the world, a sheltered environment in which I grew up as part of an innocent generation when girls were still virgins on their wedding day" (31). When Ruff-O'Herne turns to the narrative of forced incarceration after the Japanese occupation, she provides an ethnography of internment camp life, describing the fight for physical and emotional survival and for the survival of Christian values in the midst of hunger, sickness, and degrading living conditions. Always she represents herself as an unfailing Catholic, turning to the Bible and to other prayer books for support, giving to others with Christian generosity, and maintaining the values of family love and protection. When she tells of her forced removal from the prison camp and her subsequent life in the comfort station, she emphasizes the solidarity among the girls and women as they confronted and endured forced prostitution, and her continual resistance to being raped: "Never once did any Japanese rape me without a violent struggle" (93). She also testifies to the redemptive power of her Catholic faith and her unfailing belief in God: "My inner strength came from my faith, from prayer and from God" (101).

Henson and Ruff-O'Herne write radically different narratives of childhood and adolescence. Henson's is a narrative of poverty and illegitimacy; Ruff-O'Herne's of privilege, wealth, and comfort. Henson's is a narrative emphasizing resistance to colonialism; Ruff-O'Herne's represents Dutch Indonesia as paradise, failing to comment on issues of colonial relations. But they share discursive frameworks through which they reframe the prostitution script into the violation of rights script and make it part of a larger narrative. As devoted Catholics they entwine rights discourse with the discourse of Christian faith, including its language of redemption and forgiveness. They situate themselves in their roles as daughter, wife, mother, and grandmother, identifying their survival with traditional female roles sanctioned by the church, writing themselves into social subjectivity out of the social death they experienced as sex prisoners.

Critically, Henson and Ruff-O'Herne come from cultures in which the concept of human rights is yoked to Christian concepts of betterment and redemption and to Enlightenment liberalism, traditions that place primary value on the individual and her moral worth, regardless of gender, race, ethnicity, age, and social status—in other words, regardless of social location (Weatherley 18). These cultural values sanction and legitimate extended autobiographical acts through which the narrator claims that integrity, and enacts self-determination, in these two cases within the context of Catholicism. As a result of the difference of their cultural location, Henson and O'Herne write beyond ur-testimony, telling the story of a life and its multiple meanings. In this way they find a way to write beyond the fixed script and fixed identity of former "comfort woman," even as they testify to the anguished experience of social death.

Chunghee Sarah Soh notes that, "because of the historical and cultural legacy of the hierarchical social relational patterns, many Koreans have yet to learn how to practice in everyday life the rhetoric of human rights in the sense of respecting personal autonomy of the individual regardless their gender, age, and social status" (1998). Soh, in this instance analyzing the ways in which survivors from Korea, Taiwan, and Indonesia are being urged by some activists *not* to accept money from the Asian Women's Fund, points to the cultural differences separating the diverse women whose acts of witnessing collectively produced the identity of "comfort woman." Located in cultures influenced by the legacies of Confucianism and Islam, subjects of cultures that privilege role-based and duty-based morality in service to social harmony through a hierarchical concept of social order, activists and survivors in some communities approach the discourse of rights differently than those activists and survivors located in cultures influenced by Western liberal notions of autonomy and self-determination.

CIRCULATING THE PAST OF SEXUAL VIOLENCE

Released into the global flows of the rights regime, the narratives of survivors circulate beyond the local sites of telling to connect with audiences in governmental and civic spheres elsewhere. These audiences put the stories to various, often contradictory, uses. The increasingly public exchange around stories of sexual slavery and demands for reparation in South Korea, for instance, has exposed the imbrications of hetero-national masculinity and pan-Asian economic relationships. Government leaders have remained resistant to claiming compensation from the Japanese government, due perhaps to "patriarchal-national pride" in an ennobling nationalist narrative of virile resistance and to the government's desire to channel Japanese money to other national projects (Field 24–5). If the stories told by the former sex prisoners test the political stakes in publicly remembering a compromised past of shame and complicity (Korean brokers, after all, provided young girls and women to the Japanese military), they also test and unsettle contemporary gender relations in the nation. "For both the Japanese and South Korean governments," suggests Hyun Sook Kim, "the women survivors of sexual slavery may pose a serious threat precisely because these women are new subjects who have stepped out of their class-gender positions and who are revealing a partial truth about the nations' hidden past that has officially been rendered invisible" (100).

In Japan, the issue of forced military prostitution "has become a litmus test of attitudes about war responsibility and the construction of public memory" (Ueno 129).[19] Narratives of survivors have been invoked in the context of feminist critiques of patriarchal nationalism and the masculinist state and leftist critiques of resurgent state fascism. Most prominently, they have provoked textbook debates about how the national past should be remembered. In an extended discussion of the politics of apology and reparation, Field notes that "education" becomes the contested site of enacting or rejecting responsibility for past actions. To teach about past actions and events is to establish the "truth of the past," to accept the need for reflection upon that past, and to ensure national acceptance of responsibility (37–39). In this "civil war over memory" (Ueno 132), over what information about World War II should be included in primary- and secondary-level history books, progressive historians give credence to the testimony of the former sex prisoners, which they read for its evidentiary value. Their antagonists from the Liberalist History Research Group debunk the truthfulness of the narratives, arguing that the evidence available does not indicate that there was sex slavery, only that there was prostitution with willing prostitutes.[20] Both sides approach survivor narratives through a positivist methodology (Ueno 133–5). Thus the debate focuses not on the problem of suffering but on historiography—the means by which facts are asserted, verified, and interpreted. The narratives released by former sex prisoners into the public sphere in Japan are in this instance relegated to the category of "damaged truth-telling."

The narratives of survivors also circulate to audiences in broadly dispersed diasporic Asian civil spheres. In the United States, where the Asian American population stands at some ten million, up dramatically from the numbers in the immediate post–World War II era, the anguished history of Korean survivors has become a defining site of political activism and consciousness-raising.[21] Public testimony by women who are positioned within the diasporic community in the United States as "mothers" and "grandmothers" (Hein 1998, 110) have become occasions for reclaiming a diasporic history, a transnational "nationalist" identity, and a shared past characterized by poverty and racial discrimination (Hein 1998, 111).[22] The "ethnic" identity galvanized around the informational displays, the archives, and the testimonies of former sex prisoners on college campuses composes a new "global" ethnicity. The young second-generation Korean Americans who organize campus events, such as the one on the University of Michigan campus, may understand themselves anew as former colonials (of Japan) even if they have never lived outside the United States. In effect, the intense transnational interest in the memories of Japanese actions in World War II reveals the ways in which human rights discourse energizes diasporic communities of affiliation.

Survivor narratives have also reached diverse feminist communities, energizing nationally-and transnationally-based activism. For Japanese feminists, writes Hein, "the extreme misery of the military comfort women…has become part of a larger critique of gender relations in Japan, both past and present" (Hein 1999, 349–50). For feminists organizing nationally in Japan and South Korea and others organizing globally to recognize and challenge contemporary institutionalized forms of sexual exploitation of girls and women and other forms of "traffic in women," the narratives of survivors have sparked feminist critiques of sex tourism and military sex systems as aspects of the contemporary global flows of people, capital, and power. For other feminists working transnationally, they have provided occasions for challenging the sovereignty of the nation-state and its authority over women's lives (Thoma 120). In Western nations such as the United States, the narratives have offered occasions to enact an Asian American transnational feminism (Thoma 121) in a way that places issues of Asian American feminism at the center of a U.S.-based feminist agenda. As a result, stories of former sex prisoners seed pan-Asian alliances and feed into and challenge the imperial discourses of a Western feminism that considers itself the site for universal understanding of and remedies for the violations of the rights of women around the world.

Finally, in the late 1990s another site of circulation, reception, and subsequent reproduction of the stories of former sex prisoners emerged in the West. Novels by young writers in Western nations began to circulate that take the history of forced military prostitution as background and/or survivors as their protagonists, among them Nora Okja Keller's *Comfort Woman* (1997); Simone Lazaroo's *An Australian Fiancé* (2000); Chang-rae Lee's *Gesture Life* (1999); and Teo Hsu-Ming's *Love and Vertigo* (2000). Imaginative literature now offers more latitude for the exploration of possible subjectivities for former sex prisoners and greater aesthetic and affective license to imagine alternative forms of experiencing and surviving structures of feeling under the duress of the silenced past. In *Comfort Woman*, for instance, the Asian-Hawaiian Keller invokes the indigenous Korean tradition of shamanism as she situates the survivor of forced prostitution as a medium connecting immigrant South Koreans in the United States and the ghosts of the spirit world carried across the Pacific.

Keller draws on a cultural history in which women, mostly from impoverished backgrounds, become shamans after profound suffering that signals spirit possession (See Chen n.p.). What these novels collectively mine is the diasporic condition in which immigrants struggle to bring the past with them in the traversals of time and space, and children struggle to understand the difference of their parents in the context of their own multicultural identifications.

In sum, the personal narratives of former sex prisoners, as they have circulated around the globe in the last decade via personal testimony, official testimony at hearings and tribunals, in print, in visual media, on websites, and in such scattered venues as campus lecture halls, have energized and reproduced the international order based on human rights and at the same time spurred localized critiques and defenses of nation-state sovereignty, new forms of identity at once national and transnational, new debates about memory, and imaginative genres of reproduction. We can situate the accumulated force of these narratives in interlocking cultural formations having to do with the scattered effects of the international order of human rights, but we must also recognize how the narratives, as they are invoked and refused, are caught up and oftentimes recuperated "into dominant scripts and cultural fantasies" (Hesford 1999, 211)—whether dominant scripts about women's inherent sexual contamination or scripts about women's victimization.

MULTIPLE CONCLUSIONS

We return to the testimony of Kap Soon-Choi on the campus of the University of Michigan on March 11, 2002. "We were so very poor," Kap Soon-Choi began. Introducing her impoverished childhood she told of being given to recruiters by her mother who sought to satisfy the police who had come for her father. She moved quickly to her induction into the routines of the comfort station, becoming more expressive gesturally as she did so and crying periodically.

As an event, Kap Soon-Choi's appearance on this college campus was designed to make the reality of the former sex prisoners and their horrifying past visible to the privileged audience in the United States. At the University of Michigan, the audience confronted Kap Soon-Choi's physical fragility; the uncontrollable affect charging her narration of past events; the layered story of exploitation (by her mother, by the traffickers in women, by her keepers, and by the soldier-clients); and the uncanny conjunction of the "grandmother's" presentation and the translator's youthful voice narrating the story of sexual degradation. The appeals in this intense sensory environment were multiple—horror at the suffering of this woman; anger at the perpetrators; empathy with her suffering; critical awareness and activism.

Organized to build support in the United States for the demands of the former sex prisoners, sponsored campus events like this one can, however, turn witnessing to less ethical effect. In this instance, the survivor was inserted in a programmed format of witnessing. Activist/experts provided historical information for an uninformed audience; a questioner led the testimony through a prepared set of questions; a translator turned testimony into language, phrases, and a narrative that the audience could easily understand. As witness, Kap Soon-Choi was fixed in her narrative of victimization as a subject of human rights, required to take up an essentialized subject position as "former comfort woman," consumed by the audience as an "authentic" victim of rights abuse. Displayed to view, in bodily form and in narrative form, the former comfort woman was made to participate in the repetition of her own social death. For some in the audience she may have figured as a melodramatic spectacle of the "other" who suffers. For others, her story may have elicited exhaustion or impatience.

In the midst of her narrative of intolerable degradation, Kap Soon-Choi inserted another self-figuration that exposed the remainder of shame. Throughout, she positioned herself as more virtuous than the other girls in the comfort station. "My vagina would be torn," she testified, "but I never had an STD." She told of washing the sheets of the other girls to raise money to buy herself out of the comfort station. She told of how some of the other girls would not pay her for the clean sheets. She told of saving all her money and not squandering what little money she made on make-up. Throughout her testimony she kept repeating that she sought to pay her debt so that she could return to see her beloved grandmother. In these rhetorical moves, the older woman, asked to rehearse her narrative of exploitation and degradation, located herself in a story of filial duty, hard work, austerity, self-sacrifice, and physical cleanliness. She attempted to reclaim her body and her character before the audience, to claim, that is, some characterological agency.

Kap Soon-Choi claimed bits of agency, however, by distinguishing herself from other sex prisoners. In rendering unnamed sex slaves as abject "other," she unsettled the bond of collective social identity. Distinguishing herself, she opened a space for members of the audience to respond to her story as an individualized narrative of victimization and survival. Wendy Hesford argues that, to the extent that sites of personal storytelling and rights activism "get caught up in the individualization of injury," they can "foster a kind of passive empathy on the part of viewers predicated on viewer's moral judgments and projected sense of vulnerability and fear for their own lives" (212). The ethical call for collective action on behalf of systematic injustice can be rerouted into a commodified story of individual adversity and survival, especially when the scene of witnessing takes place far away from Southeast Asia in nations founded on individualist ideologies of identity. Looking again at Kap Soon-Choi's moment of witness prompts these cautionary reminders about the ways in which human rights campaigns frame acts of personal witness, thereby constraining the kinds of stories survivors can tell and complicating the narrative and cultural politics attending their reception.

However heterogeneous and unpredictable their reception, however imbricated in the commodification of suffering, courageous acts of public witness such as Kap Soon-Choi's have motivated new formations within the global circuits of rights activism. In December 2000, seventy-four survivors from nine countries testified at the Women's International War Crimes Tribunal on Japan's Military Sexual Slavery that took place in Tokyo. The Tribunal's express charge was the prosecution of Japan for crimes against humanity that were not part of the Tokyo Tribunal held in 1946–48. On December 12, 2000, tribunal judges rendered their decision based on international law in effect during World War II. They found Emperor Hirohito and nine other Japanese officials guilty of sexual slavery and rape, named as crimes against humanity. They also found Japan liable for reparations. Claiming moral but not legal authority in the name of international law and the regime of human rights, the Tribunal condemned Japan for its state-sponsored violence against women. Emerging out of networks and meshworks of local activism and transnational NGO activism in Pacific Rim countries, this "people's tribunal set up by the voices of global civil society" represents a "quasi-legal system" that "engages in distinctive practices of constructing and supporting rights" (Merry 84).

The narratives of former sex prisoners have been authorized by this new "global language of social justice in the world" (Merry 84) and in turn have spurred new alliances and structures for pursuing social justice. The personal narratives of these "grandmothers," all of them in their sixties and seventies, all of them marginalized in so many ways, thus circulate as so many collapsible and rebuildable bridges linking local and global flows: crossing between the everyday acts of remembering the past and larger sociopolitical forces such as the effects of the end of the Cold War and the economic alignments of the economies of the Pacific Rim; between activism in the nationalist context of Korea or Japan or the Philippines and the diasporic imagination of communities in the United States and elsewhere in countries beyond the Pacific Rim region.

To date, there has been no official apology from the Japanese prime minister. While the Japanese government has officially acknowledged the existence of the comfort station system, it has not accepted *legal* responsibility for military sexual slavery before and during World War II. Certain government officials have accepted *moral* responsibility. Prime Minister Obuchi issued an apology to the former comfort women for their forced sexual slavery during World War II in 1998.[23] In 1995, the Japanese government launched the Asian Women's Fund, a private fund established to raise monies from Japanese individuals committed to offering reparations to survivors.[24] Few women have accepted the monies. Many *refuse* to take monies from a private fund, demanding instead formal apology and reparation, including compensation and pledges to educate the young about this history. Unfortunately, the Fund has precipitated rifts within various NGOs working on behalf of former sex prisoners (Soh 1998).[25] Many survivors, who were active in the campaign for apology and reparations, have died. Those still alive are left with their collective identity and what psychic release might come from the reinterpretation of the past.

CHAPTER 6

LIFE SENTENCES: NARRATED LIVES
AND PRISONER RIGHTS IN THE
UNITED STATES

No one shall be subjected to torture or to cruel, inhuman or degrading treatment or punishment.

—International Covenant on Civil and Political Rights

They keep you wrapped up in civil rights. And you spend so much time barking up the civil-rights tree, you don't even know there's a human-rights tree on the same floor.

—*Malcolm X*, "The Ballot or the Bullet"

Ultimately, when a society fails to care what happens to some of its members, believes that certain human beings have forfeited their human rights because of their actions, or fails to hold officials to account for their misdeeds, then it creates the conditions in which human rights violations can thrive.

—*Amnesty International*, United States of America:
Rights for All

Oₙ September 8, 2000, Nelson Mandela stood before a cheering crowd of young Australians in Melbourne's Colonial Stadium to address the World Reconciliation Day tribute concert. World Reconciliation Day had begun as a social studies project of ninth graders at Melbourne's Trinity Grammar School. Here was grassroots activism in practice, a human rights initiative spearheaded by local teenagers who had studied Mandela's life and decided to enlist him in their effort to promote reconciliation between Australia's Indigenous and non-Indigenous peoples.

Prime Minister John Howard, fearing the political repercussions of Mandela's Australian tour, chose not to stand with Mandela that day. Two days before Mandela had told an audience at the Australian National University in Canberra that "the scars of the past remain and fester unless they are addressed," directly alluding to the plight of Australia's Indigenous people. For his part, Howard had been fending off UN charges condemning the living conditions of Indigenous Australians. In response to the charges, Howard denounced the United Nations for its criticism of Australia, called for the reorganization of its committee system, and snubbed Mandela as a way to avoid political embarrassment over Liberal Party policies.

American rights activist and celebrity Rubin "Hurricane" Carter did stand with Mandela, joining him before the estimated crowd of 40,000 present at the benefit concert. Millions more around the world watched the concert on television, and an estimated 300 million people logged on to the simultaneous webcast of the event. Carter's appearance beside Mandela projected to audiences in Australia and around the world intersecting filiations of rights activism: campaigns for black civil rights; for indigenous rights; and for prisoner rights.

Carter stood before the crowd as a former welterweight boxer, convicted murderer, cause célèbre of Bob Dylan's haunting "Hurricane," now human rights activist, who, in the words of Dylan's song "coulda been the champion of the world" but for a miscarriage of the American justice system. Three-and-a-half decades earlier, with the civil rights movement, the growing antiwar movement, the long summers of urban unrest, and the newly empowered Black Panther Party challenging the complacencies of American society, Carter, a rising middleweight boxer in training for the World Championship fight, was arrested for a triple murder in a New Jersey bar. Convicted in 1967, Carter entered prison to serve three life terms.

While incarcerated, Carter began writing his life story, chronicling his impoverished childhood and his adolescence lived in and out of reformatories and jails, chronicling as well the racism of the police and justice systems. In 1974, Viking Press published *The Sixteenth Round: From Number 1 Contender To #45472*. At the same moment, two of the state's key witnesses in his trial reversed their testimony. Carter's cause was joined by celebrity advocates, among them Joan Baez,

Muhammad Ali, Roberta Flack, and Bob Dylan whose top-selling "Hurricane" made Carter's name a household word across the airwaves of the United States. Carter's life narrative brought his story to a broad public, spurred celebrity activism, and motivated a young African American teenager Lazarus Martin to urge his Canadian guardians (Sam Chaiton and Terry Swinton) to dedicate themselves to securing Carter's release. Chaiton has said that *The Sixteenth Round* "was the first book Lazarus had ever bought. He read it, and was very moved and inspired by Rubin's story. He decided to write Rubin Carter a letter. Rubin Carter, who was serving a triple life sentence in a New Jersey state prison at the time for three murders that he did not commit, wrote Lazarus back. Thus began a friendship between the two of them, and the rest of us, our Canadian group, slowly got drawn into Rubin's life as well" (CNN.com). It would take twenty-four years, and the tireless advocacy of Chaiton and Swinton, working in concert with the self-educated Carter, for Carter's indictment to be dismissed and for him to be released from prison in 1988 on the grounds that the prosecution had withheld evidence in the trial. Upon his release Carter immigrated to Canada and has since toured the United States and the world as a spokesperson for human rights. In his capacity as a human rights activist he joined Mandela on the stage in Melbourne.

News accounts of Carter's appearance with Mandela at the World Reconciliation Day concert were not all positive. Writing in the Australian *Herald Sun* the next week, the conservative columnist Andrew Bolt condemned organizers of the event for bringing Carter to the stage to stand beside Mandela. For this reporter Mandela's aura, his moral authority, was unassailable; but Carter's moral authority remained dubious. Bolt offered up a counter-narrative to the narrative projected in the Dylan song and in the 1999 film *The Hurricane* of Carter as a victim of a racist American justice system. Bolt's Carter remained a far more violent man, his life story a far more sordid affair. Begging the question of his innocence, Bolt qualified Carter's claim to the identity of victim of injustice, and figured him as a perpetrator of violence.

Two ex-prisoners stood beside one another on that Melbourne platform. One of them remains a revered citizen of the world whose narrative of his life, *The Long Walk to Freedom*, charted his rise to political and moral leadership, incarceration as a political prisoner, and vision of the future, modeling both heroism and reconciliation for his country and for those fighting injustice around the world. The other remains an ambivalent figure. For many people, Carter is a former "political" prisoner of a racist justice system, who has dedicated his life to helping others wrongly convicted. For others, Carter remains a naively lionized criminal, whose gritty life narrative spoke to leftists, intellectuals, and celebrities only too eager to discredit the American justice system as racist. This doubled projection confuses the roles of victim and perpetrator, roles central to the regime of human rights. It is this confusion that complicates the ways in which narrated lives circulate in human rights campaigns on behalf of prisoners in the United States.

THE RIGHTS REGIME IN THE UNITED STATES

For decades, the United States has been a major nexus in the transnational flows of the international regime of human rights. The UN headquarters in New York, as the iconic symbol and material locus for rights projects, constantly focuses attention on the United States as the preeminent hub for human rights debates and campaigns. People from around the world travel to and through the United States, looking to the country for its great potential to provide platforms, media outlets, and the human resources necessary for promoting recognition and advocacy, even when their campaigns challenge the individualistic norms of the American ethos.

Stories of abuse elsewhere are mobilized by the U.S. government to reinforce American claims to the moral high ground as champion of human rights around the world, thereby turning other peoples' testimonies into parables of America's ethical commitment to the betterment of all people. Stories of rights abuse elsewhere also serve America's economic and political interests, turning the contemporary regime of human rights into a conduit for U.S. neo-imperial global extension. But this is only part of the story of the United States and the international regime of human rights. Certainly, the U.S. government participated fully and centrally in the debates that eventuated in the UDHR in 1948. But it has been slow in most cases, and has refused in others, to ratify UN covenants and conventions. Even in cases where the United States has signed and ratified treaties, it continues to evade certain terms of those treaties, effectively undermining their international force. "It is a paradox," writes Amnesty International, "that the nation that did so much to articulate and codify human rights in its foundation documents has so consistently resisted the effective functioning of an international framework to protect these principles and values" (133). Indeed, for many Americans, the U.S. Constitution takes precedence over any international document, treaty, convention, or covenant. Michael Ignatieff attributes this position to "rights narcissism," which he parses as "the conviction that the land of Jefferson and Lincoln has nothing to learn from international rights norms" (2001b, 13).

As the world's most powerful nation, the United States imagines and positions itself as the exporter and guarantor of democratic freedoms and the civil and political rights of peoples around the globe, especially those in developing countries. Yet the United States has often been challenged by its own citizens and by politicians and activists around the world for its failure to live up to its espoused values, for its support of perpetrators of human rights violations, and for its imposition of Western-based right norms upon the rest of the world. The *realpolitik* of national interest, the myth of American exceptionalism, and the unassailable principle of state sovereignty complicate and render inconsistent the role of the United States in the international order of human rights. While the government, the media, and the people of the United States report and expose rights violations elsewhere, they frequently have difficulty acknowledging rights violations at home.

Our previous case studies focused on the publication, circulation, and reception of stories told by people suffering abuses elsewhere than the United States. In these contexts the U.S. government and its citizens have variously acted to defend the rights of others. In this chapter, we turn the lens back on the United States to explore an arena of human rights violations largely invisible within the country. This fourth case study finds stories of human rights abuses coming from within the prisons of "homeland" America.

PUNISHING RIGHTS

Before the war on terrorism grabbed daily headlines and focused attention on the threat of Islamic fundamentalists and terrorist organizations such as al-Qaeda, America's longest-lived, albeit undeclared, wars were the wars on drugs and crime. Fear of crime is pervasive in American society, and for good reason. The United States has the highest per capita crime rate of all the developed countries. Periodically, the media blare out stories of mass killings—at schools and on campuses, inside private offices and public buildings, in people's homes. Americans exhibit multiple forms of anxiety about the levels of violent and nonviolent crime with which they live, adding locks to doors, buying guns, disappearing inside gated communities. People everywhere demand a vigorous war on crime. A large number of them support the death penalty. The American public wants to be protected by the State from the eruptions of violence and the loss of property. It wants the convicted locked up and kept out of sight.

If fear of crime is pervasive in American society, so too is the culture of punishment. At the beginning of the twenty-first century, the United States incarcerates the highest proportion of its citizenry of all the industrial democracies and the developing countries of the world. In 1996, 427 out of every 100,000 people lived life behind bars (an average across all states); in 2001 the rate was 690 per 100,000 (Sentencing Project figure). In 2003, the *New York Times* reported on its editorial page that the incarceration rate had reached "a staggering 1 in 143" (August 1, 2003, A22). The U.S. incarceration rate bests that of Russia, which in 2001 stood at 644 out of every 100,000 people. It exceeds by five to eight times that of other industrial democracies such as Australia, Germany, and Japan. In 2003, approximately 2.16 million people were living life behind bars, an increasing number of them awaiting execution. In 2001, a total of 5.6 million people in the United States were either in prison or had been imprisoned, a figure representing 2.7 of the adult population of 210 million (Bureau of Justice Statistics).

These figures tell only part of the story. Another part has to do with who lives behind bars. By the end of the 1990s approximately one of three young black men were subjects of various kinds of "supervision" within the criminal justice system (Currie 13). The proportion of men of color currently in the penal system far exceeds the proportion of men of color in the population. From 1970 to 1996 the number of women in prison increased thirteenfold, from 5,600 to 75,000, and the proportion of incarcerated women has continued to increase. In 2003 the Bureau of Justice Statistics of the Department of Justice predicted that one of every fifteen persons (or 6.6 percent of the population) will do time in America's prisons sometime in their lifetime, if recent rates hold constant. The Bureau estimated that 32 percent of black males and 17 percent of Hispanic males will do time, as compared to 5.9 percent of white males.

In the last twenty years harsh sentencing guidelines, prompted by three-strikes laws requiring incarceration for a third conviction, have been responsible for the phenomenal rate of growth of the U.S. prison population. This expansion of the prison population at all levels, local, state, and federal, has been accompanied by the building boom in maximum-security facilities, the elimination of educational opportunities within the prisons, and the curb on access to legal counsel and legal recourse for complaints. The privatization of prison facilities has brought the expansion of the prison workforce, including chain gangs. Outside the prison system, racial profiling and racism in the justice system ensures that the proportion of prisoners of color, including the fastest-growing group, women of color, remains far in excess of the proportion of people of color in the general population. And since the mid-1980s, the pace of executions has accelerated, taking the lives of juveniles and the mentally handicapped. As Elliot Currie has argued, "Short of major wars, mass incarceration has been the most thoroughly implemented government social program of our time" (Currie 21).

The "modern" penal system had begun in post-Enlightenment America as a new system of penitence. Instead of the public spectacles of the scaffold or the pillory and the executions that attended many offenses, reformers called for a new kind of prison where, through work, silence, isolation, and self-regulation, the criminal could be remade into a productive citizen of the republic. Thus was born the project of betterment, the "house of repentance," the "penitentiary" imagined, designed, and first introduced in the state of Pennsylvania.[1] Actual conditions in the penal system, however, came under constant scrutiny, inspiring successive waves of reform.

Despite reform movements, the judicial system of the United States adopted a "hand's off doctrine" toward the treatment of prisoners in penitentiaries well into the mid-twentieth century, tacitly sanctioning a zone of the despotic where subjects were denied civil rights and recourse to legal action. After the Attica rebellion of 1971,[2] the courts began to chip away at this doctrine in a series of rulings that recognized the degrading conditions of penal life in specific states. In 1974 the Supreme Court held in Wolff versus McDonnell that "there is no iron curtain drawn between the Constitution and the prisons of this country," and accorded prisoners some basic civil rights—the right to litigation and the right to due process among them (Specter and Kupers 240–1).[3] A steady stream of litigation on inhumane treatment and the emergence of law firms dedicated to prisoner rights followed.[4] In the last decade, however, the courts have reversed that trend, making it easier for prison officials to counter prisoner lawsuits, restricting access to law libraries, and reducing funds available for attorney fees (Specter and Kupers 245). This retreat took place at the same time the war on crime sent more and more people to the nation's prisons.

By the last decades of the twentieth century, the nation's penal system had become a system without any myths of penitence and transformation. Talk of the penal project as one of rehabilitation has long given way to talk of "incapacitation" and retribution in a system that effectively "warehouses" a large segment of the population (Parenti 247).[5] Increasingly, prisoner rights activists and scholars argue that it is time to accept that "the purpose of imprisonment is punishment" and that "prisons simply cannot be reformed" (Dodge 266). They point to the increasing number of prisoners who have been exonerated by DNA evidence. They call for a moratorium on executions. They call, as does Angela Davis, for the abolishment of the prison, given the penal system's use in relegating large proportions of people of color to a life of degradation under state surveillance and state-administered dehumanization (Davis 2003 n.p.). On the other side, however, those who have suffered and survived violent crimes build an ever more effective network of activists working on behalf of victims' rights. They bring their own personal stories of anguish and anger to the public.

THE SUBJECT OF PRISON RIGHTS

How likely is it that the general public will be moved to concern and action by personal narratives coming from the convicted and incarcerated when many Americans believe that people who are incarcerated deserve whatever punishment they receive, including, for those convicted of murder, state-sanctioned death by various means; when many believe that "the country," understood abstractly, is safer when criminals are locked up and "keys thrown away"? Such responses register anxiety about the high level of crime in the United States and the high levels of recidivism (measured at 65 percent). They also expose the stereotypes people bring to their engagements with the stories of the convicted and incarcerated. As one death row inmate writes, "we're the new vampires and ghosts. We're the people who've been completely transformed by the legends and myths. We're now the replacements, the ones they warn their children about" (Arriens 85).

In the culture of fear that pervades the United States, the convicted and incarcerated are represented in the justice and penal systems, in the media, and in public exchanges through the rhetoric of "otherness." They are labeled "unruly" and "intractable," and in some cases as "barbarous" and "uncivilized." Male prisoners are projected as embodying the essentially brutal and violent sides of a hypermasculinity read through ongoing stereotypes from slavery and colonialism (most often the masculinities of the poor and of minority communities) (Sabo et al. 14). Female inmates are projected as embodying the essentially errant forms of a patriarchally defined femininity, failed motherhood, unloving wifehood, sexual profligacy, and degraded, out-of-control addiction. Their otherness is marked as failed nurturing and failed heterosexuality. In America's imaginary, the derelict, the down-and-out, the chronically impoverished, the youth of minority communities, reckless and sexually licentious women—peoples projected as threats to the "proper" norms of middle-class America—deserve to be sent away and forgotten in prison. Moreover, in the popularization of scientific discourses, criminality becomes for many an essentialist category of character, a genetic predisposition, an inescapable destiny, a fixed identity. These attitudes toward perpetrators of crime affect the stories that people want to hear from the convicted and incarcerated and the ethical responsiveness of audiences to them.

Justice system professionals, prison officials, and members of the public expect and demand to hear from the convicted personal stories confessing to crimes, admitting guilt, expressing remorse. In early stages of investigation, the confession, putting the personal signature to a statement of guilt, paves the way for conviction, sentencing, and plea-bargaining. After incarceration, confession ensures that the system has exacted justice and that the convicted can be led to an efficacious self-policing and a moral renewal. At the parole hearing, confession proves critical to a positive outcome. Confession sustains both justice and penal systems by reproducing the master narrative of responsibility and guilt (see Knox note 8). In fact, the performativity of confession becomes an end in itself, more efficacious for the convicted and incarcerated than the truth of confession. That one confesses becomes more important than whether or not one tells the truth in one's confession.

Confession maintains the boundary "divid[ing] the guilty from the innocent, and the 'socially valuable' from the 'socially dangerous'" (Knox para. 30).[6] That is, whether truthful or false, it marks the boundary between victim and perpetrator so critical to the state's agenda of punishment, and the agenda of human rights campaigns. The subject of human rights is commonly understood as the victim-subject, deserving of dignity, inviolate physical integrity, changed conditions and changed status within the nation. He or she is the subject to be educated, to be healed, the subject to whom restitution is owed. Human rights campaigns rely for their moral force on "victims of injustice" to make their case. In effect, then, storytellers in the context of rights campaigns are expected to take up the subject position of "innocent" victims; they are expected to be able to occupy that position unambiguously.

And yet the person whose rights are violated cannot always be assumed to occupy the subject position of innocent victim. This is indeed the case with prison inmates claiming violation of their human rights. Many of those convicted have confessed to crimes. Many are guilty of crimes. All have been "found guilty" of their crimes in the legal jurisdiction of the courts, stripped of their defining citizenship rights, and "reduced to bodies absorbing mandatory labor and institutionalized punishment" (Rodríguez 417). But here they are, "perpetrators" telling stories in which they are positioned as victims of injustice and abuse, of cruel and unusual punishment, asking the audience to accord them humanity and demand redress on their behalf. Telling stories of victimization, inmates and their advocates confound the differentiated identities of victim and perpetrator, confuse the alignment of innocence and victimization. Appealing for recognition, they provoke confusion about the affective grounds upon which the intersubjective exchange between victim/survivor and reader/listener takes place. In effect, they test the limits of the human rights paradigm for judgment and action.

The contexts of production, circulation, and reception of personal stories become particularly vexed when those convicted as perpetrators or their advocates make claims about unjust and inhumane treatment in the justice and penal systems. How can the convicted make their appeal to an audience without eliciting abhorrence, rage, fear, or antipathy? How can they claim universal human rights when they have been stripped of citizenship rights by virtue of their conviction? How can activists involved in campaigns for prisoner rights put a human face on suffering inside prisons when the evidentiary witness of the convicted remains suspicious? How can the incarcerated and their advocates expect any kind of audience for their testimony to victimization? In what follows, we pursue these questions as we survey sites of personal narrating in campaigns for prisoner rights.

Prison Narratives and Political Prisoners

In the 1960s and early 1970s, the U.S. prison system became the site of activism, the ground of narrative, and the object of analysis as convicts and ex-convicts of color analyzed the systems of oppression that made prison the social institution it had become, especially in the lives of America's minorities. Activists inside and outside prison were reading Frantz Fanon's *Wretched of the Earth*, adopting his analysis of the psychological processes of colonialism's degradation of its subject peoples and heeding his call to a cathartically revolutionary violence.

Some 750,000 copies of Fanon's book were sold in the latter half of the decade (Rushdy 46). Liberation movements in Asia, Africa, Indonesia, and Latin America, some violent, some peaceful, invoked the UN principle of the self-determination of peoples. Ché Guevara, Fidel Castro, and Patrice Lumumba galvanized leftist intellectuals and black activists in the United States with their calls for antiracist and anticolonial struggles. And the escalating war in Vietnam radicalized youth, civil rights workers, and black activists who analyzed just who was fighting and dying in America's war against an underground army of resistance. Amidst these local, national, and global activisms, men in America's prisons began locating the connections linking their own histories to the systemic conditions of their incarceration and the nation's institutionalization of violence at home and abroad.

A new kind of writing emerged from the prisons, those "critical space[s]" prompting "alternative social and political practices of counterhegemonic resistance movements" (Harlow 10). Authored primarily by African American prisoners (former and current), it offered a radically different point of departure for writing. According to H. Bruce Franklin, there were "two overlapping groups of prison authors" discernible: "the political activist thrust into prison, and the common criminal thrust into political activism" (242). The most famous of the former were Martin Luther King and Angela Davis. The latter category included Malcolm X, Eldridge Cleaver, and George Jackson. With their passionate, angry, and exhortatory rhetoric, these prison activists began to write a new history of the system that, from its inception, had functioned to control large segments of the American population considered unruly, less than fully reformable, notably escaped, freed, and then emancipated blacks who were subject to a racist legal system from the Dred Scott decision to the Black Codes of the Jim Crow south to the harsher sentences of the mid-twentieth century; the poor and immigrant; and the "wayward," particularly unwed women. In extending their analysis from personal history to the history of imprisonment in the United States, African American prison writers began to understand "imprisonment" as "first of all the loss of a *people's* freedom." "From this point of view," Franklin notes, "American society as a whole constitutes the primary prison" (Franklin 1978, 244). In *The Sixteenth Round*, for instance, Carter denounced the United States as "a penitentiary with a flag" (210), thereby issuing a radical indictment of a system that had evolved to keep the poor and people of color under the surveillance of the State.

Through their life writing, radical black activists at once bore witness to this history and engaged in the production of "radical knowledge," what Dylan Rodríguez describes as "new vernaculars of social truth" (411). Collectively, the personal narratives of black radical activists of the 1960s and 1970s functioned as so many experiential manifestoes, bearing the prominent features of manifesto as a "sign of political combat" (Lyon 29). While each individual narrative unfolded through its own logic, sometimes essayistic, sometimes epistolary, sometimes chronologically organized autobiography, most incorporated the three conventions Janet Lyon identifies as features of the manifesto. They placed the contemporary moment in a foreshortened history of oppression; they listed grievances or demands; and their exhortatory rhetoric called people to collective action (15). As they exposed the forces of oppression and disadvantage to light, they also called for a new future. Writing under the sign of hope (Smith 1993, 159), they invoked a millennial present (Lyon 30) and a future that was "now." Moreover, in their statement of grievances and call for new futures, manifestoes commanded affective response—shame, anger, and rage prominent among them—through their own charged affect.

Undisputedly, the most influential of the narratives of prison house conversion was and continues to be *The Autobiography of Malcolm X* (1965), "must" reading for incarcerated men (and common reading for minority peoples around the world). In this as-told-to narrative, the story of transformation unfolds schematically in the very succession of names and identities attached to a series of chapter titles. Malcolm X reconstructs his past as a journey of discovery and revelation that takes him from the identity of "Mascot," through Homeboy, Harlemite, Detroit Red, Hustler, and Satan, his moniker in prison, to Minister Malcolm X, Icarus, and the internationalist El-Hajj Malik El-Shabazz. But Malcolm X's narrative is far more than an individualist fable of a Franklinian protagonist who through dint of hard work, intelligence, and opportunistic acumen makes his way from impoverished child to the influential leader of America's Black Muslims. Issued in the midst of the turbulent 1960s, this personal narrative was about far more than the reform of the individual. Its appeal attracted audiences within the African American community, other minority communities in the United States and elsewhere, white liberals and leftists active in civil rights and social justice campaigns, and people engaged in anticolonial and antiracist struggles throughout the world. Malcolm offered a story of reform within the prison system, but reform whose end game was black pride, black self-help, and black resistance to a corrupt and rights-denying state.

The Autobiography of Malcolm X, and the narratives that followed, *Soul on Ice* (1968), *Soledad Brother* (1970), and *Angela Davis: An Autobiography* (1974), turned the experiential ground of prison into performative sites of radical resistance. Through these autobiographical texts, the black radical activists forged what Janet Lyon identifies as the "signature pronoun" of manifesto, the "we" of "we the people" (11). Witnessing to the failures of modern representative democracy, they called multiple audiences into being—fellow prisoners of color, the larger community of color within the United States, the community of the dispossessed around the world, the comfortable and complacent beneficiaries of the oppressive state, the prison authorities— but most importantly a "we" that was asked to understand the State, American society, and "they" in radically new terms. Such communicative exchange with the outside world, about the world inside and its meanings in American society, transported narrators out of their cells and into the public sphere, constituting an imaginative community of listeners whose listening conferred authority and power back upon the writers (Ross 1996, 90). Critically, this collective identification motivated prison intellectuals and activists to call for solidarity among inmates "protest[ing] conditions rather than attacking one another" (Chevigny xiv).

In *Soul On Ice*, Eldridge Cleaver meditated, through the prism of discrete autobiographical essays, on black masculinity, by the way charting the transformation from an angry, violent, and psychically enslaved manhood through politicization to rebirth into a new subjectivity as socialist prophet. As he develops an increasingly complex analysis of American racism, Cleaver situates the conditions of psychic enslavement within the nation to events and forces unfolding without the nation. "The police do on the domestic level," he writes, "what the armed forces do on the international level: protect the way of life of those in power" (129). Announcing *Angela Davis: An Autobiography* as "a political autobiography" (x), Davis chronicled her involvement in the Black Liberation movement. In her *Preface*, she forged the universal "we" of manifesto when she explained her reluctance to write an individualizing narrative of an extraordinary woman: "I felt that such a book might end up obscuring the most essential fact: the forces that have made my life what it is are the very same forces that have shaped and misshaped the lives of millions of my people" (ix). In the letters collected in *Soledad Brother*, George Jackson at once developed an argument for revolution through black empowerment, prison reform, and the destabilization of capitalism, and traced his own fitful project of unlearning "Western habits."

Answering a call "toward history" which, he writes, he must "follow" (98), he expanded his field of attention to global struggles around the world, attaching his awakening to events in such places as the Congo and Vietnam. With every letter, Jackson projected the "we" of collective struggle and projected himself as educator in a rhetoric overflowing with anger and rage. The narrated lives of Cleaver and Jackson, like Malcolm X's, presented versions of the conversion narrative, struggles of reform not toward individualist triumph so much as toward the agency of communal resistance.

Locating struggle globally, as contemporary narratives in Australia have done, these autobiographical manifestoes invoked the language of human rights in their histories, grievances, claims, and agendas for action. Early in the 1960s, Malcolm X spoke forcefully about the importance of linking struggles in the United States to the human rights regime, as Marcus Garvey and W.E.B. Dubois had done before him (U.S. Human Rights Network 5). In "The Ballot or the Bullet," delivered in 1964, he urged black activists to turn from the language of civil rights to the language of human rights as the ground of their analyses and their appeals. To remain tethered to a civil rights agenda, he argued, limited the arena of political activism to the national boundaries of the United States and "the jurisdiction of Uncle Sam." Civil rights struggles foreclosed the possibility of international support from "our African brothers and our Asian brothers and our Latin-American brothers" who "cannot open their mouths and interfere in the domestic affairs of the United States." "When you expand the civil-rights struggle to the level of human rights," he continued, "you can then take the case of the black man in this country before the nations in the UN. You can take it before the General Assembly. You can take Uncle Sam before a world court. But the only level you can do it on is the level of human rights" (58). Speaking as a "man of the world," as El-Hajj Malik El-Shabazz, Malcolm X linked the political activism of the black community within the United States to the anti-colonial struggles for self-determination elsewhere in the world, thus expanding the arena of demand for acknowledging and addressing grievances. In the 1970s, prison activists would petition the United Nation's Human Rights Commission regarding the conditions in American prisons, asserting "colonized people's right to fight against alien domination and racist regimes as codified in the Geneva Convention" (Acoli 151). Their actions would inspire human rights activism elsewhere, particularly in communities with high rates of incarceration, as in indigenous communities in Australia and black communities in South Africa.

As important to prison activists as international discourse on self-determination, genocide, and torture, was the international attention focused on "political prisoners" held in detention around the world. The imprisonment, transportation, and torture of political dissidents became for the decades of the Cold War a particularly telling site for charges of human rights abuses (Neier 368). Leaders in the West charged the Soviet Union and its satellite states with gross violations of the rights of dissidents. Leaders in the Communist bloc charged the West with supporting regimes, most notably those in Latin America, which secured their rule through the incarceration, torture, and murder of political dissidents. As the concern about the fate of political dissidents in repressive regimes increased, organizations emerged to galvanize activism on behalf of dissidents languishing behind prison walls. In 1961 British lawyer Peter Berenson placed a notice for "An Appeal for Amnesty 1961" in the *London Observer*, calling for the release of what he termed "prisoners of conscience" around the world. With that notice, AI came into being, serving as a lightening rod in campaigns to identify and to support prisoners as political dissidents.

Prison activists not only traced the genealogy of the contemporary penal system to the system of chattel slavery and its legacies in the lives of blacks, but they also began to proclaim themselves "political prisoners" (Chevigny xiv). Those targeted by the FBI's counterintelligence project (COINTELPRO) for their political activities in various resistance movements, among them the Nation of Islam, the Black Liberation Movement, the Black Panther Party, the Republic of New Afrika, the Puerto Rican *independentistas*, and the American Indian Movement, defined themselves as victims of an unjust, repressive State bent on eliminating them. So too did prisoners who, while incarcerated, "converted" through the testimony and the analysis of black activists who came into the system. Analyzing "the connection between political prisoners and the prison as a state apparatus of repression" (Davis, "Interview" website), activist writers inside and outside the prisons, among them Davis, Jackson, and Daniel Berrigan, called the world to attention and made the case nationally and internationally that the United States incarcerated people for their political views and actions. They produced a counter-identity and counter-narrative to that of the State that the only people in America's prisons were common criminals and terrorists.

Individually and collectively, these life narratives from the 1960s and 1970s contested the modernist, democratic project as they "critique[d] the uneven implementations of universalism" (Lyon 32). "The manifesto makes legible the recidivist failures of the

Enlightenment," comments Lyon, "and in so doing seems to rededicate the as yet incomplete projects of modernity." "At the same time," she continues, "it constitutes a repudiation of modernity, whose contradictions it bares" (Lyon 34). Paradoxically, as prison activists invoked human rights frameworks and identities, either implicitly or explicitly, they exposed the failure of the modernist democratic project by cataloguing its exclusions. But they failed to critique the gendered stakes of incarceration, conversion, activism, and universalism. In this they projected the legacy of an exclusionary gender politics, an exclusionary project carried forward through the critiques themselves.

LEGACIES

After the late 1970s, the Reagan presidency brought the wars on crime and drugs, "get tough" sentencing policies with their reduction of sentencing flexibility, and a political climate that muted the voices of radical prison activists and dispersed citizen concern for the rights of the accused. The cause of prisoners identifying, and identified by their advocates, as "political" and "social" prisoners became less publicized. Yet that cause has persisted and continues to yoke personal narrative and the discourse of human rights as incarcerated intellectuals continue "to map out new 'cognitive territories' within which ways of knowing, feeling, and living the Experience of prison create new spaces of dissent" (Rodríguez 413). Mumia Abu Jamal, Leonard Peltier, Geronimo Pratt, Assata Shakur, Susan Rosenberg (now released), Sundiato Acoli, Alejandrina Torres, Marilyn Buck, Timothy Little Rock Reed (released and now dead)[7] are some but by no means all of the inmates whose names have continued to spark advocacy.

Stories of political detention have been kept in circulation by activist organizations, such as Freedom Now, primarily through websites designed to inform, inspire, politicize, organize, and merchandize. Particularly for inmates who cannot circulate among their partisans, websites have become, since the mid-1990s, the critical venue for promulgating the cause of prisoner rights, functioning as a virtual zone of public appearance. As do many others, the International Office of the Leonard Peltier Defense Committee website includes a biographical portrait of Peltier, information about the Defense Committee, updates on legal actions taken, a compendium of recent news articles, an archive of legal materials and articles, agendas for activism, links to other Peltier websites and sites on indigenous activism, and a marketing division raising money for legal fees by selling reproductions of Peltier paintings. "Leonard Peltier" here functions as person, legal case, and activist cause. The website for Mumia lists his recent writings from prison, and perhaps more importantly, offers visitors the opportunity to listen to a voice recording of his articles. The voice recording, heightening intimacy, immediacy, and intensity, keeps Mumia in circulation, not as silenced prisoner but as an active subject-in-dialogue with the world.

Just as with the slave narratives of the first half of the nineteenth century, the published narratives of "political" prisoners and the websites dedicated to their stories involve multilayered formats of legitimation. Activist lawyers provide up-to-date news on actions taken; rights activists provide contextualizing introductions; celebrities often add the authority of their names to the case. On the Peltier website the Reverend Desmond Tutu testifies to his unjust incarceration. "I have been reading in Leonard Peltier's book," Tutu is reported as saying, "and about an hour ago I spoke with him.... He is a remarkable person and the depth of his spirituality shows.... I would hope that the campaign to have him freed will succeed. I certainly support it very passionately.... [b]ecause it is a blot on the judicial system of this country that ought to be corrected as quickly as possible" (Degiya'göh Resources 2003). The moral authority of Tutu, familiar as the voice of truth and reconciliation around the world, affirms Peltier's identity as political prisoner.

Websites enable the flows of advocacy to run in multiple, overlapping directions. Organized efforts to free individuals can have a catalyzing effect on activist campaigns, especially in cases where the celebrity political prisoner is articulate and professionally skilled as a writer, as is the case with Mumia. America's political prisoners gain attention and credibility as their stories are taken up and dispersed in organized rights campaigns around the world. Peltier's narrative, for instance, circulates through the networks and meshworks of indigenous rights campaigns elsewhere. In reverse, transnational rights campaigns gain international purchase through identification with "celebrity" political prisoners identified with the movement. The unpredictable flows of advocacy also turn upside-down the direction of benevolent and enlightened activism. Tutu advocates on behalf of Peltier; a South African brings his moral suasion to bear on a case of rights violations in the United States.

The writings and narratives of those claiming political prisoner status, a diverse group of differently aligned radical prison intellectuals, always enter a contested field as they move beyond the prison, for there are multiple reading publics available to respond to their calls to recognition and action and their indictment of the "nation-state itself and the legitimacy of its legal and moral standing" (James 6). Some readers may fix the inmate in a fantasy of heroic resistance (James 7); some may actually help free prisoners, as happened in the case of Carter. But with a large portion of the public, "there is," as Dylan Rodríguez notes, "a rather widespread, normalized *disavowal* of the political and theoretical substance of the work generated by imprisoned radical intellectuals" (qtd. in James 7).

CONVERSIONS

In the 1960s and 1970s, the Left had accorded prison intellectuals, such as Cleaver, Jackson, and Davis, celebrity status and accorded their writings status as revolutionary manifestoes. But in the early 1980s the case of Jack Henry Abbott and his much-hailed prison writing defused the Left's romance with the celebrity prison writer. Abbott had been in and out of reformatories as an adolescent, and by the time he was twenty-five had been given a nineteen-year federal sentence for killing another inmate. In 1978 he began corresponding with Norman Mailer, then writing *The Executioner's Song*, his book on convicted killer Gary Gillmore. Through his connections, Mailer convinced the *New York Review of Books* to publish some of Abbott's letters, which led in turn to the publication in 1981 of *In the Belly of the Beast*. Attracted to Abbott's hypermasculinized writing style, Mailer promoted Abbott as a wounded artist languishing in prison, redeemed by writing itself. He even served as Abbott's advocate at his parole hearing, rallying support for him among artists and writers. In 1981 Abbott was released to a halfway house in New York City, where he was interviewed on television and touted in the literary world. Then six weeks after his release, Abbott stabbed a waiter outside a restaurant and returned to prison on a fifteen-to-life sentence. The case of Abbott discredited prison writing programs, undermining the legitimacy of PEN's[8] prisoner writing project and exposing the instability of the moral equation of powerful writing and redemption. A backlash against prison writers and angry prison writing followed.

Abbott's prison writing evidenced some of the same powerful stylistics as the manifestos of the 1960s, but his cause was not a political one. His was a far more individualistic self-presentation, a trend in keeping with the shifts in the political culture within the prisons after the 1970s. Reviewing the recent collection of contemporary prison writing entitled *Doing Time*, Mumia notes the transition from "the high-water mark of prison activism and social rebellion of the early to mid-1970s to the more individualistic, less politicized, and more repressive 1990s" (1999, 59). The transition from politicized writing, manifesto, and collective resistance to a more individualized, nonpoliticized confessional writing was underway. Without political outlets or leftist activism prompted by political and cultural turmoil, inmates sought expression through other avenues, primary among them religion. As former prisoner John Mack noted in his critique of this move to a nonpolitical storytelling mode, "Eldridge Cleaver's conversion [to Christianity] seems to have symbolized a turning point in the consciousness of the Black underclass—a surrender to the inevitability of their degradation in American society. Having lost all faith in their own ability to change their circumstances, they are 'turning to Jesus'" (50). Cleaver had published his *Soul On Fire* in 1978; by the mid-1980s a powerful call within prisons was the call not to organized resistance but to conversion through "born-again" theology, a call coincident with the rise of 12-step self-help programs in the United States.

Again, a particular personal narrative captured this move to religious as opposed to political conversion and modeled that move in a way that shifted the critical edge of the prison experience from collective social critique to individualist relationship to God. Chuck Colson's *Born Again* (1976) has since its publication served as a "Bible" for the prison ministry movement. Colson, who had served several years in prison for his role in the Watergate cover-up, narrates his conversion story in the language of born-again teleology. "Witnessing" to Christ's healing power, and also to the events of Watergate and to his own version of responsibility, he represents incarceration as a necessity for reform. "I was in prison," he writes, "because I had to be there, an essential step, a price I had to pay to complete the shedding of my old life and to be free to live the new.... Just as God felt it necessary to become man to help His children, could it be that I had to become a prisoner the better to understand suffering and deprivations" (283–4).

Conversion narratives such as Colson's are fables of individualist autonomy, responsibility, and self-improvement. The subject who speaks in these narratives is the postconversion, reformed subject whose authority derives from the truth-effect of the culturally credible fable of individualist conversion and redemption, the "I once was lost but now I'm found" plot. Recent versions of this fable can be found in Patrice Gaines's *Laughing in the Dark: From Colored Girl to*

Woman of Color—A Journey from Prison to Power (1994), a story of conversion from a life of crime, self-hatred, and violence to a life of self-love, social meaning, and aspirational achievement. Gaines concludes her narrative with an epiphanic moment of redemption: "A voice in my head said, *Now you see? This is why you snorted dope. This is why you went to jail. This is why you were lost. So that you could one day go out and spread the word, that there is no greater love than love of self*" (295).

These narratives find ready audiences in the United States, reinforcing as they do the sense of moral rightness of the justice and penal systems and reproducing the national fable of individualist responsibility. They offer assurance to readers that those who have fallen outside the law can reenter society and take up their positions as law-abiding citizens. In effect they testify to the penitentiary's efficacy as a site of reform, what Rodríguez describes as "the prison's pedagogical capacities" (409), thereby sustaining the rationale for this modern institution. They do not make their appeals to the State, nor do they make their appeals to an international community of activists pursuing projects within the international regime of human rights.

Contemporary Rights Activism and the Project of Representation

Only a limited number of inmates can or do make the claim to their advocates and to the world that they are political prisoners. An even smaller number can keep their stories in circulation through websites and documentaries. Nor do many inmates tell individualist fables of conversion and reform, easily recognized and acknowledged by those on the outside. Many have limited literacy skills and little inclination to write their personal stories. Some inmates do become involved in prison writing programs, as did Gaines, but these programs are now much curtailed by the decrease in federal funding. Thus, inmates continue to depend upon advocates and activists to make their case before the public only too willing to contest their claims or to forget them entirely.

In the last two decades, there has been a dramatic increase in prison activism, joining national organizations such as The Sentencing Project, Critical Resistance, The Moratorium Campaign, and The National Roundtable on Women in Prison, with the large international NGOs such as AI and HRW. In the first half of the 1990s, many activists working on prisoner rights began to shift their advocacy strategies by adopting an invigorated human rights framework for bringing claims of unjust treatment. They did so for several reasons: activists organizing interventions in specific prisons recognized that the arguments they were making were generalizable to actions elsewhere; they began to question the sufficiency of legal and administrative remedies applied domestically; and they found it difficult, and in some cases impossible, to convince state and federal governments and officials to recognize their appeals for prisoner rights, especially appeals concerning women inmates (Ford Foundation 98). Of appeals on behalf of women inmates, a Ford Foundation Report, entitled *Something Inside So Strong*, notes how through a " 'confluence of factors,' including new initiatives by domestic human rights groups and the United Nations, the use of human rights as a potentially transformative framework to improve the conditions for women in U.S. prisons gradually took shape" (100). Deborah LaBelle, a lawyer activist litigating on behalf of systemic discrimination in women's prisons, remarks that "the introduction of human rights allowed [lawyers] to talk to the court in a different manner," invoking international human rights law, such as the UN Standard Minimum Rules for the Treatment of Prisoners, and connecting with UN mechanisms such as special rapporteur reports. "We were trying to represent clients in a socially marginalized class," recalls Labelle, "and we didn't want to keep using socially marginalized law" (qtd. in Ford Foundation 101). The invocation and deployment of human rights discourse, platforms, and mechanisms enabled activists on behalf of U.S. inmates to garner broad media attention, to frame their cases in a "more expansive intellectual framework," and to connect themselves and their claimants in an international community of advocates (Ford Foundation 101–2).

Whether working within local, national, or internationally-based organizations, or as individuals, activists recognize the importance and the difficulty of getting inmate stories to the public in ways that humanize the convicted and criminalized. They have deployed multiple modes of storytelling to personalize the suffering of those living behind bars: documents and websites, published collections of prison writings, memoirs of activism, documentary and feature films, and public performances staged by activists and pressure groups. Many of these modes of presentation are collaborative in the sense that they are coproduced by witness and activist, and to the degree that they are collaborative such modes cannot escape the inequalities in control exercised over the story. Within these genres of presentation, activists have developed various strategies for framing inmate stories so as to target their affective appeals to audiences, strategies that often include embedding inmate stories inside other peoples' stories. In what follows, we look to three arenas of rights activism—inhuman conditions within prisons, the situation of incarcerated women, and the death penalty—to explore the ways in which advocates invoke and frame the personal stories of inmates.

NGOs, Common Criminals, and Conditions in America's Prisons

NGOs building the case for the cruel and unusual treatment of America's prisoners face a dilemma in making their claims that inmates who have been "proven guilty" should be legitimate subjects of universal human rights. On the one hand, they understand that the effect of their appeal to a broad audience depends upon making the suffering of others palpable through first-person witness. On the other, they know how complicated it is to turn the inmate into victim. In the context of this dilemma, prisoner narratives are activated or erased within formal reports, depending upon the kinds of appeals groups are making as they circulate their claims through the global circuits in the regime of human rights.

Amnesty International's 1998 Report on the American justice and penal systems, issued on the fiftieth anniversary of the signing of the UDHR, offers one strategy for negotiating this dilemma. In this instance, report and website deploy visuals rather than personal narratives to tell a persuasive story of victimization and expose the degrading and inhumane conditions within the prisons. Some photographs present visual evidence (assumed to be objective and indisputable) of inhumane prison practices. Anonymous, naked men stand in line as prison guards subject them to a massive strip search. An unidentified prisoner, his head partially obscured by his arms and hands, is shown cuffed to an immobile fence. A group of anonymous women prisoners chained together in leg irons carry the coffin of a dead inmate. A juvenile sits in leg irons, waiting. Other photos offer stark evidence of inhumane punishment; photos of a steel restraining bed, for instance, and of the emptied rooms and corridors of a super-max prison. Collectively, these photos, and the absence of personal voices witnessing to inhumane treatment, tell the story of the anonymity and radical deindividualization of the state of detention, precisely the charges the Report lodges against the U.S. government in administering its penal system.

The Report also includes select photographs of individually named prisoners. These photos, putting a human face on the victims of rights violations, accompany stories of persons unjustly killed or tortured by police, or of men exonerated of their crime after serving years on death row. In terms of the affective appeal of the Report, these men can be legitimately figured as victims of rights abuses, their stories uncompromised by a doubled identity as victim and perpetrator. This Report offers one strategy for overcoming the challenge of issuing an appeal to the reader from the perpetrator as victim; and yet, in not including stories of specific inmates, and not naming individuals photographed, except of those unjustly sentenced, the Report reproduces the invisibility and anonymity of "the inmate" even as it seeks to make the conditions of his or her life visible.

A second tactic deployed by NGOs involves the careful culling and framing of inmate testimony. We see this tactical deployment of narrated lives in a 2001 HRW Report on rape in men's prisons entitled "No Escape: Male Rapes in U.S. Prisons" (April, 2001). To build its case of human rights violations in America's prison, HRW gathered testimony from the field, soliciting stories from inmates through advertisements in prison publications. In its Report, however, only a small number of testimonies are selected as exemplary narratives, strategically deployed to personalize the story of rape in prison, lend specificity to the suffering attached to this particular rights violation, and increase the Report's affective power to elicit empathy and spur action. (In the on-line version of the Report, HRW includes a sidebar linking the reader to the oral testimony of inmates who recorded their stories on tape.)

"No Escape" incorporates eleven biographical portraits of rape victims, supplemented with their first-person witness to rape culture inside prisons. In all but one case, victim portraits open with first-person inmate testimony to being raped, often repeatedly.[9] The individualized narrative voices of the inmates expose the world of prison inmates to audiences often unaware of the realities of rape culture in America's prisons, taking the reader inside prison through the language of incarceration—often ungrammatical, fitful, brutally direct, visceral. The authors of the HRW Report limit the first-person testimony to brief passages through which a composite portrait of victimization within the prison system can be produced. They also embed the testimony in biographical narratives they tell of the inmates and their victimization. Embedding the personal testimonies in biographical sketches, the HRW authors keep the focus on conditions and avoid turning the inmate into a pornographic spectacle of violent male sexual predation. The authoritative voice of HRW keeps the story on its track and away from a titillating melodrama of degradation through recourse to a social science discourse of objectivity.

The authors of the Report also interweave throughout the biographical sketches stories of inmate agency, narratives in which inmates take action to bring the conditions inside the prison to the attention of authorities and prisoner rights advocates. Stories of inmate agency contest the stereotype of the degraded inmate who wallows in, and deserves, his degradation. Such stories also contest the stereotype of the feminized inmate, the one who should have resisted, the one who, unresisting, can be held accountable for his own rape. These biographical stories present the inmate as the subject of human rights, and a subject who claims those rights.

The selection of inmate profiles underscores the importance to an activist agenda of turning the inmate/perpetrator into victim/ activist. For one, the authors of the Report are strategic in the crime for which the inmate was convicted. Those profiled did not commit violent crimes against persons. Several committed property crimes while juveniles, implicitly raising questions about the incarceration of juveniles in the United States and the warehousing of juveniles with hardened criminals. The authors are also strategic in foregrounding multiple differences among inmates in terms of sexual orientation, ethnicity, age, and crime committed, thereby unsettling the stereotype of the criminal as an uneducated "underclass" man of color. Through these strategic choices, the HRW Report interrupts the ease with which the reader can dismiss the inmate's claims of victimization and thus intervenes in the stereotyping of the inmate as hardened criminal who deserves whatever degradation he endures.

The Plight of Women Inmates

In the 1990s, human rights activists turned considerable attention to the most invisible population within America's prisons, women. Prison activists such as Angela Davis had long been working on behalf of women in America's prisons, a source of concern evident in the attention she paid to women inmates in her 1974 autobiography. But it took until the early 1990s for a groundswell of concern for women inmates to materialize in documentaries, personal narratives, and NGO reports. As in the case of the former World War II sex prisoners, the new interest in women's narratives of incarceration accompanied the dispersed global movements to claim women's rights as human rights and confront the role of everyday violence and acts of torture in constraining women's lives. More particularly, feminist activists within the United States had begun exploring the affects and legacies of traumatic abuse—childhood sexual abuse and violent and psychological domestic abuse—in the lives of women living life behind bars. Moreover, as more and more women were incarcerated for three-strikes drug violations, activists began to focus on the condition of the children of incarcerated women, the majority of whom are mothers.

Women prisoners are the most invisible of those serving time in America's prisons. They remain far more isolated than incarcerated men and receive far fewer visitors. Often their own families do not support them. Far fewer lawyers represent them. Once incarcerated, their sustained invisibility is an effect of their relative nonresistant and nonlitigious behavior. Women prisoners rarely riot. They do not file the number of lawsuits male prisoners do. Moreover, women prisoners are rarely the focus of extensive studies. Nor have women prisoners gained public recognition as prison writers or prison journalists. While they contribute to the prison writing contests run by PEN, they do so at a far lower rate than their male counterparts.[10] Given this situation, it has been incumbent on activist artists and scholars to bring the stories of incarcerated women to a broader public through documentaries and published narratives.

Over the last decade, for instance, videographer Carol Jacobsen has advocated for women serving life sentences in Michigan prisons for killing their abusive partners. In her 1994 video *From One Prison* Jacobsen interweaves fragments of interviews with four of these women, Violet Allen, Juanita Thomas, Geraldine Gordon, and Linda Hamilton, who tell about their family relationships, describe the circumstances of their abusive relationships, recall the killings, and offer their own analyses of their treatment within the criminal justice system. *From One Prison* presents women who have not so much reformed, in terms of confessing and acknowledging their criminality, as women who have begun to understand and articulate the ways in which the criminal subject is produced by social structures (of marriage, justice, and punishment). In the inter-cutting of multiple stories, the women become at once four individuals, with different stories to tell, and a chorus whose collective narrative accumulates the force of truth through repetition (but always with differences). Neither the videographer nor the women make claims of innocence; they do, however, make claims about the systems that put them on a life sentence. Critical to Jacobsen's project is enabling the women to position themselves not as passive victims of domestic violence and State indifference but as critics of the justice and penal systems and of the institution of the family itself. Thus, she listens for, and edits to capture, the public voice of the social critic rather than the personal voice of the victim.

In 1995, HRW, a sponsor of the project, took *From One Prison* to the International Women's Conference in Beijing. The video has been used as an organizing tool within rights organizations; it circulates in galleries, museums, and arts festivals where it is mobilized in efforts to spur activism on behalf of women's rights. In this way, the four women who tell their personal stories speak to a broad international audience far beyond the confines of Scott correctional facility in Michigan. They enter their stories into circulation within the field of NGOs active on behalf of women prisoners, among them the Clemency Project (the activist arm of Jacobsen's work)[11]; Critical Resistance in California (in which Angela Davis has been active), American Friends Active, the California Coalition for Battered Women's Defense, and the New York–based Women in Prisons Association. In circulation, their stories participate in "the social and global contextualization of violence against women" so "central to 'locating' it within the human rights framework" (Youngs 1216).

In *Women on the Row: Revelations from Both Sides of the Bars* (2000), Kathleen O'Shea entwines her own narrative of childhood, adolescence, and adulthood with the personal narratives of ten women living on death rows throughout the United States. As a doctoral student at the University of Oklahoma, O'Shea participated in a research project on the reasons for high recidivism rates for women in prison. After struggling to find the names of women on death rows, many of whom she discovered through word-of-mouth passed on by other women on death row, and after initiating communication with them and between them, O'Shea decided to write a personal narrative about her relationship to the women and about their influence on her life. *Women on the Row* becomes at once a personal narrative of O'Shea's childhood, adolescence, and experience in a Catholic order of nuns, and an interspersed collection of personal narratives of women serving time on death row.

As O'Shea says in her introduction, most of the women admit their guilt in the crimes for which they were convicted. Theirs are not narratives of innocence and justice miscarried. Nor, however, are they confessions. They are narratives of childhood, family, and relationships; they are narratives about prison conditions, including lack of affection and touching. Through their personal narratives, these women on death row, isolated, often forgotten by those on the outside, and living under constant surveillance, offer critiques of the prison and justice systems. In their descriptions of relationships and their critiques of the prison system, O'Shea recognizes aspects of her own history. She tells the story of her violent relationships; she tells of her own experiential history of life inside the "total institution" (Goffman xii) of the religious order. Through recourse to the authority of Erving Goffman, noted sociologist of the relationship of selves to institutions, O'Shea projects and claims the commonality of aspects of everyday lives in institutional settings and enfolds the self-understandings of nuns and prisoners within one another, the former figures of chastity and goodness, the latter figures of errancy and criminality. Linking the prison to the total institution of the convent, with its surveillance, formal rules, pervasive authorities, spectacles of convention and control, and enforced activities (Goffman 6), O'Shea finds a means to understand her life in relation to the lives of the women with whom she corresponds. The women on death row become agents of O'Shea's transformation, and she becomes an agent of their communication with one another and themselves.

As O'Shea makes clear in her final chapter, the intent of her narrative project is to blur the distinction between the convicted murderer on death row and the researcher/academic in a way that challenges readers to forgo their conventional understandings of the differences between those inside and those outside the bars of a prison, and in a way that challenges the readers' stereotypes about women who act violently. *Revelations from Both Sides of the Bars* is O'Shea's performative witnessing to the ethical responsibility of seeing oneself in the other and the other in oneself. In its refusal of the self/other binary, it models an ethics of recognition that places the self in proximity to women prisoners. In effect, O'Shea confuses the boundary between the innocent and the guilty, the criminalized subject and the noncriminalized subject, in order to extract the subjects of incarceration from the degrading and dehumanizing zone of no-rights.

Anti-Death-Penalty Activism

Death row narratives have become a specific category of narrated lives that find contemporary audiences, moving them, haunting them. National media, artists, and human rights activists are drawn particularly to the stories of those sentenced to death and later exonerated of their crimes. In 2002, *The Exonerated*, written and directed by Jessica Blank and Erik Jenson and based on their interviews with former death row inmates, opened off Broadway and subsequently played (and continues to play) to packed houses.[12] The play braids the personal narratives of six people speaking directly to the audience of their arrests, wrongful conviction, and survival on death row, as well as of their exoneration. When performed in New York and across the country, *The Exonerated* has moved actors (many of them international celebrities such as Susan Sarandon and Richard Dreyfuss) and audience members to empathy, anger, and anti-death-penalty activism. At the conclusion of the performance, audiences are enlisted in a reparation project: cast members inform them that the State does not offer reparations payments to those wrongly convicted and then solicit donations.

Elsewhere around the country stories of exoneration—by means of new investigative or DNA evidence—grab headlines in national and local papers. At Northwestern University Law Professor Lawrence Marshall, now working with the Center for Wrongful Convictions, catapulted wrongful convictions into public consciousness in 1998 when he organized a national conference at which thirty-one exonerated death row inmates appeared. At Northwestern as well, David Protess, professor of journalism, has guided journalism students, sometimes referred to as "the Angels of Death Row," in their efforts to expose wrongful convictions. In December of 2002, the New York papers began running numerous articles about the exoneration of five young black men, imprisoned while teenagers, who had been convicted of the infamous 1989 Central Park jogger case involving the brutal rape and assault of a young white woman. Exoneration came when another prisoner confessed to the rape and brutal beating, thereby calling attention to the politics of racial profiling and of false confessions and their "extortion" during unrecorded interrogations. In January 2003, outgoing Illinois governor George Ryan commuted the sentences of Illinois's death row inmates after the Northwestern journalism students cleared Anthony Porter of the murder for which he received the death penalty and exposed other cases of wrongful conviction. As of September, 2003, 132 convicted inmates had been exonerated of their crimes based on DNA evidence (*New York Times*, September 1, 2003).

Wrongly convicted, the exonerated can claim status as victims of the miscarriage of American justice. Their stories can be counted on to gain a sympathetic reception. But not all anti-death-penalty stories can elicit empathic response, especially when the person serving time on death row is neither exonerated nor especially attractive as a "victim" of America's cruel and unusual punishment. As in O'Shea's case, human rights advocates engaged in anti-death-penalty activism are challenged to tell a convincing story, and they often experiment with hybrid genres to frame the stories they tell of murderers.

Perhaps the most widely read and influential narrative written by an activist has been Sister Helen Prejean's *Dead Man Walking*, published in 1994 and subsequently adapted for film, starring Susan Sarandon and Sean Penn. In 1982, Helen Prejean, of the Sisters of St. Joseph of Medaille order, was asked by members of an activist organization to be pen pal for Elmo Patrick Sonnier, "number 95281, Death Row, Louisiana State Penitentiary, Angola." Prejean's personal relationship of witness lasted until Sonnier's execution in 1984. Several months later, she became spiritual advisor for death row inmate Robert Willie until he was executed in December 1984. *Dead Man Walking*, which she subtitles "an eyewitness account of the death penalty in the United States," is Sister Prejean's account of her relationship with these two convicted men and her extended argument for the abolition of the death penalty in the United States. A hybrid text, it is at once a memoir of her two-plus years as spiritual advisor to two death row inmates; a conversion narrative tracing her transformation into anti-death-penalty activist; a sustained argument against the death penalty; an extended meditation on violence, punishment, forgiveness, and their affective dimensions; and a performative act of witness, modeling empathetic listening for the reader.

The multilayered density of the text derives from the inter-articulation of multiple voices. There is Prejean the narrator whose authority derives from several sources. She speaks as a religious whose purpose is to serve the indigent, alleviate suffering and pain, and witness to God's presence in people's lives. With this aura of religious authority, she commands the reader's respect and willingness to listen to her story of murderers. She also positions herself as an innocent who is being educated, and as someone struggling with the reality of violence and issues of justice. Her continual use of the present tense of narration reinforces the reader's sense that Prejean is in the midst of this struggle, as she imagines her readers to be. At the same time that she presents herself as a subject of struggle, as one who needs education, she does the work of educating, building her case against capital punishment. As she witnesses to life on death row and to the experience of execution, she also offers a history of capital punishment in the United States; an exposé of the workings of the death penalty, in prosecution and exaction; an analysis of the effects of the death penalty on guards and executioners, many of whom question its morality but maintain its legality; statistical and polling data about the American public and its attitudes about crime. She joins the authority of her voice to that of such intellectual figures as Camus and joins her arguments to the discourses of the constitution and the UN conventions and covenants on cruel and unusual punishment (113). In this way her authority is supplemented with the authority attached to objective data, other moral authorities, and to history.

At the center of *Dead Man Walking* are the portraits of Prejean's two interlocutors, Pat Sonnier and Robert Willie. The reading audience in the United States is familiar with biographies of criminals; these are the fare of sensational biopics and crime news reporting. Provoking fascination and horror, stories of violent criminals terrify and titillate at once. The portraits drawn of Sonnier and Willie, however, are never sensationalized. Nor are they portraits of the innocent, nor even the likeable. Sonnier is the perpetrator of the crime along with his brother. Willie is the perpetrator of the murders. He is also a racist (150). Their crimes are heinous. Yet these convicted murderers are given their own voices through her narrative, and Prejean listens to them, always assuming their humanity and their capacity to change. She listens to them as she listens to the voices of the impoverished and the marginalized, for, as she tells her reader, the death penalty is meted out disproportionately to the poor and marginalized (197).

As her narrative proceeds, Prejean makes increasing room for the voices of the victim/survivors of the crimes perpetrated by Sonnier and Willie. Describing her confusion after meeting the parents of the young couple Sonnier and his brother murdered, she confesses: "I had not thought seriously enough about what murder means to victims' families and to society. I had not considered how difficult the issue of capital punishment is. My response had been far too simplistic" (65). Her spiritual journey involves the struggle of compassions—for those condemned to die and for the parent/victims (175). In humility, she suggests her own inadequacy in confronting the pain and suffering of victims. Even as she foregrounds the pain of victims of murders (145), however, she foregrounds the possibility of forgiveness. She closes with the narrative of her last meeting with Lloyd LeBlanc, the father of one of Sonnier's victims: "He went to the execution, he says, not for revenge, but hoping for an apology. Patrick Sonnier had not disappointed him" (244). As a religious, Prejean joins perpetrator and victim in this final scene of apology, redemption, and forgiveness. Having struggled with the ethics of beginning and sustaining a friendship with a killer who would himself be executed by the State, this witness and human rights activist finds a common ground of recognition for the perpetrator, the victim, and herself as intermediary.

Telling sites such as *Women on the Row* and *Dead Man Walking* participate in what Leigh Gilmore terms "the auto/biographical demand, in which the demands of autobiography (to tell my story) and the demands of biography (to tell your story) coincide" (2001, 72). Researcher, spiritual advisor, these narrators, whose authority derives from their positioning on this side of the bars, on this side of criminalization, tell a doubled story through which they confront the violence of the other, and the profound ethical responsibility of witnessing and telling within themselves. Entering into a generic mode through this demand, such narrators open themselves to the "irresolvable narrative dilemma"—"whose story is this? mine? ours? how can I tell them all?" (Gilmore 2001, 72). In this dilemma lies the ethical possibility of responsibility in the struggle for prisoner human rights.

SOME CAUTIONARY NOTES

As in our other telling sites, we need to sound some cautionary notes about the deployment of narrated lives in campaigns for prisoner rights. We referred earlier to the challenge of crediting the inmate's story in a regime where innocence accumulates great moral force. The purchase of personal testimony in campaigns for prisoner rights is almost always qualified by the identification of the inmate as perpetrator. Stories of innocence and victimization coming from inmates remain suspicious, easily dismissed as self-serving. A reader, an audience can all too easily refuse the ethical responsibility to accord subjectivity to the other. But there are additional constraints on the uses of personal narrative in campaigns for prisoner rights in the United States.

State Regulation of Storytelling

For one, the State can and does regulate personal storytelling as part of punishment. State regulations control what kinds of access activists have to inmates and their stories. Inmate writing can be censored, writing materials confiscated, manuscripts and their narratives destroyed. In addition, the State controls inmates' rights to their personal stories and the extent to which inmates can be professional writers while in prison, as it has done in the case of Mumia. In 1977, after rumors surfaced that convicted murderer David Berkowitz (a.k.a. Son of Sam) was negotiating with publishers for a hefty advance on his life story, the New York legislature passed a statute making it illegal for the convicted to profit from writing or selling movie rights to their personal stories of crime. The law allowed the State to capture earnings from book and movie deals for an escrow account to be made available to victims through civil action. Subsequently forty-three states passed "Son-of-Sam" laws; so too did the federal government. That law was ruled unconstitutional in 1991 when the Supreme Court held that the Son-of-Sam laws violate the First Amendment freedom of speech rights of writers and publishers, but in some states, Son-of-Sam laws have been rewritten to withstand constitutional challenge.

Victim's Rights Narratives

The rise of the victim's rights movement throughout the 1990s puts other viscerally compelling and affectively charged narratives in circulation. If, in 1990s, the Victim's Rights Movement had barely hit the radar screen in terms of national consciousness, throughout the 1990s it gained momentum as victims' rights organizations tapped the sense of disenfranchisement and isolation of crime victims, who often feel that they are the ones treated as criminals during the prosecution process. Collectively, victim advocates work for the passage of a Victims' Rights Amendment to the U.S. Constitution, an amendment seen as a necessary counter-balance to what the Victims' Rights Movement considers the unreasonable rights of the accused. As victims of crime witness to their experiences across the country, they set in motion competing, and incommensurable stories of victimization, ones with greater moral purchase than those told by inmates. It is important to note, however, that survivor/victims respond differently to their suffering and that some become anti-death-penalty activists, as have those represented in the anthology *Don't Kill in Our Name* (see Cooper n.p.).

DNA Speaking

With the advance in the technologies of genetic testing, DNA is now used to speak the truth of guilt and innocence within the prison industrial complex, transforming the body itself into a confessing or exonerating machine. And yet the jury is still out on the willingness of prison officials, prosecutors, and judges to credit the evidentiary basis of DNA. In summer 2003, the newspapers reported stories of prosecutors in Florida arguing that DNA should not be inviolate as exonerating evidence of innocence, that it remains one of many kinds of evidence and should not be privileged as the source of truth telling. The power of DNA testing to distinguish the guilty from the innocent may short-circuit the claims of rights violations by offering a surety bond for the protection of innocence. At the same time, equal access of inmates to DNA testing may become one of the major "rights" that future campaigns for prisoner rights put on the table.

Terrorism Discourse

The U.S. government has never recognized the category "political prisoner," assigning individuals identities as "subversives" or "terrorists."

In the post–September 11 environment, the term "terrorist" has become ever more usable and politically efficacious as a State descriptor overwriting the term "political prisoner." In the name of homeland security and the war on terror, individuals claiming political prisoner status can be and are put in isolation in maximum-security prisons. They are placed *incommunicado*, made even more invisible than those considered common criminals. And in Guantanamo Bay, Cuba, the United States has been holding alleged al-Qaeda fighters *incommunicado* without charging them or giving them access to counsel by deploying the designation "enemy combatant." That term carries specific meaning in international humanitarian law, designating those detained in the armed conflict in Afghanistan for the duration of that conflict. Human rights NGOs such as HRW have argued vigorously that the term should not be used to designate those identified with al-Qaeda detained within the United States nor as a defense for holding them indefinitely (HRW 2002).

CONCLUSION

The convicted are understood to be those who have forfeited their place inside the domain of civil and political rights. And, as noted above, the convicted do forfeit their citizenship rights for the duration of their sentences, and sometimes beyond. Sentencing places the incarcerated subject in a despotic zone, an "economy of force" (Douzinas and Warrington 213). Through entry into this state-sponsored economy of force, the inmate moves to the position of the legalized (because named thus in the law) "other" to the citizen-subject. Thus, despite the nomination as an "outlaw," the prisoner is never outside the law, never the outsider to the law, but rather the subject within the law, the subject without which the law would not have legitimacy as the institution policing the realm of civil and political rights. "The other," argue Costas Douzinas and Ronnie Warrington, "is used to underpin the superiority of the law (and) of belonging" (227). State violence directed to the convicted and incarcerated is thus "entangled," suggests Rodríguez, "with common notions of personal liberty, community welfare, and social peace" (424). This entangled relationship of the outlaw to the law, of state violence to notions of freedom, suggests why inmates and ex-inmates, advocates and activists have such difficulty circulating stories of degradation, claims for human rights, and calls to action to audiences that may be unreceptive to their demands for recognition and unwilling to concede that the United States is a gross violator of human rights.

Ignatieff points to America's "highly paradoxical relation to an emerging international legal order based on human rights principles," when he writes, "America has promoted human rights norms around the world, while also resisting the idea that these norms apply to American citizens and American institutions" (2001, 13). As the superpower "champion" of the regime of human rights elsewhere, the United States (its government and many of its people) refuses to imagine itself as "perpetrator" in the conditions it enforces or allows to persist in the nation's prisons. This rights narcissism at the confluence of cultural, economic, and political currents, inevitably affects what kinds of stories can be told by the incarcerated and their advocates about "cruel and unusual punishment" within governmental and civic spheres.

As noted throughout this chapter, in campaigns for prisoner rights the affective appeal of stories soliciting empathy, critical awareness, identification, or activism is difficult, if not impossible to make successfully, especially in the context of contemporary America's psychic economy of fear. The narrated lives of inmates, whether told autobiographically or within someone else's narrative, confound the differentiated identities of victim and perpetrator. In the hierarchy of the "deserving" those already placed outside civil and political rights as "criminals" provoke more disgust and fear than interest and empathy. Moreover, campaigns for prisoner rights encode their own hierarchies of the deserving: political prisoners often garner celebrity status for their heroic dissidence (at least within certain communities of advocacy); the exonerated garner pity and prompt horror for their unjust suffering; the remorseful, especially those invoking the discourse of self-help and Christian redemption, reassure outsiders that the justice system works to instill an individualist ethic of responsibility in the reformed; and then there are the recalcitrant guilty.

Nonetheless, narrated lives telling of violations of prisoner rights and of cruel and unusual punishment have circulated within the United States and out from the United States to other parts of the globe, here to enter into the politics of apartheid resistance in South Africa; there to enter into the campaign to force the government to study the deaths in custody of Indigenous prisoners in Australia. They have reached Chinese dissidents beginning to form protest movements and challenge involuntary detention as a strategy of state control. In our final case study, we turn to China and look at a nascent human rights discourse that among other forms includes the writings of dissident Wei Jingsheng.

CHAPTER 7

POST-TIANANMEN NARRATIVES
AND THE NEW CHINA

No one who has suppressed a student movement ever came to a good end.

—*Mao Zedong*

The whole Democracy Movement is the key to understanding China today. The government showed they have no legitimacy except brute force. Everything they do now is designed to reestablish legitimacy.

—*Xiao Qiang*, New York director of
Human Rights in China

For many Chinese writers and thinkers, coming to terms with such concepts as democracy and personal freedom (whether expressed through fiction, poetry or essays) is tantamount to a struggle to be released from Mao's hold over them.

—*Geremie Barmé and Linda Jaivin*, New Ghosts,
Old Dreams: Chinese Rebel Voices

In the late twentieth century, student protest movements sparked massive campaigns for human rights across the world. None, however, would eclipse the June 4 Movement in China. In terms of sheer numbers alone, the event was monumental.

In mid-May of 1989 large numbers of students, frustrated by the slow progress of liberal reforms in China, amassed on university campuses in Beijing and elsewhere in Guangzhou, Shanghai, and other mainland cities. On May 14, students moved from the university to Tiananmen Square and declared a hunger strike. On May 16, three hundred thousand students marched. By May 18, more than a million people were demonstrating in and around the Square. By June 4, more than two hundred Chinese journalists and tens of millions of intellectuals, workers, civil servants, peasants, police, and soldiers had joined the student demonstrations. Frustrated by inflation and corruption and sympathetically engaged by the students' actions, masses of people rallied in more than three hundred cities in a nationwide demand for reform. They staged their protests in the streets, on town squares, and on university campuses around the country.

Eventually, and fatally, the demonstrators met with massive resistance. On May 20 the government, declaring Martial Law, sent troops to surround the Square. By this action the Party signaled that moderates, among them Party Chief and Deng's heir apparent Zhao Ziyang 赵紫阳,[1] who had earlier visited the hunger strikers in hospitals and protestors on the Square and promised reforms, had been defeated by hard-liners. On the evening of June 3, the government moved in thousands of troops. Shocked audiences watched in horror as armed soldiers and Army tanks quelled the protests with mass killings. By nightfall on June 5, somewhere between 1,000 and 3,000 protestors and innocent bystanders had been killed and tens of thousands more injured (Chung 296; Miles 19; Buruma 5).[2] The June 4 Movement had come to an end.

As fate would have it, the foreign press broadcast the events as they unfolded over a six-week period to an audience of millions around the world. About fifteen hundred members of the international media and more than two hundred Chinese journalists had amassed in Beijing in mid-May to report on the state visit of Soviet President Gorbachev, for whom the government had planned a ceremonial march through Tiananmen Square. For two weeks viewers in China, as well as overseas BBC viewers and Voice of America listeners, had access to unprecedented coverage of the demonstrations on radio and television. As one of the foreign journalists present noted, reportage by the foreign media constituted "the most detailed and sustained foreign coverage of any episode in Chinese history. And it came about largely by chance" (Chung 277–8). Both within and outside of China, commentators called the protest movement a life-and-death struggle between the Chinese Communist Party and the swelling ranks of citizenry demanding democratic liberalization and making claims for human rights.

RESPONSES TO TIANANMEN SQUARE

News of the demonstrations and the massacre reverberated around the world. In the weeks preceding the Massacre over one million Hong Kong civilians had held massive rallies; donated blood, tents, and supplies; organized a rock concert; and raised $14 million (USD) to support the demonstrators. During the massacre Hong Kong people took to the streets in outpourings of grief, expressing rage against the violence. Following the June 4 media purge in Beijing, Hong Kong sympathizers countered mainland censorship by faxing reports from the BBC and Voice of America to foreign businesses in China. Hong Kong broadcasting networks interrupted local television and radio programs to provide independent documentation of Beijing's "act of insanity" (Chung 286). For Hong Kong supporters of the Tiananmen Square protestors, the political stakes of the Massacre were high. In its aftermath, they feared that the planned Chinese takeover of the territory would bring measures of totalitarian repression to Hong Kong.

In Eastern Europe the event brought back memories of the Prague spring of 1968, the terrorist purges and liberalization campaigns of the intervening years, the student movements in Hungary and East Germany, and the rise of the Solidarity movement in Poland. The election of Lech Walesa as the new president of Poland occurred on the same day as the Tiananmen Square Massacre. Americans received the news of the demonstrations with the "shock of recognition" (Woodward 3 of 10) born of the scars of mass protest throughout the 1960s and early 1970s—the remembered traumas of the anti-Vietnam War protest demonstrations on university campuses in 1968 and the murder of four students by police at Kent State. In Australia, Prime Minister Robert J. Hawke appeared before Parliament in arm with Jin Zhefei, a Chinese student representative, to deliver with her a tearful plea to the Chinese government to stop the killing of unarmed civilians. Western leaders promised shelter to those who found means to escape the mainland. Prime Minister Hawke granted permanent resident visas to Chinese students studying in Australia.

The Massacre as event was seared into the cultural memory of hundreds of millions of people around the world through the enduring photographic image of "the man and the tank." Released by the Associated Press, this photo made front-page coverage on June 5,

1989, in major newspapers around the world. This striking, iconic photograph, featuring a fearless young man in pursuit of democratic freedoms standing alone on a wide boulevard, halting the advance of a convoy of army tanks, and calling for peace, seemed to encapsulate the event. For foreign observers, this image symbolized the meaning of the Tiananmen Square Massacre as a failure of the State to respect the will of its citizens. The image of that one man signaled, at least for Western democratic nations, the courage of the individual standing up to the power of the authoritarian State and marked China as the limit case for human rights in the late twentieth century.

Inside China, however, that same image took on a different set of meanings. At the time of the Massacre the Chinese government closed all radio and television stations and ordered a total ban on reporting. In its aftermath, government-controlled media presented "the man and the tank" photograph as evidence of military restraint in the face of terrible social unrest and riots (Vervoorn 241–2). For the Chinese government, the final use of military force was deemed necessary to restore order and stability to a country of some 1.2 billion people veering dangerously out of control. Press reports in China told of soldiers bravely putting down a counterrevolutionary uprising. Communist Party Chairman Deng Xiaoping 邓小平 appeared on television to congratulate the generals for their support during the "turmoil," designed, in his words, to "topple the Chinese Communist Party, negate socialism and establish a capitalist country" (Chung 299).

China's defense of the value of social stability was the ideological position that held sway over the rights demanded by the protestors. In its justification, China argued that, in keeping with pan-Asian values, the State recognized a different set of fundamental principles and traditions from those of democratic nations of the Western world. In China, the citizen's duties to the State held priority over the State's guarantee of individual expression (Vervoorn 240; Aziz 39).

While the Western world equated "Tiananmen Square" with the limit case for human rights in China, inside China government forces quickly suppressed not only the movement but also any discussion of the June 4 event. The Party continued its crackdown on what it described as social provocateurs by enlisting more than six million people in China into Neighborhood Watch campaigns to spy on neighbors and report suspicious activities. Police rounded up thousands of dissidents who were summarily jailed or sent to labor camps. What became an iconic moment of human rights abuse for the rest of the world was effaced from the body politic of China, leaving a deep scar, an absent presence, an indelible trace memory.

During the demonstrations, students had clamored to tell their stories to Western journalists. After the purge, the event could be neither spoken nor written about. As Chinese-Canadian journalist, Jan Wong, reports, participants and sympathizers held their stories in their hearts and hid their news clippings in treasure boxes, awaiting better times (Wong 13). Years passed. Still fearing reprisal, people remained silent about the event, even with their children. Some, like Ding Zilin 丁子霖, the mother of a slain student and a retired philosophy professor, covertly defied the ban. Forming a Tiananmen Mothers group,[3] she endeavored surreptitiously to contact parents of the victims of the Beijing Massacre. As a visible gesture of remembrance and commemoration, she began to attend Qing Ming, the annual grave-sweeping festival, dressed in black and wearing a white headscarf (as the Madres de Plaza de Mayo had done in Argentina) as a signal to other mothers to come forward. In 1994, to mark the fifth anniversary of June 4, she published a book listing 96 names of victims; by 1999 the list had grown to 155. During the ten-year commemoration of the Tiananmen Square Massacre in Hong Kong in 1999, Ding Zilin, for the first time, spoke publicly on behalf of parents of the lost children (Buruma 322–33). But, for the most part, people maintained their silence.

The Chinese government has never acknowledged any wrongdoing for the event. Unlike our other sites of trauma discussed in this study, traumas that were revisited in human rights narratives and campaigns for redress, there has been no transformation of common knowledge into public discourse about the Massacre on the Square, no survivor-as-victim testimonies, no campaigns for redress, no recognition of the suffering of Chinese citizens, no reparations, no tribunals, no reflection, no apologies, no healing processes. The "truth" of the past has been buried in an amnesiacal fold of history, held in memory through the production and circulation of narratives beyond China's borders. Indeed, when Jan Wong, a foreign journalist who covered the story in 1989, returned to China a decade later, students she met at the university asked her if the whole event had been an invention of the foreign media (Wong 283).

The event was far from forgotten in the West, however. Widespread reporting, including editorial and academic commentary, represented the Massacre as a campaign of terror, a repetition of the repressive regimes of the Old China.[4] In journalistic reports of the massacre, readers were reminded of the Boxer rebellion, Mao's reeducation campaigns, and the disappearance of millions of Chinese during the Cultural Revolution. Headlines proclaimed that the "Betrayal in Beijing" had once again left "blood on the hands of the Old Men of China" (Bernstein 33). The foreign press aligned the "student innocents" with western hopes, fears, and fantasies for democratic reform in China. And Westerners embraced exiled student demonstrators, like the "elected" leader of the demonstrations, Chai Ling 柴玲, and leader of the hunger strike, Wuer Kaixi 吾尔开希, who on arrival in the United States were greeted with great fanfare.

In the years following the 1989 Massacre, tales from Tiananmen Square have emerged, but they have not come out of China. Rather, they have become public in different contexts—geographic, linguistic, cultural, and temporal—and through different fields of recovery—interviews, stories, documentaries, film, art, music, and silence. While official China closed down its remembering processes, the transnational Chinese intellectual diaspora,[5] made up in part of dissident exiles in residency in the United States, Canada, Australia, Japan, and England, participated in "world remembering" in another place.[6] Their stories, recovered in particular in and through the Western media, were translated into new landscapes of memory where they were subjected to new meanings, interpretations, controversies, and usages.

DISSIDENT STORIES AFTER TIANANMEN

Soon after the events at Tiananmen Square, anthologies incorporating personal stories of participants appeared in the West, among them *Children of the Dragon: The Story of Tiananmen Square* (1990) and *New Ghosts, Old Dreams* (1992), both edited by China scholars and human rights advocates. These anthologies, the former focused on the protest itself, the latter inspired by but not limited to it, explore "the social and cultural roots of the 1989 Protest Movement" (Barmé and Jaivin xv). They offer a pastiche of perspectives, including testimony of student participants, views of sympathetic Chinese intellectuals and foreign observers, journalistic pieces, speeches, petitions, songs, essays, poetry, prose, and artwork by Chinese dissidents living mainly in the West in the aftermath of the disaster. Shaped and framed by advocates in the West, these collections recirculate Tiananmen Square memories within the dominant liberal humanist discourse on human rights. Personalizing human rights abuse in China, the anthologies call readers to a recognition of violations, enable empathy for and identification with the protestors and their claims, spur activism, and lend international support to Western governments intent on pressing for continued reforms in China.

In the decade following the Massacre, stories about Tiananmen also circulated through media interviews with dissidents in exile. After their arrival in the United States, key leaders and known "public enemies" of the Communist State generated intense media interest. Su Xaiokang 苏晓康's *A Memoir of Misfortune* (2001) comments, wryly, on the fate of many dissidents. Describing the typical daily life of exiled families, Su writes: "Journalists flew in from all over the world, with their cameras and recorders and flashlights, flashing their way right up to Fox Run (a suburb of Princeton, New Jersey, where many exiles settled), following their subjects even to their English lessons and driving tests.... This kind of exile," he muses, "must be unprecedented in world history" (180). Despite their halting English, limited understanding of "human rights" as promulgated in the West, and struggles with psychological adjustment to exile, many key dissidents took up offers of lecture tours, made guest appearances on television talk shows, and gave frequent interviews with journalists.

Circulating in such media venues, the exiles were caught up in the Western media's prescripted narrative of the events in Tiananmen Square. Embodying the West's story of Tiananmen, they were fetishized as personifications at once of the betrayed youth of China and of a new generation whose hopes were harnessed to a human rights agenda. Although young, politically inexperienced, and only vaguely aware of the historical significance of the event, they were positioned as dissidents in exile (even though they did not necessarily fit the profile), heralded as "experts" on human rights in China, and asked for their opinions on unfolding world events. Su depicts the mainly male enclave of exiles, whose ideals had been shattered by the Massacre, as a young, naïve, and arrogant band of survivors who were surprised, and then quickly spoiled, by the fawning adoration of the international media and the American public.

More recently, Ian Buruma updates the personal stories of dissident exiles, focusing on how they subsequently coped "with disappointed idealism" (15). After traveling around the world in search of the diasporic exiles from 1996 to 2001, Buruma tells some of their stories in *Bad Elements* (2001). Some, like the Tiananamen Square "leaders" Chai Ling and Li Lu 李录, finished business degrees and went on to brokerage firms and computer companies (10). Some, like the intellectual Henry Wu, who escaped to England, continued to speak passionately on university campuses around the world, telling stories of brutal labor camps, detention centers and prisons, and denouncing China as a "miserable country" (Buruma xxii). A few, like Wuer Kaixi, quickly opted for the high life in the United States, engaging in rock-star behavior and pursuing money-making schemes to sustain his desire for high fashion and fast cars (Buruma 15). Intermittently through the decade of the 1990s, international media attention offered exiles a lucrative way to live off the seemingly insatiable interest in their personal stories. Ultimately, many were spurned by others in the international Chinese diaspora for using the Massacre to promote themselves.

Although the dissidents themselves were often not prepared to act as spokespersons for human rights in China, they did, through their appearances, effect a recognition of China's record of human rights abuse, especially in relation to dissidents incarcerated in Chinese prisons. In the years after the Massacre, whenever the Tiananmen Square exiles, based mainly in the United States, spoke publicly, they reminded Americans of the fate of political prisoners still being held in China.[7] Foremost among them was imprisoned Democracy Wall leader, Wei Jingsheng 魏京生, who had been imprisoned in China since 1979.

Wei Jingsheng

Wei was neither a student nor an artist at Tiananmen but an electrician and activist worker who had been the leader of the earlier Democracy Wall Movement (1979–81) a decade before the Tiananmen Square demonstrations of 1989. Where other dissidents talked of civil rights, political reform, and liberalization, Wei had been using the Western-inflected discourse of human rights that became available inside China as the partial thaw in the Party's hard-line policies opened China to the outside world in the late 1970s. He used the discourse of human rights in the essay entitled "The Fifth Modernization," a radical statement of principles he posted on the Democracy Wall in December 1978. Written in response to the famous "Four Modernizations" of Deng Xiaoping (agriculture, industry, science and technology, and defense), "The Fifth Modernization" encouraged the Party to add democracy to the list of national objectives. The Democracy Wall movement demanded, amongst other things, protections for pro-democratic movements; reexamination of Marxism; freedom of the press; liberalization within the media, arts, and politics; and the end to corruption within Party ranks. For his activism, Wei received two consecutive fifteen-year prison sentences.[8]

By 1981 the Chinese government had quelled the Democracy Wall Movement. Yet the movement became part of a "silent history" that resurfaced nearly a decade later in the June 4 (Tiananmen Square) Movement. As Buruma comments, students of the later June 4

Movement may not have known the history of the Democracy Wall, but they utilized the same rhetoric of freedom from slavery and respect for human dignity that had charged the political atmosphere and had inspired readers at the Wall ten years earlier (98–100).

Although only sporadic news of Wei reached the West from 1979 to 1997,[9] demands for his release punctuated virtually every diplomatic exchange between China and the United States. Human rights groups such as AI, HRW/Asia, and PEN International joined Wei's cause. This public advocacy over a twenty-seven-year period afforded Wei three nominations for the Nobel Peace Prize and further successful nominations for the Gleitsman International Activist Award (won with Nelson Mandela) and the 1996 Sakharov Prize for Freedom of Thought, means through which human rights organizations kept the spotlight on his imprisonment.[10] Advocacy also intensified in the 1990s as the Tiananmen Square exiles brought continual attention to the fate of political dissidents inside China. Such advocacy was one of the means through which the U.S. government kept human rights on the agenda during its diplomatic negotiations with China. Time and again, the United States used demands for the release of Wei and other dissidents as levers in foreign diplomacy and the negotiations through which it secured lucrative contracts for trade and joint ventures in exchange for granting China "most-favored nation" status.

Wei's continued presence in the human rights regime was in part the result of his writings, most prominently his autobiographical essay and his prison letters. The autobiographical essay, "From Maoist Fanatic to Political Dissident," and several letters from prison were published in *The New York Times* and other overseas newspapers after his initial arrest. Both the early essay and his accumulated prison letters were subsequently published in 1997 in the United States in *The Courage to Stand Alone: Letters from Prison and Other Writings*, which appeared a few weeks before Wei's final release from prison. The publication came about as a result of a massive public campaigns directed by China scholars and human rights groups. Compiled with the active commitment of human rights advocates in the United States, *Courage* underscores the critical importance of outside advocates for political prisoners. Indeed, an appendix provides sample letters and petitions and instructs readers to send letters to political leaders in China and the United States calling for Wei's release. Wei's international celebrity may have spared his life. As Buruma relates. "Deng Xiaoping is said to have wanted him shot. The fact that we know what happened during the trial is one of the reasons he was spared" (102). Rights activists and scholars also recognized the importance of this publication in assisting the U.S. government in exerting maximum pressure on China in the lead up to President Clinton's 1998 visit to negotiate bilateral trade agreements and consider China's bid for most-favored nation status.

Wei's prison writings, like those of Martin Luther King, Jr., Ariel Dorfmann, Nelson Mandela, Aung San Suu Kyi, and other imprisoned dissidents, offer a powerful testimony to human endurance and resilience in the face of seemingly insurmountable injustice. In them, Wei engages in a sardonic dialogue with Chinese authorities, relentlessly arguing for democratic reforms in China. Although a strong defender of universal human rights standards, in his writings, ostensibly addressed to Chinese authorities, he utilizes the wisdom of Marxist–Leninist–Mao Zedong thought—not the language of human rights in the West—against Chinese Communist Party practice, demanding that the government honor its own laws; respect human dignity, justice and freedom; and rectify its prior political mistakes.

Wei's prison writings, however, are framed in particular ways by the activists engaged in making his writings and his case more public. In the preface and testimonials bracketing his writings, Wei's advocates frame the text through an American ethos of individualist freedom. Liu Qing 刘青, Chairman of the U.S.-based NGO, Human Rights in China (HRIC), and Wei's Democracy Wall colleague and friend, writes a laudatory preface that underscores Wei's endurance in the face of brutal oppression. "Chinese prisons try to break idealists," he writes: "They failed with Wei." Liu testifies that his friend's strong sense of self as "a dissident speaking out alone against a totalitarian society" (xxi) enabled him to overcome illness, confinement, persecution, threats, taunts, and promises. In her testimonial, Sophia Woodman notes that Wei's daily life in prison was "a microcosm of the struggle for democracy in China: One man upholding his integrity against the unfettered power of the state" (Woodman 249). Her remarks link Wei's symbolic status to that of the unnamed "man and the tank," whose photograph provided the most enduring iconic image that represents the Tiananmen Square Massacre to the outside world.

While the publication of Wei's letters feeds into and sustains hegemonic U.S. narratives of rights politics that position China as a gross violator of "universal human rights," and positions the dissident as the lone individualist railing against the injustices of the State, the publication of his letters nonetheless challenges readers to attend to the cultural, philosophic, and nationalist differences between Western and Asian rights values and to consider the common ground of rights discourses across those differences. Carried through the agency of human rights organizations and supporters at home and abroad, the narrative keeps alive a Chinese-inflected human rights discourse, one engaged in active and ongoing dialogue with rights discourses in democratic nations.

Through his voice, his writings, his faith in China's democratic future, his indomitable commitment, and the sheer force of his personality, Wei kept the hopes of overseas Chinese for democratic reform inside China alive. Pragmatically, his antiauthoritarian stance against the Chinese government facilitated the West's pursuit of human rights, attached to an economic and political agenda, which maintained pressure on China to address, justify, and modify its human rights record. Through his interviews and activism, which include a recently established Foundation that supports a newsletter and a website, he has dedicated his life in exile to maintaining international pressure on China. One of his first gestures after a brief period of recovery of his health in the United States was to call together the exiled dissidents for a forum held at Niagara Falls in an attempt to heal wounds, overcome dissension, and forge new political campaigns through the newly formed Overseas Chinese Democracy Coalition. As he told a reporter recently, no matter how many barriers the government erects, the news gets through to China. It remains an important means of educating Chinese citizens about human rights. Ultimately, however, he believes that change must come from within, through grassroots political resistance.

The cases of Wei and other Chinese nationals living abroad demonstrate how diplomacy, economics, politics, publishing, mass culture, independent media, and international information flows all intersect to shape, in profound but confounding ways, the kinds of stories produced, reproduced, circulated, and reframed in the field of human rights. Here, local stories go global in a global moment dominated by the United States, but transnational circuits have the potential to reach and impact mass audiences, not only in the West but also increasingly in China, through travel, tourism, the Internet, and the underground press.

HUMAN RIGHTS IN CHINA

In a host of sites, from television interviews and newspaper reports, to published anthologies and NGO activism, to the published letters of Wei Jingsheng, personal stories of the events at Tiananmen Square activated interest in extending human rights in China and contributed to a decade of pressure on China for reform. In the years immediately after Tiananmen, China became a pariah nation and found itself "confronted with fierce and unprecedented international criticism of its human rights record" (Svenssen 265). A new NGO, Human Rights in China (HRIC), was founded in the United States in March 1989, in response to Fang Lizhi 方励之 's[11] open letter calling on the Chinese government to respect human rights and release political prisoners. HRIC joined a number of human rights groups, including AI and HRW, to document widespread, serious, and ongoing human rights violations. The list of offences is long. It includes charges of ill-treatment, torture, and the death of political prisoners; arbitrary detention, forced prison labor, and "Re-education through Labor"; suppression of unionism and new political parties; involuntary sterilizations; trade in human body parts and experimentation on human fetuses; and the denial of ethnic, religious, and self-determining rights, particularly in regard to Tibet and the Xinjiang Uighur Autonomous Region.

In response to Western pressure, China issued a series of White Papers on human rights.[12] Directed mainly to a Western audience, these papers argue that China's foremost human rights goal is to "promote people's rights to subsistence and development" (1999). Against the assumption of a moral high ground of human rights practice in the West, China charges the West with hypocrisy, arrogance, and blindness to its own need to reform and lambasts the United States for its record of violence, gun possession, crime, and poverty, as well as race and sex discrimination, child abuse, nuclear testing, arms dealing, and sexual violations by army personnel in foreign countries, all in direct violation of UN conventions.[13] The early white paper (1991) pursues the argument that economic development, tied to political stability, will lead to greater freedoms (even if, as cynical critics were to point out, economic development occurs at the expense of environmental protections, civil and political liberties, democracy and human rights). Later White Papers (1995, 1999), issued as China awaited approval for membership in the WTO, made more concessions. The 1999 paper points out that since 1989 China had signed, ratified, and acceded to seven human rights conventions (albeit with some reservations). These include an International Labor Organization (ILO) agreement (signed with a reservation precluding any union organizing in China) and several UN conventions, including the Convention on the Elimination of Discrimination Against Women (CEDAW), the International Convention on Economic, Social and Cultural Rights (ICESCR), and the International Convention on Civil and Political Rights (ICCPR).[14] The 1999 paper concedes that although China's road to economic development offers enhanced opportunities for China's population, human rights problems exist. It promises "dialogues and cooperation among countries in terms of human rights" (1999) so that China might learn from the experience of the West as it attempts to extend human freedoms.

By 2002, however, the tide had turned. HRW, AI, and HRIC all reported that practices that contravene international covenants continue to occur in China. In response to the growing use of the Internet for purposes not approved by the government,[15] China introduced Strike Hard, a campaign initiated in April 2001 to "safeguard social stability." Leading academics were arrested, magazines and newspapers closed, Internet cafe licenses revoked, website access patrolled and controlled, and suspected criminals, terrorists, and religious extremists denied legal safeguards. The government hired a virtual army of information technology specialists to patrol web usage, blocking access to sites supporting human rights (among other forbidden topics).

Since Strike Hard began, HRW estimates that more than ten thousand people have been arrested and 1,800 executed, with twice that number receiving death sentences (2002 Report). Despite its limited adoption of human rights conventions, in 2002 China rejected UN requests to investigate claims of human rights abuse within its own borders, charging that such investigations violate national sovereignty. Officially, the government absolves itself from charges of human rights violations, continuing to argue that collective rights to subsistence must take priority over individual civil and political rights. But the country is clearly conscious of its need to address its critics. While cracking down on dissident political activities, it has encouraged academic discussions, conferences, and debates on human rights. As Marina, Svensson notes, human rights discourses in China have an extended history, one that has tempered the legacies of the British enlightenment with Confucianism, communist socialism, and the Cultural Revolution.

Outside China, Asian studies scholars concede that some progress has been made in response to continued criticisms by the United Nations, as well as monitoring by NGOs, pressure from China's diasporic communities, and diplomatic pressure from the United States. But most note that concessions, when offered, too often come as a trade-off to gain economic advantage, such as the need to maintain most-favored nation status with the United States, to join and then protect membership in the WTO, or to win the Olympic Games bid, all designed to enhance China's growing dominance in the global economy. These sobering observations remind us that the whole notion of "human rights" is capable of becoming a bargaining chip between domestic and foreign actors, a chip of fluctuating, and highly ideological, currency in the charged international atmosphere of expanding marketplaces and international alliances.

Nevertheless, in light of China's strong economic growth, coupled with widespread dissatisfactions in urban and rural areas, new media and information flows, porous national boundaries, and transformations made possible by global modernities, some proponents of human rights both within and outside of the country suggest that further political liberalization may be possible as a result of successful and ongoing economic, social, and cultural advances (Sullivan 124; Weatherley 137).

CULTURAL REVOLUTION LITERATURE

Although public storytelling about the events at Tiananmen Square remained off limits inside China, the Chinese government continued modernization campaigns that opened opportunities for new kinds of stories to be told in the post-Tiananmen period. From the end of the Mao era and the arrest and trial of the Gang of Four in 1978–79, when Deng Xiaoping initiated the policy to "let a hundred flowers bloom," new literary experimentation, tied to the modernization agenda, flourished. In the decades of the 1980s and 1990s, the government encouraged an open-door policy in arts and education even as it enacted continuous purges and issued condemnations of "spiritual pollution" and "bourgeois liberal influences." These new policies in the arts were designed to open China to the world, enhance the State within a global economy, and counter its inferiority complex vis à vis the West (Barmé 7–12). In this context, cultural workers, whom the State recognized as important to its agenda, entered into a new partnership with the government. Encouraged to absorb fifty years of modernism in less than a decade, cultural workers engaged in a process that did not so much involve absorption of European forms as the consumption and production of imported cultural and political images, carefully managed and under the surveillance of the State (J. Wang 2001, 86–7).

In the aftermath of the Democracy Wall Movement in the 1980s, writers, artists, students, and intellectuals met at various Democracy Salons throughout China, and particularly in Beijing and Shanghai. Although after 1989 the Salons closed and intellectuals and artists abandoned overt political talk of democratic reforms, artists continued to engage with Western cultural forms in aesthetic terms, carefully avoiding political critique (Dutton 1998; Harootunian). Colluding in an uneasy partnership with the government, they enjoyed security as long as they maintained a kind of aesthetic self-censorship. The government also tolerated, even encouraged, new artistic movements as it steered the country into a global cultural and economic marketplace. With the youth movements also came new modes of storytelling and new stories of a modernized China. Thus, while stories of Tiananmen Square witnesses could not be told, personal exposés critical of Mao's Cultural Revolution of the 1960s and 1970s found government support.

In the decade of the 1980s, stories and memoirs of the Cultural Revolution began to emerge, written by former Red Guards and educated youth (*zhiqing* 知青) who had been "sent down" to the countryside at Mao's directive (1966–77). These stories became popular in China and in the West, but they served different ends in the two locations. For the first time in Chinese history, personal stories exposing the dark side of socialist society became public. Leading Chinese intellectuals published confessional narratives, like Yang Jiang 杨绛 who, in *Six Chapters from my Life Downunder* (1984), accepts personal responsibility for her aquiescent participation in the Cultural Revolution and asks forgiveness, before the disgraceful events "slip through our minds and vanish without a trace" (2–3). Museums sponsored exhibitions of memorabilia; libraries published directories of writings; and associations of former *zhiqing* were formed. New anthologies of *zhiqing* writing appeared. Scores of anonymous confessors came forward to reveal their shame at having betrayed the formative ideals of the Revolution. Personal reminiscences fueled scripts for several television series, theatrical performances, and new memoirs.

After Tiananmen, narratives of the Cultural Revolution proliferated, taking on a nostalgic and sentimental quality as elegies for a lost but shared past. These previously silenced stories of separated families, rustication of the urban elites, and their subjection to abuse, persecution, imprisonment, torture, and death at the hands of the Red Guards provided a collective outlet for the grief for loved ones lost and the beginnings of a healing process for individuals and families. They also contributed to a healing process in the nation. In a phenomenon similar to the writing of Afrikaners in post-apartheid South Africa, writers began to split themselves off from the past to signal their own reform and the country's shift to a new era and a new political agenda. These texts reframe the Cultural Revolution as a dark era, historicized, shielded, and sealed off from the "new," secular, and modern China. Although the experiences of people during the Cultural Revolution had been much more complicated than the stories allowed, the narratives echoed the popular refrain in China that the evils of the Mao era had passed, that in China a bright future had dawned.

Officially, the Chinese government welcomed and promoted what came to be called wounded or scar literature (*shanghen wenxue*) as part of a new political regime intent on "thoroughly negat[ing] the Cultural Revolution" (Zhong et al. xx). As these stories, taken collectively, redirected political critique to China's past, they had the potential to unite the masses, spur a new nationalism, and signal social change. Made possible by the new government discourse of reform, of "leaving the past behind," the genre of scar literature contributed to a resurgent, progressive nationalism. Affecting an historical disjunction, relegating policies aimed at producing docile followers of Mao to an earlier era, these personal narratives kept in circulation a narrative of national progress and enlightenment through acts of remembering the faults of the old government on which the new China had turned its back.

THE CIRCULATION OF CULTURAL REVOLUTION NARRATIVES IN THE WEST

Scar literature also circulated in overseas avenues—where stories were received and interpreted differently. In the 1990s scores of Cultural Revolution memoirs and films appeared in the West, among them Nien Cheng's *Life and Death in Shanghai* (1986), Chang Jung's *Wild Swans: Three Daughters of China* (1991), and Anchee Min's *Red Azaleas* (1994); films like Chen Kaige's *Farewell, My Concubine* (1993), and Joan Chen's *Xiu Xiu, the Sent Down Girl* (1998). Narratives that claimed to represent the lives of the victims of China's communist past, these memoirs told audiences in the West of the gross violations of people's rights during the "dark years" of Mao's Cultural Revolution. Published with "one eye on the Western market" (Giffone, website) these memoirs and films fed into the West's fascination with narratives of victimhood of all sorts,[16] with their "dark age master narrative" and their drama of "'helpless' (therefore good) Chinese vs. 'evil' Chinese" (Xueping et al. xviii). Commodified and marketed in the West, they reaffirmed outmoded fantasies of

China's past. Zhong Xueping, Wang Zheng, and Bai Di suggest that "Western" tales of victimization during the Cultural Revolution "produce yet another set of exotic stories that cater to the expectations of Western readers, that is, political campaigns, political persecutions, sexual repression, and so forth" (xvi).

Often conveyed in a mood of exilic melancholy, the Cultural Revolution narratives published in the West produced precisely the opposite effect of similar tales circulating in China. Written mainly by Chinese women in exile and read overseas, they offered Western readers evidence of China's moral degeneracy, paradoxically reifying outmoded notions of Red Guard China and reproducing historical understanding devoid of complexity. Like trauma narratives produced elsewhere, these Chinese memoirs were adapted in Western sites to promote empathetic identification but in a way that confirmed previously established beliefs and fantasies. Cultural Revolution narratives chosen for publication in the West conform to a narrowly focused story of one victim's courage against the horrors of the Mao era, reproducing the iconic "man and the tank" stance for Western consumption. Individually and collectively, they reproduce a common tale, as narrators chronicle the horrors of the Cultural Revolution, including separations from family, exile to the remote countryside, persecution, brutality and rape, and other forms of sexual violation at the hands of the Red Guards. *Life and Death in Shanghai* is a typical example. The narrator, a wealthy, well-educated Nationalist, opens the memoir on a melancholy note: "The past is forever with me and I remember it all" (1). Cheng tells of being victimized by the government for refusing to admit to being a bourgeois "enemy of the people," of being intimidated, humiliated, and terrorized by the Red Guards, and made to suffer in solitary confinement for six years. Jung Chang's immensely popular *Wild Swans* details generations of women's suffering, confirming for Western readers China's status as one of the world's worst abusers of human rights. Not only does the three generational saga detail the horrors of China's feudal, patriarchal, and totalitarian past, it also provides ample evidence of ongoing human rights violations, including references to the takeover of Tibet, forced abortion, the one-child policy, government spying, corruption, and greed. Popular with both human rights advocates on the left and anti-communist activists on the right, this "dark age narrative commands a stronger popular imagination in the United States than even in China" (Zhong et al. xxi).

The reiteration of the horrors of Communist China for Western consumption raises several issues about the commodification of suffering, the transmission and legitimacy of cultural memory, and the resonance of certain voices in different locales as they convey authority over the stories they tell. As the editors of *Some of Us* note, China favored Cultural Revolution narratives by male intellectuals. Their stories carried moral authority and assisted the government's reform policy, signaling a break from the past. In the West victimized women wrote the most popular narratives. Their stories of suffering and abuse were taken by English-speaking readers to be representative of China's ongoing history of patriarchal treatment of women (xx–xxii). In China, narratives authored by privileged male intellectuals lent legitimacy to the condemnation of the excesses of the Mao era; the Western sagas authored by women allowed for readers' empathetic identification with the victim as survivor while also directing attention toward individual suffering and remedy. In the West, the stories reinforced the reductive good–bad dichotomies of Cold War politics: the West versus the East, democracy versus communism, liberation versus oppression, victims versus persecutors, individuals versus the totalitarian State. They maintained China's reputation in the West, closing off examinations of the complex, multilayered histories of the Mao era, of multiple social, political, and personal contradictions, of ordinary lives, and of those with different, often positive, experiences as Chinese people living through the period engaged "in their quest to become modern subjects" (Zhong et al. xxvii).

Some diasporic Chinese intellectuals resisted the West's ready acceptance of Cultural Revolution literature as indicative of China's record of human rights abuse. They began to use alternative media outlets to challenge naive interpretations of the scar literature genre, both within China and beyond its borders. *Some of Us*, a recent compilation by Chinese diasporic women in the United States, presents nine narratives about the Mao era, recollected in another place and refracted through a new set of rhetorics. A number of these personal narratives of the Cultural Revolution tell counter-narratives of happy childhoods lived in the promise of Mao's vision for a fully-matured socialist State. Others tell of childhoods spent as sent-down girls whose social worlds were extended by the experience of working in the countryside. Collectively, these narratives refuse the story of victimization and project more complex, reflexive, and critically nuanced accounts that defy the wounded victim model. But *Some of Us* was accepted and published by Rutgers University Press rather than a trade press like Random House, and directed toward an academic, often feminist, readership, rather than the popular audience targeted by mainstream trade presses.

Inside China, the expansion of public access to national and international media outlets allowed access to a range of formerly silenced stories of China's past, particularly stories of rural women often living in semifeudal conditions. In the 1980s, radio journalist Xinran launched a late night talkback radio show, "Words on the Night Breeze," and attracted a steadily growing and largely uncensored remote and rural audience of listeners. Over the eight-year period of the show's success, the anonymity of the media enabled thousands of women to report horrendous stories of brutality, rape, and injustice at the hands of China's men, many of whom had been Party members or *appuratchiks*. These rural women witnessed to their restricted knowledge of sexuality, limited awareness of rights, and lack of protections of any kind from abuse—be they legal, ethical, civil, or communal. Given the absence of protections, anonymity remained a founding condition of witnessing.

After moving to London, Xinran reassembled the women's stories into a book, *The Good Women of China* (2002), framed and translated for a Western audience. As she traveled overseas to promote the book, she generated an international forum for discussion of rural women's lives in China. In this global context, the radio host became an agent of discourse on behalf of the anonymous women who themselves had been denied public personhood. The penetration of modern technology into the remote countryside in the form of the radio gave these women a platform for recognition and change. Their stories, later put in circulation in Western locales, placed those voices in an international public sphere where stories of sexual abuse became part of an international feminist agenda for action.

The publication of *The Good Women of China* inserted the witness voices of rural Chinese women within the global politics of the human rights regime and the culture of commodification surrounding Western fantasies of China. Many of the stories concern sexual violation and abuse of rural women dating back to the Cultural Revolution and to a China where women continue to have limited access to education, employment, or opportunity. Xinran herself participates in a commodification of Cultural Revolution narratives that feed the seemingly insatiable appetites of Western readers for Chinese horror stories. In a central chapter of the anthology, the radio hosts tells her own Cultural Revolution story, structured in keeping with the "dark era" script. Moreover, the appalling nature of the women's victimization and the popularity of the radio program gave Xinran a platform to be received as an heroic saviour of rural women, a stance transferred into a Western framework. Through the media hype surrounding her book, Xinran becomes a new hero, a female equivalent to Wei Jingsheng, an individual speaking out against oppression.

On the one hand, the production, circulation, and reception of Cultural Revolution narratives throughout the West framed and constrained witness voices and stories of suffering within the culture of consumption and its tropes of individualist hardship, survival, and triumph. On the other, alternative technologies of storytelling and witnessing, coupled with the circulation of the women's collective stories globally, made possible, for some victimized listeners and readers, new knowledge, recognition, and rescue. The contexts of production and reception provoke different readings of China to itself (within a government-approved framework) and to the West (within Western ideologies and fantasies). In an age of media access, the national and international transmission of stories like those told by Xinran enabled rural women to voice their ongoing oppression in backward rural communities and offered those dissident voices a platform within an international feminist community.

THE NEW LITERATURE OF YOUNG CHINA

Scar literature, as it is produced and circulated within and outside China in the post-Tiananmen era, is the literature of the generations who came of age during the 1960s and 1970s. Their narratives have contributed to the political and cultural work of disavowing a dark past in service to a modern and progressive future, even as the State maintained tight censorship over the more recent trauma of the Massacre at Tiananmen Square. For the generation born of the 1980s, however, the trauma and betrayal of the ideals of the June 4 Movement at Tiananmen Square gave rise to a disillusionment with politics that marked the post-Tiananmen era in China. This loss of faith in political processes of liberalization begun in the 1980s, coupled with the crosscurrents of a global modernity, impacts new forms of storytelling.

Young China's dissident writers and artists of the late 1990s, denied a public political forum, sought alternative outlets for their passions, away from the political arena. In their music, poetry, and prose they reveal a lost faith in any unifying discourse, political philosophy, or national allegiance. Echoing the songs of the dissident Tiananmen rock stars Cui Jian 崔健 ("I Have Nothing to My Name") and Taiwanese-born Hou Dejian 侯德健 ("Howl" and "Descendants of the Dragon"), they exchanged protest for hedonism, nihilism, and desire for oblivion. Like followers of popular writer Wang Shuo 王朔, the founder of the genre known as "hooligan literature," contemporary Chinese urban youth began to espouse an "aesthetics of debauchery" in their lives and their writing (Wang 1996, 271–2).

Forbidden to engage in political critique and urged to join a global capitalist market, China's youth yoked their desires to consumerist identities within a globalized international youth culture. In urban centers an underground grunge music culture (*pengke*) emerged, along with a counterculture of drugs, prostitution, and sexual experimentation. Internet cafes proliferated, especially around university districts. For a time, chatrooms allowed exploration of previously tabooed subjects. For example, Mian Mian 棉棉 and Wei Hui 卫慧, two well-connected urban grunge artists, went on-line in a chat room conversation and achieved immediate notoriety when one accused the other of plagiarizing from her work and masturbating as she wrote. Punk and grunge artists, musicians, and writers exploited their celebrity status on Internet sites, exported their desirable products around the world, and expanded their fame through international promotional tours, thus becoming part of a global youth culture.

A host of popular writers emerged in the 1990s in China, promoting a literature of rebellion with an eye on the market. Young women raised in the modernizing aftermath of Tiananmen joined the craze. In urban areas, political and economic reforms offered young women unprecedented employment opportunities, which they exploited to achieve a means of personal, social, and economic autonomy. Labeled the "Bad Girls" of Chinese literature by Western publicists, these defiant young women used fiction to explore new subjectivities. They gained international attention with their outrageous exhibitionism on the web, narcissistic self-regard, and hedonistic literary explorations.

This latest wave of "bad girl" literature explores a new generation of women's desires for freedom and autonomy not through a politics of resistance but through a poetics of embodied pleasures. Borrowing from recent translations of Anglo and French feminisms, fused with Chinese traditions and mythologies, and honed to deliver a specifically Asian critique of patriarchal values, these Beijing- or Shanghai-based women authorize themselves through explorations of narcissistic individualism tied to libidinous desires. Given China's reputation for patriarchal and repressive sexual codes for women, the new assertions shocked overseas readers and critics while being received with enthusiasm among China's globally-connected trendsetters. Wei Hui, author of the international best seller, *Shanghai Baby* (2001), and Mian Mian, author of *Candy* (2003), are among the most celebrated practitioners. This "personal" literature, notes Jing Wang with some opprobrium, eschews politics, instead celebrating hedonism and "riotous rebellion" through underworld themes of drug-taking, prostitution, sadomasochism, pornography, and personal freedom through "consumerism and self-conscious individualism" (1996, 219). Wang comments that these writers, far from being iconoclastic, actually collude with the government by promoting a culture of consumption, turning rebellion into a new consumer trend. But the possibilities of autonomy, professional careers, international celebrity, and new wealth that writing offers to the young authors exceed the dictates of the State. Marketed for their defiance of feminine codes, these women gained international notoriety through lucrative overseas publishing contracts, international publicity tours, network television interviews, and syndicated newspaper stories. Advertised as "Banned in China,"[17] their mainland narratives gain a kind of symbolic capital that, itself, promotes the writers in an international marketplace. These spunky chroniclers of new China "*linking up with the tracks of the world*" ([italics in original] Zhang Zhen 2000, 93) are lauded on the covers of English editions as "the original voices of *fin-de-siecle* fiction" that is "leaving the past behind."

Reviewers of the so-called banned books deploy descriptors such as dirty realism, Glam Lit, Pretty Girl Lit, or Oriental Grunge to characterize the works. Such descriptors serve several functions. They promote sales in the West, heighten attention to China's youth, and promote China as a progressive, secular, modern nation. Self-fashioned orientalist cover illustrations of glamorous, "China doll" fashion model faces and provocative blurbs on English-language editions present an alluring package, commodifying for an expanding global youth market a supposedly new group of young women writers who presently occupy the space of its most spectacular sexual excesses.

English-speaking China scholars are divided on the question of whether new literature eschews politics or is another mode of resistance, Surprisingly, a number of established China watchers give the trend a positive valence. Michael Dutton, for example, argues in *Streetlife China* that the youth cultures of subalternity, in which some of these authors play a part, occupy a critical space in which today's young artists explore and come to terms with the everyday tactics of resistance (*á la* Michel de Certeau) and move beyond narratives that valorize political dissent. John Sheng, in opposition to critics who demean the consumer-oriented literature, remarks that the ban of

Shanghai Baby in China prompted widespread social commentary and in-depth discussions about the nature of literature in promoting social change, philosophic debates about concepts of human nature, and analyses of social problems brought about by China's economic reforms (Sheng). Not the text itself, but the social effects of its banning, he argues, promoted social and cultural diversity and discussions of intellectual maturity amongst China's youth. These China commentators provide perspectives beyond the "shock of the new" that challenge the binary categories that structured East–West cultural debates of the 1980s.

Many diasporic Chinese intellectuals in the West treat the new popular literature with hostility. In *High Culture Fever*, Wang maintains a fidelity to the dashed hopes of Tiananmen, arguing forcefully that the rebellious youth of the 1990s were not rebels, "for there was no purpose for their rebellion. It was just a lifestyle, decadent and cool" (Wang 1996, 271–2). Zhang Zhen cynically assesses the new literature as indicative of the expansion of consumer culture that has been an official policy of the State designed to prevent further unrest since the Tiananmen Square disaster (2000, 94). Zhang concedes, nonetheless, that the new literature can also exceed the intentions of the State by offering new opportunities to explore previously tabooed topics in China; defy China's repressive patriarchal traditions; engage with Western feminisms; and explore an embodied female interiority never before possible. For Zhang, the new literature, in defiance of patriarchal repressions, writes the subject into a new political and libidinal economy, partaking of a transnational female consciousness, "a new powerful sensibility that challenges the identification of Chinese national culture with masculinity" (1999, 334).

In the post-Tiananmen era, individualistically motivated literature seems to promote individualist desire and autonomy, and to challenge past cultural traditions and practices. This literature writes a new female subject into existence, the modern citizen-subject desirous of personal autonomy and conscious of civil rights. Yet questions linger concerning the potential of the literature of Young China to spur social change, speed democratic reforms, and extend human rights.

CHINA AND THE POLITICS OF GLOBALIZATION

Chinese's turn to a capacious culture of consumption results not so much from a national attachment to or adoption of Western notions of bourgeois liberalism but as a response to new state-initiated policies designed to encourage mass consumption to drive the economic engine of globally inflected modernization. As part of this modernization project, the Chinese government enlists intellectuals and writers in both high and popular culture venues in its image-making apparatuses. Through their production of new cultural forms, writers and intellectuals present to the world new images of China, particularly images of Beijing and Shanghai, figured as world-class cosmopolitan centers, and thereby contribute to the promotion of business markets inside the country. In this way, the State, the markets, the media, and the writers collude in "reinvent[ing] the national capital into a world-class center of cultural consumption" (Wang 2000, 87). In constant negotiation, or collusion, with the Chinese State, young intellectuals and writers help direct China into a global market economy.

The new narratives, mining the field of the individual and personal, construct a citizen-self that is a private, consuming subject, one far removed from the socialist cadres of comrades advocated by the Marxist agenda of the past. In this sense, the literature of Young China offers consumers ways of imagining, enacting, and becoming new kinds of citizen-subjects for a globally-marketed and marketing China. Although the new cultural formations of Young China seem to be devoid of any politics of reform, they construct a consuming subject who also becomes an individualized subject and a subject of property rights. As Wang recognizes, consumer desires rebound on the State, pressuring government to evolve a "new international intellectual property regime" organized to protect and ensure people's rights, but more specifically the rights of urban elites in the new "consumerist democracy" (2000, 94–5). The pressure to protect citizen's rights to property has become critical to demands for the evolution of civil rights protections by the Chinese government. This move is particularly urgent since the earlier Marxist–Leninist–Maoist linkage of the authoritarian State's control over citizens and the State's control and provision of housing and employment has been severed in post-socialist China.

Thus, while the Chinese government has encouraged experimentation in the arts and attempted to maintain control over literary production in service to the State, it cannot fully control the proliferating effects of narrative experimentation on producers, consumers, and the larger society of mainland, exiled, and diasporic Chinese, ever more thoroughly entangled through the interconnectedness made possible by the Internet. The forces of modernization enable new examinations of subjectivity, interiority, privacy, sexuality, and private property ownership that were not previously part of a Chinese cultural and literary scene. State policies also generate an emergent privileged, highly educated leisure class available to consume narratives, imagine new forms of individualized subjectivity, assume new subject positions as subjects of property, and gain access to rights discourse. Ironically for some, in today's global economy, capitalism, not socialism, is driving the push for (limited and elite serving) democratic citizen rights in China.

While the downside of this relationship of complicity is that the State continues to channel the energies of Tiananmen-style social critique into vigorous engagement with the global marketplace, the upside is that a new citizen-subject capable of demanding rights has entered the social, personal, and political imaginary within China. Yet, it must be noted that the cultural transformation of the old socialist citizen-subject into a new consumerist citizen-subject has been taking place primarily in the cosmopolitan centers of Beijing and Shanghai, producing disparities between notions of citizenship in cities and citizenship in regional centers and the countryside. However, unpredictable changes are also occurring in rural and remote areas. Many factors influence this change: among them the introduction of the Internet, investigative reporting by an international media, and traveling sites of protest made possible, for example, by writers like Xinran through her book promotions outside of China. Journalists traveling to remote areas of China report an increase in political protests around wages, safety, and housing as people in the country become irate about the increasing disparity in income levels between city and country (Armitage 2002; Armitage 2003a,b). In addition, a discourse on human rights, already widely debated in the academy, percolates down in practical and pragmatic ways into sites of foment through NGO-supported Internet sites. Despite the State's resistance to rights discourse outside an Asian-values framework, new cultural formations in cities and protests in the countryside open up avenues for human rights discourse to enter and transform China from within.

RE-PRESENTING TIANANMEN SQUARE

Having considered the kinds of personal stories coming out of China and the Chinese diaspora in the decade after the Tiananmen Square Massacre, and the politics of their production, circulation, and reception in and outside China, we return now to narratives of the event itself in order to investigate how the cultural memory of Tiananmen translates into contemporary culture. We noted earlier that, in the years after the Massacre, dissidents in exile made their tours of college and university campuses in the United States, Japan, Canada, England, and the Netherlands, among other Western nations. Throughout the 1990s, as China bid for the Olympic Games, gained most-favored nation status with the United States, membership in the WTO, attracted joint business ventures and overseas loans, and exacted numerous trade concessions from the West, its human rights record remained open to intense scrutiny in the international news.[18] Whenever and wherever these issues were taken up in the Western media, journalists inevitably invited Tiananmen Square dissidents to comment on China's rights record. Tiananmen remained a signal event in the West, contested and reinvented throughout the 1990s and into the twenty-first century through cultural interchange and the global politics of negotiation. Yet, few memoirs of dissidents who participated in the demonstrations appeared until the 2001 publication of Su Xiaokang's *A Memoir of Misfortune* and the 2002 publication of Zhang Boli 张博立's *Escape from China*. Neither narrative, however, details the June 4 Movement, the Tiananmen Square Massacre, or the narrators' participation in the demonstrations.

The Gate of Heavenly Peace

Personal narratives of Tiananmen Square have circulated in the West in the latter half of the 1990s, primarily through the documentary film *The Gate of Heavenly Peace* (1995) and two autobiographical novels, Hong Ying 虹影's *Summer of Betrayal* (1997) and Annie Wang's *Lili: A Novel of Tiananmen* (2002). In 1995 *The Gate of Heavenly Peace*, created a scandal even before it premiered at the New York Film Festival. The three-hour-long documentary, produced and directed by Carma Hinton and Richard Gordon, created the most comprehensive account ever to emerge from the events of Spring 1989.[19] Hinton and Gordon interviewed a diverse pool of participants, both in and outside of China, including student leaders, academics, union leaders, the parent of a slain student, government officials, and Cui Jian, the Taiwanese rock star who returned to Beijing to join the demonstrators and participate in the hunger strike. In the final mix, the filmmakers interspersed the personal testimony of witnesses with Western and Chinese news footage, home video footage, and music videos. Hinton and Gordon claimed that their primary goal in making the documentary was "to get the facts straight" about the Massacre and to enable participants in the events to speak for themselves, rather than have their voices muted in journalist reports where reporters spoke for them (White 2–3 of 5). Their "truth," culled from interviews and documentary footage and cinematographically constructed from a particular point of view, prompted intense discussion about the politics of "voice," about who speaks for the students, and in what contexts.

Gate's cinematographic trajectory challenged received wisdom about the lessons of Tiananmen. It suggested that radical students like Chai Ling, the democratically elected leader of the protest and key spokesperson in the film, actually may have invited and encouraged police violence. For the first time, a narrative of blame implicating the victims of the Massacre entered the discourse of Tiananmen Square, splitting the ranks of dissidents and sparking heated controversy. Dissident students, China scholars, and Chinese government officials discussed (and condemned) the film even before its release.

The most controversial aspect of the film concerned the debate between student leaders on the eve of the Massacre as to whether they should stay in the Square or disperse the crowds to avoid possible bloodshed. Juxtaposing "radical" and "moderate" students, the directors imputed blame for the Massacre to the radicals, like Chai Ling, who, in opposition to more moderate students like Wang Dan 王丹, refused to leave the Square. The film highlights Chai's leadership and assigns her a strategic role in inciting the violence that led to the Massacre at key points throughout the narrative.

The intensity of controversy induced by the film's apparently revisionist politics called the past into question, creating a fissure in the accepted wisdom that the students were innocent victims. In response to these unexpected resonances, critics and commentators took sides, contesting the film's constructed boundaries between the moderates and the radicals. Journalists took up the issue of students' culpability. In virtually every interview with dissident leaders in the United States after the release of *Gate*, dissident students were challenged about their behavior on the Square. In preparation for President Clinton's visit to China for talks on China's most-favored nation status in 1998, news channels across the nation returned to the history and memory of the Massacre. Jim Lehrer separately interviewed recently released Democracy Wall activists Wang Dan and Wei Jingsheng. *The News Hour* featured a debate between three Chinese dissidents, Li Lu, Harry Wu, and Xiao Qiang 肖强, asking them how they thought Clinton should deal with China during his visit. Scores of "exiles" were invited once again to tour university campuses, revisiting their personal stories of the bloodshed of June 4.[20]

Interviewers also asked former student leaders to comment and to judge the behavior of Chai Ling and Wuer Kaixi, whom the *Gate* documentary characterized as "radical." As noted earlier, Chai and Wuer shunned the media and abjured the political stage, opting, instead, to take advantage of their position in the United States to make money. For this, reporters implicitly accused them of selling out their socialist values and commitments. In other words, the U.S. media, by promoting a romantic notion of dissidence and criticizing the former protestors for pursuing economic gain, seeded dissension among the dissident students, maintained binary divisions between American democracy and Chinese communism, accused exiles of failing their ideals when they succeeded in their American entrepreneurial quests, and shielded Americans from the vast forces of modernization that were overtaking China.

This particular controversy affected other political agendas as well. The introduction of a narrative of culpability in *Gate*, in shifting attention away from the government and to the students for the bloodshed, took pressure off Clinton to respond to exiled students' demands that he secure an apology for the Tiananmen Square Massacre in return for trade agreements. Clinton did not press for human rights reforms as a condition of bilateral agreements that gave China most-favored nation status during his visit, nor have President Bush or leaders of the European Union in response to the latest round of post-9/11 UN monitoring of human rights violations in China.[21] Clinton did, however, visit students at Beijing University to discuss human rights and deliver a speech in support of human rights that was broadcast on public television in China.

Novels of Tiananmen

If *Gate* put in circulation alternative interpretations of the heroism and actions of dissidents during the event, *Summer of Betrayal* and *Lili*, both written by women in exile, return to the scene of the Tiananmen Square Massacre to take the events of Tiananmen as backdrop for explorations of women's desire in post-socialist China. These narratives disguise the historical details in order to protect family members and offer alternative venues for acts of remembrance. Emerging in different geographic, linguistic, cultural, and temporal contexts, they convey the memories of the event and embody the trauma through a pastiche of personal memory, fictionalized history, new philosophic underpinnings, traditional Chinese mythologies, contemporary Western allusions, and documentary scenes. They carry the memory into new cultural landscapes in which memory exceeds the personal.

More about personal relationships than about politics, both novels revolve around women's relationship to the State and to the West as exemplified in their relationships to the men in their lives. The betrayal of the State to live up to the ideals of the citizenry forms the backdrop of the narrative of love and sexuality. Both novels begin with the Tiananmen Square turmoil in order to imagine a future beyond the Massacre in which China is radically transformed by the processes of modernization, modernization that makes possible female autonomy, private desire, and consumer pleasures, and participation in a global civic sphere. Published in the West when Cultural Revolution memoirs were reaching a saturation point, these narratives have sparked a new awareness for Western readers of a modern, secular, post-socialist China.

Hong Ying's widely marketed *Summer of Betrayal* opens to scenes of violence in Beijing as the Tiananmen Square Massacre unfolds. Taking place between June 4 and August 2, 1989, the narrative involves a group of post-Tiananmen protesters and students who call themselves the "Degraded Survivors"—political dissidents, artists, and intellectuals associated in the text with the June 4 Movement (but in all probability more reminiscent of similar salon-styled groups associated with the Democracy Wall movement of an earlier decade).[22] Hong's "survivors" include a feuding band of insecure, damaged, opportunistic males and a lesser number of savvy, self-confident women. Incorporating aspects of political and artistic dissidence known to have occurred during the Democracy Wall movement and in Beijing at the time of the Massacre, the narrative traces the group's underground world, gradually exposing the chauvinism and shallow pretenses of the male band of bohemian artists and intellectuals, all of whom eventually betray the women. In this, Hong deploys the trope of betrayal to parallel that experienced by dissident students in the wake of Tiananmen.

In a situation fueled by danger and desperation, the women grow strong, defying the dictates of both their male companions and the State. But their defiance is one of embodied libidinous desire rather than of political action. In the final scene of the narrative, the protagonist Lin Ying defiantly flaunts her naked body before the police who come to arrest the group. Released from social and psychic constraints, Lin performs a specifically feminine dance of embodied psychic resistance. The prose bears echoings from the existential philosophy of the beat generation and from the philosophy of desire of contemporary French feminism as Hong Ying offers a reading of

Tiananmen in which political activism is rerouted through a libidinous poetics of female desire.

If Tiananmen Square is the event and backdrop of *Summer of Betrayal*, the imaginative and philosophical foreground derives from the new interest in psychoanalysis and feminism brought into intellectual China initially during the opening up of the 1980s but even more pervasively in the aftermath of the UN-sponsored International Women's Conference held in Beijing in 1995. First published in Taiwan in 1992, and widely circulated in mainland China despite the ban imposed one year after Hong Ying's departure from China, *Summer of Betrayal* has been translated into ten languages. English press reviewers enthusiastically praised the novel, presenting Hong as representative of the new generation of cosmopolitan Chinese women, within a new Western imaginary. In the West, the novel's shock value had to do with its exploration of privacy, sexuality, and feminist resistance, aspects of Chinese culture unfamiliar and unexpected in the contexts of Western understandings of China.

In its erotic dimensions and frank explorations of female sexuality, *Summer of Betrayal* partakes of a transnational female consciousness that is a feature of a plethora of other contemporary diasporic Chinese women's writing, such as London-based Liu Hong's *Startling Moon* (2001), Canadian Evelyn Lau's *Runaway: Diary of a Street Kid* (1989) and *Other Women* (1995), and Australian Lillian Ng's *Swallowing Clouds* (1997). These autobiographical novels explore new narratives of identity that establish transglobal connections between diasporic Chinese intellectuals dispersed in communities throughout the Western world.

Annie Wang's parodic novel *Lili: A Novel of Tiananmen* (2001) explores the complex layerings of contemporary China, the divisions between Eastern and Western perceptions, the transience of modern China, the pervasiveness of Western influences, the horrors of the political situation, and the possibilities for change.[23] Written on the edge of satire and far removed from Cultural Revolution literature, although echoing back to it, it opens with the arrest of the anti-heroine in a Beijing hangout in 1989 and moves inexorably toward the tragedy of Tiananmen Square. Arrested on charges of "having a corrupt lifestyle and hooliganism," Lili is sentenced, without trial, to three months "rehabilitation through labor" (3). After her release Lili drifts into disillusionment, by chance meeting an American journalist, Roy, a rebel from his middle-class bourgeois life, who becomes her lover, father of her child, spokesperson for Western human rights values of liberty and autonomy, and her eventual means of escape.

The love story of Roy and Lili encodes complex relationships of East and West, of ying and yang, transiting across the imaginary binary previously dividing the West and the East. The two travel through China, opening a travelogue that witnesses many of the horrors of degraded and dehumanizing life in the cities as well as the countryside. Roy's deep appreciation of Chinese traditional culture and his commitment to human rights ideals offers hope to a despairing Lili who, while remaining clear-sighted about his failings, his innocence, and his naiveté, opens herself to new perceptions about human rights and democracy. Through the travel episodes the narrative explores the American's idealism, while also exposing his propensity to intrude on the lives of others and blunder into potentially fateful situations.

The final third of the narrative details the events leading up to the fatal days of early June 1989. Although a bystander, Lili is drawn to the students' desires for a better China and the eloquence of their demands for "democracy now." Through Lili's eyes, the narrative records the "moment of destiny" when students declared the hunger strike, demanding political reform and equality in what she knows is a patriotic movement, not a "turmoil." Lili witnesses the growing support of intellectuals who entered the Square wearing white sashes for easy identification, the swelling participation of police, peasants, military officers, and Buddhist nuns, the mesmerizing performance of the students' anthem, "Heirs of the Dragon," the arrival of the Goddess of Democracy "holding her torch in a face off [sic] with Chairman Mao" (Wang 2001, 297), and finally the bloodshed. In this moment of transformation, the narrator announces that "the Lili of Beijing died that night, but a new Lili was born somewhere else. Somewhere where freedom and respect bloom" (Wang 2001, 307).

In her narrative of remembering, Wang expands the notion of contemporary China by offering snapshots of the country as economically, politically, geographically, and culturally diverse. Doing so, she renders China as a vast space of transition, permeable to new discourses coming from the West and returning to the West rerouted from an Asian perspective. Wang has explicitly linked her literary project with the possibilities for a China penetrated by the discourse of human rights. "The ultimate success of China's civil rights movement," she has stated, "is its power to awaken the small and uneducated people like Lili and make them realize they are equal to intellectuals when it comes to deciding how the country should be governed" (Wang 2003).

While Wang was only sixteen at the time of the Tiananmen Square Massacre, she nevertheless carried its traumatic legacies with her as she immigrated to the United States. If *Summer of Betrayal* is about disillusionment and self-assertion, Annie Wang's *Lili* is a novel of transformation and faith in the possibilities for China's political future, including enhanced rights, dignity, and justice for its citizens. *Lili* transposes the "impossible memory" of Tiananmen Square into a new cultural landscape. It portends new futures born out of a global cultural politics of interpenetration and fusion. Written at the interface between aesthetics and politics, fiction and documentary, Eastern and Western imaginings, it re-presents the Tiananmen Square Massacre to readers around the world, transforming the trauma into a promise of new beginnings and new geographic interfaces to produce new cultural realities.

Contemporary Chinese women's texts are characterized by a return to the Massacre as a scene of trauma. The new texts take forward Hong Ying's perception that "our generation was born to enact a tragedy" (1997, 131). The literature circles an absence, a void of meaning, a crisis of legitimacy for the wounded survivors. Sometimes, as in the case of *Summer of Betrayal*, that void is breeched with narrative assertions of selfhood elementalized into erotica. Sometimes, as in the case of *Lili*, it is recaptured and bitterly recalled through parody and satire. These narratives, projecting multilayered cultural, geographic, linguistic, political, and aesthetic journeys into a rediscovered selfhood, represent a necessary if not sufficient condition for personal, social, and cultural transformations. In the words of Dai Qing, the only way to break the government's hold on freedom of speech is to continue to tell stories: "To break through the lies. To tell the truth. To tell stories...To give a different view from the orthodoxy" (Buruma 330). Given the censorship in China, and the need to protect families and friends still living at home, these diasporic, semiautobiographical novels transmit an "impossible memory" to another cultural space. Each example, in its own way, speaks to the rupture affected by the Massacre, the betrayal of youth, the limits of politics, and the interplay of identity and desire. In particular ways, contemporary diasporic novelists participate in a politics that extends the regime of human rights into China and back to the West again by telling stories.

These autobiographical novels, personal stories fictionalized in transit, might be understood to constitute new aspects of a "cultural China" of overseas writers and intellectuals. Some cultural analysts have speculated that since the Tiananmen Square Massacre, China has become increasingly decentered and divided between the so-called center and periphery, not so much in political but in cultural terms. Harvard Professor Tu Wei-ming, for example, puts forth the concept of a "cultural China," comprising several symbolic universes (13–4).[24] Speculating that China now occupies a newly constructed cultural space "that both encompasses and transcends the ethnic, territorial, linguistic, and religious boundaries that normally define Chineseness," Tu "challenge[s] the claims of political leadership (in Beijing, Taipei, Hong Kong, or Singapore) to be the ultimate authority in a matter as significant as 'Chineseness' " (viii). In his view, the transnational intellectual diaspora, now numbering over thirty-six million people worldwide, has a great transformative potential "that will significantly shape the intellectual discourse on cultural China for years to come" (Tu 34). In other words, "China" is far more fluid as a space of production, circulation, and consumption than the State.

With their cosmopolitan approach, the new novels by women shocked Western audiences when they appeared. They revealed a rapidly modernizing China that surprised Euro-centric readers, fed on a diet of prescriptive media representations and Cultural Revolution narratives. Directed to an English-speaking audience, they depicted China as a violator of human rights an outmoded socialist state. In a sense, the publication, circulation, and reception of these representations of Tiananmen invited Western readers and audiences to reimagine a new kind of China, at once an authoritarian State only partially opened to the claims of rights violations and a vast, diverse, and modernizing country whose citizens are inevitably engaged in local negotiations of Western humanist human rights principles and practices fused with Chinese traditions, transforming and permutating ideologies and lives through those negotiations. Yet, the popularity of *Summer of Betrayal* and *Lili* remains dependent on a Western-based publishing industry that fetishizes China, turns suffering into a salable commodity, and privatizes the narrative of resistance as an individualist tale of survival and triumph.

CONCLUSION

The desires of a younger, post-Tiananmen Square generation may not be commensurate with those of their elders; the urban-based, elite group of spoiled sons and daughters of corrupt party officials may benefit from China's modernization to the detriment of the rest of China's disaffected youth; young women in the cities may find sexual liberation, social autonomy, and economic independence while their country sisters continue to suffer exploitation and abuse; the "freedom of religion of the marketplace" may assuage the soul of the upwardly mobile in Shanghai and Beijing but provide no escape from persecution for ethnic and religious minorities in Tibet and the Uighur Region. Although the Chinese government must now cope with a population of disaffected citizenry, there are many Chinas. Even if new freedoms become available to an expanding elite of urban youth of means, this extension of human rights may or may not extend far beyond their privileged circle. Or China may respond to the numerous, ongoing localized rights-based campaigns, coupled with international pressures to reform, and expand the possibilities for civil and political liberties.

Despite widespread liberalization and a willingness to take on previously tabooed subjects in the arts and culture, discussions of the Tiananmen Square Massacre in China remain off limits. As we have seen in earlier chapters, social transformations sometimes give voice to previously marginalized victims of civil rights abuse through a legitimation of their testimony in national or internationally sponsored forums, thereby giving victims an occasion and a place for recovery of memories of trauma. But in contemporary China there has been no recovery of the history of Tiananmen Square Massacre. China has yet to deal with the trauma perpetrated on the nation during those terrible days of bloodshed. The high ideals of the millions of citizens who participated in the Movement were brutally crushed. Betrayed by their government, they turned pain into cynicism. It is unlikely that student movements will return to that kind of political activism; but change may come through local micropolitics.

As this book goes to print, the Chinese people anticipate the fifteenth anniversary of the Tiananmen Square Massacre. On March 4, 2004, the *New York Times* reported that Dr. Jiang Yanyong, the respected physician who exposed the Chinese government's cover-up of the SARS epidemic, had written a letter to the Politburo calling for a revision of China's hardline stance on the Tiananmen Square Massacre. Jiang asked the Politburo to conduct a review and "a correct evaluation" of the June 4 Movement that, according to the doctor, "should be reappraised as a patriotic movement" (Yardley 2004, A-3). Jiang's letter was banned from circulation in China but widely reported in the international media. When asked for comment at a press conference to mark the closing of the tenth National Party Congress, Chinese Premier Wen Jiabao reiterated the official government stance that the student-led protests were "a very serious political disturbance" (Shi Jiangtao 2004). Although noticeably milder in his remarks than his predecessors, Wen defended the actions of the government in 1989 as necessary in order to restore unity and stability to the country (Shi Jiangtao). It is unlikely that Jiang's recent letter, like those sent yearly by Ding Zilin on behalf of the Tiananmen

Mothers group, will force the Politburo to re-open a discussion of the Tiananmen Square "incident," at least in the short term.

At its March 2004 meeting, the National Party Congress did, however, pass two amendments to the constitution to protect human rights and property rights. China experts caution that the constitutional reforms, although historically significant in signalling China's awareness of the need to improve its human rights record, may be more symbolic than real, given the ineffectiveness of court judges, especially on the local level, in applying Constitutional principles (Wan). Nonetheless, these developments and their reportage in the international press do indicate rifts within the country made more visible through their circulation in a global media at a time when China seeks to extend its economic, trade, and diplomatic relations with the West.

Since Deng's reform policies were announced in 1992, numerous individual, local, and national rights campaigns have emerged. Although none would rival the 1989 protests, they continue to open up spaces within China to seek redress for the violation of rights, air grievances, and raise awareness of rights abuse and claims. While little evidence of the protests is available by way of political tracts, public posters, or protest literature, *per se*, individual protests, tied to Internet campaigns, global information flows, and transnational activism, remain ongoing and insistent. Furthermore, according to Xiaojiang Li, although contemporary campaigns for extended freedoms seldom invoke the discourse on human rights, indeed they deliberately avoid the term due to its controversial nature, they contribute to the evolution of a rights consciousness and practice in contemporary China.

These local movements, coupled with international attention to China's human rights record, impact the government's growing sensitivity to criticism and acceptance of responsibility for international covenants. Internet access has brought unprecedented opportunities for students, intellectuals, artists, workers, and ordinary citizens to interact, organize for political and religious purposes, evolve a distinctive and iconoclastic youth culture, and build transnational alliances. Internet technologies effectively shatter the traditional opposition between politics and aesthetics, connecting users and enabling a fusion of artistic and political endeavors both within China and beyond its borders.

The Party is not conceding however. As previously noted, the current official "Strike Hard" campaign has brought about an intensification of repression of political and civil liberties in favor of social stability and continued economic and social development. Although the Internet is notoriously difficult to police effectively, the government has issued regulations to control its use. Since Strike Hard began, citizens have been regularly detained for illegal downloading from the web or for use of the web for political or religious purposes. Recent regulations forbidding the promulgation of pornography led to the censoring of "the shock sisters," Wei Hui and Mian Mian, whose erotically-charged websites and Internet chat spats had been widely publicized. Nonetheless, the government recognizes, albeit with caution, the need for web-based technologies to further its aims of domestic and international economic dominance. But the Internet, notoriously impossible to control, continues to support a plethora of "illegal" activities. Sites disappear and reappear overnight; members of the student-initiated Chinese Hackers Union regularly breach firewalls; U.S.-based websites, like that of Wei Jingsheng, even when officially blocked, can be accessed through the offices of the Voice of America, the BBC, and Radio Free Asia; and international Internet groups like the Digital Free Network maintain connections to ensure the flow of information within China and beyond its borders.

The Chinese government continues to maintain a tight hold on politics, but the State is only one of many influences—local, transnational, and global. And the political arena, narrowly defined, is only one of many arenas capable of effecting social transformations within the State. New cultural formations and human rights networks are emerging, beyond economic and political realms. In the last chapter of *Bad Elements*, Ian Buruma makes his assessment of China since the Tiananmen Square tragedy. He reflects on the effects of the national suppression of the Tiananmen Square story that went underground, focusing on the affective dimensions of this tragedy and arguing that "the truth about June 4 [is] still a smoldering political issue that could yet explode" (319). Ultimately, no matter how brutal China's controls may be, Buruma and other China scholars concur that no nation can be up to the task of controlling 1.3 billion people (318). In addition, the desires of China's youth for new private-sphere freedoms cannot be separated from a volatile transnational public sphere, presaging the emergence of new subjectivities and demands for civil and political rights. These local to global transits effect micropolitical realignments within China. They reconfigure the culturally organized boundaries between the personal and the political, the local and the global, the national and transnational communities. The affective-moral and politico-ethical intensities called into play influence the dynamics of modern Chinese culture and the Chinese diaspora and have the capacity to shape both internal and external engagements between China and the rest of the world.

Conclusion

*Human rights must be theorized in a way that privileges stories
and lived experiences of individuals and peoples. It is as these stories
are personally engaged with, reflected upon and lived out by
becoming part of our lives that we are most likely to find the
resources to respect others.*

—*Anthony Langlois*, The Politics of Justice
and Human Rights

*If rights are what historically subjugated peoples most need, rights
may also be one of the cruelest social objects of desire dangled above
those who lack them.*

—*Wendy Brown*, "Rights and Identity in
Modernity: Revisiting the 'Jewish Question'"

Witnessing to dislocation, exploitation, violence, resilience, and
survival, personal storytelling, as it is produced, circulated, and
received around the globe, lends particularity to abstract principles of
human rights and keeps the passage of time and forgetting at bay.
And yet, as the five case studies elaborated in *Human Rights and
Narrated Lives* have revealed, the efficacy of personal narrating in
human rights campaigns defies simple analyses.

Rights Stories in Global Flows

We introduced a number of our chapters with significant events—the
release of Nelson Mandela after serving twenty-seven years in prison,
the Bicentennial protests in Sydney, and the Tiananmen Square
Massacre in China—as examples of deeply unsettling events that
made visible fissures in the body politic. These events unleashed
unpredictable energies and affective forces that were sometimes channeled into human rights campaigns at home. At other times, the

events resonated with international audiences and movements far removed from the home site in ways that then rebounded back onto the local context, as happened in post-Tiananmen China. The South African case provides the most dramatic instance of a nation coming to terms with its oppressive past. More than any other modern nation, South Africa models the importance of personal witness as it attaches to human rights discourse. In Australia the campaign that resulted in the recognition of Indigenous claims and proposals for avenues of redress was radically forestalled by a change in government. With its election to power in the mid-1990s, the Liberal Government denied responsibility for assimilationist policies of the past and their effects on succeeding generations. Nonetheless, Indigenous groups found alternative channels for addressing their claims for self-determination and for preserving cultural traditions. In the case of China, the government resolutely refused to acknowledge that any crime had taken place at Tiananmen Square, necessitating dissident students to air their claims elsewhere where they were taken up in countries of exile and subterranean circuits of the Internet. In exile, dissidents became pawns in political and diplomatic negotiations primarily between the United States and China. In these exchanges China argued for Asian values of social cohesion and stability that contradicted the individualist Enlightenment principles foundational to human rights in the West. In this case rights discourse was suppressed and life writing censored, thereby forestalling the possibility of telling and listening. Even in South Africa, where local witnessing translated through global circuits affected a radical transformation of political culture and an end to apartheid oppression, the results have been less than expected. The promises set in motion by the TRC have yet to be realized.

We began other chapters with moments of witnessing in scattered venues, on campuses or in benefit concerts. These sites of witnessing appear far removed from the formal networks in which human rights activism takes place and far distant from the local contexts that the chapters address. In both of these instances, the appearance of Kap Soon-Choi on the University of Michigan campus and the appearance of Rubin "Hurricane" Carter with Nelson Mandela on a stage in Melbourne, rights activism disperses into informal meshworks foliating outward through international channels of affect, awareness, and action. Through these transnational crossings, unpredictable alliances for social justice emerge. The witnessing of Kap Soon-Choi inaugurates an alliance of the former sex prisoners with Asian American students seeking to fill in the gaps of family histories implicated in the stories the women tell. The appearance of Carter and Mandela together links the figure of the political prisoner, the unassailable hero of the South African Struggle, with a former "common" prisoner to whom the status of political prisoner has been accorded by activists inside the United States. Yoking the two former prisoners together on stage, the event in Melbourne calls attention to the intersection of race and incarceration that is critical to the understanding of prisoner rights activism in the United States and to the push for human rights for black populations in South Africa and Australia as well. No matter what the rights claim or where the origins, the efficacies of stories circulating through campaigns evolve in unpredictable ways, by chance occurrences as much as by planned activities.

Narratives circulating locally, nationally, and transnationally in the field of human rights tell stories of difference. As the discourse of rights circulates around the globe, here to be taken up by one kind of campaign, there by another, here to tell one kind of story of violation, there to tell another, witnesses to human rights violations tell stories of difference and incommensurability. Indeed they often give witness to disturbingly incommensurable usages, responses, receptions, and meanings: across indigenous and settler versions of history; between Western and Asian cultures; for law-abiding citizens and sentenced inmates; among mainland and diasporic Chinese.

Global cultural flows of stories in action might be viewed as a series of overlapping, overdetermined, complex, and chaotic conditions that coalesce, often unexpectedly, as campaigns "travel." Chinese dissidents sent reports of the events at Tiananmen via fax machines to the Hong Kong Chinese and to diasporic Chinese in the West. Activists organizing around sex tourism in Asia solicited stories from former sex prisoners by radio, and then brought women from disparate nations together via transnational organizations. In South Africa and elsewhere around the world, people could listen to live broadcasts of the TRC hearings and, after the hearings ended, could purchase a CD recording of the hearings. Post-Tiananmen writers known as the Young China Group promote liberalization campaigns through auto-biographical novels, stories, and chat room wars that circulate over the Internet, through an international youth underground, and through proxied channels to the Western world. At the same time, those texts and conversations are banned in their home country where the writers face very real threats of political prosecution. As Anthony Giddens notes, these global information flows, particularly aided by new technologies, allow for cultural transactions to be conducted across time and space where any given place is penetrated and shaped by social influences quite distant from it (1991).

Global technologies have changed the ways people listen to and respond to other people's stories. At the turn of the twenty-first century, narratives can circulate around the globe instantaneously, moving readers in Istanbul and Indianapolis at the same time. The globalization of cultural forms has the capacity to render an often Western uniformity to diverse sites around the globe, but it also has the capacity to keep in circulation a diversity of experiences and identities, keeping the forces of uniformity and difference in dynamic tension. Further, the unpredictable patterns of dissemination of stories to multiple audiences, the mixed responses to them, and the diverse uses to which they are put, all contribute to what is developing as a different politics of social change.

As we have seen in several of our case studies, personal stories galvanize global networks, circulating within them, binding them in new and newly intense organized and hierarchical networks and more dispersed, informal meshworks of activism. Personal narratives expand audiences of people around the globe educated about human rights abuses. As they reach larger and larger audiences, they can affect readers and prompt acts of engagement with persons having experienced rights abuses. Within the context of life narrating, claims take on a human dimension, calling for the listener/reader to become more self-reflexive, more informed, more active. Acts of listening and reading, however diverse in location and purpose, seed new awareness, recognition, respect, and willingness to understand, acknowledge, and seek redress for rights violations. While such narrative acts and readings are not a sufficient ground for social change, they are a necessary ground.

The meanings generated by individual narratives, and by the collective culture of personal narratives, can become commodified as they enter the global marketplace, but they can also exceed the processes of commodification. There is no ensuring how stories will be read, interpreted, and recirculated by individuals or within communities. Furthermore, as Mariam Ticktin cautions, "sometimes it may be better to commodify incompletely rather than not to commodify at all" (34). Even experiences of traumatic upheaval can be transected by contradictions and transformed by desires attached to forces of global capital (36), as in the case of the new feminist-inflected narratives coming out of China. Commodified narratives can also keep a human rights agenda in the public eye when local campaigns fail, as happened when the Australian Prime Minister denied

Human Rights Commission charges of genocide and refused to apologize. The nation shut down its processes of remembering at the same time as international audiences registered shock and disbelief at the brutality of practices of childhood separation, presented evocatively to the world in the film *Rabbit-Proof Fence*.

By looking carefully at stories in action in specific rights contexts, we have been better able to understand the confounding complexities of campaigns for social justice. Critics of the human rights regime have pointed to the ways in which human rights discourse is a globalizing discourse, part of a Western and particularly American-oriented imperial project that emphasizes individual freedoms and civil and political rights. They often conceptualize the problem in terms of a binary relationship between the universal and the particular (or relative). But as Margaret Jolly has cautioned, that critique is too simplistic (124–46). A binary schematic cannot sufficiently illuminate the efficacies of storytelling in the field of human rights. Invocation of universals spurs activism in specific, local contexts. Rights advocates and activists in the West argue for collective rights, particularly for women and minority groups. Groups in the South (as opposed to North) and East (as opposed to West) blend an insistence on individual rights with the call for collective rights (often raised by women and minorities contesting the State or particular cultural practices). Human rights challenges mounted by minority groups, indigenous peoples, women, and Asian scholars and activists push the parameters for interpreting what constitutes a right and understanding how rights claims take shape in the dynamic tensions between the modern and the traditional, the universal and the particular (Langlois). In effect, the invocation of universal principles paradoxically makes certain local particularities visible. Simultaneously, the local inflections of universal principles attached to the concept of universal human rights generate implicit and explicit critiques of the exclusionary terms of the universal, thereby accounting for, making visible, and claiming particularities in the local.

New stories bring with them their own social and cultural imperatives. They emerge in specific contexts and are contested, mediated, and negotiated within those contexts. Ultimately, global flows through which the regime of human rights circulates via personal storytelling impact a constellation of forces in the public and private domains of governmentality, civil-sphere affiliation, and identity formation. Stories in action illuminate, even exacerbate, the tensions between the jurisdictions of international law, established through

UN covenants, and the internal laws, policies, and practices of member States.

THE MOVING TARGET OF RIGHTS

Every term in the phrase "universal human rights" has been under debate since the drafting of the UDHR at the end of World War II. For us, there has been no adequate or uncontested way to understand "human rights" at this historical moment. Thus we have taken a non-foundational, minimalist, and situational approach to definitions.

Discourses on human rights, mechanisms for adjudication and redress, and specific campaigns evolve in the midst of conflicting and contested zones of power within and between communities and nations. As our case studies suggest, in the West the language of rights, so imbricated in modernist philosophical traditions and values, has been pervasive and pervasively mobilized to serve the interests of developed nations and to maintain their privileged status in a hierarchy of nations. While the Western language of rights may appear to be globally dominant, however, it is neither fully pervasive nor the only language of rights in circulation around the globe. People within privileged nations, even if not committed to a liberal politics or philosophy, mobilize the liberal discourse of rights and tell stories that critique the inhumane acts and institutions in their own country, if often unsuccessfully. In other cultural contexts, stories of suffering, abuse, and violation may not always be framed within a recognizable "rights" discourse. In such instances, human rights campaigns may be yoked to cultural values that derive from "differing moral schemas" (Stacy 197). In fact, they may emanate from cultures with radically different traditions of justice and social well-being. "In some places," Anthony Langlois reminds us, "human rights language is not spoken at all; other forms of expression mediate people's moral self-understandings" (161).

Such heterogeneous forms of expression can extend international concerns for human justice and dignity beyond Western frameworks and expand ways of imagining a variety of avenues to achieve just societies. In local contexts, sometimes far removed from centers of human rights activism and sometimes from disempowered or disenfranchised communities within sovereign nation-states, discussions of what constitutes rights and their violations exceed the modernist presumptions of UDHR principles. In diverse local sites human rights discourse may be reconceived beyond the modernist framework to serve the needs of and acknowledge the differences between peoples engaged in local struggles. Local actors, Maila Stivens suggests, may draw upon "long-circulating, quintessentially 'modern' ideas about democracy, rights, equality and justice" to understand, frame, and make their own claims for recognition and redress (3). In these locations, the language of rights can be attached to local praxis, whether impelled by nationalist, religious, revolutionary, modernist, communal, subaltern, anticolonial, or some combination of forces. Such entwining of discourse and praxis signals that there are "multiple, divergent modernities" (Stivens 9) throughout the world, where human rights practices exceed the universal-relativist model. In effect, "these ideas [about democracy, rights, equality and justice] are being reclaimed and reimagined in an often exuberant transforming of the notion of 'rights' within a new world order of 'global modernities' " (3).

Personal narratives in action, emanating from local sites of activism, can trouble established interpretations of rights violations, shift definitions and framings of human rights, and test modes of advocacy. Genres of life writing become forums through which people lodge their concerns and claim rights in the name of the "human." In doing so, they both affirm something called "human rights," always a moving target rather than a fixed concept, and redefine the grounds upon which those rights are asserted. A number of critical legal scholars, including Costas Douzinas, Anne Barron, and Eric Yamamoto, argue that the language of rights advocated by newly mobilized, heterogeneous rights claimants invokes an ethics of care that "challenge[s] and overtak[es] the limits of self and law" (Douzinas 369). According to Barron, the liberal conception of law inscribed by the UDHR assumes a unitary view, "a place of convergence in the midst of difference, a place simultaneously available to all and capable of affording a perspective from which the whole chaotic field of social life might be apprehended and dominated" (1990, 108). These rights theorists insist that the claims to justice made by new rights claimants might be best addressed not through universalist prescriptions nor through the judicial mechanisms of the nation-state but through alternative frameworks, including special legislative enactments or executive policies that invoke goal-oriented tactics to achieve limited, concrete ends.

At dispersed sites, in diverse ways, actions on the local, national, and global level and critiques coming from within and outside the United Nations destabilize founding assumptions and spur social change. They reframe the principles and apparatuses available for redress in the national and international arenas. They allow for recognition of cultural differences. They expand the bases upon which rights can be claimed. In this fluid climate, the principles upon which human rights are founded are continually being asserted, challenged, redefined, and resisted. This is all to suggest that the global flows of rights discourse extend into and are transformed by multiple contact zones where ideas, institutions, cultural practices, and peoples mingle and contend with one another, with Enlightenment legacies, with other traditions of philosophical and religious principles, with global transformations, and with ongoing struggles through which people take responsibility for the "global quest for justice" (Quillen 109).

HOPE

The world has changed dramatically in the four years since we began this project in late summer of 2000. Then, on the cusp of a new millennium, we could look back on advances in human rights in the late twentieth century with some degree of optimism. While we recognized that the international regime of human rights did not promise continual advance for emancipatory struggles on behalf of the oppressed, the displaced and dispossessed, and the politically dissident, we could see some positive signs of advancement. Granted, that atrocities continued to occur all too often; that everyday forms of economic, social, and political inequality and disempowerment continued to stunt the life choices and the very bodies of massive numbers of the world's peoples; that dissidents continued to be prosecuted, jailed, and exiled. But these realities were counterpoised by a number of developments, including the advancement of the idea of women's rights as human rights, the advancement of claims by First Nations peoples, the experiment in reconciliation of South Africa's TRC, among them.

Then came September 11, 2001, and the attack on the World Trade Center in New York City and the Pentagon in Washington, D.C. The post–September 11 era ushered into existence a new kind of international politics and realignments of the world order. State-sponsored assaults on civil rights have gained momentum in the United States and countries aligned with its war on terror. As we write, the U.S. Justice Department holds prisoners of the war on terror *incommunicado* in Guantanamo Bay, Cuba, and shrouds the proceedings in secrecy. Increasingly, even conservative political commentators have condemned the assault on civil rights in this strange time of "war." The new global politics brings in its wake

attacks on individual freedom of speech, the return of repressive
politics, heightened military build-up to protect domestic security,
new police powers, including house arrest and mandatory detention
for citizens and residents suspected of collusion with the Enemy. In
some Western countries, individual freedoms are curbed for the
"common good" and international relations crafted in service to an
amorphous war on terror. In Islamic countries, activists working on
behalf of modernization and democratization have to negotiate the
contested terrain of fundamentalist Islamic politics.

Equally disturbing, the president of the United States and his sen-
ior advisors and cabinet officers have challenged the legitimacy of the
United Nations as a viable international institution for the new
geopolitics of terrorism. U.S. unilateralism threatens to derail the
multinational struggle for human dignity, equality, and justice
launched with the adoption of the UDHR more than fifty years ago
and to defeat the promising efforts of the last thirty years toward
international cooperation in pursuit of the goals of that historic
Declaration. In a time of unpredictable global and local realignments,
however, there can be no clear overarching analysis of globalization,
no predicting the long-term effects of this particular historical juncture, even as the UN finds itself with diminished political and moral
purchase as an arbiter of struggles around the world.

While there appears to be an erosion of human rights principles
and mechanisms and a loss of moral authority for the international,
national, and local institutions charged with promoting justice, there
remain in place, in many and dispersed places, a multitude of witnesses, activisms, alliances, and challenges, erupting both within and
across the borders of nation states. Victims and survivors of abuse
continue to tell stories that affirm the UDHR, attaching their claims
to the freedoms guaranteed in the document as their horizon of hope
or asserting new utopian principles beyond its intended universalisms,
directed towards "a promise of justice always still to come" (Douzanis
368). As new stories circulate, they reveal new sites of rights violations, seeding new campaigns for recognition and redress. These personal narratives bring into existence desires, feelings, sensibilities, and
perceptions that connect with diverse cultural energies, link with
other domains of cultural and political activity, mutate and transform
themselves through multiple forms of engagement—ethical, aesthetic, legal, and political—in multiple contexts. As they enter and
alter personal, national, and international imaginings, these stories
have the capacity to shatter and transform, to find their way through

cracks and fissures within dominant cultures in unpredictable ways, through unexpected horizontal micropolitical forces that are both visible and subterranean. Thus, despite the challenges to the philosophies and politics that attend the international regime of human rights, calls for justice, dignity, and freedom continue to urge listeners and readers to respond ethically, to join with disempowered and disenfranchised people worldwide in campaigns for social justice.

The human rights regime can only offer an imperfect response to the problem of human suffering in the world. It reifies the identities of "victim" and "perpetrator." It stages the plurality of voices but controls the terms of their witnessing. It attempts to manage the chaotic forces of affect, thereby directing political awareness into privatized emotional response. It depends on the politics of shame. It reproduces a circuit of demand in which the powerful and relatively privileged retain the right to confer or refuse recognition, thereby short-circuiting the "mutual obligation" of an intersubjective project of caring (Hage 148).

These problems exist, in part, because the human rights regime rests on a secular humanist tradition that eschews cultural pluralism. William B. Connolly, an "anti-secular" advocate of human rights and the pursuit of justice, considers the premises of humanism obstructive to an ethics of recognition because of humanism's investment in an identity politics that requires difference for its definition (141–5). An ethics of recognition grounded in identity sustains asymmetries of power: the powerful bestow recognition onto the powerless. Paradoxically, then, a humanist ethics of recognition mobilizes at once a stabilizing construct (seeking a universal or unified identity) and a threat to that stability (dispersing sureties of a unified self through difference). Reconfiguring this pattern of response requires readers and listeners to accept and relate to difference at the expense of a certain and secure sense of self.

In addition, a secular humanist tradition relies on political processes at the macro level as the mainstay of political change. This reliance obscures the visceral forces always attending an ethic of engagement. Connolly notes the often-unacknowledged importance of "the regular effects that culturally organized, thought-imbued intensities and feelings have on the *active world of intersubjective thought and political action*" (181). In Connolly's conception of the micropolitical, "detail, desire, feeling, perception, and sensibility" (149) are all political and relational forces that motivate people's capacity for critical responsiveness to an other. With thinking and judgment configured in these terms, a new space for justice opens up, one attentive to different kinds of suffering and subordination that, for a secular world, lie fallow and ignored, "below the register of justice" (10).

Although Connolly's concerns about secularism take us beyond the scope of this book, the conundrums he articulates resonate with those we encountered and explored in our five case studies. Human rights in action challenge the political and philosophical foundations of the human rights regime and call for reconceptualizations in response to suffering and ethical engagement. As Langlois suggests, personal narratives and witnessing spur critical awareness of cultural difference and initiate possibilities for intersubjective exchange beyond the certainties of a secure sense of selfhood. They bring into play practices that potentially exceed the political as presently constituted.

Despite limitations, contradictions, and insufficiencies, then, evolving human rights discourse, mechanisms, and platforms also offer hope to the disempowered and the oppressed. Claimants and their communities find through the rights regime a context, a purpose, a forum, and a platform for making meaning out of their experiential histories of suffering, activism, and survival; for seeking recognition and redress; and for remaking the past and the not-yet-to-come. People who come forward to tell their stories in rights venues engage in acts of witnessing that can inaugurate a healing process, for individuals and the community as a whole. Through rights mechanisms, among them inquiries, commissions, and rapporteur hearings, witnesses find listeners to affirm their story and recognize the suffering and dignity of the teller. Through such occasions and means, human rights claimants may (inevitably) become caught in a politics of otherness, but they also engage in new modes of intersubjective exchange that open out rather than foreclose the radical relationalities possible within social life, generating hope and opening new futures.

Principally, this book is a testimony to the efficacy of stories: stories silenced by and emerging from fear, shame, trauma, and repression; stories enlivened by hope, connection, commitment, and affiliation; stories fed by calls for justice, fueled by empathy and an ethics of equality and human dignity; stories framed by faith in international covenants calling for dignity, justice, and freedom. The chapters, taken together, mount a powerful argument for the efficacy of storytelling in advancing the ongoing and constantly transforming pursuit of social justice, emanating from, but not limited to, the human rights project inaugurated with the UDHR. Although subject to reinterpretation and contestation, the dynamics that attend the human rights campaigns taken up here suggest to us that at this historical moment human rights activism, and the discourse sustaining it, remains the most viable hope for extending democracy, social justice, and freedom.

NOTES

INTRODUCTION

1. It is arguable that the vocabulary of human rights has now been displaced, in the wake of September 11, 2001, by the discourse of terrorism and counter-terrorism both globally and domestically within many nations of the world.
2. Freedom as understood variously: the freedom of negative rights (freedom from state intervention and coercion); and the freedom of positive rights, (freedom to live in conditions sustaining a dignified life).
3. Afghanistan, Iraq, and North Korea have displaced China as "worst cases" in the wake of September 11. It is also the case that China has had effective ways of defending its position while other nations have been silenced or dismissed. Thus the dominant, but not the only, international discourse surrounding China for the last decade has been that of economic "development miracle" rather than that of "human rights violator."

1 CONJUNCTIONS: LIFE NARRATIVES IN THE FIELD OF HUMAN RIGHTS

1. The West is obviously a contested concept. By it, we mean to imply not a geographic location but a locus of symbolic and grounded power relations, emanating mainly from the United States, Europe, and the English-speaking world, sharing Enlightenment traditions and (post)colonial histories. The term entails a complex and often contradictory set of philosophic, political, economic, and social relations. There is no ground for identifying an essential "Western" subject, discourse, or nation. The Western subject shares many attributes of modern, or modernizing, subjects, nations, and cultures across the globe. Often, critics in non-Western countries who are contesting Western frameworks use hybridized Western-based political, legal, and cultural theory to make their case. Often those living in and identifying with the West inflect their arguments with theories and analyses contrary to Western traditions. We will try to work with some of these complications in our analyses of storytelling in a human rights field.

2. As Leigh Gilmore recently noted, the number of books published in English and labeled as "autobiography or memoir" tripled from the 1940s to 1990s (Gilmore 2001, 1). Gilmore goes on to discuss factors contributing to the memoir boom, particularly in the United States. Jay Winter notes that in the last twenty years historians in France, Germany, Italy, and Portugal have sought and published numerous collections of memoirs as ways of understanding historical legacies of events in the twentieth century (52).

3. The Sisters in Islam is a case in point. Working in Malaysia, but connected to reformist Islamic women's groups throughout the world, Sisters in Islam solicits testimony from abused Muslim women with a view to promoting equality and justice in accord with the teaching of the Koran. Although the group adopts modernist philosophies and feminist practices from the West that are "not welcomed" by conservatives and traditionalists (Langlois 2001, 60), it has nonetheless been influential in a number of spheres, particularly in relation to law reform and advocacy for Islamic women suffering domestic violence. Working between democratic states rights and religious obligations of the Islamic state, Sisters in Islam argues that grounds can be found in the Koran to promote equality, justice, and freedom for women through democratic Shari'a (or religious) law reform.

4. Elie Wiesel and Primo Levi were two of the more widely circulated witnesses from the 1960s and 1970s, contributing their testimony to public Holocaust remembrance.

5. Hirsch defines postmemory as "the relationship of children of survivors of cultural or collective trauma to the experiences of their parents, experiences that they 'remember' only as stories and images with which they grew up, but that are so powerful, so monumental, as to constitute memories in their own right" (8).

6. Films include documentaries like Claude Lanzmann's *Shoah*, and features such as Steven Spielberg's *Schindler's List*. Representative exhibitions and archives include the Spielberg Shoah Visual History Foundation, the Fortunoff Video Archive at Yale University, and the dramatic scenes of witness in the Holocaust Museum in Washington, D.C.

7. The reception of Holocaust narratives by different audiences both inside and outside of Israel suggests how critical location is to reception. In Israel, the dominant mode of response is to receive these narratives as examples of heroic resistance and survival. In the United States Holocaust literature is consumed and interpreted within national narratives of redemption, as stories that tell "of the wider struggle for tolerance, for freedom of religion, for freedom from persecution: they locate the Holocaust within the American narrative, itself configured as universal" (Winter 2001, 54).

8. See, e.g., Caruth (1995); Felman and Laub (1992); and LaCapra (2001), among others.

9. For some social commentators, however, "the global reach of the media and of power mechanisms with which they are in complicity dwarf local efforts to fight back" (see Massumi 1993, 30).
10. Dunant shared the first Nobel Peace Prize (1901) with Frédéric Passy.
11. See *The Rigoberta Menchú Controversy*, edited by Arturo Arias; with a response by David Stoll (2001).

2 THE VENUES OF STORYTELLING

1. For the emotional and ethical difficulties of this positioning, see Sen 110 and Langer 195.
2. In the midst of this fieldwork, fact-finders' and witness's lives may be put at risk. Witnesses in particular face the possibility of reprisal if they give personal testimony or, in the case of indigenous people, if they reveal sacred secret knowledge. Anonymity, however, limits the truth-value of the testimony, often rendering it suspect.
3. In 2002, *Witness* documentary testimony was offered into evidence at the World Court during the International Criminal Tribunal for the former Yugoslavia (ICTY) in which two former army officers were found guilty of crimes against women.
4. Media links with Hong Kong also resulted in massive street demonstrations in which one million of the city's 5.5 million residents marched in solidarity with the students. A Hong Kong rock concert for protestors raised valuable cash to maintain the protest.
5. To avoid surveillance, radios were set up under surgical beds in gynecological clinics. When police raids occurred, officers would be put off in their investigations by the sight of undressed women lying on the beds in stirrups.
6. Bethaney Turner explains that in contrast to the Marxist–Leninist diatribes of the past, the Zapatistas "employed a simplistic vernacular used to convey information in an often lyrical, story-like manner, rich with poetic imagery" (5). Subcommandante Marcos adopted a language familiar to the Tzeltales, Tzotziles, and Choles so that freedom fighters and people in indigenous communities found common ground for resistance.
7. One disadvantage of the advanced technological features of *Witness* is that full access also requires sophisticated hardware. Other sites, like Universalrights.net offer access to stories and invite viewer dialogue in ways that require minimal hardware.

3 TRUTH, RECONCILIATION, AND THE TRAUMATIC PAST OF SOUTH AFRICA

* This chapter could not have been written without our interactions with a number of South African scholars. Of particular note, we wish to thank Dorothy Driver and Joan Wardrop who generously shared their knowledge and research materials, commented on drafts as they developed, and, along with Colin Muller, engaged us in conversations that refined our thinking and provided countless insights as the research progressed.

1. Our discussion here is indebted to Alexis de Veaux's published recollections of the event in "Walking into Freedom" (1990); Mark Gibson's retrospective assessment of this "moment of radical opening and possibility as well as repression and cynicism" (Gibson 2001, 66); and the recollections of Dorothy Driver and Joan Wardrop.

2. In his ghostwritten autobiography *The Long Walk to Freedom*, Mandela reports on the conflict between the ANC and Inkatha that ensued shortly after his release. He notes that the ANC refused his attempts to meet with Chief Buthelezi and that the Zulu king retaliated by refusing to become involved in negotiations to bring about the end of white rule. This impasse between the ANC and the Inkatha led to violence, demonstrations, and police killings in the townships of Johannesburg and brought a temporary end to talks with President de Klerk (Mandela 1994, 561–64).

3. The MDM included the Congress of South African Trade Unions (COSATU), the United Democratic Front (UDF), the South African Youth Congress (SAYCO), and the Congress of South African Writers (COSAW).

4. Personal correspondence with Joan Wardrop, 4 August 2003. Albert Tambo had been the ANC President in exile for decades.

5. Collections of worker stories and prisoner narratives had been issued by publishers testing the limits on censorship; but these narratives, fuelling the Struggle, were seldom couched within a human rights framework. In addition, the South African Institute of Race Relations, the Black Sash, the Federation of Transvaal Women (FEDTRAW), and other anti-apartheid organizations had kept records of violations (Driver, pers. comm.).

6. Pass laws required every black adult to carry a pass at all times. Originally required by men (and women in the Orange Free State from 1913), they were extended to all black women in the 1950s, prompting active defiance (See Ngoyi 240–44). Without passes, black South Africans remained outside the law and vulnerable to arrest, detention without trial, relocation, disappearance, and death.

7. As the editors of *Women Writing Africa* explain, "In South Africa, the racial category 'coloured' was applied to people of certain mixtures of descent since colonial times. Gradually it was formalized to serve apartheid and white domination; officially the South African government declared it to include all people of 'mixed race,' but the category soon came to include the many peoples who could not be placed in the rest of the irrational system. Thus San, Khoe, and Griqua people, as well as those of "Malay" origin (the descendants of slaves brought to

the Cape from Java and neighboring islands), were categorized as coloured, as were the Chinese people" (Daymond et al. 61, footnote 36).

8. The apartheid state organized intersubjective exchange and relationships. Whiteness was reproduced in white families whose participation in the apartheid system confirmed white superiority and privilege and to whom the benefits of the apartheid system accrued. The laws of miscegenation meant that people could not marry across their racial classifications. Thus, after the passage of the apartheid laws, many affective relationships were suddenly made illegal, as children of crossracial marriages became "coloured." Black family life suffered from fragmentation, dislocation, and the pressures of state violence.

9. After being released from prison, First went into exile. She was killed in 1982 in Mozambique by a letter bomb sent by the South African Security Police.

10. Other notable prison narratives included Albie Sach's *Jail Diary* (1966), Quentin Jacobsen's *Solitary in Johannesburg* (1973), Hugh Lewin's *Bandiet: Seven Years in a South African Prison* (1974), Winnie Madikizela Mandela's "Detention Alone is a Trial in Itself" (1975), Breyten Breytenbach's *The True Confessions of an Albino Terrorist* (1984), Tim Jenkins' *Escape From Pretoria* (1987), and Caesarina Kona Makoere's *No Child's Play: In Prison Under Apartheid* (1988).

11. Later critics would claim that far from portraying "everyday life," such narratives produced only "the spectacular" of oppression. See Ndeble, "The Rediscovery of the Ordinary."

12. For many international readers in the United Kingdom, the United States, Australia, and other white settler nations, anti-apartheid advocacy displaced anti-racist action against oppression in their own countries, like that suffered by black Britons and African Americans, Indigenous Australians, and other minority cultures struggling for recognition in postcolonial contexts. Nonetheless, these stories promoted international campaigns and UN motions of censure that led to measures against South Africa.

13. "History from below" projects, evolving from the Black Consciousness Movement, gained momentum and cultural force in the 1980s and involved gathering, transcribing, and disseminating oral histories and promoting street poetry and performance as a way of making the stories of people's everyday lives available to a broader public. These were projects involving people whose stories were unlikely to become fare for novels, television series, or films made inside the country.

14. As Hofmeyr (1996) reminds us, what had primarily been male oral traditions were sustained by women in the absence of male storytellers due to the National Party's policies of forced removal of black men from the homelands to migrant barracks, where, in the absence of

courtyards, the storytelling tradition could find no constitutive space. Women's storytelling, however, "which was associated with the kitchen and the hearth area, transplanted quite well" (92).

15. "Necklacing," a particularly cruel form of violence, involves the practice of filling a tire with petrol and setting it alight around the neck of a black person suspected of colluding with the police.

16. We are endebted to Dorothy Driver for this information.

17. McClintock critiques Joubert's depoliticization of the narrative through her editorial framing. See *Imperial Leather* (30 f.f.).

18. For Guattari, a "singular event" is "a point, or presence in the world that comes into contact with other singularities." Here, Guattari points to the release of energy that the viewer, as subject coming into contact and "if need be, in open conflict" (36) with alterity, occasions and generates. The singular event propels different configurations of knowledge and, in turn, gives rise to uncertain and unsettling effects. It is this energy that calls attention—as a politically mobilizing force— to what is in the midst of happening and to what may be yet to come. There is risk involved in this recognition, but it is propulsive risk, moving the subject and its environment into transformed relations that evade formula. "[I]t's sometimes necessary to jump at the opportunity," Guattari writes, "to approve, to run the risk of being wrong," and, in doing so, "[to] respond to the event as the potential bearer of new constellations of Universes of reference" (18). We thank Emily Potter for her assistance in the formulation of this discussion.

19. Beginning in 1974 in Uganda, Truth Commissions have occurred in more than twenty-one countries, including Chile, Argentina, Uruguay, the Philippines, Chad, Bolivia, Zimbabwe, Ethiopia, Germany, Uganda, El Salvador, Guatemala, Malawi, South Africa, Australia, and Peru.

20. In their submission to the Commission on behalf of the Gender Research Project of the Centre for Applied Legal Studies at the University of Witwatersrand, Beth Goldblatt and Sheila Meintjes catalogued a set of interlocking effects of the TRC's exclusive terms of reference. These terms of reference precluded addressing the systemic effects of gender inequalities and the realities of sexual violence (1996, subsequently published 1998).

21. Albie Sachs, referring to the demands for justice, asks: "What does this word 'justice' mean? In terms of social processes, is that the beginning and end of justice? Is there no justice if you do not send someone to jail?" (99). He asserts that perpetrators did pay a price, and continue to live with the legacy of the public confession to their crimes.

22. Other features of the TRC in practice impeded the goal of healing wounds opened by giving witness to the truth of the past: the differential sums paid to lawyers for perpetrators as opposed to victims; the limits of investigatory and prosecutorial powers of the

Commission; the perceived leniency in the treatment of ANC perpetrators; and the murky permeability of boundaries between personal
and political motives for killing.

23. The Amnesty Committee continued its work for another two years.

24. Notable here is the South African Broadcasting Company's dramatic
    presentation of TRC testimony through the emotive and dramatized
    production of a special set of CDs entitled *South Africa's Human
    Spirit*. For a critical assessment of the package, see Libin (2003).

25. After the democratic elections in 1994, Ramphele became the first
    black Vice Chancellor of the University of Cape Town. She has been
    followed by Njabulo Ndebele.

26. Heyns notes that J.M. Coetzee's autobiographical narrative *Boyhood*
    (1997) is a notable exception to the conversion narratives that have
    appeared. Coetzee does not split the protagonist off from his past,
    nor protect him from the knowledge of complicity (52, 55).

27. For a discussion of the "drama of hospitality," see Derrida and
    Dufourmantelle.

28. In addition to Morgan, the storytellers in the book are Virginia
    Maubane, Robert Buys, Valentine Cascarino, Sipho Madini, David
    Majoka, Steven Kannetjie, Gert, Patrick Nemahunguni, Pinky
    Siphamele, and Fresew Feleke. We are told before the title page that
    one of the storytellers, Sipho Madini, has gone missing. His picture
    appears with the request printed underneath: "Can you help?"

4   INDIGENOUS HUMAN RIGHTS
IN AUSTRALIA: WHO SPEAKS FOR
THE STOLEN GENERATIONS?

1. On the encoding of legal fictions, see Goodrich 1990.

2. This was a position articulated by the Aboriginal Provisional
   Government, founded in 1990 by Tasmanian lawyer Michael Mansell.
   Mansell, along with Roberta Sykes, Paul Coe, and other activists, had
   erected an Aboriginal Tent Embassy on the lawns of Parliament
   House in 1972 as a symbol of sovereignty claims. From the early
   1970s Mansell engaged many performative acts to assert his belief and
   commitment to justice and the sovereignty of Aboriginal nations,
   including the design of an Aboriginal flag and the issue of passports.
   He traveled to Cuba and Libya for independent talks with Fidel
   Castro and Colonel Gadaffi. These dramatic gestures captured the
   attention of an international media and maintained pressure on the
   government at home. See APG 1992b (324–29), and Nicoll.

3. In 1938 Indigenous people had been bussed into town and forced to
   play their appointed roles in a reenactment of the coming of the First
   Fleet to Sydney Cove, under threat of starvation. That confrontation
   led to the first Day of Mourning and Protest, organized later that year

by William Cooper and the Aborigines Progressive Association, to commemorate 150 years of grief since the Anglo-invasion of 1788. In 1954 when Queen Elizabeth visited Australia, Aborigines were coerced into providing "exotic" entertainment, dancing a corroboree in the Melbourne stadium. (See Goodall 2002 and Kleinert 1999.)

4. In addition, incarceration rates vary across the nation. In Western Australia an Aboriginal person is 7.5 times more likely to be serving a non-custodial sentence than a non-Aboriginal person (RCADIC 126).

5. Enraged Aboriginal activists vented their anger in protests and renewed political claims for self-determination (McDonald 1999). By 1995 Indigenous detention rates had risen a further 25 percent, another ninety-seven deaths in custody had occurred, and few of the RCADIC recommendations had been implemented (Harris 208). Although larger in scope than any previous government inquiry, RCADIC had little practical impact on the nation or the lives of Indigenous Australians.

6. The quotes from the review appear on the front and back covers of the first edition.

7. Colin Johnson, later known as the writer and critic Mudrooroo Narogin and Mudrooroo, grew up in government institutions believing himself to be Aboriginal. His claims to an Aboriginal identity have since been challenged. *Wild Cat Falling* was presumed to be the first modern Indigenous narrative, predating the "foundational" texts of Oodgeroo Nunuccal, Monica Clare, Kevin Gilbert, Margaret Tucker, and others.

8. See, e.g., the collection of essays on *My Place* in Delys Bird and Dennis Haskell's (eds.) *Whose Place?* (1992), the discussion of *My Place* along side other Australian autobiographical narratives in Rosamund Daziell's *Shameful Autobiographies* (1999), and the objections concerning the representativeness of the memoir voiced by Jackie Huggins (1993).

9. Narratives continued to be published in the years following the Bicentennial. They include Glenyse Ward's *Unna You Fullas* (1991), Torres Strait Islander Ellie Gaffney's *Somebody Now* (1989), Alice Nannup's *When the Pelican Laughed* (with Lauren March and Stephen Kinnane, 1992), Evelyn Crawford's *Over My Tracks* (1993), Rita Huggins and Jackie Huggins's intergenerational narrative, *Auntie Rita* (1994) and Doris Pilkington Garimara's *Follow the Rabbit-Proof Fence* (1996).

10. For a discussion of the collaborative framing of foundational women's narratives and the politics of their production and reception, see Jones (2000a, b, c; and 2001).

11. Jill Bennett and Rosanne Kennedy detail the politics of cultural memory in their "Introduction" to *World Memory: Personal Trajectories in Global Time* (2003).

12. The positive reception of the film in Australia was echoed globally. Overseas reviewers, however, framed the film within their own previously established popular myths of exile and belonging, variously comparing the film to *E.T.* and *The Wizard of Oz*, *Schindler's List*, and prison-escape films. Most reviews provided historical information about the child removal practices. In the United States and Canada particularly, reviewers frequently drew comparisons with their own colonial past and similar experiences of racial oppression and human rights violations against indigenous populations (See Potter and Schaffer 2004).

13. There is a major absence of critical texts authored by black or Indigenous Australians. Mudrooroo Narogin published his landmark study *Writing From the Fringe: A Study of Modern Aboriginal Literature* (1990). Marcia Langton's influential, extended essay on constructions of "Aboriginality," "*Well, I Heard it on the Radio and saw it on the Television—*": *An Essay for the Australian Film Commission on the Politics and Aesthetics of Filmmaking by and about Aboriginal People and Things* appeared in 1993, followed by Aileen Moreton-Robinson's searing critique of white women's privilege in *Talkin' Up to the White Woman: Indigenous Women and Feminism* in 2000. The first anthology of critical writings, *Blacklines: Contemporary Critical Writing by Indigenous Australians* (with Michelle Grossman as contributing editor) appeared in 2003.

14. The referendum is sometimes said to have given Aborigines citizenship status. This is not entirely accurate. Aboriginal people had had voting and other citizenship rights in some states prior to this time, but their status was both insecure and highly variable. In 1967 the Commonwealth assumed conjoint jurisdiction with the States over Aboriginal and Torres Strait Islander peoples and, for the first time, began to count them in the national census.

15. The Mabo decision on land rights overturned the doctrine of *terra nullius* thus allowing Indigenous groups who could claim continuous occupation on Crown lands to attain land rights, as was the case of the Mer Island people who were the subjects of the Mabo claim. The decision did not, however, restore traditional Indigenous customary law nor did it cede national sovereignty. For an extended discussion on Indigenous claims to sovereignty see Reynolds (1999).

16. These included Ted Koppel's *Nightline*, which aired in the United States shortly after the release of the Report, and John Pilger's documentary, *Welcome to Australia*, which aired in the United Kingdom in 1999.

17. The government responded by refusing to allow a visit by a United Nations special rapporteur and by issuing a warning to the UN that it would not support UN Committees unless the entire appeals process was radically overhauled and no longer capable of being "hijacked by minority groups."

18. See also Rosanne Kennedy (2001).
19. The Report set up conditions for reparations and compensation through Court processes. Several test cases, presented to State Courts, have met with limited success. In 1999 Joy Williams sought compensation from the New South Wales government, charging the State with breaches of duty of care. In 2000 Lorna Cubillo and Peter Gunner claimed against the Commonwealth of Australia, citing gross mistreatment that resulted in long-term suffering. Both claims were dismissed. In Queensland, Aboriginal workers sought compensation for stolen wages, kept in government-held "trust" accounts. Since the 1980s these workers have waited for wage claim adjudication, which could amount to as much as $500 million (AUD). In May 2002 the government offered $55.6 million (AUD). as a "take it or leave it" deal. The "Stolen Wages" campaign continues.
20. Some human rights advocates see apology as an empty symbolic gesture in the absence of substantive, structural changes. Around the world too many apologies were forthcoming—with too little action. Eric Yamamoto (1997, 80–8) has drawn up an "apology catalogue" detailing over forty-eight instances in the 1990s to which governments, religious organizations, businesses, individual public figures, institutions, and private actors issued apologies for race or ethnically related crimes.
21. The Wukindi Rom Project is one of those initiatives. Based on Yolngu protocols of conflict resolution aimed at restoring relationships between individual, groups and clan nations, it offers an ancient ceremony, strongly linked to non-Indigenous mediation, conflict-resolution, and decision-making processes. Offered as an annual event, the Rom Project provides "a positive and practical way towards national reconciliation as well as providing an opportunity to exchange dispute resolution understandings and skills between... 'western' and indigenous sources of learning" (Wukindi, accessed March 4, 2004).
22. Witnessing offered people who had been objectified through various rights-violating processes an opportunity to take up enabling subject positions through which they might become agents of history and claim legitimate positions within the sociality. "Through the processes of bearing witness to oppression and subordination," suggests Oliver, "those othered can begin to repair damaged subjectivity by taking up a position as speaking subjects" (7).
23. See Judy Atkinson for a discussion of the use of Aboriginal healing practices of *dadirri*, or deep listening, growing out of indigenous cultural protocols.
24. This is not to say that none of these elements were present in pre-HREOC life narratives. Rather the new narratives combine many elements in ways that signal important shifts in narrative voice, collective identifications, and modes of audience address.

25. The Hindmarsh Island Bridge controversy concerns Njarrindjeri objections to plans to build a bridge over the Hindmarsh River south of Adelaide, South Australia. After a group of Njarrindjeri women claimed the proposed bridge would interfere with a women's secret site, the Labor government imposed a twenty-five year ban on construction that was overturned when the Liberal government came to office in 1996. A Royal Commission deemed the women's claims to be fabricated and approved the bridge construction. The findings of the Royal Commission continue to be contested. For a full account, see Simons.

26. Stephen Kinnane, in his Writer's Week talk at the Adelaide International Festival of the Arts (First Nations Writing panel, March 10, 2004), used this phrase to describe the general situation faced by contemporary researchers tracing family heritage through anthropological, medical, mission, and government records. We are indebted to Stephen for comments on how contemporary Indigenous lives are transected by multiple community identifications, a concept which we adapt in this discussion.

27. Grant was the first Indigenous newsreader, then host of a current affairs program, in Australia. His private life attracted widespread attention in the popular media when his marriage broke down after he fell in love with a white broadcaster, Tracey Holmes, whom he met when they both covered the Olympic games in Sydney. He is now located in Hong Kong where he works as a media journalist and presenter for CNN.

28. Here Grant refers to the so-called "history wars" and debates about historical representation, responsibility, and blame that arose after the publication of the *Bringing Them Home* Report. See Windschuttle (2001) and Manne (2003).

5   BELATED NARRATING: "GRANDMOTHERS" TELLING STORIES OF FORCED SEXUAL SLAVERY DURING WORLD WAR II

1. Most people writing on the former "comfort women" explain the vexed use of the term. We have put the term in scare quotes here in order to call attention to the ethics and politics of naming. On the one hand, the use of the term reproduces the dehumanization of the women and renders invisible the violence of women's sexual slavery during the Pacific War. On the other hand, the term has transnational political salience at this historical juncture and can be understood as a collective term of identification among women from very different geographical locations. We sometimes use the term sex prisoner and sometimes the term survivor. We often use the phrase sexual slavery to mark, as Vera Mackie does in her discussion of the issue of discursive reference,

"the institutional aspect of this form of violence" (39). But we do use the phrase "comfort women" at times so as not to lose the charge of the irony of the naming of these women subjected to repeated rapes as "comfort women."

2. See Ustinia Dolgopol for an exploration of the history of the UN War Crimes Commission (created on October 20, 1943) and its recommendations on the prosecution of Japan for war crimes.

3. For an extended discussion of the history of Japanese compensation to Southeast Asian nations after the Pacific War and issues of reparations, see Won Soon Park.

4. The Korean Council is an umbrella group of some twenty-three feminist organizations in South Korea.

5. Recent research suggests that Japan's organized system of brothels for soldiers dates back to the turn of the twentieth century (Watanabe 4) and certainly was expanded after the Nanking massacre in 1937 in China. The military system of enforced sexual slavery can also be historicized in terms of the far longer system of licensed prostitution dating to the Tokugawa Shogunate (1603–1867). For further historization of the brothels, see Fujime Yuki; and Chin Sung Chung.

6. During the early twentieth century, Japanese women were recruited by sex brokers primarily from Kyushu, where impoverished parents sold daughters to support their families. The *karayuki* lived as captives while they worked as prostitutes and then were often rejected and disowned by their families when their usefulness came to an end (Freiberg 232). Also see Chin Sung Chung and Watanabe for discussions of the development of military sexual slavery in Imperial Japan.

7. Lee is glossing the work of medical anthropologists Arthur and Joan Kleinman (1994) on the body as a somatic site of traumatic remembering (716).

8. Stetz notes the long history of "rape culture," organized systems of state prostitution for fighting men, reaching back at least to the imperial powers in the classical world (91–2). She argues that the "systematic sexual violence by invading or occupying military forces has been disguised as 'prostitution,' to mitigate atrocities by dismissing them as ordinary commerce" (Stetz 92).

9. Vera Mackie comments that "a feminist consciousness of the linkage between gender and militarism, and the relationship between sexuality and human rights is necessary before militarized sexual violence can be seen as a fit topic for public discourse, and an issue which must be considered alongside other aspects of international relations" (38).

10. The upsurge in women's activism in Korea had to do in part with the international attention focused on Korea before and during the 1988 Seoul Olympic Games (Barkan 54).

11. In the 1980s, Yun Chong-ok, a civilian who had almost been forced into sexual slavery during World War II, joined forces with the Korean

Church Women's Federation to call attention to the history of sexual exploitation of Korean women. In 1988 she read a paper on former sex prisoners at a conference on Japanese sex tourism in Korea. See Japan Anti-Prostitution Association paper, 1995; cited in Chunghee Sarah Soh's lecture, "Human Rights and Humanity: The Case of the 'Comfort Women,'" delivered at the University of Pennsylvania, December 4, 1998. The Federation began protesting Japanese sex tours in Korea. In 1988 women from the group visited a former comfort station. In 1990 the group joined with others to call on the Korean president Roh Tae Woo to bring up the history of military sex slavery on his next official visit to Japan (Chin Sung Chung 1997, 234).

12. Since 1991 the Korean Council has taken the lead in supporting and advocating on behalf of former sex prisoners (Chin Sung Chung 1997, 235–6).

13. In 1990, the Japanese Diet refused to acknowledge Japanese military involvement in the comfort station system. In 1991 the Japanese government, in reply to demands made by the Korean Council for the Women Drafted for Military Sexual Slavery in Japan, denied the need for public apology and stated that all Korean claims against Japan for wartime deeds had been compensated in the treaty of 1965 (Soh 2001).

14. See Rumiko (1998) for a more detailed analysis of official and unofficial Japanese responses to the claims of the former sex prisoners.

15. Feminist scholars and activists contest the ways in which rights discourses and mechanisms reproduce the gendered distinction between private and public spheres, assigning women's experience to the private sphere of household and family and failing to frame their issues as issues of rights. "The marginalization of women's rights," suggest Brunet and Rousseau, "inevitably reflects the position of inferiority held by women in all countries, societies and communities" (35).

16. For an exploration of the tension between feminist and cultural relativist critiques of the human rights system, and the implications for issues having to do with violence against women, see Brems.

17. Despite the publication history, the narrative included in *Comfort Women Speak* was recorded in 1994 in Seoul, the narrative included in *Silence Broken* was recorded in 1995.

18. The profound irony of this scene of rape is that the father's home is appropriated by the Japanese military during the occupation and used as a headquarters where Henson herself is raped by officers.

19. After the 1992 international hearing on compensation for war crimes held in Tokyo, for instance, the historian Yoshimi Yoshiaki studied the archive of the Imperial Army in the Self-Defense Agency (which had been returned to Japan from the United States during the Cold War era). Through archival documentation, he exposed to the public the extent of imperial culpability in establishing and maintaining the

system of comfort stations throughout Japan's empire and named it a "war crime."

20. For an analysis of the ways in which the testimony of survivors at the 2000 Tokyo Tribunal was framed and altered on Japan's public education television in February of 2001, see Yoneyama (2002). Yoneyama describes how the program "disgraced the survivors" who had witnessed at the Tribunal by adding a caption insinuating that they were giving false testimony and by intercutting an interview in which a person active in the textbook debates denies that there had been a "comfort station" system.

21. Paradoxically, the successful suit on behalf of Japanese Americans rounded up and held in detention during World War II focused national and world attention on the unsettled war crimes from the Pacific War of World War II.

22. For a discussion of transnational state-building across diasporic communities, see Kim (n.p.).

23. One small victory has been won: In 1996 the U.S. government instituted a ban on entry into the country of sixteen former perpetrators of this crime against humanity.

24. The Asian Peace and Friendship Fund for Women was set up as a way to negotiate the tension between Japan's position that reparations had been made to South Korea in 1965 and Japan's recognition that contemporary pressure was building to make some gesture in response to the history of sexual slavery during the Pacific War, to show a kind face toward the now old women (Hyunah 1997, 55).

25. Soh notes, "the individual survivors in the Philippines and the Netherlands have been given the freedom to make a personal decision to accept or reject the atonement money, while in Korea, Taiwan, and Indonesia, the actions of the leadership or the government have disallowed the survivors to decide on their own" (Soh 1998).

6   LIFE SENTENCES: NARRATED LIVES AND PRISONER RIGHTS IN THE UNITED STATES

1. The reform of modes of punishment emerged out of the American Revolution, engendered in part in resistance to the continued transportation of convict labor to the colonies and to the "Bloody Code" that called for execution for as many as 200 crimes (Franklin 1998, 2).

2. The Attica Rebellion began on September 9, 1971, when approximately 1,200 inmates at the Attica prison in upstate New York took action against the conditions of their incarceration. Then Governor Nelson Rockefeller sent 500 state troopers to quell the rebellion. In the end thirty-nine people died, including ten guards held as hostages.

3. Indeed, the right to litigation, earned piecemeal during the 1970s and eroded throughout the 1990s, conferred agency upon prisoners.

"Prisoners who believe that their constitutional rights are being respected and that they have some legal recourse," write Specter and Kupers, "are less likely to resort to illegal or violent means to attain some control over their situation" (242–3).

4. "Without these kinds of lawsuits," conclude Specter and Kupers, "there is little doubt that the absence of outside scrutiny would permit correctional officials to return to the barbaric practices that the courts discovered when they began to review conditions in the prisons in the 1970s" (241).

5. As Elliott Currie observes: "In a very real sense, we have been engaged in an experiment, testing the degree to which a modern industrial society can maintain public order through the threat of punishment. That is the more profound meaning of the charge that America is an unusually punitive country" (21).

6. Knox is here reading the fate of Karla Faye Tucker against the fate of Henry Lee Lucas in order to understand why the former was executed for murder while the latter, falsely confessing to hundreds of serial killings, had his death sentence commuted.

7. For a discussion of Little Rock Reed's status as a political prisoner and his affadavit on his behalf, see Garlin.

8. According to its website, PEN is "the worldwide association of writers" that "exists to promote friendship and intellectual co-operation among writers everywhere, regardless of their political or other views; to fight for freedom of expression and to defend vigorously writers suffering from oppressive regimes. PEN is strictly non-political, a Non Governmental Organization with Category A status at UNESCO" (http://www.internatpen.org/). In 1973 PEN American Center inaugurated the Prison Writing Project, which sponsored an annual literary competition for prisoners. The competition continues until this day, though it languished in the 1980s after Abbott killed a restaurant waiter while on parole.

9. In one case, the father of the inmate victim who committed suicide tells his son's story of repeated sexual assaults.

10. Chevigny notes that women "who write seem to send their work out more reluctantly than men unless they have political backgrounds" (xviii).

11. Jacobsen is the coordinator, with three attorneys and a former prisoner. Two of the four women profiled in "From One Prison" have been released: Violet Allen and Juanita Thomas. Geraldine Gordon (not on a life sentence) was released on parole at thirteen years. Linda Hamilton has now served 26 years. The Clemency Project has filed two clemency petitions and motion for relief from judgment with no results thus far.

12. *The Exonerated* was initially produced by The Culture Project, a grantee of the George Soros funded Open Society Institute and its Criminal Justice Initiative.

7 POST-TIANANMEN NARRATIVES AND THE NEW CHINA

1. Wherever possible, Chinese characters are provided for Romanised Chinese names in *pinyin* appearing in the text for the first time.
2. Official Chinese estimates were that that 300 soldiers and 23 civilians lost their lives in the "turmoil". A host of Western journalists, using both photographs and eyewitness accounts, estimate that between 1,000 and 3,000 people were killed (Chung 1988, 294).
3. The Tiananmen Mothers have petitioned the Supreme People's Protectorate to open a criminal investigation of the Tiananmen Square killings and determine legal responsibility. They also brought a lawsuit in the United States against the former Premier Li Peng for his role in the crackdown (see Swenssen 2002, 303–5).
4. Notes here refer to news reports in *The New York Times*, *The Times (London)*, *The Age (Melbourne)*, and *The Australian* newspapers on June 5, 1989. See also note 24.
5. Wanning Sun reports, "according to official figures released by the Chinese Ministry of Education, since the start of economic reform, 370,000 Chinese students...have gone overseas, with a return rate of one in three...roughly 40 percent went to the United States, 22 percent to Japan, and 6 percent to Australia, followed by Canada, France and the UK" (Sun 2002, 3). See also note 23.
6. For discussions of the transmission of "world memory," see essays in Bennett and Kennedy (2003).
7. By the mid-1990s, in what seemed at least a partial recognition of human rights activists' demands in the West, most jailed political activists from the Democracy Wall and Tiananmen Square movements were released. Of the thousands of other people arrested after the Massacre, little is known. They have been lost to history.
8. Wei was sentenced to fifteen years in prison in March 1979, released on parole in September 1993, rearrested in March 1994, and finally released into exile in the United States in November 1997. He was first released in 1993, along with Tiananmen Square protestor Wang Dan and other prominent dissidents partially in a gesture of concession to the United States and partially out of China's self-interest (see Nathan 1997, xiii). The release came only nine days before the International Olympic Committee announced the winner of the 2000 Olympics bid, which Australia won over China by the thinnest of margins.
9. After his arrest in 1979, a brief autobiographical essay was smuggled out of China and published in the *New York Times Magazine* (November 18, 1980) and overseas Chinese newspapers. After his 1993 release, two letters from prison (September 5, 1990 and June 15, 1991) were published in the U.S. press with Chinese government approval. After his rearrest in 1994, Liu Qing, Wei's friend and fellow Democracy Wall

protestor, smuggled the transcript of his trial and other articles out of China, for which Liu received a ten-year jail sentence.

10. While Wei was in prison he received the Sakharov Prize for Freedom of Thought (1996), and was corecipient (with Nelson Mandela) of the Gleitsman International Activist Award. He also was nominated three times for a Nobel Peace Prize. He received $50,000 (USD) for the Gleitsman Award, money that enabled him to survive after his exile to New York (Wong 1999, 29).

11. Fang Litzi, China's most outspoken human rights advocate, is an astrophysicist and Professor at Peking University.

12. For the most part, the Chinese deliberately avoid the term "human rights," tied as it is to Western liberal principles deemed "imperialistic" within government circles. (See Weatherley 151.)

13. See also Ran Yanshi (1997).

14. As of May 2002, according to HRW, the ICESCR had been ratified (with reservations) but the ICCPR had not.

15. A host of (unstable) Internet sites support human rights campaigns, including those of the Tiananmen Square Mothers, the Free Tibet Movement, the "illegal" religious activities of the Falun Gong and the demands for religious and ethnic freedoms by the Xinjiang Uighur Autonomous Region (XUAR), HIV/AIDS, gay and lesbian rights, and those of other pro-democratic activists (Buruma 2001, 108–23).

16. For more on the commodification of suffering in the West, see critiques by Karen Ball (2000), Megan Boler (1997), and Lauren Berlant (1999).

17. The concept of banning in China is complex. It means that a book cannot be officially published or sold in official government bookshops. Although subject to censorship, such titles often continue to circulate widely through the Chinese underground. Western promoters utilize the "ban" to different ends, e.g., advertising it in order to promote sales of controversial books like *Shanghai Baby* to an overseas audience (See www.chinaguide.org/e-white).

18. In fact attention to China's human rights record has been overdetermined in the news. For example, *The New York Times* in 1996 ran fifty-seven articles about human rights in China, compared to three on Pakistan and one on India (Finnane 101).

19. The film was made possible through the resources of the U.S. media, which contributed some 1.4 million dollars to its production.

20. For further details of the controversy, see the website for *The Gate of Heavenly Peace* (www.tsquare.tv).

21. In April 2003, both the United States and the European Union chose not to support resolutions censoring China on its human rights record in exchange for China's support for the war against Iraq (HRW April 16, 2003 press release).

22. Personal communication with Nicholas Jose, author and Australian Cultural Counselor to Beijing from 1987 to 1990.

23. *Lili* is Annie Wang's first novel in English. She is presently preparing a text drawn from her weekly satirical columns appearing in the Hong Kong news. Wang's cast of shallow, name-dropping, trend-hopping, urban chic characters offers a farcical antidote to the high seriousness of the "shock sisters" and their crowd.

24. For various perspectives on the nature and dynamics of the Chinese diaspora see Tu Wei-Ming's "Introduction" and "Cultural China: The Periphery as the Center" in his book, *The Living Tree: The Changing Meaning of Being Chinese Today;* Wang Gungwu and Annette Shun Wah, *Imagining the Chinese Diaspora: Two Perspectives;* Ien Ang, *On Not Speaking Chinese: Living between Asia and the West;* and Wanning Sun, *Leaving China: Media, Migration and Transnational Imagination.*

Bibliography

Abbott, Jack Henry. *In the Belly of the Beast: Letters from Prison.* New York: Random House, 1981.

Aboriginal and Torres Strait Islander Commission. *International Year Speeches.* Canberra: ATSIC, 1993.

Abu-Jamal, Mumia. "Prison Sentences." *Monthly Review* 51 (1999): 59–60.

———. *All Things Censored.* New York, Toronto, London, and Sydney: Seven Stories Press, 2000.

Acoli, Sundiata. "An Updated History of the New Afrikan Prison Struggle (*Abridged*)," in *Imprisoned Intellectuals: America's Political Prisoners Write on Life, Liberation, and Rebellion.* Ed. Joy James. Oxford: Rowman & Littlefield Publishers, Inc., 2003, 138–64.

Age. "Black Leaders to Seek UN Action Over Jail Deaths," July 6, 1989, in *The Struggle for Aboriginal Rights: A Documentary History.* Ed. Bain Attwood and Andrew Markus. Sydney: Allen & Unwin, 1999, 317–8.

Agger, Inger. *The Blue Room: Trauma and Testimony among Refugee Women: A Psycho-Social Exploration.* London: Zed Books, 1994.

Altbach, Philip G. "Publishing in the Third World: Issues and Trends for the 21st Century," in *Publishing and Development in the Third World.* Ed. Philip G. Altbach. London, Melbourne, Munich, and New York: Hans Zell Publishers, 1992, 1–28.

Amnesty International. *United States of America: Rights for All.* New York: Amnesty International Publications, 1998.

Ang, Ien. *On Not Speaking Chinese: Living Between Asia and the West.* London and New York: Routledge, 2001.

APG (Aboriginal Provisional Government). "APG Papers: Intellectual Prisoners," 1992a in *The Struggle for Aboriginal Rights: A Documentary History.* Ed. Bain Attwood and Andrew Markus. Sydney: Allen & Unwin, 1999, 323–4.

——— (1992b). "APG Papers: Towards Aboriginal Sovereignty," 1992b in *The Struggle for Aboriginal Rights: A Documentary History.* Ed. Bain Attwood and Andrew Markus. Sydney: Allen & Unwin, 1999, 324–9.

Appadurai, Arjun. "Disjuncture and Difference in the Global Cultural Economy," in *Colonial Discourse and Post-Colonial Theory: A Reader.* Ed Patrick Williams and Laura Chrisman. New York: Columbia University Press, 1997, 324–38.

———. *Globalization.* Durham and London: Duke University Press, 2000.

Arendt, Hannah. *Eichmann in Jerusalem: A Report on the Banality of Evil.* London: Faber & Faber, 1963.

Arias, Arturo (ed.). *The Rigoberta Menchú Controversy,* with a response by David Stoll. Minneapolis and London: University of Minnesota Press, 2001.

Armitage, Catherine. "Jian Pushes Accelerated Market Reform: Toeing Party Line Takes Great Leap of Faith." *The Australian,* November 9–10, 2002: 16.

———. "China's 'Wild West' Leads Push for True Democracy." *The Australian,* January 3, 2003a: 14.

———. "Hu's Red Light on Student Protest." *The Australian,* January 11–12, 2003b: 9.

Arriens, Jan (ed.). *Welcome to Hell: Letters and Writings from Death Row.* Boston: Northeastern University Press, 1997.

Askin, Kelly Dawn. *War Crimes Against Women: Prosecution in International War Crimes Tribunals.* The Hague, Netherlands: Martinus Nijhoff Publishers, 1997.

Atkinson, Judy. *Trauma Trails: Recreating Song Lines: The Transgenerational Effects of Trauma in Indigenous Australia.* Melbourne: Spinifex Press, 2002.

Attwell, David and Barbara Harlow. "Introduction: South African Fiction after Apartheid." *Modern Fiction Studies* 46.1 (2000): 1–9.

Attwood, Bain. *Rights for Aborigines.* Sydney, Allen & Unwin, 2003.

Attwood, Bain and Fiona Magowan (eds.). *Telling Stories: Indigenous History and Memory in Australia and New Zealand.* Sydney: Allen & Unwin, 2001.

Attwood, Bain and Andrew Markus (eds.). *The Struggle for Aboriginal Rights: A Documentary History.* Sydney: Allen & Unwin, 1992.

Australian. "Native Title Isolates Urban Blacks: Activist," October 6, 1994, in *The Struggle for Aboriginal Rights: A Documentary History.* Ed. Bain Attwood and Andrew Markus Sydney: Allen & Unwin, 1992, 341–2.

Aziz, Nikhil. "The Human Rights Debate in an Era of Globalization: Hegemony of Discourse," in *Debating Human Rights: Critical Essays from the United States and Asia.* Ed. Peter Van Ness. London and New York: Routledge, 1999, 32–55.

Baca, Jimmy Santiago. *A Place to Stand: The Making of a Poet.* New York: Grove Press, 2001.

Bal, Mieke, Leo Spitzer, and Jonathan V. Crewe (eds.). *Acts of Memory: Cultural Recall in the Present.* Hanover, NH: Dartmouth College-University Press of New England, 1999.

Ball, Karyn. "Trauma and Its Institutional Destinies." *Cultural Critique* 46 (Fall 2000): 1–44.

Barkan, Elazar. *The Guilt of Nations: Restitution and Negotiating Historical Injustices.* New York and London: W.W. Norton, 2000.

Barmé, Geremie. *In the Red: On Contemporary Chinese Culture.* New York: Columbia University Press, 1999.

Barmé, Geremie and Linda Jaivin (eds.). *New Ghosts, Old Dreams: Chinese Rebel Voices.* New York: Times Books, 1992.

Barnes, Nancy. *Munyi's Daughter: A Spirited Brumby.* Henley Beach, S. Australia: Seaview Press, 2000.

Barron, Anne. "Legal Discourse and the Colonisation of the Self in the Modern State," in *Post-Modern Law: Enlightenment, Revolution, and the Death of Man.* Ed. A. Carty. Edinburgh: Edinburgh University Press, 1990, 107–25.

Baucom, Ian. "Globalit, Inc.; or, The Cultural Logic of Global Literary Studies." *PMLA* 116.1 (2001): 158–72.

Baxi, Upendra. "Human Rights: Suffering Between Movements and Markets," in *Global Social Movements.* Ed. Robin Cohen and Shirin M. Rai. London and New Brunswick: The Athlone Press, 2000, 33–45.

Bayet-Charlton, Fabienne. *Finding Ullagundahi Island.* Sydney: Allen & Unwin, 2002.

Behr, Mark. *The Smell of Apples.* New York: St. Martin's Press, 1995.

Bennett, Jill. "Tenebrae after September 11: Art, Empathy, and the Global Politics of Belonging," in *World Memory: Personal Trajectories in Global Time.* Ed. Jill Bennett and Rosanne Kennedy. London and New York: Palgrave Macmillan, 2003, 177–94.

Bennett, Jill and Rosanne Kennedy (eds.). *World Memory: Personal Trajectories in Global Time.* London and New York: Palgrave Macmillan, 2003.

Berlant, Lauren. "The Subject of True Feeling: Pain, Privacy, and Politics," in *Cultural Pluralism, Identity Politics, and the Law.* Ed. Austin Sasat and Thomas R. Kearns. Ann Arbor: University of Michigan Press, 1999, 49–84.

Bernstein, Richard. "Betrayal in Beijing." *The Age Good Weekend Magazine* (1989): 33–38.

Birch, Tony. "'This is a True Story': *Rabbit-Proof Fence*, 'Mr. Devil,' and the Desire to Forget." *Cultural Studies Review* 8.1 (2002): 117–29.

Bird, Carmel. "Freedom of Speech." *Island* 59 (Winter 1994): 38–41.

———. (ed.). *The Stolen Children: Their Stories.* Sydney: Random House, 1998.

Bird, Delys and Dennis Haskell (eds.). *Whose Place?: A Study of Sally Morgan's "My Place."* Sydney: Angus and Robinson, 1992.

Bird, Greta, Gary Martin, et al. (eds.). *Majah: Indigenous Peoples and the Law.* Sydney: The Federation Press, 1996.

Blank, Jessica and Eric Jenson. *The Exonerated.* New York: Faber and Faber, 2004.

Boler, Megan. "The Risks of Empathy: Interrogating Multiculturalism's Gaze." *Cultural Studies* 11.2 (1997): 253–73.

Bolt, Andrew. "Aboriginal Leader Sorry for Stolen Children." *Herald Sun*, February 23, 2001a. Accessed March 2003 at http://www.news.com/common/printpage/ 06093,739936,00.

———. "The Truth—and Nothing But." *Herald Sun*, February 24, 2001b. Accessed March 2003 at http://www.news.com/common/printpage/ 06093,739936,00.

Bozzoli, Belinda. "Public Ritual and Private Transition: The Truth Commission in Alexandra Township, South Africa 1996." *African Studies* 57.2 (1998): 167–95.

Breines, Paul. *Tough Jews: Political Fantasies and the Moral Dilemma of American Jewry.* New York: Basic Books, 1990.

Brems, Eva. "Enemies or Allies? Feminism and Cultural Relativism as Dissident Voices in Human Rights Discourse." *Human Rights Quarterly* 19.1 (1997): 136–64.

Brewster, Anne. "The Poetics of Memory." ASAL (Association for the Study of Australian Literature) Conference: unpublished paper, 2003.

Breytenbach, Breyten. *The True Confessions of an Albino Terrorist.* London and Boston: Faber and Faber, 1984.

Brodie, Veronica and Mary-Anne Gale. *My Side of the Bridge: The Life Story of Veronica Brodie.* Kent Town, South Africa: Wakefield Press, 2002.

Bropho, Robert. *Fringedweller.* Chippendale: Alternative Publishing Co-operative with the Assistance of Aboriginal Arts Board, Australia Council, 1980.

Brown, A. Widney and Laura Grenfell. "The International Crime of Gender-Based Persecution and the Taliban." *Melbourne Journal of International Law* 4.2 (2003): 347–75.

Brown, David Maughan. "Black Criticism and Black Aesthetics (1979)." *Soweto Poetry.* Ed. Michael Chapman. Johannesburg: McGraw-Hill, 1982, 46–55.

Brown, Wendy. "Rights and Identity in Modernity: Revisiting the 'Jewish Question,'" in *Identities, Politics, and Rights.* Ed. Austin Sarat and Thomas R. Kearns. Ann Arbor: University of Michigan Press, 1997, 85–130.

Bruhn, Kathleen. "Antonio Gramsci and the 'Palabra Verdadera': The Political Discourse of Mexico's Guerilla Forces." *Journal of InterAmerican Studies and World Affairs* 41.2 (1999): 29–55.

Brunet, Ariane and Stephanie Rousseau. "Acknowledging Violations, Struggling Against Impunity: Women's Rights, Human Rights," in *Common Grounds: Violence Against Women in War and Armed Conflict Situations.* Ed. Indai Lóurdes Sajor. Quezon, Philippines: ASCENT-Asian Center for Women's Human Rights, 1998, 33–60.

Bureau of Justice Statistics. "Criminal Offenders Statistics." Accessed April 2003 at http://www.ojp.usdoj.gov/bjs/crimoff.htm.

Burgoyne, Iris. *The Mirning: We are the Whales.* Broome, WA: Magabala, 2000.

Buruma, Ian. *Bad Elements: Chinese Rebels from Los Angeles to Beijing.* New York: Random House, 2001.

Calling the Ghosts: A Story about Rape, War and Women. Directed by Mandy Jacobson and Karmen Jelinicic. Produced by Julia Ormond. Women Make Movies, 1996.

Camfoo, Tex and Nelly. *Love Against the Law: The Autobiographies of Tex and Nelly Camfoo.* Recorded and Ed. Gillian Cowlishaw. Canberra: Aboriginal Studies Press, 2000.

Carter, Rubin. *The Sixteenth Round: From Number 1 Contender to #45472.* New York: Viking Press, 1974.

Caruth, Cathy. *Trauma: Explorations in Memory.* Baltimore: Johns Hopkins University Press, 1995.

Chalarimeri, Ambrose Mungala. *The Man from the Sunrise Side.* Broome, WA: Magabala, 2001.

Charlesworth, Hilary and Christine Chinkin. *The Boundaries of International Law: A Feminist Analysis.* Executive Park, NY: Juris Pub, 2000.

Chen, Tina Yih-Ting. "From the Word to the World: Writing about Korean Comfort Women." Paper presented at 118th MLA Annual Convention, New York, December 29, 2002.

Cheng, Nien. *Life and Death in Shanghai.* New York: Grove Press, 1987.

Chevigny, Bell Gale (ed.). *Doing Time: Twenty-Five Years of Prison Writing.* New York: Arcade Pub, 1999.

Chin, Sung Chung. "The Origin and Development of the Military Sexual Slavery Problem in Imperial Japan." *positions* 5.1 (1997): 219–53.

Cho, Eunice, et al. *Something Inside So Strong: A Resource Guide on Human Rights in the United States.* Washington DC: U.S. Human Rights Network, 2004.

Chung, Helene. *Shouting from China.* Ringwood, Vic: Penguin, 1988.

Chungmoo Choi. "The Politics of War Memories Toward Healing," in *Perilous Memories: The Asia-Pacific War(s).* Ed. T. Fujitani, Geoffrey M. White and Lisa Yoneyama. Durham and London: Duke University Press, 2001, 395–409.

Clare, Monica. *Karobran: The Story of an Aboriginal Girl.* Sydney: Alternative Publishing Co-operative Ltd, 1978.

Clarke, David. "Contemporary Asian Art and Its Western Reception." *Third Text* 16.3 (2002): 237–42.

Cleaver, Eldridge. *Soul On Ice.* New York: McGraw-Hill, 1968.

——. *Soul on fire,* Waco, Tx: World Books, 1978.

CNN.com. "Sam Chaiton and Terry Swinton: A Chat with the Authors of *Lazarus and the Hurricane: The Inside Story of the Freeing of Rubin 'Hurricane' Carter.*" February 2, 2000. Accessed at http://www.cnn.com/COMMUNITY/transcripts/2000/2/chaitonswinton/.

Coetzee, J.M. *White Writing: On the Culture of Letters in South Africa.* New Haven, CT and London: Yale University Press, 1988.

——. *Boyhood: Scenes from Provincial Life.* New York: Viking, 1997.

Colson, Charles W. *Born Again.* Old Tappan, NJ: Chosen Books, 1976.

Connolly, William E. *Why I Am Not a Secularist.* Minneapolis and London: University of Minnesota Press, 1999.

Cooper, Helen Margaret. "Not in My Name." Paper presented at 119th MLA Annual Convention, San Diego, CA, December 30, 2003.

Coplan, David. *The Time of Cannibals: The Word Music of South Africa's Basotho Migrants.* Chicago: Chicago University Press, 1994.

Coullie, Judith Lütge. "Apartheid and Post-Apartheid Life Writing," in *Encyclopedia of Life Writing: Autobiographical and Biographical Forms, 1 (A-K).* Ed. Margaretta Jolly. London and Chicago: Fitzroy Dearborn Publishers, 2001, 43–44.

Cox, Larry and Dorothy Q. Thomas (eds.). *Close to Home: Case Studies of Human Rights Work in the United States.* New York: The Ford Foundation, 2004.

Crawford, Evelyn as told to Chris. Walsh. *Over My Tracks: A Remarkable Life.* Ringwood, Vic: Penguin, 1993.

Currie, Elliott. *Crime and Punishment in America: Why the Solutions to America's Most Stubborn Social Crisis Have Not Worked—and What Will.* New York: Henry Holt and Company, 1998.

Curthoys, Ann. *Freedom Ride: A Freedom Rider Remembers.* Sydney: Allen & Unwin, 2002.

Davis, Angela Yvonne. *Angela Davis: An Autobiography.* New York: Random House, 1974.

———. "Political Prisoners, Prisons, and Black Liberation." *Imprisoned Intellectuals: America's Political Prisoners Write on Life, Liberation, and Rebellion.* Ed. Joy James. Oxford: Rowman & Littlefield Publishers, Inc., 2003, 64–77.

Davis, Jack. *John Pat and Other Poems.* Ferntree Gully: Dent, 1988.

Davis, Stephen M. *Apartheid's Rebels: Inside South Africa's Hidden War.* New Haven, CT and London: Yale University Press, 1987.

Davis, Therese. "Becoming Unrecognizable." *UTS Review* 4.1 (May 1998): 169–79.

Daymond, M.J., Dorothy Driver, et al. (eds.). *Women Writing Africa: The Southern Region.* New York: Feminist Press, 2003.

Daziell, Rosamund. *Shameful Autobiographies: Shame in Contemporary Australian Autobiographies and Culture.* Melbourne: Melbourne University Press, 1999.

Degiya'göh Resources. "The Case of Leonard Peltier: Native American Political Prisoner." Accessed February 2003 at http://www.freepeltier.org.

De Klerk, F.W. *The Last Trek: A New Beginning: The Autobiography.* London and Basingstoke: Macmillan, 1998.

De Kock, Eugene. *Long Night's Damage: Working for the Apartheid State.* Saxonwold, RSA: Contra Press, 1998.

Delgado, Richard. "Storytelling for Oppositionists and Others: A Plea for Narrative." *Michigan Law Review* 87.6 (1989): 2411–41.

Derrida, Jacques and Anne Dufourmantelle. *De l'hospitalité.* Paris: Calmann-Lévy, 1997.

DeVeaux, Alexis. "Walking Into Freedom." *Essence* 21.2 (1990): 48–59.

Dodge, L. Mara. *"Whores and Thieves of the Worst Kind": A Study of Women, Crime, and Prisons, 1835–2000*. DeKlab: Northern Illinois University Press, 2002.

Dodson, Michael. *Social Justice Commission: First Report*. Canberra: Human Rights and Equal Opportunity Commission, 1993.

Dolgopol, Ustinia. "Rape as a War Crime—Mythology and History," in *Common Grounds: Violence Against Women in War and Armed Conflict*. Ed. Indai Lourdes Sajor. Quezon City, Philippines: Asian Center for Women's Human Rights (ASCENT), 1998, 122–47.

Douzinas, Costas and Ronnie Warrington. *Justice Miscarried: Ethics and Aesthetics in Law*. New York: Harvester Wheatsheaf, 1994.

Driver, Dorothy. "Transformation Through Art: Writing, Representation, and Subjectivity in Recent South African Fiction." *World Literature Today* 70.1 (1996a): 45–51.

———. "Modern South African Literature in English: A Reader's Guide to Some Recent Critical and Bibliographic Sources." *World Literature Today* 70.1 (1996b): 99–107.

———. "Changing Landscapes" *Recreating Memory After Apartheid*. Adelaide: Australasian Universities Language and Literature Association, Thirty-First Congress, unpublished keynote address, 2001.

———. "Truth, Reconciliation, Gender: The South African Truth and Reconciliation Commission." Leeds University: Centre for Cultural Analysis, Theory and History, unpublished conference paper, 2002.

———. Personal communication. 24 Feb. 2004.

Dube, Pamela Sethunya. "The Story of Thandi Shezi," in *Commissioning the Past: Understanding South Africa's Truth and Reconciliation Commission*. Ed. Deborah Posel and Graeme Simpson. Johannesburg: Witwatersrand University Press, 2002, 117–30.

Duiker, K. Sello. *The Quiet Violence of Dreams*. Cape Town: Kwela Books, 2001.

Dunant, Henry. *A Memory of Solferino*. Washington, DC: American National Red Cross, 1939.

Dutton, Michael. *Streetlife China*. Cambridge: Cambridge University Press, 1998.

———. "Street Scenes of Subalternity: China, Globalization, and Rights." *Social Text* 17.3 (1999): 63–86.

Edelstein, Jillian. *Truth and Lies: Stories from the Truth and Reconciliation Commission in South Africa*. London and Johannesburg: Granta, and M&G Books, 2001.

Fang, Lizhi (1989). "Open Letter to Deng Xiaoping." *The Chinese Human Rights Reader: Documents and Commentary, 1900–2000*. Armonk, NY and London: M.E. Sharpe, 2001.

Fanon, Frantz. *The Wretched of the Earth*. New York: Grove Press, 1963.

Farewell, My Concubine. Directed by Chen Kaige. Screenplay by Lilian Lee and Lu Wei. Produced by Hsu Feng. Burbank, CA: Miramax, 1993.

Farrell, Kirby. *Post-Traumatic Culture: Injury and Interpretation in the Nineties.* Baltimore and London: Johns Hopkins University Press, 1998.

Felman, Shoshana and Dori Laub (eds.). *Testimony: Crises of Witnessing in Literature, Psychoanalysis, and History.* London and New York: Routledge, 1992.

Field, Norma. "War and Apology: Japan, Asia, the Fiftieth, and After." *positions* 5.1 (1997): 1–49.

Finnane, Antonia (2000). "Dead Daughters, Dissident Sons, and Human Rights in China," in *Human Rights and Gender Politics: Asia-Pacific Perspectives.* Ed. Anne-Marie Hilsdon, Martha Macintyre, Vera Mackie, and Maila Stivens. London and New York: Routledge, 2000, 83–106.

First, Ruth. *117 Days: An Account of Confinement and Interrogation Under the South African 90-Day Detention Law.* Harmondsworth, Middlesex: Penguin Books, 1965.

Foucault, Michel. *Power/Knowledge: Selected Interviews and Other Writings, 1972–1977.* Ed. Colin Gorden. New York: Pantheon, 1980.

Franklin, Bruce H. *Prison Literature in America: The Victim as Criminal and Artist.* Westport, CT: Lawrence Hill & Company, 1978; rev. ed. 1982.

———. "Introduction," in *Prison Writing in 20th-Century America.* Ed. H. Bruce Franklin. New York: Penguin Books, 1998, 1–18.

Freiberg, Freda. "Blame and Shame: The Hidden History of the Comfort Women of World War II," in *Body Trade,* Ed. Barbara Creed and Jeanette Hoorn. New York: Routledge, 2001, 231–38.

From One Prison. Directed and produced by Carol Jacobsen. Berkeley, CA: University of California Extension Center for Media and Independent Learning, 1994.

Frow, John. "A Politics of Stolen Time." *Meanjin* 57.2 (1998): 351–68.

Fugard, Athol. *Boesman and Lena and Other Plays.* Oxford and New York: Oxford University Press, 1978.

———. *Statements: Siswe Bansi Is Dead, the Island, Statements After an Arrest Under the Immorality Act / 3 Plays.* New York: Theatre Communications Group, 1988.

———. *My Children! My Africa!* London: Faber, 1990.

Fujime Yuki. "The Licensed Prostitution System and the Prostitution Abolition Movement in Modern Japan." *positions* 5.1 (1997): 135–70.

Gabriel, John. *Whitewash: Racialized Politics and the Media.* London and New York: Routledge, 1998.

Gaffney, Ellie. *Somebody Now: The Autobiography of Ellie Gaffney, a Woman of Torres Strait.* Canberra: Aboriginal Studies Press, 1989.

Gaines, Patrice. *Laughing in the Dark: From Colored Girl to Woman of Color—A Journey from Prison to Power.* New York: Crown, 1994.

Galgut, Damon. *The Beautiful Screaming of Pigs.* London: Abacus, 1992.

Gallagher, Anne. "Ending the Marginalization: Strategies for Incorporating Women into the United Nations Human Rights System." *Human Rights Quarterly* 19.2 (1997): 283–333.

Garlin, Deborah L. "A Political Fugitive: The Case of Little Rock Reed (A Story of Due Process the American Way." *Social Justice* 20.3–4 (1993): 163.

The Gate of Heavenly Peace. Directed and produced by Carma Hinton and Richard Gordon. Scripted by Geremie Barmé and John Crowley. San Francisco: NAATA/CrossCurrent Media, 1995.

Gibson, Andrew. *Postmodernity, Ethics and the Novel: From Leavis to Levinas.* London and New York: Routledge, 1996.

Gibson, Nigel. "Transition from Apartheid." *Journal of Asian and African Studies* 36.1 (2001): 65–85.

Giddens, Anthony. *The Consequences of Modernity.* Cambridge: Polity Press, 1990.

———. *Modernity and Self-Identity: Self and Society in the Late Modern Age.* Cambridge: Polity Press, 1991.

Giffone, Tony. "Book Review: The Lily Theatre." *Persimmon Magazine* Spring 2001, Accessed at www.persimmon-mag.com/spring2001/ bre_sp2001_8.html.

Gilbert, Kevin. *Living Black: Blacks Talk to Kevin Gilbert.* Ringwood, Vic: Penguin Books, 1977.

Gilmore, Leigh. *The Limits of Autobiography: Trauma and Testimony.* Ithaca, NY and London: Cornell University Press, 2001.

———. "Jurisdictions: I, Rigoberta Menchú, The Kiss, and Scandalous Self-Representation in the Age of Memoir and Trauma." *Signs: Journal of Women in Culture and Society* 28.2 (2002): 695–718.

Ginibi, Ruby Langford. *Don't Take Your Love to Town.* Ringwood, Vic: Penguin Books Ltd, 1988.

Gleeson, Kim. "Universal Rights Network." Accessed at http://www.universalrights.net. Produced by Kim Gleeson, 2002.

Goffman, Erving. *Asylums: Essays on the Social Situation of Mental Patients and Other Inmates.* Chicago: Aldine, 1961.

Goldblatt, Beth and Sheila Meintjes. "Gender and the Truth Reconciliation Commission: A Submission to the Truth and Reconciliation Commission," in *What Women Do in Wartime: Gender and Conflict in Africa.* Ed. Meredith Turshen and Clothilde Twagiramariya. London: Zed Books, 1998.

Goodall, Heather. *Invasion to Embassy: Land in Aboriginal Politics in New South Wales, 1770–1972.* Sydney: Allen & Unwin, 1996.

Goodrich, Peter. *Languages of Law: From Logics of Memory to Nomadic Masks.* London: Weidenfeld and Nicolson, 1990.

Gordimer, Nadine. *A World of Strangers.* New York: Simon and Schuster, 1958.

———. *The Late Bourgeois World.* New York: Viking Press, 1966.

———. *Burger's Daughter.* New York: Viking Press, 1979.

———. "April 27: The First Time (1994)," in *Women Writing Africa: The Southern Region.* Ed. M.J. Daymond, Dorothy Driver, Sheila Neintjeset et al. New York: Feminist Press, 2003, 467–9.

Grant, Stan. *The Tears of Strangers: A Memoir.* Pymble: Harper Collins, 2002.

Gregory, James with Bob Graham. *Goodbye Bafana: Nelson Mandela, My Prisoner, My Friend.* London: Headline, 1995.

Grossman, Michelle (coordinating ed.). *Blacklines: Contemporary Critical Writing by Indigenous Australians*. Melbourne: Melbourne University Press, 2003.

Grunebaum, Heidi and Yazir Henri. "Re-membering Bodies, Producing Histories: Holocaust Survivor Narrative and Truth and Reconciliation Commission," in *World Memory: Personal Trajectories in Global Time*. Eds. Jill Bennett and Rosanne Kennedy. London and New York: Palgrave Macmillan, 2003, 101–18.

Guattari, Félix. *Chaosmosis: An Ethico-Aesthetic Paradigm*. Bloomington: Indiana University Press, 1995.

Hage, Ghassan. Against Paranoid Nationalism: Searching for Hope in a Shrinking Society. Annandule, NSW and London. Sydney: Pluto Press and Merlin Press 2003.

Hames-García, Michael. *Fugitive Thought: Prison Movements, Race, and the Meaning of Justice*. Minneapolis and London: University of Minnesota Press, 2004.

Harcourt, Wendy. "Women Refiguring Globalisation: Gender and the Politics of Place." Adelaide, University of South Australia: unpublished paper, 2002.

Harding, Richard W., Roderick Broadhurst, et al. *Aboriginal Contact with the Criminal Justice System and the Impact of the Royal Commission into Aboriginal Deaths in Custody*. Perth: Crime Research Centre, University of Western Australia-Hawkins Press, 1995.

Harlow, Barbara. *Barred: Women, Writing, and Political Detention*. Hanover, NH: Wesleyan University Press, 1992.

Harootunian, Harry D. "In the Tiger's Lair: Socialist Everydayness Enters Post-Mao China." *Postcolonial Studies* 3.2 (2000): 339–47.

Harris, Mark. "Deconstructing the Royal Commission—Representations of 'Aboriginality' in the Royal Commission into Aboriginal Deaths in Custody," in *Majah: Indigenous Peoples and the Law*. Eds. Greta Bird, Gary Martin, and Jennifer Nielsen. Sydney: The Federation Press, 1996, 192–214.

Harrison, Jane. *Stolen*. Sydney: Currency Press in Association with Playbox Theatre Centre, Monash University, Melbourne, 1998.

Havemann, Paul. *Indigenous Peoples' Rights in Australia, Canada and New Zealand*. Oxford and New York: Oxford University Press, 1999.

———. "Enmeshed in the Web? Indigenous Peoples' Rights in the Network Society," in *Global Social Movements*. Ed. Robin Cohen and Shirin M Rai. London and New Brunswick: The Athlone Press, 2000, 18–32.

Hayner, Priscilla B. "Fifteen Truth Commissions—1974–1994: A Comparative Study." *Human Rights Quarterly* 16 (1994): 597–655.

Hegarty, Ruth. *Is That You Ruthie?* St. Lucia: University of Queensland Press, 1999.

Hein, Laura. "American Media and Military Comfort Women: A Comparative Analysis of News Reports," in *Japan Made in USA: Warawareru Nihonjin*. Ed. Zipangu Henshubu. New York: Zipangu, 1998, 109–13.

———. "Savage Irony: The Imaginative Power of the 'Military Comfort Women' in the 1990s." *Gender & History* 11.2 (1999): 336–72.

Henson, Maria Rosa. *Comfort Woman: A Filipina's Story of Prostitution and Slavery Under the Japanese Military.* New York and Oxford: Rowman & Littlefield Publishers Inc., 1999.

Hesford, Wendy S. "Reading Rape Stories: Material Rhetoric and the Trauma of Representation." *College English* 62.2 (1999): 192–221.

Hesford, Wendy S. and Wendy Kozol (eds.). *Haunting Violations: Feminist Criticism and the Crisis of the "Real."* Urbana and Chicago: University of Illinois Press, 2001.

Heyns, Michiel. "The Whole Country's Truth: Confession and Narrative in Recent White South African Writing." *Modern Fiction Studies* 46.1 (2000): 42–66.

Hicks, George. *The Comfort Women: Sex Slaves of the Japanese Imperial Forces.* Singapore: Heinemann Asia, 1995.

Hirsch, Marianne. "Projected Memory: Holocaust Photographs in Personal and Public Fantasy," in *Acts of Memory: Cultural Recall in the Present.* Ed. Mieke Bal, Leo Spitzer, and Jonathan V. Crewe. Hanover, NH: Dartmouth College- University Press of New England, 1999.

Hofmeyr, Isabel. "Not the Magic Talisman: Rethinking Oral Literature in South Africa." *World Literature Today* 70.1 (1996): 88–95.

Holiday, Anthony. "Forgiving and Forgetting: the Truth and Reconciliation Commission," in *Negotiating the Past: The Making of Memory in South Africa.* Ed. Sarah Nuttall and Carli Coetzee. Oxford and New York: Oxford University Press, 1998, 43–56.

Holt, Albert. *Forcibly Removed.* Broome, WA: Magabala, 2001.

Honeysett, Stewart. "Aborigines Reclaim Identity Through Literature." *The Australian*, August 7, 1996: 9.

Hong, Ying. *Summer of Betrayal.* New York: Grove Press, 1997.

———. *Daughter of the River: An Autobiography.* London: Bloomsbury, 1998.

Hosking, Susan. "Breaking the Silence: Aboriginal Life Narratives in South Australia." *CRNLE (Centre for Research in the New Literatures in English)* (2001): 9–24.

Howard, Keith. *True Stories of the Korean Comfort Women.* London: Cassell, 1995.

Huggins, Jackie. "Always Was Always Will Be." *Australian Historical Studies* 25.100 (1993): 459–64.

Huggins, Rita and Jackie Huggins. *Auntie Rita.* Canberra: Aboriginal Studies Press, 1994.

Hughes-D'Aeth, Tony. "Which *Rabbit-Proof Fence?*: Empathy, Assimilation, Hollywood." *Australian Humanities Review* 27 (2002), Accessed at http://www.lib.latrobe.edu.au/AHR/archive/Issue-September2002/hughesdaeth. html.

Human Rights in China. *Children of the Dragon: The Story of Tiananmen Square.* New York and London: Collier Macmillan Publishers, 1990.

Human Rights Watch. "No Escape: Male Rapes in U.S. Prisons." Accessed at http://www.hrw.org/reports/2001/prison.

———. "U.S. Circumvents Courts with Enemy Combatant Tag." June 12, 2002. Accessed at http://www.hrw.org/press/ 2002/06/ us0612.htm.

The Hurricane. Directed by Norman Jewison. Screenplay by Armyan Bernstein and Dan Gordon. Produced by Armyan Bernstein, John Ketcham, and Norman Jewison. Universal City, CA: Universal Studios, 1999.

Huyssen, Andreas. "Present Pasts: Media, Politics, Amnesia." *Public Culture* 12.1 (2000): 21–38.

———. "Trauma and Memory: A New Imaginary of Temporality," in *World Memory: Personal Trajectories in Global Time*. Eds. Jill Bennett and Roseanne Kennedy. London and New York: Palgrave Macmillan, 2003, 16–29.

Hyun Sook Kim. "History and Memory: The 'Comfort Women' Controversy." *positions* 5.1 (1997): 73–106.

Hyunah Yang. "Revisiting the Issue of Korean 'Military Comfort Women': The Question of Truth and Positionality." *Positions* 5.1 (1997): 51–71.

Ignatieff, Michael. "Introduction," in *Truth and Lies: Stories from the Truth and Reconciliation Commission in South Africa*. Ed. Jillian Edelstein. London and Johannesburg: 2001a, 15–21.

———. *Human Rights as Politics and Idolatry*. Princeton, NY: Princeton University Press, 2001b.

———. "Is the Human Rights Era Ending?" *New York Times*, Granta and M&G Books February 5, 2002, A29.

Iman, David Bowie, et al. *I Am Iman*. New York: Universe Books, 2001.

Jackson, George. *Soledad Brother: The Prison Letters of George Jackson*. New York: Bantam Books, Inc., 1970.

Jacobsen, Quentin. *Solitary in Johannesburg*. London: Joseph, 1973.

Jakobson, Linda. *"Lies In Ink, Truth In Blood": The Role and Impact of the Chinese Media During the Beijing Spring of '89*. The Joan Shorenstein Barone Center, John F. Kennedy School of Government at Harvard University, Cambridge, MA, 1990. Accessed March 2003 at http://www.tsquare.tv/themes/liesink.html.

James, Joy. "Introduction," in *Imprisoned Intellectuals: America's Political Prisoners Write on Life, Liberation, and Rebellion*. Ed. Joy James. Lanham, Boulder, New York, and Oxford: Rowman & Littlefield Publishers, Inc., 2003, 3–27.

Jefferson, LaShawn. Paper presented during a "Women's Rights as Human Rights" session at the Censoring Feminism Conference, University of Michigan, March 22, 2002.

Jenkin, Tim. *Escape from Pretoria*. London: Kliptown Books, 1987.

Jiang Yang. *Six Chapters from my Life Downunder*. Seattle and London: University of Washington Press, 1984.

Johnson, Colin. *Wild Cat Falling*. Sydney: Angus and Robertson, 1965.

Johnson, Elliot. *Royal Commission into Aboriginal Deaths in Custody: National Report.* 11 vols. Canberra: Australian Government Printing Office, 1991.

Jolly, Margaret. "*Woman Ikat Raet Long Human Raet O No*?: Women's Rights, Human Rights, and Domestic Violence in Vanuatu," in *Human Rights and Gender Politics: Asia-Pacific Perspectives.* Ed. Anne-Marie Hilsdon, Martha Macintyre, Vera Mackie, and Maila Stivens. London and New York: Routledge, 2000, 124–46.

Jones, Jennifer Anne. " 'Yesterday's Words,' The Beautiful and the Damned." *Journal of Australian Studies* 64 (2000a): 128–234.

———. "Reading 'Karobran' by Monica Clare." *Overland* 161 (2000b): 67–71.

———. "The Black Communist: The Contested Memory of Margaret Tucker." *Hecate* 26.2 (2000c): 135–45.

———. *Aboriginal Women's Autobiographical Narratives and the Politics of Collaboration.* Doctoral Thesis, Department of Social Inquiry. Adelaide: University of Adelaide, 2001.

Joubert, Elsa. *Poppie Nongena.* New York: Norton, 1980.

Jui Dan. *Crows: The Singapore Dream of a Group of China Women.* Singapore: Lingzi Media, 2001.

Jung Chang. *Wild Swans: Three Daughters of China.* New York: Simon & Schuster, 1991.

Kako Senda. *Jugun Ianfu.* Tokyo: Futabasha Showa, 1973.

Kalathil, Shanthi. "Dot Com for Dictators" in *Foreign Policy: The Magazine of Global Politics, Economics, and Ideas,* Accessed at http://www. foreign-policy.com/story/story.php?storyID = 13542, 2002.

Kann, Mark E. "Penitence for the Privileged: Manhood, Race, and Penitentiaries in Early America," in *Prison Masculinities.* Ed. Don Sabo, Terry A. Kupers, and Willie London. Philadelphia: Temple University Press, 2001, 21–34.

Kano Mikiyo. "The Problem with the 'Comfort Women Problem.' " *AMPO: Japan-Asia Quarterly Review* 24.2 (1993): 40–43.

Kap Soon-Choi, Kap. "A Testimony on the Mass Rape and Sexual Enslavement of Women and Girls." University of Michigan—Ann Arbor, March 11, 2002.

Keating, Paul. "The Redfern Statement." International Human Rights Day— Australian Launch of the United Nations International Year for the World's Indigenous People at Redfern Park, Sydney, 1992. Accessed 28 Oct, 2003 at www.antar-org.uu/keating-redfern.html.

Keenan, Thomas. "Left to Our Own Devices: On the Impossibility of Justice," in *Fables of Responsibility: Aberrations and Predicaments in Ethics and Politics.* Stanford: Stanford University Press, 1997, 7–42.

Keller, Nora Okja. *Comfort Woman.* New York: Viking, 1997.

Kennedy, Rosanne. "The Narrator as Witness: Testimony, Trauma and Narrative Form in *My Place.*" *Meridian* 16.2 (1997): 235–60.

———. "Stolen Generation Testimony: Trauma, Historiography and the Question of Truth." *Aboriginal History* 25 (2001): 116–31.

Kennedy, Rosanne and Jan Tikka Wilson. "Constructing Shared Histories: Stolen Generations Testimony, Narrative Therapy and Address," in *World Memory: Personal Trajectories in Global Time*. Ed. Jill Bennett and Rosanne Kennedy. London and New York: Palgrave Macmillan, 2003, 119–40.

Kim, Il Myon. *Nihon Josei Aishi*. Tokyo: Tokuma Shoten, 1980.

Kim, Richard S. "Chapter 3—The Diasporic Dilemmas of Transnational State-Building." Paper presented at Global Ethnic Literatures Seminar, University of Michigan, Fall 2002.

Kim-Gibson, Dai Sil. "They Are Our Grandmas." *positions* 5.1 (1997): 256–74.

———. *Silence Broken: Korean Comfort Women*. Parkersburg, Iowa: Mid-Prairie Books, 1999.

King, Rachel (ed.). *Don't Kill in Our Names: Families of Murder Victims Speak Out Against the Death Penalty*. New Brunswick, NJ and London: Rutgers University Press, 2003.

Kinnane, Stephen. *Shadow Lines*. Fremantle: Fremantle Arts Centre Press, 2003.

Kleinert, Sylvia. "An Aboriginal Moomba: Remaking History." *Continuum: Journal of Media and Cultural Studies* 13.3 (1999): 345–57.

Kleinman, Arthur and Joan Kleinman. "How Bodies Remember." New Literacy History, 25(1994): 707–25.

Knox, Sara L. "The Productive Power of Confessions of Cruelty." *Postmodern Culture: An Electronic Journal of Interdisciplinary Criticism* 11.3 (2001). Accessed February 2003 at http://www.iath.virginia.edu/pmc/text/only/issue.501/ 11.3knox.txt.

Knudson, Jerry. "Rebellion in Chiapas: Insurrection by Internet and Public Relations." *Media, Culture and Society* 20.3 (1998): 507–18.

Krog, Antjie. *Country of My Skull*. New York: Three Rivers Press, 1998.

Kushner, Tony. *Angels in America: A Gay Fantasia on National Themes*. New York: Theatre Communications Group, 1993.

LaCapra, Dominick. *History and Memory after Auschwitz*. Ithaca, NY and London: Cornell University Press, 1998.

———. *Writing History, Writing Trauma*. Baltimore and London: Johns Hopkins University Press, 2001.

La Jornada. On-line general director, Carmen Lira Saade. Accessed March 2003 at http://www.jornada.unam.mx.

Langer, Beryl. "Mothers of the Disappeared in the Diaspora: Globalization and Human Rights," in *Human Rights and Gender Politics: Asia-Pacific Perspectives*. Ed. Anne-Marie Hilsdon, Martha Macintyre, Vera Mackie, and Maila Stivens. London and New York: Routledge, 2000, 193–210.

Langlois, Anthony J. *The Politics of Justice and Human Rights: Southeast Asia and Universalist Theory*. Cambridge: Cambridge University Press, 2001.

Langton, Marcia. *"Well, I Heard it on the Radio and Saw it on the Television—": An Essay for the Australian Film Commission on the Politics and Aesthetics of Filmmaking by and about Aboriginal People and Things*. North Sydney: Australian Film Commission, 1993.

Lau, Evelyn. *Runaway: Diary of a Street Kid*. Toronto: Harper Collins, 1989.
———. *Other Women: A Novel*. Toronto: Random House of Canada, 1995.
Laub, Dori. "Bearing Witness, or the Vicissitudes of Listening and An Event
    Without a Witness: Truth, Testimony and Survival," in *Testimony: Crisis
    of Witnessing in Literature, Psychoanalysis, and History*. Ed. Soshana
    Felman and Dori Laub. London and New York: Routledge, 1992, 57–74.
Layton, Kelly. *Punks in Beijing: Practices of Consumption, Parody and
    Ambiguity in Contemporary China*. Honours Thesis, Centre for Asian
    Studies. Adelaide: University of Adelaide, 2001.
Lazaroo, Simone. *The Australian Fiancé*. Sydney: Picador, 2000.
Lee, Jennifer Hong Yub. "Japanese Comfort Stations: Sites of Revelation and
    Instruction." *East Asian Studies Journal* 23 (1998): 30–9.
Lee, Chang-rae. *A Gesture Life*. New York: Riverhead Books, 1999.
Lennon, Jessie. *I'm the One that Know this Country!: The Story of Jessie
    Lennon and Coober Pedy*. Canberra: Aboriginal Studies Press, 2000.
Lentin, Ronit. "The Feminisation of Catastrophe: Narrating Women's
    Silences," in *Global Feminist Politics: Identities in a Changing World*. Ed.
    Suki Ali, Kelly Coate, and Wangui wa Goro. London and New York:
    Routledge, 2000, 92–106.
Lessing, Dorothy. *African Stories*. London: M. Joseph, 1964.
Lewin, Hugh (1974). *Bandiet: Seven Years in a South African Prison*. Cape
    Town: David. Philip, 1981.
Libin, Mark. "Can the Subaltern be Heard? Response and Responsibility in
    'South Africa's Human Spirit.'" *Textual Practice* 17.1 (2003): 119–40.
Liu Hong. *Startling Moon*. London: Review Books, 2001.
Lyon, Janet. *Manifestoes: Provocations of the Modern*. Ithaca, NY and London:
    Cornell University Press, 1999.
Mack, John. "God and Man in Jail." *The Progressive* 49 (1985): 50.
Mackie, Vera. "Sexual Violence, Silence, and Human Rights Discourse: The
    Emergence of the Military Prostitution Issue," in *Human Rights and
    Gender Politics: Asia-Pacific Perspectives*. Eds. Anne-Marie Hilsdon,
    Martha Macintyre, and Vera Mackie. London and New York: Routledge,
    2000, 37–59.
Mah, Adeline Yen. *Falling Leaves: The True Story of an Unwanted Chinese
    Daughter*. New York: Wiley, 1998.
Mailer, Norman. *The Executioner's Song*. New York: Modern Library, 1993.
Makhoere, Caesarina Kona. *No Child's Play: In Prison Under Apartheid*.
    London: Women's Press, 1988.
Malcolm. X, *The Autobiography of Malcolm X*. New York: Grove Press, 1965.
———. "The Ballot or the Bullet (*Abridged*)," in *Imprisoned Intellectuals:
    America's Political Prisoners Write on Life, Liberation, and Rebellion*.
    Ed. Joy James. Lanham, Boulder, New York, and Oxford: Rowman &
    Littlefield Publishers, Inc., 2003, 51–61.
Mandela, Nelson. "Address to the Nation on the Assassination of Martin
    Thembisile (Chris) Hani (1993)." Accessed at the African National

Congress website, http://www.anc.org.za/ancdocs/history/mandela/ 1993/sp930410.html.

———. *The Long Walk to Freedom: The Autobiography of Nelson Mandela.* London: Little, Brown and Company, 1994.

Mandela, Winnie Madikizela. "Detention Alone is a Trial in Itself." in *Women Writing Africa: The Southern Region* Ed. M. J. Daymond, Dorothy Driver, et al. New York, feminist Press, 2003: 344–6.

Manne, Robert. "In Denial: The Stolen Generations and the Right." *The Australian Quarterly Essay* 1.1 (2001): 1–113.

———. (ed.). *Whitewash: On Keith Windschuttle's Fabrication of Aboriginal History.* Melbourne: Black Inc., 2003.

Manzo, Kathryn A. *Domination, Resistance, and Social Change in South Africa: The Local Effects of Global Power.* Westport, CT and London: Praeger, 1992.

Marshall-Stoneking, Billy. "Review: Ruby Langford Ginibi *My Bundjalung People* (also Bain Attwood et al. *A Life Together, A Life Apart*, Christine Stevens *A White Man's Dreaming—Killalpaninna Mission 1866–95*, and Kathie Cochrane *Oodgeroo*." *Overland* (1995): 138.

Martin, Dannie M. and Peter Y. Sussman. *Committing Journalism: The Prison Writings of Red Hog.* New York: W.W. Norton & Co., 1993.

Mashinini, Emma. *Strikes Have Followed Me All My Life: A South African Autobiography.* London: Women's Press, 1989.

Massumi, Brian. "Everywhere You Want to Be: Introduction to Fear," in *The Politics of Everyday Fear.* Ed. Brian Massumi. Minneapolis and London: University of Minnesota Press, 1993, 3–38.

———. "The Autonomy of Effect," in *Deleuze: A Critical Reader.* Ed. Paul Patton. Oxford: Blackwell, 1996, 217–40.

Mathabane, Mark. *Kaffir Boy: The True Story of a Black Youth's Coming of Age in Apartheid South Africa.* New York: Macmillan, 1986.

———. *Kaffir Boy in America.* New York: Scribner's, 1989.

Mathabane, Mark and Miriam Mathabane. *Miriam's Song.* London and New York: Verso, 2000.

Mattera, Don. *Sophiatown: Coming of Age in South Africa.* Johannesburg and Boston: Junction Avenue Press, and Beacon Press 1986 and 1989.

———. *Memory is the Weapon.* Johannesburg: Ravan Press, 1987.

Maupin, Armistead. *Tales of the City.* New York: Harper & Row, 1978.

McClintock, Anne. "The Scandal of Hybridity," in *Imperial Leather: Race, Gender and Sexuality in the Colonial Contest.* London and New York: Routledge, 1995, 299–328.

McCourt, Frank. *Angela's Ashes: A Memoir.* New York: Scribner's, 1996.

———. *'Tis: A Memoir.* New York: Scribner's, 1999.

McDonald, David. "Australia: Royal Commission into Aboriginal Deaths in Custody," in *Indigenous People's Rights in Australia, Canada and New Zealand.* Ed. Paul Havermann. Oxford and New York: Oxford University Press, 1999, 283–301.

McDougall, Gay J. "International Legal Approaches Toward the Issue of Japan's Military Sexual Slavery and the Liability of the Government of Japan." Accessed September 2002 at http://witness.peacenet.or.kr/symegay.htm.

Mellor, Doreen and Anna Haebich, (eds.). *Many Voices: Reflections on Experiences of Indigenous Child Separation.* Canberra: National Library of Australia, 2002.

Menchú, Rigoberta with Elisabeth Burgos-Debray. *I, Rigoberta Menchú: An Indian Woman in Guatemala.* London and New York: Verso, 1984.

Merry, Sally Engle. "Women, Violence, and the Human Rights System," in *Women, Gender, and Human Rights: A Global Perspective.* Ed. Marjorie Agosin. New Brunswick, NJ and London: Rutgers University Press, 2001, 83–97.

Mian Mian. *Candy.* Boston: Little, Brown and Company/Back Bay Books, 2003.

Mickler, Steve. *The Myth of Privilege: Aboriginal Status, Media Visions, Public Ideas.* Fremantle: Fremantle Arts Centre Press, 1998.

Miles, James. *The Legacy of Tiananmen: China in Disarray.* Ann Arbor: University of Michigan Press, 1996.

Min, Anchee. *Red Azaleas.* New York: Pantheon, 1994.

Modisane, Bloke. *Blame Me on History.* New York: Dutton, 1963.

Modjeska, Drusilla. "A Bitter Wind," in *Essays on Australian Reconciliation.* Ed. Michelle Grattan. Melbourne: Bookman Press, 2000, 158–64.

Moreton-Robinson, Aileen. *Talkin' Up to the White Women: Indigenous Women and Feminism.* St. Lucia: University of Queensland Press, 2000.

Morgan, Sally. *My Place.* Fremantle: Fremantle Arts Centre Press, 1987.

Morgan, Jonathan (director) and The Great African Spider Writers (eds.). *Finding Mr. Madini.* Claremont: Ink Inc., 1999.

Nannup, Alice, with Lauren March and Stephan Kinnane. *When the Pelican Laughed.* Fremantle: Fremantle Arts Centre Press, 1992.

Narogin, Mudrooroo. *Writing from the Fringe: A Study of Modern Aboriginal Literature.* Melbourne: Hyland House, 1990.

Nathan, Andrew J. "Foreward," in *The Courage to Stand Alone: Letters from Prison and Other Writings.* By Wei Jingsheng Ed. and trans. Kristina M. Torgeson, New York: Viking, 1997, xi–xvi.

Ndebele, Njabulo. "Memory, Metaphor, and the Triumph of Narrative," in *Negotiating the Past: The Making of Memory in South Africa.* Ed. Sarah Nuttall and Carli Coetzee. Cape Town: Oxford, 1998, 19–28.

———. *The Rediscovery of the Ordinary: Essays on South African Literature and Culture.* Manchester: Manchester University Press, 1994.

Neier, Aryeh. "Confining Dissent: The Political Prison," in *The Oxford History of the Prison: The Practice of Punishment in Western Society.* Ed. Norval Morris and David J. Rothman. Oxford and New York : Oxford University Press, 1998, 350–80.

New York Times. "The Growing Inmate Population," August 1, 2003: A20.

———. "The Real Problem with DNA Tests," September 1, 2003: A16.

Ng, Lillian. *Swallowing Clouds.* Hopewell, NJ: The Ecco Press, 1997.

Ngoyi, Lilian. "Presidential Address to the African National Congress Women's League, Transvaal," in *Women Writing Africa: The Southern Region.* Eds. M.J. Daymond, Dorothy Driver, et al. New York: Feminist Press, 2003, 240–44.

Nicoll, Fiona. "De-Facing *Terra Nullius* and Facing the Public Secret of Indigenous Sovereignty in Australia." *borderlands e-journal* 1.2 (2002): 13 pp.

Nishino, Rumiko. "The Comfort Women Issue and Responses of the Japanese Government," in *Common Grounds: Violence Against Women in War and Armed Conflict Situations.* Ed. Indai Lourdes Sajor. Quezon City, Philippines: Asina Center for Women's Human Rights (ASCENT), 1998, 214–25.

Noonuccal, Oodgeroo [Kath Walker]. *Stradbroke Dreamtime.* Sydney: Angus and Robertson, 1972.

Novick, Peter. *The Holocaust in American Life.* Boston: Houghton Mifflin, 1999.

Nuttall, Sarah and Carli Coetzee. "Introduction," in *Negotiating the Past: The Making of Memory in South Africa.* Ed. Sarah Nuttall and Carli Coetzee. Cape Town: Oxford University Press, 1998, 1–15.

O'Shea, Kathleen. *Women on the Row: Revelations from Both Sides of the Bars.* Ithaca, NY: Firebrand Books, 2000.

Oliver, Kelly. *Witnessing: Beyond Recognition.* Minneapolis and London: University of Minnesota Press, 2001.

Orr, Wendy. *From Biko to Basson: Wendy Orr's Search for the Soul of South Africa as a Commisioner of the TRC.* Saxonwold: Contra, 2000.

Pakendorf, Gunther. "What If the Truth is a Woman? Reflections on Antjie Krog's TRC Report *Country of My Skull.*" TRC: Commissioning the Past, Seminar at the University of the Witwatersrand Centre for the Study of Violence & Reconciliation, 1999.

Parenti, Christian. *Lockdown America: Police and Prisons in the Age of Crisis.* London and New York: Verso, 1999.

Park, Won Soon. *The Role of NGOs for Human Rights in Asian Countries.* Thesis on International Law. London: London School of Economics and Political Science, 1992.

Paton, Alan. *Cry, the Beloved Country.* New York and London: Scribner's and Jonathan Cape, 1948.

People's Republic of China. *White Papers.* State Council of People's Republic of China, 1999. Accessed March 2002 at http://www.chinaguide.org/ e-white.

Pigou, Piers. "The Murder of Sicelo Dlomo," in *Commissioning the Past: Understanding South Africa's Truth and Reconciliation Commission.* Eds. Deborah Posel and Graeme Simpson. Johannesburg: Witwatersrand University Press, 2002, 97–116.

Pilkington, Doris (Nugi Garimara). *Follow the Rabbit-Proof Fence*. Brisbane: University of Queensland Press, 1996.

Posel, Deborah. *The Making of Apartheid 1948–1961*. Oxford: Clarendon, 1991.

———— and Graeme Simpson (eds.). *Commissioning the Past: Understanding South Africa's Truth and Reconciliation Commission*. Johannesburg: Witwatersrand University Press, 2002.

————. "The Power of Truth: South Africa's Truth and Reconciliation Commission in Context," in *Commissioning the Past: Understanding South Africa's Truth and Reconciliation Commission*. Eds. Deborah Posel and Graeme Simpson. Johannesburg: Witwatersrand University Press, 2002, 1–13.

Potier, Beth. "Abolish Prisons, Says Angela Davis. Questions the Efficacy, Morality of Incarceration." *Harvard University Gazette* March 13, 2003 Accessed http://www.news.harvard.edu/gazette/2003/03.13/ 09-davis.html.

Potter, Emily and Kay Schaffer. "*Rabbit-Proof Fence*, Relational Ecologies, and the Commodification of Indigenous Experience." *Australian Humanities Review* 31–32 (2004). Accessed at http://www.lib.latrobe. edu.au/AHR/current.html.

Povinelli, Elizabeth A. "The Cunning of Recognition: Real Being and Aboriginal Recognition in Settler Australia." *Australian Feminist Law Journal* 11 (April 1998): 3–27.

————. "Bound and Gagged: The State of Morality in the Politics of Recognition." *UTS Review* 7.1 (May 2001): 74–95.

————. *The Cunning of Recognition: Indigenous Alterities and the Making of Australian Multiculturalism*. Durham and London: Duke University Press, 2002.

Power, Katrina. "Keynote Address." AWSA (Australian Women's Studies Association) Conference in Adelaide, 1998.

Prejean, Helen, C.S.J. *Dead Man Walking: An Eyewitness Account of the Death Penalty in the United States*. New York: Vintage Books, 1994.

Promotion of National Unity and Reconciliation Act of 1995. "Chapter 3: Truth and Reconciliation Commission, sec. 3.1: Objectives of Commission." Accessed at http://www.doj.gov. za/trc/legal.act9534.htm.

Qing, Liu. "Preface," in *The Courage to Stand Alone: Letters from Prison and Other Writings*. By Wei Jingsheng Ed. and trans. Kristina M. Torgeson. New York: Viking, 1997, xvii–xxx.

Quillen, Carol. "Feminist Theory, Justice, and the Lure of the Human." *Signs: Journal of Women in Culture and Society* 27.1 (2001): 87–122.

Rabbit-Proof Fence. Directed by Phillip Noyce. Screenplay by Christine Olsen. Produced by Phillip Noyce, Christine Olsen, and John Winter. Burbank, CA: Miramax Films, 2002.

Rall, Ann. "Trauma and the Myth of the Superwoman: Gender, Class and Counseling in Post-War Rwanda." Paper presented at the Institute for Research on Women and Gender, University of Michigan, January 30, 2003.

Ramphele, Mamphela. *Mamphela Ramphele: A Life.* Cape Town: D. Philip, 1995.

Ran Yanshi. "A Look at the US Human Rights Record." *Beijing Review* (March 17–23, 1997): 12–19.

Ravindran, D.J., Manuel Guzman, et al. (eds.). *Handbook on Fact-Finding and Documentation of Human Rights Violations.* Bangkok, Thailand: Asian Forum for Human Rights and Development (FORUM-ASIA), 1994.

Read, Peter. *The Stolen Generations: The Removal of Aboriginal Children in New South Wales, 1883–1969.* Sydney: New South Wales Ministry of Aboriginal Affairs, n.d. (1988).

Reconciliation and Social Justice Library. "Aboriginal Land Trusts" (1998). Accessed March 12, 2004 at *Austlit,* www.austlit.edu.au.

Reynolds, Henry. *Aborigines and Settlers.* Sydney: Allen & Unwin, 1987.

———. *The Law of the Land.* Melbourne: Penguin, 1992.

———. *Aboriginal Sovereignty.* Sydney: Allen & Unwin, 1996.

———. *This Whispering in Our Hearts.* Sydney: Allen & Unwin, 1998.

———. "New Frontiers: Australia," in *Indigenous Peoples' Rights in Australia, Canada, and New Zealand.* Ed. Paul Havemann. Oxford and New York: Oxford University Press, 1999, 129–40.

Richards, Jo-Anne. *The Innocence of Roast Chicken.* London: Hodder Headline, 1996.

Ridgeway, Aden. "An Impasse or a Relationship in the Making?" in *Reconciliation: Essays on Australian Reconciliation.* Ed. Michelle Grattan. Melbourne: Bookman Press, 2000, 12–18.

Rieff, David. *A Bed for the Night: Humanitarianism in Crisis.* New York: Simon & Schuster, 2002.

Robbins, Jill. "Visage, Figure: Reading Levinas' *Totality and Infinity.*" *Yale French Studies* 79 (1991): 135–49.

Rodríguez, Dylan. "Against the Discipline of 'Prison Writing': Toward a Theoretical Conception of Contemporary Radical Prison Praxis." *Genre: Forms of Discourse and Culture* 35.3/4 (2002): 407–28.

Rose, Deborah Bird. "Rupture and the Ethics of Care in Colonized Space," in *Prehistory to Politics: John Mulvaney, the Humanities and the Public Intellectual.* Eds. Tim Bonyhady and Tom Griffiths. Melbourne: Melbourne University Press, 1996.

Rose, Jacqueline. "Apathy and Accountability: The Challenge of South Africa's Truth and Reconciliation Commission to the Intellectual in the Modern World," in *On Not Being Able to Sleep: Psychoanalysis and the Modern World.* Princeton, NJ: Princeton University Press, 2003.

Ross, Fiona C. *Bearing Witness: Women and the Truth and Reconciliation Commission in South Africa.* London: Pluto, 2003a.

———. "Bearing Witness to Ripples of Pain," in *World Memory: Personal Trajectories in Global Time.* Eds. Jill Bennett and Rosanne Kennedy. London and New York: Palgrave Macmillan, 2003b, 143–59.

Ross, Susan. "The Writings of Women Prisoners: Voices from the Margins," in *Mainstream(s) and Margins: Cultural Politics in the 90s.* Ed. Michael Morgan and Susan Leggett. Westport, CT: Greenwood Press, 1996, 85–100.

Roughsey, Elsie (Labumore). *An Aboriginal Mother Tells of the Old and the New*. Fitzroy: McPhee Gribble/Penguin Books, 1984.

Ruff-O'Herne, Jan. *50 Years of Silence: Comfort Women of Indonesia*. Singapore: Toppan Company, 1996.

Rumiko, Nishino. "The Comfort Women Issue and Responses of the Japanese Government," in *Common Grounds: Violence Against Women in War and Armed Conflict*. Ed. Indai Lourdes Sajor. Quezon City, Philippines: ASCENT-Asian Center for Women's Human Rights, 1998, 214–25.

Rushdy, Ashraf H.A. *Neo-Slave Narratives: Studies in the Social Logic of a Literary Form*. Oxford and New York: Oxford University Press, 1999.

Ryang, Sonia. "Inscribed (Men's) Bodies, Silent (Women's) Words: Rethinking Colonial Displacement of Koreans in Japan." *Bulletin of Concerned Asian Scholars* 30.4 (1998): 3–15.

Rymhs, Deena. "Discursive Delinquency in Leonard Peltier's *Prison Writings*." *Genre: Forms of Discourse and Culture* 35.3/4 (2002): 563–74.

Sabo, Don, Terry A. Kupers, and Willie London (eds.). *Prison Masculinities*. Philadelphia: Temple University Press, 2001.

Sachs, Albie *Jail Diary*. London: Sphere, 1969.

———. "His Name was Henry," in *After the TRC: Reflections on Truth and Reconciliation in South Africa*. Ed. Wilmot James and Linda Van De Vijver. Athens, OH, and Cape Town: Ohio University Press and David Philip, 2000, 94–100.

Sanders, Mark. "Responding to the 'Situation' of Modisane's *Blame Me on History*: Towards an Ethics of Reading in South Africa." *Research in African Literatures* 25.4 (1994): 51–67.

———. "Ambiguities of Mourning: Law, Custom, Literature and Women Before South Africa's Truth and Reconciliation Commission." *Law, Text, Culture* 4.2 (1998): 105–51.

———. "Reading Lessons." *Diacritics* 29.3 (1999): 3–20.

———. "Truth, Telling, Questioning: The Truth and Reconciliation Commission, Antjie Krog's *Country of My Skull*, and Literature after Apartheid." *Modern Fiction Studies* 46.1 (2000): 13–41.

Saul, John. "Free at Last? The Next Round in South Africa." *Monthly Review* 42.3 (1990): 63–72.

Scarry, Elaine. *The Body in Pain: The Making and Unmaking of the World*. Oxford and New York: Oxford University Press, 1985.

Schaffer, Kay. "Narrated Lives and Human Rights: Stolen Generation/s Narratives and the Ethics of Recognition." ASAL (Association for the Study of Australian Literature) Conference at Brisbane, 2003.

Schellstede, Sangmie Choi (ed.). *Comfort Women Speak: Testimony of Sex Slaves of the Japanese Military*. New York and London: Holmes & Meier, 2000.

Schindler's List. Directed by Steven Spielberg. Screenplay by Steven Zaillan, based on the novel by Thomas Keneally. Produced by Steven Spielberg, Gerald R. Molen, and Branko Lustig. Universal City, CA: Universal Pictures, 1993.

Sen, Krishna. "The Human Rights of Gendered Citizens: Notes from Indonesia," in *Human Rights and Gender Politics: Asia-Pacific Perspectives*. Eds. Anne-Marie Hilsdon, Martha Macintyre, Vera Mackie, and Maila Stivens. London and New York: Routledge, 2000, 107–21.

Sheng, John. "Afterthoughts on the Banning of 'Shanghai Baby.'" *Perspectives* 2.2 (2000). Accessed at http://www.otcf.org/magazine_8_ 10312000/ afterthoughts_on_the_banning_of.html.

Shi Jiantao. "Tiananmen Crackdown Justified, Says Wen." *South China Morning Post* (Hong Kong). March 15, 2004, sec. A-5.

Senso Daughters: "Daughters of War." Produced and directed by Noriko Sekiguchi. New York: West Glen Communications, Inc., 1989.

Shoah: An Oral History of the Holocaust. Directed by Claude Lanzmann. Coproduction by Les Films Aleph and Historia Films. New York: New Yorker Films, 1985.

Simon, Ella. *Through My Eyes.* Adelaide: Rigby, 1978.

Simons, Marian. *Meeting of the Waters: The Hindmarsh Island Affair.* Sydney: Sceptre, 2002.

Slaughter, Joseph. "A Question of Narration: The Voice in International Human Rights Law." *Human Rights Quarterly* 19.2 (1997): 406–30.

Slovo, Joe. *Slovo: The Unfinished Autobiography.* Randburg: Ravan Press, 1995.

Slovo, Gillian. *Every Secret Thing: My Family, My Country.* London: Little, Brown and Company, 1997.

Smith, Charlene. *Proud of Me: Speaking Out Against Sexual Violence and HIV.* London: Penguin Books, 2001.

Smith, Shirley with Bobbi Sykes. *Mum Shirl: An Autobiography.* Richmond, Vic: Heinemann, 1981.

Smith, Sidonie. *Women, Identity, and the Body: Women's Autobiographical Practices in the Twentieth Century.* Bloomington: Indiana University Press, 1993.

Soh, Chungee Sarah. "The Comfort Women Project." Written by Chungee Sarah Soh. Coded and designed by Jerry D. Boucher. Accessed October 2003 at http://online.sfsu.edu/~soh/comfortwomen.html.

———. "Human Rights and Humanity: The Case of the 'Comfort Women.'" Lecture, University of Pennsylvania, Philadelphia, December 4, 1998. Reprinted on-line by Institute for Corean-American Studies, Inc., Accessed at http://www.icansinc.org/lectures/ cssl1998.html.

———. "Prostitutes Versus Sex Slaves: The Politics of Representing the 'Comfort Women,'" in *Legacies of the Comfort Women of World War II*. Eds. Margaret Stetz and Bonnie B.C. Oh. Armonk, NY and London: M.E. Sharpe, 2001, 69–87.

Specter, Donald and Terry A. Kupers. "Litigation, Advocacy, and Self-Respect," in *Prison Masculinities*. Eds. Don Sabo, Terry A. Kupers, and Willie London. Philadelphia: Temple University Press, 2001, 239–46.

Stacy, Helen. "Western Triumphalism: The Crisis of Human Rights in the Global Era." *Macquarie Law Journal* 2 (2002): 193–200.

Staunton, Marie and Sally Fenn (eds.). *Amnesty International Handbook*. Claremont, CA: Hunter House, 1991.

Stetz, Margaret. "Wartime Sexual Violence Against Women: A Feminist Response" in Legacies of the Comfort. Women of World War II Ed. Margaret Stetz and Bonnie B.C Oh. Armonk, New York and London: M. E. Sharpe, 2001, 91–100.

Stetz, Margaret and Bonnie B.C. Oh (eds.). *Legacies of the Comfort Women of World War II*. Armonk, NY and London: M.E. Sharpe, 2001.

Stivens, Maila. "Introduction: Gender Politics and the Reimagining of Human Rights in the Asia-Pacific," in *Human Rights and Gender Politics: Asia-Pacific Perspectives*. Eds. Anne-Marie Hilsdon, Martha Macintyre, Vera Mackie, and Maila Stivens. London and New York: Routledge, 2000, 1–36.

Stoll, David. *Rigoberta Menchú and the Story of All Poor Guatemalans*. Boulder: Westview, 1998.

Stratton, Jon. "Before Holocaust Memory: Making Sense of Trauma Between Postmemory and Cultural Memory." Unpublished paper, 2003.

Su Xiaokang. *A Memoir of Misfortune*. New York: Random House/Vintage, 2001.

Sullivan, Michael J. "Developmentalism and China's Human Right's Policy," in *Debating Human Rights: Critical Essays from the United States and Asia*. Ed. Peter Van Ness. London and New York: Routledge, 1999, 120–43.

Sun (Melbourne), "Black Power on the March," January 27, 1988, in *The Struggle for Aboriginal Rights: A Documentary History*. Ed. Bain Attwood and Andrew Markus. Sydney: Allen & Unwin, 1999, 315–16.

Sun, Wanning. *Leaving China: Media, Migration and Transnational Imagination*. Oxford: Rowman and Littlefield, 2002.

Svensson, Marina. *Debating Human Rights in China: A Conceptual and Political History*. Lanham, Boulder, New York, and Oxford: Rowman and Littlefield Publishers, Inc., 2002.

Sydney Morning Herald, "One Man's Gulf War," July 6, 1996, in *The Struggle for Aboriginal Rights: A Documentary History*. Ed. Bain Attwood and Andrew Markus. Sydney: Allen & Unwin, 1999, 347–48.

Teo Hsu-Ming. *Love and Vertigo*. St Leonards, NSW: Allen & Unwin, 2000.

Thoma, Pamela. " 'Such an Unthinkable Thing': Asian American Transnational Feminism and the 'Comfort Women' of World War II Conference," in *Legacies of the Comfort Women of World War II*. Ed. Margaret Stetz and Bonnie B.C. Oh. Armonk, NY and London: M.E. Sharpe, 2001, 101.

Thompson, Janna. *Taking Responsibility for the Past: Reparation and Historical Justice*. Cambridge: Polity Press, 2002.

Thoolen, Hans and Berth Verstappen. *Human Rights Missions: A Study of the Fact-Finding Practice of Non-Governmental Organizations*. Dordrecht and Boston: M. Nijhoff, 1986.

Ticktin, Miriam. "Selling Suffering in the Courtroom and Marketplace: An Analysis of the Autobiography of Kiranjit Ahluwalia." *PoLAR* 22.1 (1999): 24–41.

Tlali, Miriam. *Muriel at Metropolitan: A Novel.* London: Longman, 1979.

———. *Amandla: A Novel.* Johannesburg: Ravan Press, 1980.

To Live. Directed by Zhang Yimou. Screenplay by Yu Hua and Lu Wei. Produced by Chiu Fusheng. Los Angeles: Samuel Goldwyn Company, 1994.

Tomkins, Silvan. "What are Affects?" in *Shame and Its Sisters: A Silvan Tomkins Reader.* Ed. Eve Kosofsky Sedgewick and Adam Frank. Durham and London: Duke University Press, 1995, 33–74.

TRC (Truth and Reconciliation Commission). *Truth and Reconciliation Commission of South Africa Report.* Cape Town: Truth and Reconciliation Commission (5 Vols.), 1998.

Tutu, Desmond. *No Future Without Forgiveness.* New York: Doubleday, 1999.

Tu Wei-Ming. "Introduction," in *The Living Tree: The Changing Meaning of Being Chinese Today.* Stanford: Stanford University Press, 1994, i–vii.

———. "Cultural China: The Periphery as the Center," in The Living Tree: The Changing Meaning of Being Chinese Today. Stanford: Stanford University Press, 1994, 1–34.

Tucker, Margaret. *If Everyone Cared: Autobiography of Margaret Tucker M.B.E.* London: Grosvenor, 1977.

Turner, Bethany. "Writing Resistance: Lessons from Mexico's Far South East," in *Resistance and Reconciliation: Writing the Commonwealth.* Ed. Bruce Bennett. Canberra: ACLALS, 2001, 1–10.

Ueno Chizuko. "The Politics of Memory: Nation, Individual and Self." *History and Memory* 11.2 (1999): 129–52.

Uys, Pieter-Dirk, with cartoons by Zapiro. *Elections and Erections: A Memoir of Fear and Fun.* Cape Town: Zebra Press, 2002.

Van Alphen, Ernst. "Symptoms of Discursivity: Experience, Memory, and Trauma," in *Acts of Memory: Cultural Recall in the Present.* Ed. Mieke Bal, Jonathan V. Crewe, and Leo Spitzer. Hanover, NH: Dartmouth College-University Press of New England, 1999, 24–38.

Van Boven, Theo. "Study Concerning the Right to Restitution, Compensation, and Rehabilitation for Victims of Gross Violations of Human Rights and Fundamental Freedoms: Final Report." New York, 1993, UN Doc E/ NC4/ sub2/1996/17.

Van der Vyver, Marita. *Entertaining Angels.* London: Joseph, 1994.

Van Schalkwyk, Annalet. "A Gendered Truth: Women's Testimonies at the TRC and Reconciliation." *Missionalia* 27.2 (1999): 165–88.

Van Toorn, Penny. "Indigenous Australian Life Writing: Tactics and Transformations," in *Telling Stories: Indigenous History and Memory in Australia and New Zealand.* Ed. Bain Attwood and Fiona Magowan. Sydney: Allen and Unwin, 2001, 1–20.

Vervoorn, Aat. *Re Orient: Change in Asian Societies.* South Melbourne: Oxford University Press, 1998.

Vienna Declaration and Programme of Action. World Conference on Human Rights, 1993, UN Doc. A/CONF. 157/23, reprinted in 32 I.L.M 1667.

Villa-Vicencio, Charles and Erik Doxtader (eds.). *The Provocation of Amnesty: Memory, Justice, and Impunity.* Cape Town: David Philip, 2003.

Wajnryb, Ruth. "The Holocaust as Unspeakable: Public Ritual Versus Private Hell." *Journal of Intercultural Studies* 20.1 (1999): 81–94.

Wan, Frieda. "Changes Could Be Just Symbolic, Observers Fear." *South China Morning Post* (Hong Kong), March 15, 2004: A-4.

Wang, Annie. *Lili: A Novel of Tiananmen.* London and New York: Macmillan, 2001.

———. "A Conversation with Annie Wang" in *Author Q & A*, randomhouse.com. Accessed March 2003 at http://www.randomhouse.com/pantheon/catalog/ display.pperl?0375420851&view=printqa.

Wang Gungwu and Annette Shun Wah. "Imagining the Chinese Diaspora: Two Australian Perspectives." Canberra: Centre for the Study of the Chinese Southern Diaspora, Australian National University, 1999.

Wang, Jing. *High Culture Fever: Politics, Aesthetics, and Ideology in Deng's China.* Berkeley: University of California Press, 1996.

———. "Culture as Leisure and Culture as Capital." *positions* 9.1 (2000): 69–104.

Wang, Lulu. *The Lily Theater: A Novel of Modern China.* New York: Nan A. Talese/Doubleday, 2000.

Ward, Glenyse. *Unna You Fellas.* Broome, WA: Magabala Books, 1991.

Watanabe Kazuko. "Militarism, Colonialism, and the Trafficking of Women: 'Comfort Women' Forced into Sexual Labor for Japanese Soldiers." *Bulletin of Concerned Asian Scholars* 26.4 (1994): 1–14.

Watson, Irene. "Aboriginal Law and the Sovereignty of *Terra Nullius*." *borderlands e-journal* 1.2 (2002), Accessed at http://www.borderlandsejournal. adelaide.edu.au/ vol1no2_2002/watson_laws.html.

Weatherley, Robert. *The Discourse of Human Rights in China: Historical and Ideological Perspectives.* London and New York: Macmillan Press and St. Martin's Press, 1999.

Wei Hui. *Shanghai Baby.* New York: Pocket Books, 2001.

Wei Jingsheng. "A Dissenter's Odyssey through Mao's China." *New York Times Magazine* (November 16, 1980): SM34.

———. *The Courage to Stand Alone: Letters from Prison and Other Writings.* Ed. and trans. Kristina M. Torgeson New York: Viking, 1997.

Welcome to Australia. Written, directed, and produced by John Pilger. Carlton Television England, 1999.

Weller, Archie. *Going Home: Stories by Archie Weller.* Sydney: Allen & Unwin, 1986.

West, Ida. *Pride Against Prejudice: Reminiscences of a Tasmanian Australian Aborigine.* Canberra: Australian Institute of Aboriginal Studies, 1984.

White, Jerry. "Squaring Off Over Tiananmen: Critics Clamor at the Gate of Heavenly Peace." *The Independent* January/February 1996. Accessed May 2002 at http://www.tsquare.tv/film/indep.html.

Whitlock, Gillian. *The Intimate Empire: Reading Women's Autobiography.* London: Cassell, 2000.

———. "In the Second Person: Narrative Transactions in Stolen Generations Testimony." *biography* 24.1 (2001): 197–214.

Wicomb, Zoë. *You Can't Get Lost in Cape Town.* London: Virago, 1987.

———. *David's Story.* New York: Feminist Press, 2001.

Wilder, Lisa. "Local Futures? From Denunciation to Revalorization of the Indigenous Other," in *Global Law without a State.* Ed. Gunther Teibner. Aldershot: Dartmouth, 1997, 215–56.

Wilson, Richard. "Reconciliation and Revenge in Post-Apartheid South Africa: Rethinking Legal Pluralism and Human Rights," *The TRC: Commissioning the Past,* University of the Witwatersand and Centre for the Study of Violence & Reconciliation, 1999.

Wilson, Sir Ronald. *Bringing Them Home: National Inquiry into the Separation of Aboriginal and Torres Strait Islander Children from Their Families.* Canberra: Human Rights and Equal Opportunity Commission, 1997.

Windschuttle, Keith. *The Fabrication of Aboriginal History.* Sydney: Macleay Press, 2002.

Winter, Jay. "The Memoir Boom in Contemporary Historical Studies." *Raritan* 21.1 (2001): 52–66.

WITNESS. "WITNESS: Using Video and Technology to Fight for Human Rights." Website produced by Peter Gabriel, the Lawyers Committee for Human Rights, and the Reebok Human Rights Foundation. Accessed at http://www.witness.org.

Women's International War Crimes Tribunal on Japan's Military Sexual Slavery. "Final Charter." 8–12 December 2000, 10 June 2004. http://iccwomen.addr.com/tokyo/finalcharter.htm.

———. "Summary Judgment." 12 Dec. 2000. Tokyo. 10 June 2004. http://iccwomen.addr.com/tokyo/summaryjudg.htm.

Wong, Jan. *Jan Wong's China: Reports from a Not-So-foreign Correspondent.* Sydney, Auckland, Toronto, New York, London: Transworld, Random House, Anchor, 1999.

Woodman, Sophia. "Wei Jingsheng's Lifelong Battle for Democracy," in *The Courage to Stand Alone: Letters from Prison and Other Writings.* By Wei Jingsheng. Ed. and trans. Kristina M. Torgeson. New York: Viking, 1997, 249–71.

Woodward, Richard B. "Anatomy of a Massacre." *Village Voice* June 4, 1996. Accessed May 2002 at http://www.tsquare.tv/film/voice.html.

Wright, Edie. *Full Circle: From Mission to Community—A Family Story.* Fremantle: Fremantle Arts Centre Press, 2001.

Wukindi Rom Project. "Wukindi Rom Project." Djiniyinii Gondarra et al. www.wukindi.com.

Xiaojiang Li. "From 'Modernization' to 'Globalization': Where Are Chinese Women?" *Signs: Journal of Women in Culture and Society* 26.4 (Summer 2001): 1274–78.

Xinran. *The Good Women of China: Hidden Voices*. London: Chatto and Windus, 2002.

Xiu Xiu, The Sent Down Girl. Directed by Joan Chen. Written by Yan Geling and Joan Chen. Produced by Joan Chen and Alice Chan. New York: Image Entertainment, 1998.

Yamamoto, Eric K. "Race Apologies." *Journal of Gender, Race & Justice* 1.1 (1997): 47–88.

———. "Racial Reparations: Japanese American Redress and African American Claims." *Boston College Law Review* 40.1 (1998): 477–523.

Yang Jiang. *Six Chapters from My Life "Downunder,* trans. Howard Goldblatt". Seattle and London: University of Washington Press, 1984.

Yanshi Ren. "A Look at the US Human Rights Record." *Beijing Review* March 17–23, 1997: 126–33.

Yardley, Jim. "Chinese SARS Hero Urges Party to Admit to Error for '89 Massacre." *New York Times*, March 3, 2003: A3.

Ye Ren. "Controversy Among Chinese Dissidents." *The 90s* July and August 1995. Website produced by Long Bow Group, Inc. 2002. Accessed May 2002 at http://www.tsquare.tv/film/YeRen.html.

Yoneyama, Lisa. "Re-Manufacturing Cold War Amnesia: Hiroshima, 'Comfort Women,' and America's 'New War' of Retaliation." Paper excerpt sent to Sidonie Smith, March 2001.

———. "NHK's Censorship of Japanese Crimes Against Humanity." *Harvard Asia Quarterly* 6.1 (2002): 15–19.

Young, James E. "America's Holocaust: Memory and the Politics of Identity," in *The Americanization of the Holocaust*. Ed. Hilene Flanzbaum. Baltimore and London: Johns Hopkins University Press, 1999, 68–82.

Youngs, Gillian. "Private Pain/Public Peace: Women's Rights as Human Rights and Amnesty International's Report on Violence Against Women." *Signs: Journal of Women in Culture and Society* 28.4 (2003): 1209–29.

Zhang Boli. *Escape from China: The Long Journey from Tiananmen to Freedom*. New York: Washington Square Press, 2002.

Zhang Zhen. "The World Map of Haunting Dreams: Reading Post-1989 Chinese Women's Diaspora Writings," in *Spaces of Their Own: Womens' Public Sphere in Transnational China, Vol. 4.* Ed. Mayfair Mei-hui Yang. Minneapolis and London: University of Minnesota Press, 1999, 308–36.

———. "Mediating Time: The 'Rice Bowl of Youth' in *Fin de Siecle* Urban China." *Public Culture* 12.1 (2000): 93–113.

Zhong, Xueping, Wang Zheng, and Bai Di (eds.). *Some of Us: Chinese Women Growing Up in the Mao Era*. New Brunswick, NJ and London: Rutgers University Press, 2002.

Index